# Economic Analysis of Pressing Social Problems

# Economic Analysis of Pressing Social Problems

**Llad Phillips and Harold L. Votey, Jr.**

The Department of Economics and
The Community and Organization Research Institute
*University of California/Santa Barbara*

**Rand McNally College Publishing Company** · Chicago

**Rand McNally Economics Series**
Ralph E. Beals, *advisory editor*


Printed in U.S.A.
Library of Congress Catalog Card Number: 73-15434

# Preface

By concentrating on current social problems instead of abstract economic principles, the authors of this volume have sought to convey vividly some of the breadth and scope of economic analysis and its relevance to both public and private decision-making. Each of the essays deals with a social problem area that calls for application of specific analytical techniques. Thus, while not concentrating on economic principles per se, the text systematically introduces the reader to basic economic theory and methodology applied to real problems.

Colleges and universities across the country are currently being criticized because their faculties spend too much time on research at the expense of effective teaching. However, it is our conviction that research is an important stimulus to creative teaching. Faculty members who stay at the forefront of their respective fields have much to say.

Each of the contributors to this volume has sought to bring to the reader the scope and depth of understanding that come only from direct involvement. Each chapter constitutes a short monograph independent of the others; however, it is recommended that they be read in the sequence in which they are presented, so that the reader can take full advantage of the cumulative experience with the special terminology and analytical tools used by economists. To further aid the reader, an "economist's tool kit" has been appended.

This book has been written from the pragmatic viewpoint that the student is entitled to a justification of the relevance of a particular scientific approach before he can be expected to embrace it with enthusiasm. We have attempted to establish the relevance of economics as a logical approach to decision-making by providing a sampling of the broad spectrum of problems with which economists deal. It is only a sampling because it would be impossible in a book of this length to provide examples of all of the types of decision-making to which economic principles can be applied. We hope that the student, as he gains in understanding of the tools of economic analysis, will discover that there are other social problems that are amenable to solution with those same tools.

This volume was made possible by the financial support of the Regents of the University of California through an undergraduate instruction improvement grant. Walter Hopper's extensive assistance at editing and as a technical adviser are very much appreciated. In addition, we acknowledge that the work could not have been completed in time to meet deadlines without the tireless efforts of Barbara Hagen in handling typing and administrative details; Cathy Barrett, who served as draftsman; and Janice de Valencia and the clerical staff of the Department of Economics, who helped in innumerable ways.

LLAD PHILLIPS
HAROLD L. VOTEY, JR.

## About the Authors

LLOYD MERCER received his Ph.D. in economics from the University of Washington (Seattle) and an M.A. in agricultural economics from Washington State University (Pullman). He taught at the University of Washington prior to accepting his current position at the University of California/Santa Barbara. He is a specialist in economic history and has published research on the development of the U.S. economy with particular reference to railroads and the automobile industry and has done research on the determination of demand and supply in grain markets.

WALTER MEAD received his M.A. in economics from Columbia University and his Ph.D. from the University of Oregon. He has taught previously at Lewis and Clark College and been All-University Lecturer of the University of California/Berkeley. He is a recognized authority on energy economics who is called upon frequently to testify before congressional committees and serve as a consultant on problems relating to natural resources. In 1972–73 he served as senior economist for the Ford Foundation's Energy Policy Project in Washington, D.C., initiated in the summer of 1972. He participates in the Environmental Studies Program at the University of California/Santa Barbara.

ROBERT McGUCKIN received his M.A. and Ph.D. in economics from the State University of New York (Buffalo). He is a specialist in industrial organization and has published research dealing with problems of industry concentration, market entry, and firm diversification.

M. BRUCE JOHNSON received his M.A. and Ph.D. in economics from Northwestern University. He taught at the University of Washington (Seattle) prior to his arrival at University of California/Santa Barbara. He is a specialist in economic theory, particularly the theory of consumer behavior. He is the author of a book on this subject and has published research dealing with peak load pricing and the efficient use of time as an economic resource. He has served as chairman of the Department of Economics.

W. DOUGLAS MORGAN received his M.A. and Ph.D. in economics from the University of California/Berkeley. He is a specialist in public finance and macroeconomic theory. His published articles deal with investment in commercial construction, railroads, and the automobile industry. Presently he is involved in a study of water allocation problems in Southern California which is being financed by the federal government.

ROBERT DEACON received his M.A. and Ph.D. in economics from the University of Washington (Seattle), where he specialized in natural resource economics and local public finance. His published research is in the areas of water resource management and fiscal patterns in state and local government. He participates in the Environmental Studies Program at University of California/Santa Barbara.

JOHN PIPPENGER received his Ph.D. in economics from the University of California/Los Angeles and has taught there as well as at University of California/Santa Barbara. He is a specialist in problems of international finance and has published theoretical and empirical research dealing with international capital flows, and spot and forward exchange rates under fixed and flexible exchange rates systems.

DONALD WINKLER received his Ph.D. in economics from the University of California at Berkeley. He was a research associate with the School of Education, Berkeley prior to joining the faculty at University of California/Santa Barbara. The problems of urban poverty and the economics of education are his specialties and he has done economic research relating to both elementary/secondary and higher education. He lectures in the Graduate School of Education as well as in the Department of Economics.

WILLIAM KENNEDY received his M.A. from Columbia University and his Ph.D. in economics from the University of Wisconsin. He was honored as a Danforth Fellow at Harvard University in 1957 and as a Guggenheim Fellow in 1959–60, has served as a consultant to the public utilities industry, and served on the War Production Board during World War II. The history of economic thought is his specialty. His writings range from a study of the economic thinking of Samuel Taylor Coleridge and Charles Knight to that of Aldous Huxley. His recent research relates to philosophical problems associated with man's relationship to economic society.

PERRY SHAPIRO received his Ph.D. from the University of California/Berkeley. He has taught at Washington University (St. Louis) and the London School of Economics prior to his arrival at University of California/Santa Barbara. Public finance and problems of urban environment are his areas of expertise and he has done both theoretical and empirical studies dealing with problems of urban location. Presently he is Director of the UCSB internship program to train (at the Master's level) decision-makers for the urban public sector.

ANTHONY BARKUME is presently completing a dissertation in urban economics at—and is a lecturer at—University of California/Santa Barbara.

HAROLD L. VOTEY, JR. received his M.B.A. at the University of Michigan and his Ph.D. in economics at the University of California at Berkeley, where he specialized in international economics and economic development. His published research is in the areas of population studies, the economics of criminal justice, and the economics of education. He is presently Director of the Community and Organization Research Institute which fosters interdisciplinary research into a number of the problems dealt with in this book.

LLAD PHILLIPS received his M.A. and Ph.D. in economics from Harvard University, where he specialized in labor economics and econometrics. His published research deals with the economics of criminal justice, education, population, and the application of spectral analysis to international and domestic monetary problems. He has conducted research for the U.S. Department of Justice, U.S. Department of Labor, and the California Council of Criminal Justice.

# Contents

# Introduction

Reading the daily newspapers, one is bound to get the feeling that the country is in a state of crisis. This sense of crisis may be stimulated in part by the tendency of the press to ignore the areas where things are going well and to give relatively greater weight to some problems than they may deserve, so far as decision-makers are concerned. Nevertheless, in a changing world there are always pressing social problems. While the substance of the problems may change, their nature will generally be such that from the point of view of analysis and evaluation, there is a certain constancy about them. This is fortunate because it means that a basic set of scientific principles can be adapted to their resolution. Decisions have to be made about these problems. Economics, which is a science of decision-making, provides us with basic concepts and tools that are needed for the task.

The laboratory of economics is the real world: the individuals and institutions, both public and private, who interact to allocate scarce resources among alternative uses. This system may or may not work in the way desired by the society. Should the expected outcomes be different from those wanted, we may wish to find alternatives for control. Thus it is important that we understand the objectives of the system, the resources available to it, and the inner workings of the various mechanisms that determine what that system can produce and how the output is distributed.

How do resources get divided up among uses in such a way that society's desires are satisfied? Is there some orderly mechanism through which this goal can be accomplished? If there were no systematic way that allocation took place, the study of economic transactions would simply be the study of random events. In reality, we find that most of the transactions that satisfy society's needs in getting those things people desire from the places they are found or produced to the point at which they are to be consumed or enjoyed occur systematically in markets.

A market may be a highly formalized activity such as a coffee exchange or a stock exchange, or it may be simply a meeting over the fence where a farmer agrees to allow a woodcutter to cut trees from his woodlot in exchange for a share of the firewood. Whatever the physical volume of the goods or services exchanged, or whatever the value of those things that change ownership, there are determinants of market transactions that can be studied in a systematic way. For example, we can study the effort that must go into the production of goods or the acquisition of control over a resource. These activities entail a cost to the producer, who, if he is to be able to gain some benefit to himself from his efforts, will want to be compensated in terms of other goods. There is, then, a systematic process of supply for which general principles can be observed. Interacting with the activities to supply goods we find individuals wishing to use, consume, or enjoy goods other than those they produce themselves, thus creating a desire for exchange. This demand has determinants that may be studied systematically as well. Finally, it is the interaction of demand forces and supply possibilities that establishes what will be produced and what society will agree is the value of those things produced.

Since much of economic activity takes the form of routine transactions within formalized markets, the obvious way to begin the study of the allocation problem is to begin with the study of markets. To introduce the reader to the topic with minimum difficulty, and within a framework unembellished with intricate complications, a logical place to begin is probably the market for farm products, one of the most crucial to our survival, as well as one of the oldest.

We might expect, if agricultural markets have been around so long, that we should know all about them and that they should consequently no longer be a problem. The economic system is constantly evolving, however, leading to new crises. For example, in the winter of 1972–73 the U.S. consumer faced an unprecedented rise in food prices, and foreign demand for our agricultural products skyrocketed to an all-time high. In Chapter 1, Professor Mercer applies market analysis to identify the economic forces that have led to this crisis and to formulate an alternative farm policy.

# 1

# The American Farm Problem: Welfare for the Rich and High Food Prices

Lloyd J. Mercer

If one listened only to farm-belt congressmen or read only the agriculture-oriented segment of the press, it would be easy to conclude that the pre-eminent farm problem in the United States is an overabundance of goods. From the farmer's point of view, this so-called excess of goods is responsible for reducing the average farm income below the welfare level prevailing in large cities. While it is a fact that a surplus exists in American agriculture, the true surplus from the point of view of society is not one of farm goods, but of farmers. This excess of farmers is the primary American farm problem.

The central issue in this problem is the effectiveness of overall resource use and the best distribution of resources among competing uses. Resource use or *production*—the matter of *what* is produced and *how* it is produced—is one of the fundamental questions considered in economics. A second major facet of the study of economics is *distribution,* or the question of *for whom* goods and services are produced. Our primary concern here will be with the production problem.

The backbone of farm policy in the United States for more than four decades has been a set of solutions to the farm problem as seen almost exclusively from the farmer's point of view. This approach has been taken because of the political power of farmers. But farmers' political power has been on the wane for some time and this decline has been accelerated by the Supreme Court's recent one-man one-vote ruling. Thus the political feasibility of a solution to the *real* farm problem is increasing. Improved understanding by the public at large should further augment the feasibility of a rational solution.

The waste of resources in attempting to solve the farm problem as seen from the farmer's point of view, and the additional cost to all of us every time we buy farm goods, act as a constraint on our ability to deal with other important problems. The magnitude of this constraint can be illustrated by a few statistics. During 1971 the United States Department of Agriculture (USDA) paid out $3.7 billion to producers of cotton, wheat, barley, grain sorghum, sugar, wool, mohair, and tobacco. Between 1956 and 1970, federal budget outlays for farm price-support programs (as subsidies) averaged $3.1 billion annually. The 1971 expense of the farm program to U.S. taxpayers, including administrative costs and related farm assistance programs, totaled almost $5 billion, or more than $25 for each man, woman, and child. In addition, economic studies estimate that U.S. consumers have recently paid as much as another $5 billion per year in higher food and fiber prices as a result of government support programs. Thus in 1971 the cost of the farm lobby's solution to the farm problem amounted to an estimated $50 for every person in the United States. Let us analyze the American farm problem from society's viewpoint, rather than the farmer's.

## Historical Development of the Problem

An oversupply of farmers has existed for at least forty years. While the basic forces producing this condition have been at work throughout most of our history, the past century has witnessed their intensification. In general terms, the overabundance of farmers results from the fact that the supply of farm products has grown more rapidly than demand. Because we are today largely an urban-industrial country, with most of our population concentrated in urban areas, we should not underestimate the historical importance of agriculture as a sector of the economy. When the Constitution was signed, approximately 95 percent of the population lived in rural areas and roughly 90 percent of the labor force was employed in agriculture. As recently as 1910 the majority of Americans still resided in rural areas. Today only about one person in four resides in a rural area, and less than 6 percent (5.8 percent in 1970) of the labor force is employed in agriculture. Figure 1–1 and Table 1–1 illustrate the long-term trends of farm labor force and rural population over the period 1810–1960. It is clear that for the first hundred years of this country's existence, agriculture was the most important sector in the total economy, but this ceased to be so by the late nineteenth century.

## Slow Growth of Demand

To study demand, the economist resorts to the notion of a demand function. The demand function for agricultural goods can be thought of as a relationship in which the quantity of agricultural goods demanded (*QF*) at

Figure 1–1. Agricultural labor force and rural population, 1810–1960.

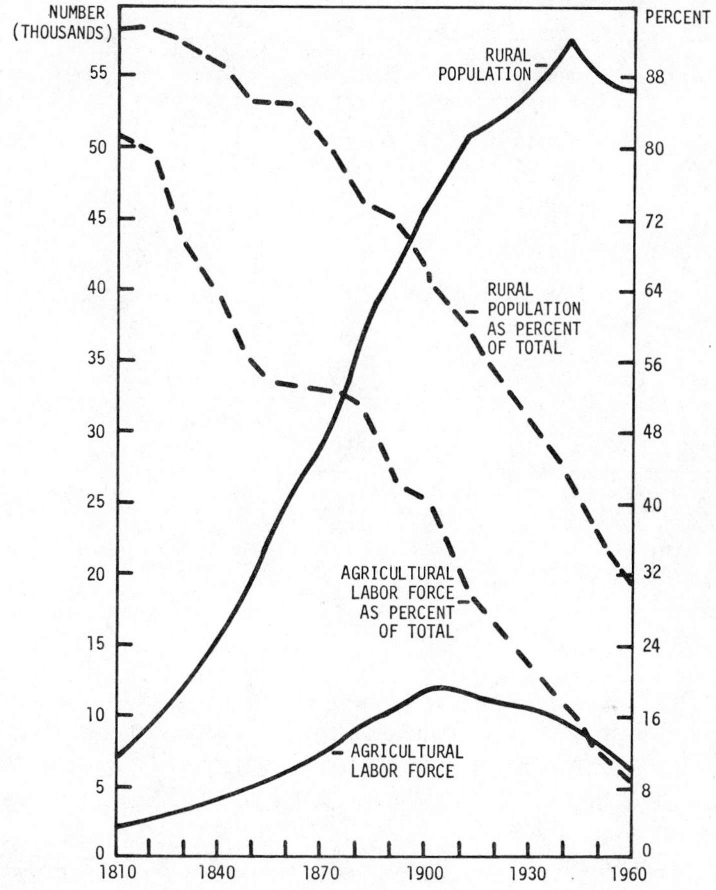


Sources: Agricultural labor force from Stanley Lebergott, "Labor Force and Employment, 1800–1960," in *Output, Employment, and Productivity in the United States After 1800,* Vol. 30 of *Studies in Income and Wealth,* by the Conference on Research in Income and Wealth (New York: National Bureau of Economic Research, 1966); rural population from U.S. Bureau of the Census, *Historical Statistics of the United States, Colonial Times to 1957* (Washington, D.C.: U.S. Government Printing Office, 1960), p. 14; *Statistical Abstract of the United States, 1970* (Washington, D.C.: U.S. Government Printing Office, 1970), p. 18.

a point in time is primarily some function ($f$) of real income ($Y$), population ($P$), and the prices of agricultural goods relative to the prices of other goods ($RP$). Real income is money income adjusted for price changes, so that a dollar of income purchases the same quantity of goods at all points in time. For brevity we can write the demand function:

$$QF = f(Y, P, RP). \tag{1}$$

Table 1–1
Agricultural Labor Force and Rural Population, 1810–1960

| | Agricultural Labor Force[a] | | Rural Population[b] | |
|---|---|---|---|---|
| Year | Number (thousands) | As Percent of Total Labor Force | Number (thousands) | As Percent of Total Population |
| 1810 | 1,950 | 80.9 | 6,714 | 92.7 |
| 1820 | 2,470 | 78.8 | 8,945 | 92.8 |
| 1830 | 2,965 | 68.8 | 11,738 | 91.2 |
| 1840 | 3,570 | 63.1 | 15,224 | 89.2 |
| 1850 | 4,520 | 54.8 | 19,648 | 84.7 |
| 1860 | 5,880 | 52.9 | 25,226 | 80.2 |
| 1870 | 6,790 | 52.5 | 28,656 | 74.3 |
| 1880 | 8,920 | 51.3 | 36,026 | 71.8 |
| 1890 | 9,960 | 42.7 | 40,841 | 64.9 |
| 1900 | 11,680 | 40.2 | 45,834 | 60.3 |
| 1910 | 11,770 | 31.4 | 49,973 | 54.3 |
| 1920 | 10,790 | 25.9 | 51,552 | 48.8 |
| 1930 | 10,560 | 21.6 | 53,820 | 43.8 |
| 1940 | 9,575 | 17.0 | 57,246 | 43.4 |
| 1950 | 7,870 | 12.0 | 54,230[c] | 36.0 |
| 1960 | 5,970 | 8.1 | 54,054[c] | 30.1 |

[a]Source: Stanley Lebergott, "Labor Force and Employment, 1800–1960," pp. 118–19 in *Output, Employment, and Productivity in the United States After 1800*, vol. 30 of *Studies in Income and Wealth*, by the Conference on Research in Income and Wealth (New York: National Bureau of Economic Research, 1966).

[b]Source: U.S. Bureau of the Census, *Historical Statistics of the United States, Colonial Times to 1957* (Washington, D.C.: U.S. Government Printing Office, 1960), p. 14; *Statistical Abstract of the United States, 1970* (Washington, D.C.: U.S. Government Printing Office, 1970), p. 18.

[c]New urban definition.

In this functional relationship, *QF* changes in the same direction as *Y* and *P*, and moves in the opposite direction from movements in *RP*. In general, changes in *Y*, *P*, and *RP* have produced a slow growth of agricultural demand in the United States over the last century.

Income has grown throughout the history of the U.S. economy, but agriculture in general has benefited proportionately less from this rise in income than other sectors of the economy. The reason for this lies in the manner in which consumers change their relative allocation of income among the various classes of goods as income rises. Budget studies that have been made of the way people at various levels of income spend their money show remarkable agreement on the general patterns of behavior.[1] The general relationships are that (1) the percentage expenditure on food declines as income increases; (2) the proportion of income spent on shelter is nearly constant over a wide range of incomes; (3) expenditures on manufactured goods increase at a faster rate than income; and (4) expenditures on services increase still more rapidly relative to income.

Despite the relationship between rising per capita income and agricultural

1. The behavior patterns are called "Engel's Laws," after the nineteenth-century Prussian statistician Ernst Engel, who first enumerated them as a result of his own studies. These so-called laws are probably the most tested ones in economics.

goods, it is clear that the quantity of agricultural goods demanded would grow as a result of the increase in population. Unfortunately for agriculture, the trend in rate of population growth has been generally downward during the past century or so, as shown in Figure 1–2 and Table 1–2. Thus, decline in the rate of growth of population has also contributed to the relatively slow growth of agricultural demand.

Although it seems hard to believe if one goes to a supermarket today, the relative price of agricultural goods has declined since about 1920, except for the period 1940–1953. One of the reasons this is not apparent in the grocery store is the great increase in services (packaging, etc.) which have been provided in response to consumer demands. The decline in relative prices has probably increased the demand for agricultural goods, but because the decline has been relatively small and slow, any resulting increase in demand for agricultural goods has also been small and slow.

Figure 1–2. Average growth rate of U.S. population, 1790–1964.

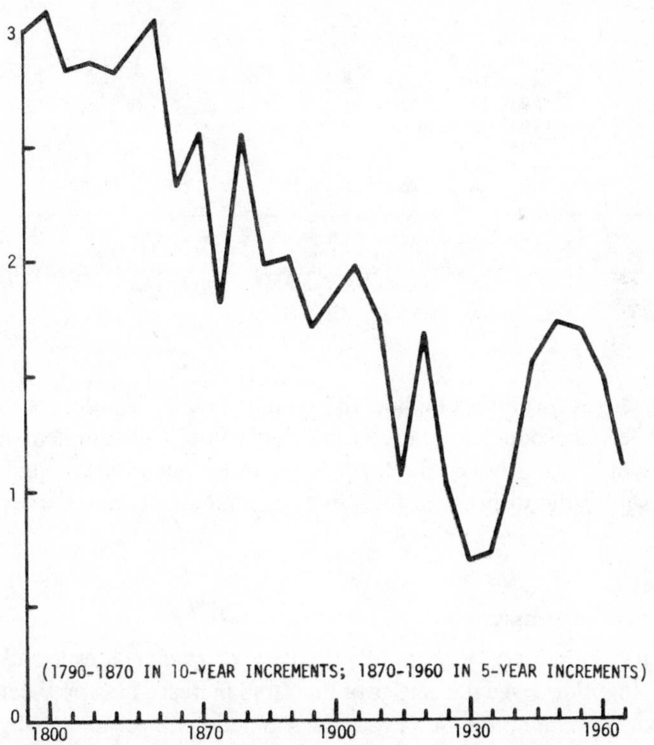


Sources: 1790–1870: Warren S. Thompson and P. K. Whelpton, *Population Trends in the United States* (New York: McGraw-Hill, 1933), pp. 1, 303; 1870–1964: Richard A. Easterlin, *Population, Labor Force and Long Swings in Economic Growth: The American Experience* (New York: Columbia University Press, 1968), p. 189.

Table 1–2
Average Growth Rate of
U.S. Population, 1790–1968

| Period | Growth Rate |
|---|---|
| 1790–1800 | 2.99% |
| 1800–1810 | 3.08 |
| 1810–1820 | 2.84 |
| 1820–1830 | 2.87 |
| 1830–1840 | 2.81 |
| 1840–1850 | 3.04 |
| 1850–1860 | 3.02 |
| 1860–1870 | 2.35 |
| 1870–1875 | 2.55 |
| 1875–1880 | 1.83 |
| 1880–1885 | 2.54 |
| 1885–1890 | 1.99 |
| 1890–1895 | 2.01 |
| 1895–1900 | 1.63 |
| 1900–1905 | 1.85 |
| 1905–1910 | 1.98 |
| 1910–1915 | 1.75 |
| 1915–1920 | 1.05 |
| 1920–1925 | 1.69 |
| 1925–1930 | 1.25 |
| 1930–1935 | 0.70 |
| 1935–1940 | 0.72 |
| 1940–1945 | 1.06 |
| 1945–1950 | 1.56 |
| 1950–1955 | 1.72 |
| 1955–1960 | 1.70 |
| 1960–1964 | 1.53 |
| 1965–1968 | 1.11 |

Sources: 1790–1870: Warren S. Thompson and P. K. Whelpton, *Population Trends in the United States* (New York: McGraw-Hill, 1933), pp. 1, 303; 1870–1964: Richard A. Easterlin, *Population, Labor Force, and Long Swings in Economic Growth: The American Experience* (New York: Columbia University Press, 1968), p. 189; 1965–1968; U.S. Bureau of the Census, *Statistical Abstract of the United States, 1969* (Washington, D.C.: U.S. Government Printing Office, 1969), p. 6.

While the major forces behind the quantity of farm products demanded have tended to produce a relatively slow growth of quantity demanded, this in itself would not produce the farm problem we have today. That problem is the result of the working of the forces of both supply and demand.

## Fast Growth of Supply

Supply has increased very rapidly relative to demand, especially in this century. In order to see the causes of the rapid increase in supply, let us begin by introducing the notion of a production function:

$$QA = g(L, K, R, T)$$

where

$QA$ = output of agricultural goods
$L$ = labor in agriculture
$K$ = capital in agriculture
$R$ = land (natural resources) in agriculture
$T$ = the state of agricultural technology, i.e., the technical knowledge about how to combine inputs to obtain output

The production function is the technical relationship between inputs (land, labor, and capital) and output given the state of technology. It tells the maximum amount of output that can be produced by each and every set of inputs per time period.

It is obvious that the vast expansion of land, labor, and capital devoted to agriculture accounts for an enormous increase in the supply of agricultural goods during the history of the United States. In recent decades, the amount of land and labor employed in agriculture has declined substantially, but the output of agricultural goods has nevertheless continued to rise. This can be explained by the substitution of capital for labor in agriculture and the enormous technological advances that have occurred in agriculture. Since the middle of the nineteenth century the effects of these changes have been augmented by the increased output per unit of input (productivity increase) resulting from growth of the market, increased specialization, and changes in the basic organization of agricultural production.

Technological change in agriculture generally appears in two ways: through mechanization and through application of discoveries in pure science. These are not entirely independent of each other, since scientific discovery may affect the invention of machines, and some scientific applications require a certain level of mechanical development. Both mechanization and application of scientific discovery in agriculture are means of applying capital to land so as to increase the productivity (output per unit of input) of farm land and farm laborers.

Historically, there have been three distinguishable periods in farm mechanization in the United States. The first, from about 1830 to 1880, was a period of basic invention. Mechanical invention in grain harvesting and improved horse-drawn implements for the row crops (corn and cotton) were especially important in the period 1830 to 1850. The second period, from about 1860 to 1910, was one of extensive use of machines dependent upon animal power. By the 1890s the possibilities of horse-drawn technology were almost fully achieved. The third period, about 1900 to the present, has witnessed the innovation of power-driven machinery. A lull in technical change through mechanization occurred from 1910 to 1940, disturbed by only one major development: the replacement of animal power by the tractor. This innovation substituted gasoline for hay and oats, which released 90 million acres of cropland (one-quarter of the acreage under cultivation) to other uses within four decades and expanded acreage available for dairy pasture and food crops by approximately one-third.

Applications of advances in pure science have affected U.S. agriculture primarily in the twentieth century. Considerable progress in fundamental science was required before standardized products (e.g., fertilizers, hybrid seeds, and insecticides) could become suitable products for commercial marketing and widespread use. These products began to appear in the 1920s. Before these products could be developed, however, a sponsor was needed to support risky and massive experiments in abstract science—experiments that could not be envisioned as leading to immediate economic gain.

In the United States, the patron was the federal government. The institutions that it established to carry out the task (the land-grant colleges and experiment stations) proved very effective in developing agricultural science and disseminating the results of research. The land grants under the Morrill Act (1863) stimulated every state to found colleges for the agricultural and mechanical arts. The experiment stations (at least one in every state) were introduced under the Hatch Act of 1887 and strengthened by the Adams Act of 1906. These institutions produced the requisite discoveries in basic science and subsequent applications. The Agricultural Extension Service made relevant developments known in a practical way to the farm population.

Since 1940, three major strands of invention have come together and intensified each other: (1) mechanical inventions designed to fit crop, terrain, and farm size; (2) biological inventions, most notably hybrid seed and improved feed and fertilization techniques for animals; and (3) the chemical and medical inventions—feeding nutrients from soil to plant, and controlling disease and natural enemies. The application of this intensified technology has become so widespread that fears are now expressed that the natural balance of the environment has been upset.[2]

The overall impact of this continuing technological change has been very great in the past two decades, as two statistics illustrate. In 1951, one farm worker supplied 16 persons with food; in 1971, he produced enough for 51 persons. The end of these cumulative developments is not at hand, but the history of technology suggests that advances along present lines are likely to terminate soon.

As a result of these changes, the growth of supply has exceeded that of demand. This is the primary cause of the American farm problem.

2. Whatever their merits, such fears are not new.

## Market Forces and the Determination of Prices

To understand fully the discussion about supply growing faster than demand and to appreciate the analysis of farm policy to date, it is necessary to acquire some detailed knowledge of the concepts of demand and supply.[3] Let us turn next to this question of concepts before taking up the details of present and past farm policies and their relation to the farm problem.

### Demand Schedules and Curves

At any point in time a definite relationship exists between the price of a good (such as beefsteak) and the quantity demanded of that good. It is a common observation that the quantity of a good that people will buy at any point in time varies inversely (is negatively related) with the price of the good. The higher the price, the smaller the quantity demanded; and, other things being equal, the lower the price, the larger the quantity demanded. The relationship between price and quantity bought is called the demand schedule or demand curve. Table 1–3 gives a hypothetical demand schedule for beefsteak. The demand schedule shows the relationship between quantity demanded and price. It shows the quantity of the good which consumers *desire* to buy at alternative prices. The demand schedule of Table 1–3 incorporates the "law of demand" referred to earlier, i.e., that the quantity demanded varies inversely with price.

It is very useful to depict the demand schedule graphically (or geometrically). Figure 1–3 shows the hypothetical demand schedule for beef-

Table 1–3
Demand Schedule for Beefsteak

| | Price ($ per lb.) | Quantity Demanded (millions of lbs. per month) |
|---|---|---|
| A | 4.0 | 6 |
| B | 3.5 | 8 |
| C | 3.0 | 12 |
| D | 2.5 | 18 |
| E | 2.0 | 25 |
| F | 1.5 | 40 |

3. According to that ubiquitous writer Anonymous, "You can make even a parrot into a learned political economist—all he must learn are the two words 'supply' and 'demand.' " It must often seem that this is the case to the uninitiated. However, as one with a brief initiation, you will, I hope, recognize that the crucial point in demand and supply analysis is recognition of the impact of the forces determining demand and supply themselves, the other things being assumed constant behind each curve.

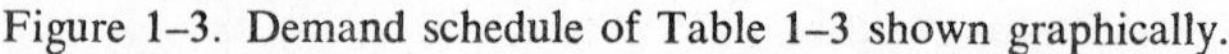

Figure 1–3. Demand schedule of Table 1–3 shown graphically.

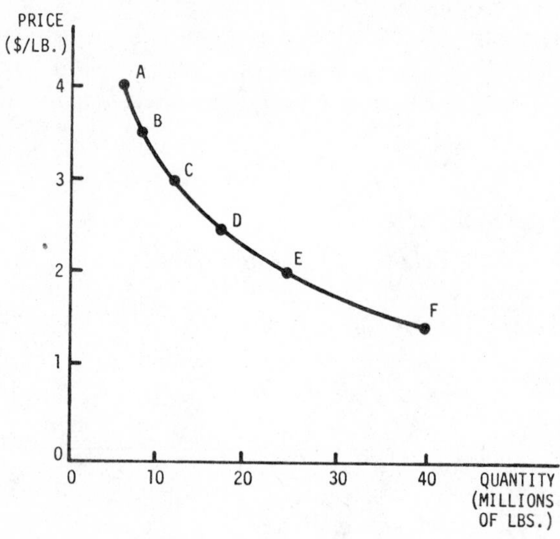


steak contained in Table 1–3. The vertical scale represents the various alternative prices of beefsteak measured in dollars per unit (in this case, dollars per pound). The horizontal scale measures the quantity of beefsteak demanded (in pounds) per time unit (in this case, per month). The locus of connecting points *A, B, C, D, E* and *F* is called the "demand curve," which is simply a graphical (or geometric) representation of a demand schedule. In Figure 1–3 the demand curve is a smooth curve drawn through the coordinates given by the price and quantity observations of Table 1–3. Thus quantity and price are inversely related on the demand curve, *Q* going down when *P* goes up, and vice versa. Because of this the demand curve slopes downward to the right, i.e., from northwest to southeast. This is an important property and is labeled the "law of downward sloping demand." It holds true for virtually all commodities.

The market demand schedule is simply the horizontal summation of the demand schedules of all consumers. An important reason for the validity of the law of downward sloping demand is that each reduction of price may result in additional purchases of a good by each of its consumers, and of course a rise in price may cause each to buy less. There are two main reasons for this. The first is that, as the price of a good (beefsteak) rises, individuals will substitute other goods (hamburger, roasts, etc.) for it, so that the quantity purchased declines. The opposite substitution occurs when the price of the good is reduced. Also, when the price of the good rises, individuals will find themselves really poorer than before. They will view their real income as being reduced by the rise in price, and will therefore consume less of most normal goods. The opposite income effect occurs when the price of beefsteak falls. These substitution and income effects are the reason for the law of downward sloping demand for individual consumers. Additionally, the market demand curve is downward sloping because the lowering (raising) of price increases (reduces) the number of individual buyers.

The demand curve for a particular good describes behavior when other things besides the price of the good are held constant (in the case of demand the other things usually considered are income, tastes, and the prices of other goods). As long as other things are held constant, changes in the quantity of a good available result in movements along the demand curve. Such movements along a demand curve are called *changes in the quantity demanded*.

Other things, of course, do not always remain constant. Income rises or falls, tastes change in favor of or against a particular good, and prices of goods that are substitutes or complements (goods used in conjunction with the particular good) rise (or fall). These changes bring about a movement in the demand curve. In general, a rise in income or prices of substitute goods, or a change in tastes favorable to a particular good, increases demand for the good as depicted by the shift from *DD to* $D_1D_1$ in Figure 1–4.

Figure 1–4. Changes in demand.

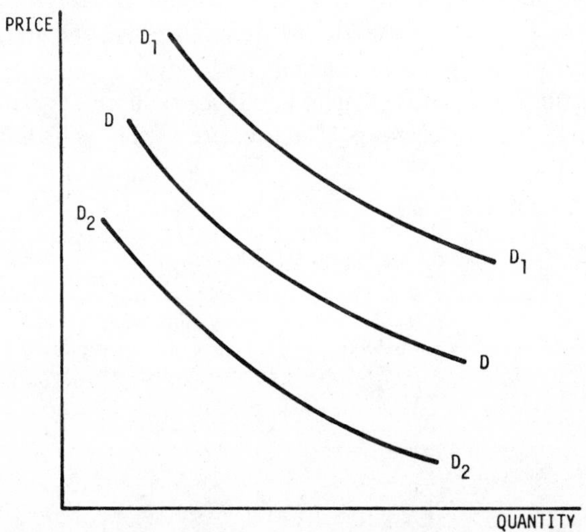

Reverse changes in the other things held constant reduces demand, as shown by the shift from *DD* to $D_2D_2$ in Figure 1–4. Such movements in demand are referred to as *changes in demand.* These shifts in the demand curve should be clearly distinguished from movements along a demand curve or *changes in quantity demanded.*

**Supply Schedules and Curves**

To evaluate the impact of agricultural programs on the market for farm products it is necessary to consider supply as well as demand. A supply schedule reflects the quantities of a particular good that producers wish to sell at alternative prices. Table 1–4 presents a hypothetical supply schedule for beefsteak. For a particular supply schedule, as well as for a specific demand schedule, it is assumed that everything that affects the quantity supplied other than price of the good in question is held constant. The other things assumed equal for supply include the goals of firms, the state of technology, prices of other goods, and the prices of factors of production. Generally a specific supply schedule is assumed to correspond to the behavior illustrated by the hypothetical supply schedule of Table 1–4. Here the quantity of the good produced and offered for sale increases as the price of the good rises and decreases as price falls. This simply says that producers wish to supply a larger quantity as price per unit rises, and vice versa. In the case of supply, price and quantity vary directly.

The supply schedule, like the demand schedule, is usually depicted graphically or geometrically for analytical purposes. The curve connecting points *A, B, C, D, E,* and *F* of Figure 1–5 is the supply schedule contained in Table 1–4, with the *P* and *Q* coordinates labeled as in the table. The vertical axis measures price per unit and the horizontal axis measures the quantity supplied (flow) per time period. Movements along the supply schedule are termed *changes in quantity supplied.*

Changes in those other things held equal for a supply schedule result in shifts of supply (i.e., movements of the entire supply schedule). Suppose

Table 1–4
Supply Schedule for Beefsteak

| | Price (\$ per lb.) | Quantity Supplied (millions of lbs. per month) |
|---|---|---|
| A | 4.0 | 24 |
| B | 3.5 | 22 |
| C | 3.0 | 20 |
| D | 2.5 | 18 |
| E | 2.0 | 15 |
| F | 1.5 | 10 |

Figure 1–5. Supply schedule for beefsteak.

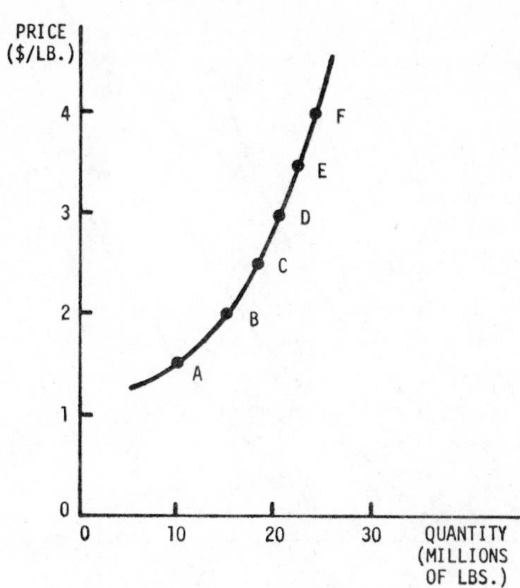


the state of technology improves or prices of factors of production decline. These changes would increase supply. An increase in supply is represented by the shift from *SS* to $S_1S_1$ in Figure 1–6. The reverse changes would result in a decrease in supply, as indicated by the shift from *SS to* $S_2S_2$. These movements in the supply schedule and curve are referred to as *changes in supply* to distinguish them from movements along a specific curve, or *changes in quantity supplied.* Note that the terminology used for supply is analogous to that used for demand. The purpose is to avoid the frequent confusion between movements along a curve and a shift in the curve.

### Price Determination

Now we are ready to combine supply and demand to see how competitive market price is determined. A competitive market is one in which buyers and sellers accept the price determined by the working of the market. No buyer or seller can affect the price in the market through his individual actions. In general terms this is a good description of most agricultural goods markets. Neither the supply nor the demand schedule alone can tell us how much will be produced and consumed and the actual level of price. To determine this we must put supply and demand together. The hypothetical schedules of demand and supply for beefsteak are presented in Table 1–5.

Figure 1–6. Changes in supply.

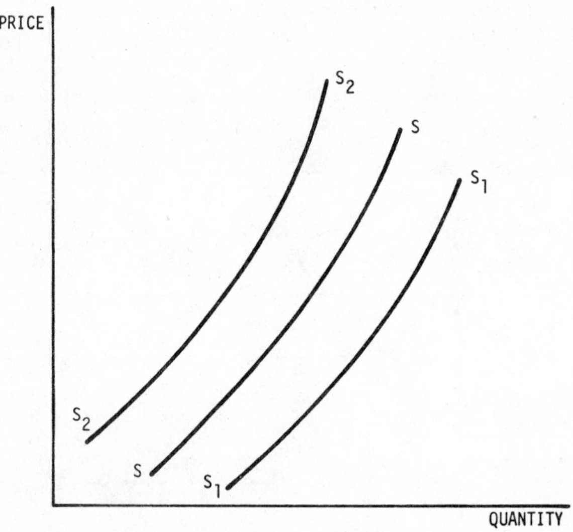


Suppose we were to use trial and error to determine the equilibrium price of beefsteak in the market represented in Table 1–5. Try situation A with the price of $4 per pound. Clearly this price cannot prevail for any extended period of time. Producers will supply 24 million pounds of beefsteak every month, but the amount demanded by consumers is only 6 million pounds per month. Eighteen million pounds of beefsteak would have to go into storage every month. As the stock of beefsteak mounts, competitive sellers will cut price. Thus if price were set at $4 per pound, downward pressure on the price would exist in the market.

Consider situation F, with beefsteak priced at $1.50 per pound. Con-

Table 1–5
Supply and Demand Schedules for Beefsteak

| | Price ($ per lb.) | Quantity Demanded (millions of lbs. per month) | Quantity Supplied (millions of lbs. per month) |
|---|---|---|---|
| A | 4.0 | 6 | 24 |
| B | 3.5 | 8 | 22 |
| C | 3.0 | 12 | 20 |
| D | 2.5 | 18 | 18 |
| E | 2.0 | 25 | 15 |
| F | 1.5 | 40 | 10 |

sumers now wish to purchase 40 million pounds per month, but producers want to supply only 10 million pounds. The previously overflowing storage facilities are soon emptied. Disappointed demanders will bid the price up. It is clear that upward pressure on price will exist in the market if the price is initially set at $1.50 per pound.

By now the equilibrium price is obvious. The quantity willingly supplied is equal to the quantity willingly demanded only in situation D, with the price at $2.50 per pound. Given the supply and demand schedules, this is the only price that can prevail for an extended period of time. Competitive equilibrium occurs at the point of intersection (*I*) of supply and demand curves (schedules), as shown graphically in Figure 1–7. Again, this kind of market situation is an accurate description, for the most part, of the agricultural sector of the economy.

If price is set at $4 in Figure 1–7, a condition of *surplus* exists. Quantity supplied exceeds quantity demanded. Downward movement of price results in a free competitive market. When price is set at $1, we have a *shortage* situation. The quantity demanded exceeds the quantity supplied. Upward movement of price results in a free competitive market when we have a shortage situation. Only at point *I* will there be a balancing of forces and an equilibrium with respect to price and quantity. It is in this manner that supply and demand play their roles.

Figure 1–7. Price and quantity in the beefsteak market as determined by supply and demand.

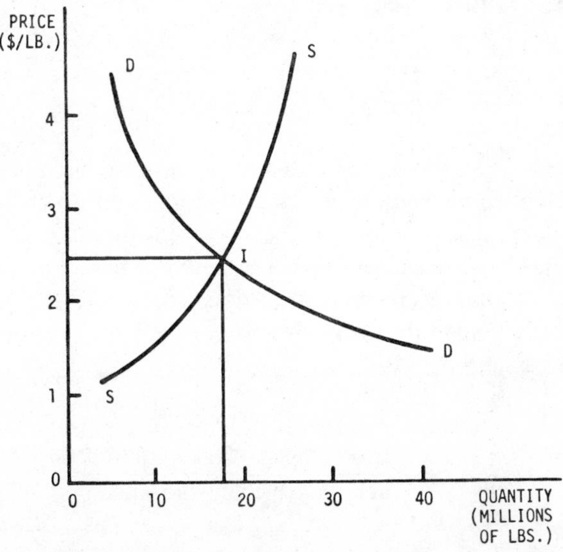

## Price Fluctuations and Income Instability

The long-run farm problem, an oversupply of farmers, is complicated by the short-run instability of income in agriculture. This instability (fluctuation) of income is the product of fluctuation in farm prices resulting from fluctuations in demand and supply. Short-run fluctuations in demand for farm goods primarily result from the instability of export demand. Demand in the rest of the world for U.S. farm products depends on weather (a highly variable factor) in the rest of the world. Export markets can also experience dramatic changes because of tariff acts or quality or sanitary restrictions imposed to benefit domestic producers. This source of instability has had a differential effect over time on the various products of American agriculture. Demand fluctuations by themselves have not had serious long-run effects on U.S. farm income, except when they were large and continued over several years.

The domestic supply of farm products has also been subject to considerable variability. Weather, insects, and disease, as well as movement of resources between regions or particular lines of production in response to market forces, can lead to fluctuations in supply.

The size of the price change resulting from fluctuations in demand or supply, or both, is dependent on the responsiveness of quantity demanded or supplied to changes in price. In economics, this responsiveness is called elasticity. An anomaly for farmers is the fact that, as a whole, they tend to receive *less* total revenue with good harvests than with poor harvests. The tendency for high $Q$ and low $P \times Q$ to go together in agriculture is an important factor with which every recent President of the United States has had to reckon. This phenomenon is a result of the "price elasticity of demand" for agricultural goods.

## Price Elasticity

Price elasticity of demand is a measure of the responsiveness of quantity demanded to price changes. A word of warning is in order here. It can be very misleading merely to inspect a single demand curve and to conclude from its general appearance (slope) something about the degree of responsiveness of quantity demanded to price changes. As a measure of the responsiveness of quantity demanded to changes in price, define the price elasticity of demand as:

$$\eta = -\frac{\text{percentage change in quantity}}{\text{percentage change in price}}$$

Where $\Delta$ stands for "a small change in," we can write:

$$\eta = -\frac{\Delta Q}{Q} \div \frac{\Delta P}{P}$$

This can be manipulated to:

$$\eta = -\frac{\Delta Q}{\Delta P} \times \frac{P}{Q}.$$

It can be shown that $\Delta Q/\Delta P$ is the reciprocal of the slope $(\Delta P/\Delta Q)$. From this it is clear why examination of the slope alone does not give us a clear indication of the responsiveness of quantity demanded to changes in price. This is given only by the price elasticity of demand. When $\eta = 0$, the demand curve is vertical; the same quantity will be demanded regardless of price. If $\eta = \infty$, the demand curve is horizontal.

One might be inclined to suppose that the revenue $(P \times Q)$ received by sellers of a good must move in the same direction as price. This is not necessarily so, as can be seen from consideration of the law of downward sloping demand and price elasticity of demand. Consider a decline in price. From the law of downward sloping demand we know that the quantity demanded will increase. What happens to total revenue depends on the proportionate change in quantity demanded relative to the proportionate change in price, i.e., on the value of price elasticity of demand. If $\eta > 1$, demand is said to be elastic with respect to price. If $\eta < 1$, demand is inelastic, and if $\eta = 1$, demand is of unitary elasticity. If price declines and demand is elastic, total revenue increases. If price rises and demand is elastic, total revenue falls. The reverse movement of total revenue occurs with price decreases and increases when demand is inelastic. If demand is of unitary elasticity, total revenue remains the same when price rises or falls.

The demand for agricultural goods in general is inelastic with respect to price. Thus a greater quantity of goods that can be sold only at a lower price, other things being equal, means that total revenue will decline. Conversely, a smaller quantity of goods sold at a higher price results in larger total revenue. In general, then, small harvests produce a greater total revenue for farmers as a whole than do large harvests. These statements do not, of course, apply to each and every individual farm product.

**Supply Elasticity**

Supply curves, like demand curves, have a measurable responsiveness of quantity change to price change at each point on the curve. In the case of supply, this responsiveness is labeled supply elasticity. The elasticity of supply ($\epsilon$) is defined as:

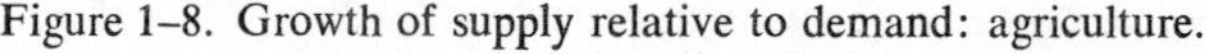

$$\epsilon = \frac{\text{percentage change in quantity supplied}}{\text{percentage change in price}}$$

Like the elasticity of demand, supply elasticity is a measure of the responsiveness of change in quantity to change in price. If $\epsilon = 0$, the quantity supplied is fixed—that is, the same quantity will be supplied at all prices—and the supply curve is vertical; when $\epsilon = \infty$, the supply curve is horizontal.

The end result of the demand and supply changes discussed earlier has been that the growth of supply has outstripped that of demand. This is illustrated in Figure 1–8 where supply has increased much more (from *SS*

Figure 1–8. Growth of supply relative to demand: agriculture.

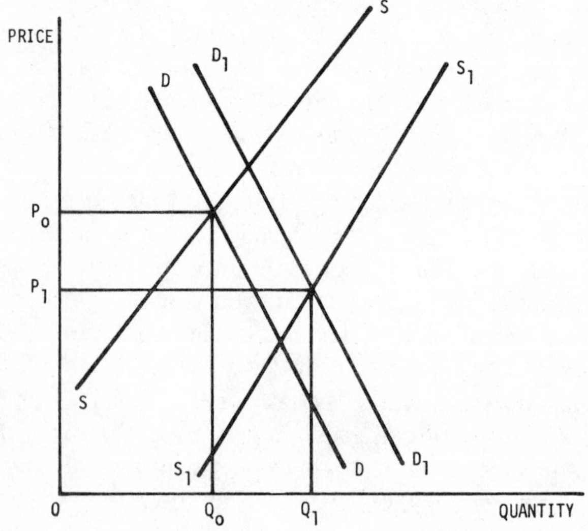


to $S_1S_1$) than demand (from *DD* to $D_1D_1$). The result of these long-term changes in demand and supply is continuing downward pressure on farm prices in general. This pressure is substantial because both demand and supply are quite inelastic with respect to price. Small shifts in inelastic curves generate large price fluctuations.

Short-run fluctuations in demand and supply also result in considerable variability of farm income because of the relative inelasticity of agricultural demand and supply curves. This short-run problem of income instability requires a different solution than does the long-run problem of an oversupply of farmers.

### Income Elasticity

Demand elasticity is considered in two parts. One is price elasticity of demand, discussed previously; the other is income elasticity of demand. Income elasticity of demand, as we might expect, is simply the responsiveness of quantity demanded of a particular good to changes in income, and it is defined in the same way as price elasticity of demand, except that income is substituted for price. Thus, income elasticity $(E)$ is

$$E = \frac{\text{percentage change in quantity demanded}}{\text{percentage change in income}}$$

For most goods, increases in income bring about an increase in demand, and income elasticity will be positive. Income elasticity of demand is negative only for what are termed inferior goods, i.e., goods that consumers demand less of as income increases.

In general, as noted previously, the responsiveness of quantity demanded to increases in income is less than proportionate for agricultural goods. In other words, the income elasticity of demand for agricultural goods is less than one.

### Farm Policy Since 1929

Federal policy (and legislation) before 1920 was not intended to have a direct effect on prices and production. Since that date, however, the "farm bloc" has obtained legislation that directly affects farm prices. Because many consider the years 1909–1914 to have been the golden age of agriculture, there has been considerable political pressure to have the government guarantee farm prices that would be as favorable to the farmer as the prices prevailing then. This is the basic idea of "parity" and parity prices. To many, it seems only fair that if a unit of farm goods sold for enough to purchase a certain market basket of city goods and services from 1909 to 1914, then in the 1970s the same relationship should hold. A major difficulty with this concept is that more rapid technical progress on the farm than in town means that a unit of rural resources produces many more units of output in 1973 than it did from 1909 to 1914. Maintenance of parity, or even 60 or 70 percent of parity, means six-figure incomes for efficient farmers, but only a pittance for the marginal farmer. The subsidy involved keeps some inefficient farmers from moving to occupations where their productivity would increase. The result of all this is that production is different, and less efficient, than it would be in a free market. Programs put in effect since 1929 have, in general, exacerbated the basic farm problem instead of resolving it. The major programs can be divided into four groups, which we will examine in some detail.

### Purchase-Loan Storage Programs

The first purchase-loan storage program was embodied in the Agricultural Marketing Act of 1929, which established a Federal Farm Board with the primary function of encouraging the formation of cooperative marketing associations. The Board was authorized to set up institutions called "stabilization corporations" to be owned by the cooperatives and funded with $500 million to carry on price-support operations. Between June 1929 and June 1932 the corporations bought surplus farm products, only to incur steadily growing losses as prices declined. The Federal Farm Board took over the operation and accepted the losses. About $676 million was spent on stabilization operations and loans to cooperatives in three years. The Board was successful only in spending the taxpayers' money and to some extent redistributing income from taxpayers in general to farmers.

The dilemma faced by price-support programs like that of the Federal Farm Board is illustrated in Figure 1–9. The government pegs the price at $OP$, above the market equilibrium price $OP_1$. At price $OP$ there is a surplus, $Q_sQ_d$, because the quantity demanded is only $OQ_d$ while the quantity supplied is $OQ_s$. The government therefore must buy $Q_sQ_d$ of the good. Consumers pay the higher price, $OP$, and get no current benefit from the $Q_sQ_d$ part of the crop. In loan-storage programs the government must also pay for storing the surplus. The owners of storage facilities, who may also be farmers, gain from this type of program at the expense of taxpayers.

One of the background ideas in this kind of program has been to establish what is called an "ever normal granary" program of stabilization. This program was to work in the following way: It was supposed that there were limitations on the growth of supply relative to demand. Thus while the government would maintain its support price of $OP$, demand ($DD$) would in time shift to the right and intersect $SS$ above point $B$. The Treasury would then have to do nothing to maintain parity, but could reverse the previous procedure. It could take food out of storage and sell it to the public to maintain price $OP$.

The problem with the "ever normal granary" concept is that supply has not stood still and waited for demand to catch up. Farmers faced with a guaranteed parity price of $OP$, which would give them higher earnings for resources than can be achieved elsewhere in the economy, would rush to increase supply. Thus supply would increase from $SS$ to $S_1S_1$. Now, the

Figure 1–9. Price support program.

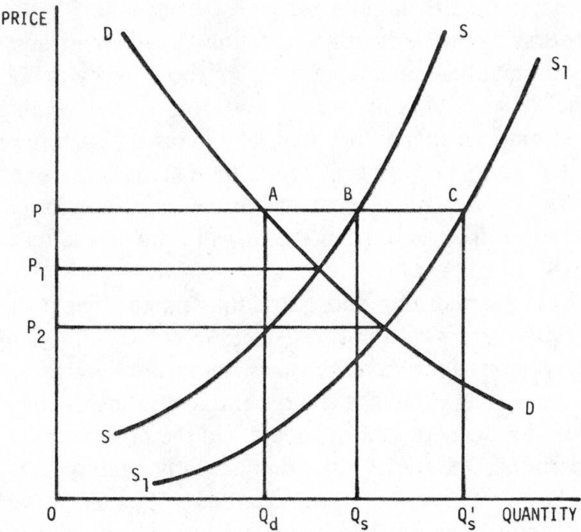


government would have to buy $Q_s'Q_d$ to maintain price at *OP*. Taxpayers would then have to pay even more for the price support program. Clearly, consumers would be worse off with this policy. Efficient farmers and owners of storage facilities would, however, gain.

### Crop Restriction Programs

The difficulty of supporting prices for farm products when supply continues to grow was quickly seen. In May of 1933 the Agricultural Adjustment Act was enacted, providing for an Agricultural Adjustment Administration (AAA) which had the responsibility of raising farm prices by restricting the supply of farm commodities. The "acreage allotment" became the most important weapon of the AAA. Considering prospective demand and carry-over from the previous season, the AAA would determine a total acreage of certain major crops to be planted in the next growing season. The total acreage would then be subdivided into state totals, which in turn would be allotted to individual farms on the basis of each farm's recent crop history. The original AAA scheme received a setback in 1936 when the Agricultural Adjustment Act was declared unconstitutional. The adverse decision did not force discontinuance of acreage allotments, but only changed the previous basis on which allotments had been made to one that presumably encouraged soil conservation.

A new Agricultural Adjustment Act was passed in 1938 which greatly increased the power of the Commodity Credit Corporation (CCC), an independent agency with the minor function of "cushioning" prices of wheat, corn, and cotton against adverse fluctuations in demand and supply. The CCC did this by making loans to farmers on the security of their crop on a "nonrecourse" basis so that the loan rates were, in effect, minimum prices.[4] The 1938 act made it mandatory that CCC loans on corn, wheat, and cotton be between 52 and 75 percent of parity. Thereafter, Congress specified support prices at a certain percent of parity or at farm prices having the same purchasing power as those prevailing in a favorable base period such as 1909–1914.

The marketing agreement and marketing quota, which came into use during the 1930s, are two additional means of restricting supply of farm products. Marketing agreements are still important for certain fruits and vegetables and milk. In this scheme a contract is entered into between an association of producers of a raw product and the processors of the product, with a Department of Agriculture representative refereeing the contract negotiations. Minimum prices, total quantity to be marketed, and allotments of marketings among processors may be set by the producers and processors. Marketing quotas involve setting an upper limit to the amount of certain crops that producers can sell. If two-thirds of the qualified producers approve in a referendum, a quota is assigned each grower. Any farmer who exceeds the marketing quota is subject to fines and penalties on the excess sold.

A new wrinkle in crop limitation was tried under the Soil Bank Act of 1956 in an effort to stem the rising carryover of feed grain and wheat. The aim was to reduce supplies of the six basic crops (wheat, corn, cotton, tobacco, rice, and peanuts) by achieving a 10 to 17 percent reduction in cropland. This was to be accomplished on a "voluntary" basis through payments for shifting land out of production into the "soil bank." The plan did not achieve its goal, since carry-overs continued to rise until 1961.

The economics of crop restriction programs can be seen in Figure 1–10. Before initiation of the crop limitation program, supply is $SS$ and market price and quantity are $OP$ and $OQ$. When government intervenes, and production controls cut supply from $SS$ to $S_1S_1$, price rises to $OP_1$ and equilibrium $Q$ declines to $OQ_1$. Because demand is inelastic with respect to price, gross farm income is increased. Moreover, since something is saved on production costs when less is produced, net revenue increases more

4. With a nonrecourse loan, the farmer could let CCC take title to the stored product and cancel the debt together with accumulated interest, if prices fell below the loan rate. If prices rose above the loan rate, the farmer could sell the commodity, pay back the loan with interest, and keep any difference.

Figure 1–10. Crop limitation program.

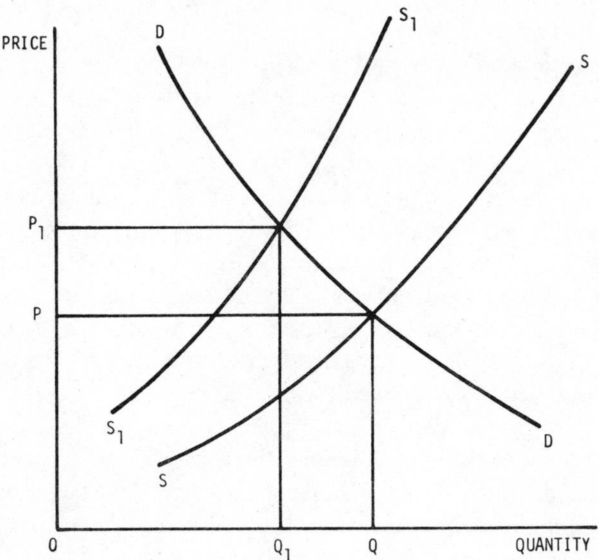


than total receipts.[5] Consumers, of course, are hurt by the scarcity of goods and higher prices.

Suppose that price $OP_1$ in Figure 1–10 is the parity price the government wishes to achieve. Can it be guaranteed that the crop restriction program will achieve an equilibrium price of $OP_1$? The obvious answer is no. Farmers are free to use tremendous doses of fertilizer to increase output on quota land under acreage allotment schemes. Thus an acreage allotment calculated to produce $OP_1$ and $OQ_1$ in the market may produce something quite different. The costs to taxpayers may not in the end be much different with

5. Thus, in the case of acreage allotment programs, the net earnings of the land that can be used in the program rise. Since the value of land is the capitalization of the earnings stream, the value of the land that has an allotment rises. That is,

$$V = \frac{NE}{r} \text{ rises under an acreage allotment program}$$

where

$V =$ value of land per unit
$NE =$ net earnings per unit
$r =$ the market interest rate

Acreage allotment programs enormously benefited the original owners of the land affected by the program.

crop restriction programs than without them. The farm problem will be no nearer solution.

### Subsidized Producer-Consumer Price Differential

A subsidized producer-consumer price differential program was advocated by President Truman's Secretary of Agriculture, Charles Brannan, as a means of providing price supports for perishable goods. The Brannan plan relied on unconcealed payment of subsidies and on that ground was opposed by farm organizations. The House of Representatives refused to give the plan a trial run on three commodities. Opponents carried the day by branding so straightforward a subsidy as "socialism." It was next proposed with respect to butter by Secretary of Agriculture Benson in the Eisenhower administration and passed by the Republican Congress for that highly perishable commodity, wool.

The Benson-Brannan plan is a two-price system: one price for farmers, another for consumers. The difference between the two (if the support price to be received by farmers is greater than the market price to consumers) is paid by the Treasury, i.e., by our friends the taxpayers. Figure 1–11 illustrates the plan. The support price guaranteed by the government is the same *OP* as in Figure 1–9. Quantity supplied at price *OP* is *OQ*. Once the output is produced and on the market, supply is fixed until the

Figure 1–11. The Benson-Brannan plan.

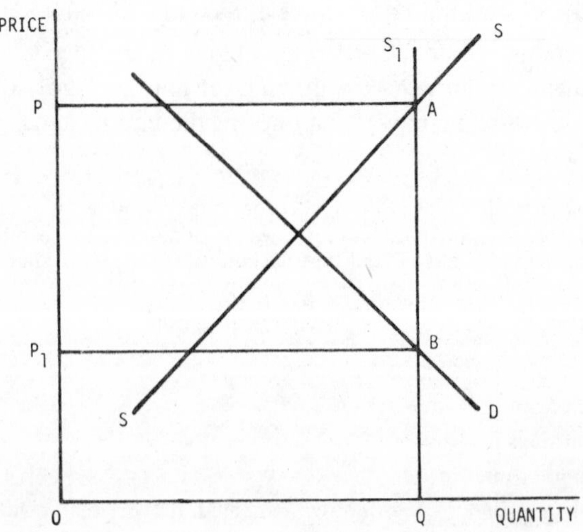

next production period, so that the supply curve (during the market period) is $S_1$. The demand curve *DD* tells us that consumers are willing to pay $OP_1$ for quantity *OQ*. Thus, to guarantee price *OP*, the Treasury (through the Department of Agriculture) must pay each farmer the amount *AB* per unit sold. The effect is the same as if the government bought the whole crop at price *OP* and sold it on the market for whatever price it would bring. The total cost to the government is shown by the area $PABP_1$.

Under the Benson-Brannan plan the farmer receives price *OP*, as in the loan-storage price support program. Producers are equally well off, receiving the same total income under both plans. With respect to overall efficiency of resource use, society is in essentially the same relative position as with a loan-storage price support program. However, consumers are now able to use the entire crop at a much lower price than under a loan-storage price support program. Agricultural goods are not left to rot in storage, thus avoiding wasteful storage costs. Of course, the "storage lobby," which includes a lot of farmers who have invested in their own storage facilities, has not been numbered among the leading supporters of the Benson-Brannan plan.

The Benson-Brannan plan has one overriding drawback from the viewpoint of political feasibility, which explains in part why it has been used only with wool, hardly a major American agricultural product. The problem is that the plan costs the Treasury more money if demand is inelastic with respect to price. Since consumers pay a lower price under this plan than under loan-storage price support programs (as shown in Figure 1–9), the total amount they pay is less than under the latter programs. Because the total amount paid to farmers is the same, by our present assumptions, the Treasury obviously pays more with the Benson-Brannan plan. From an economic viewpoint, a subsidized producer-consumer price differential program is preferable to a loan-storage program to support prices because it does not involve the wasteful storage costs of the latter, and because it makes a larger quantity of current farm products available to consumers at lower prices.

### Programs to Increase Farm Product Demand

The programs we have considered so far deal with the supply side of the market. A number of programs have also been proposed to work through the demand side. Two types of so-called surplus removal programs have been employed. The more acceptable of these have been the nutrition or direct distribution programs, which include school lunch projects, food stamp plans, and low-cost milk distribution plans. By these means, surplus commodities have been provided to those who presumably need them the most. Benefits to poor and undernourished people have been of more importance than any influence such schemes may have exerted on agricultural demand.

The second, and basically indefensible, surplus removal operation has been the export subsidy. The export subsidy is a payment to exporters to make up the difference between supported prices in the home market and lower world prices. This interference with international trade is a form of dumping which might be defended on the grounds that the rest of the world enjoys an enhancement of real income. Such an operation, however, adversely affects the income and market positions of producers of competing commodities, and hurts friendly nations that have the same goods to sell. The use of this technique by the United States, originally formulated in the Agricultural Adjustment Act of 1933, did not become significant until an amendment passed in 1935 provided that up to 30 percent of annual customs revenues could be used to finance the program. In the 1939–1940 fiscal year, export subsidies for wheat and cotton totaled $26 and $36 million, respectively.

Beginning in 1954, largely under the provisions of Public Law 480, the United States began a massive subsidy of the export of many commodities in excess supply. As a result of this program, exports in 1962 accounted for 15 percent of farm cash receipts, more than half the wheat and rice crops, and one-third the cotton crop being exported.

Cotton provides a good example of the mess created by the policies we have been examining. First, the cotton price is supported and the supply restricted so that costs of the program do not become too noticeable. Next, since at the support price we have a surplus of cotton, export subsidies are paid so that cotton can be exported, for example to Japan. The Japanese produce cotton textiles with cotton purchased through subsidized exports and then export the cotton textiles to the United States. American textile producers scream because the Japanese competition is based, in part, on U.S. cotton purchased by Japanese cotton textile producers at the world price (lower than the U.S. price) with the help of U.S. taxpayers. The United States responds with tariffs or quotas (the effect of quotas is like that of tariffs—a sales tax paid by domestic consumers) on Japanese cotton textiles. Thus does one mistaken policy breed another, and yet another, in turn.

## Efficient Use of Farm Resources

The overall objective of farm policy should be efficient use of farm resources. By this we mean that the maximum possible production should be obtained from the resources devoted to agriculture, consistent with consumer desires. Farm policy since 1929 has not achieved this goal, and has in fact led to inefficient use of agricultural resources in the United States.

We can see this and analyze the effect of past programs by developing another analytical tool—the production possibility frontier.

The production possibility frontier or transformation curve shows the maximum amount of goods that can be produced by the economy and the tradeoff between goods in production. It is derived from our knowledge of the production functions of various goods and consumers' willingness to substitute one good for another.

We can simplify the problem by considering an economy that produces only two goods, bread and cloth. Let us assume given quantities of land, labor, capital, and a stock of technical knowledge. At one extreme all of society's resources could be used to produce bread. There would still be a maximum amount of bread that could be produced per time period. That amount would, of course, depend on the quantity and quality of resources available and technological efficiency. Suppose that under these conditions 30 million pounds of bread is the maximum amount that can be produced.

At the other extreme all of society's resources could be used to produce cloth. Again, only some maximum number of bolts of cloth of a certain description could be produced. Let that number be 10 million. Between the two extremes many other production possibilities exist. If the society is willing to give up some bread, some cloth can also be produced; if it is willing to give up some cloth, it can produce some bread. Several possibilities are presented in the schedule in Table 1–6. The extreme with all bread and no cloth produced is possibility A, while that with all cloth and no bread produced is possibility F. Between these two extremes, at possibilities B, C, D, and E, bread is given up increasingly in return for more cloth. Bread is transformed into cloth, not physically, but by the use of resources to produce cloth rather than bread.

It is useful to represent the production possibility or production transformation schedule graphically, as in Figure 1–12. Cloth is measured along the horizontal axis and bread along the vertical axis. The entire range of production possibilities is shown by a smooth curve drawn through the points *A*, *B*, *C*, *D*, *E*, and *F*.

Table 1–6
Alternative Production Possibilities

| Possibility | Bread (millions of lbs.) | Cloth (millions of bolts) |
|---|---|---|
| A | 30 | 0 |
| B | 28 | 2 |
| C | 24 | 4 |
| D | 18 | 6 |
| E | 10 | 8 |
| F | 0 | 10 |

Figure 1–12. Production possibility schedule.

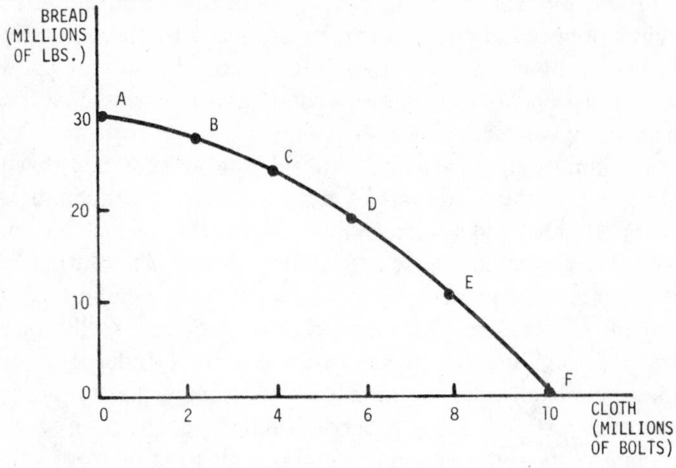


The production possibility frontier is drawn for full use (employment) of society's resources, given the state of technology. It assumes that all resources are used in the most efficient way. That is, resources are used so as to obtain the maximum output from the given stock of resources. In summary we find that a full employment economy, in producing one good, must

Figure 1–13. Shift in production possibility frontier.

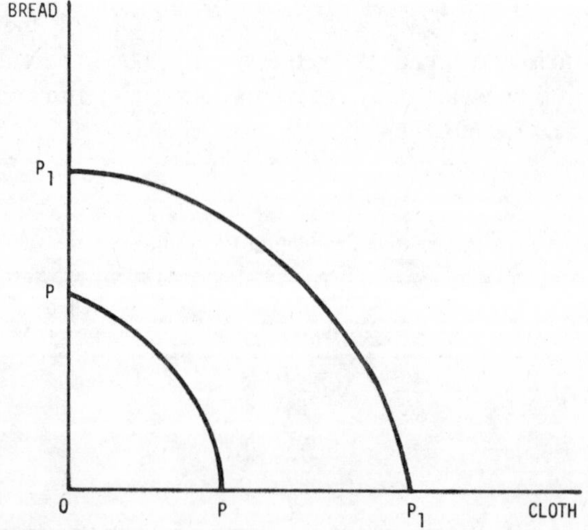

always give up some of another. The production possibility frontier shows the menu of choice available.

If either the state of technology improves or the stock of resources grows (or both), the production possibility frontier will shift outward. Thus in Figure 1–13 we have the production possibility frontier shifting from *PP* to $P_1P_1$ in a northeasterly direction. The shift may occur in a parallel fashion, but is usually biased toward one good or the other, as shown in the example.

One result of the farm policies followed since 1929 is to make the earnings on subsidized products higher than they would otherwise be. The earnings of many farmers, therefore, are higher than would be the case in the absence of such policies. Some farmers whose productivity is relatively low—that is, farmers who are relatively inefficient—are thus kept in agriculture rather than moving to occupations where their productivity would be higher. This is an inefficient use of resources (resource allocation), which means that the economy's output is not so high as it could be given available resources and technology. Society is operating inside the production frontier at some point like *U* in Figure 1–14. This is clearly inefficient, since more goods can be produced with the same resources and technology. The same inefficiency results from crop restriction programs, the soil bank, and so on.

If the outcome of price support policies is to bring about an increase in supply of the supported good, the result is inefficient in another way. Suppose that production is efficient in that the maximum possible output is obtained from the given resources and technology and that the economy operates at point *B* on the production frontier in Figure 1–14. If the economy would operate at point *A* under a free competitive market, production at *B* is not the best (efficient) solution. Consumers desire *OC* of other goods and *OD* of farm goods, but because of government interference end up with only *OE* of other goods and the larger quantity *OF* of farm goods. The well-being of society would be increased by letting the market operate, causing us to produce at point *A*. The solution at *B* is not the best. If this result is produced by a purchase-loan storage program, farmers who have goods to sell and owners of storage facilities gain, but society in general loses.

The two examples discussed illustrate the general resource allocation effect of farm policy to date. Clearly we must do better than this in the future.

## Agricultural Policy for the Future

From the foregoing discussion it is apparent that the agricultural policies of yesterday and today have failed to resolve the basic American farm problem—too many farmers. Although the underlying aim has been to support the income of poor farmers, the programs have primarily provided a boon to

Figure 1–14. Inefficient resource allocation.

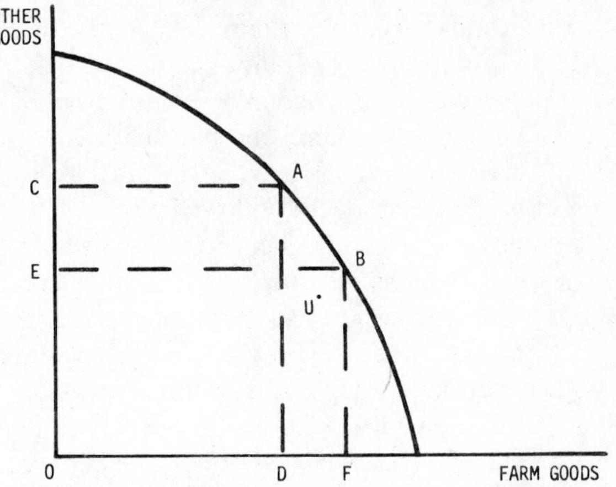


Figure 1–15. Distribution of farms by sales, 1964.

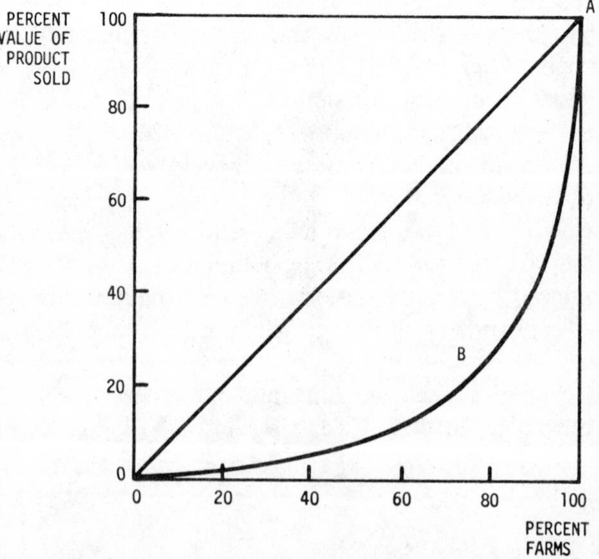


Source: Calculated from statistics in U.S. Bureau of Census, *Census of Agriculture, 1964* (Washington, D.C.: U.S. Government Printing Office, 1967).

Table 1–7
Distribution of Farms by Sales, 1964

| Value of Products Sold Per Farm (dollars) | Number of Farms (thousands) | Percentage of all Farms | Percentage of Value of Product Sold |
|---|---|---|---|
| 250–999 | 479 | 17.7 | 0.9 |
| 1,000–1,499 | 206 | 7.3 | 0.7 |
| 1,500–1,999 | 160 | 5.7 | 0.8 |
| 2,000–2,499 | 132 | 4.7 | 0.8 |
| 2,500–4,999 | 444 | 15.8 | 4.7 |
| 5,000–7,499 | 290 | 10.3 | 5.2 |
| 7,500–9,999 | 214 | 7.6 | 5.3 |
| 10,000–14,999 | 291 | 10.3 | 10.3 |
| 15,000–19,999 | 176 | 6.3 | 8.8 |
| 20,000–29,999 | 180 | 6.4 | 12.8 |
| 30,000–39,999 | 80 | 2.9 | 8.0 |
| 40,000–59,999 | 69 | 2.4 | 9.7 |
| 60,000 and over | 74 | 2.6 | 32.0 |

Source: Calculated from statistics in U.S. Bureau of the Census, *Census of Agriculture, 1964* (Washington, D.C.; U.S. Government Printing Office, 1967).

efficient farmers and especially to those who are already relatively wealthy compared to the average taxpayer (or consumer) who is paying the cost.[6] Implicitly the programs assume something like an equal distribution of volume of farm product sales over farms, which is far from the case. Table 1–7 and Figure 1–15 provide us with an illustration. If sales were distributed equally, the cumulative percentage distribution of farms and corresponding distribution of sales would lie on the line *OA*. Instead, the distribution of sales over farms is shown by the line *OBA*, indicating an extremely unequal distribution. Almost one-third of the value of sales is made by 2.6 percent of the farms in the United States. Five-eighths of total sales are made by only 14.3 percent of all farms. The subsidies involved in our farm policies basically go to those who have something to sell. Thus the subsidies are distributed among farms proportionally to sales. Truly, for the wealthy farmer this has been a "sweet land of subsidy"—welfare for the rich, taxes for the poor, and high food prices.

In summary, leaving aside the issues of price and income stability, the central problem in American agriculture is that there is a surplus not of farm goods, but of farmers. For purposes of efficiency, we should let demand and supply determine the price for farm products. Such a price will be low enough to coax resources out of agriculture and into other uses

6. In part the original purpose of price supports was to protect farmers from wildly fluctuating prices as a result of fluctuations in demand and supply and the relative inelasticity of both demand and supply. The farmers' desire to be free of this problem is understandable. However, there are far more efficient ways to accomplish this end than the programs utilized to date.

where they can produce goods and services for which there is a relatively high demand unsupported by government aid. Resources should be both forced out and attracted out of agriculture. Instead of doing this, present policies have operated to keep in agriculture resources that could be utilized more productively elsewhere. The distress that would be created by the transition back to a free market in agriculture could be alleviated by outright grants (welfare) which would not involve inefficient distortion of production and which would automatically disappear in a few years. It would be far better and cheaper to provide needed welfare to the poor in agriculture rather than gigantic subsidies (welfare) to the rich who are in agriculture. Efficient commercial agriculture would not suffer from such a policy and society as a whole would benefit.

Agricultural policy of the future should consist of programs to attract excess resources from use in farm production and measures to cushion the effects of the adjustment on property and people. Again, the central thesis is that the American agricultural sector is overstocked with both capital and labor resources, relative to its needs, and the ultimate solution is to shift these excess resources to other sectors of the economy.

The farm problem is usually not considered of great magnitude in our present world, beset by war, urban ills, and pollution. But one of the constraints on tackling these other problems is a shortage of resources (money) to do the job. Presently we are pouring $5 to $10 billion per year into misguided farm programs that make the farm problem worse instead of better. In the near future, perhaps half of this sum could be diverted to the solution of other pressing problems if we were willing to recognize the real farm problem and attack it efficiently. Surely this is sufficient incentive for reasonable people to demand that their government finally resolve the farm problem rather than prolong it.

## Suggested Reading

Benedict, Murray Reed. *Farm Policies of the United States, 1790–1950: A Study of Their Origin and Development.* New York: Twentieth Century Fund, 1953.

Bishop, C. E., and Touissant, W. D. *Introduction to Agricultural Economic Analysis.* New York: Wiley, 1958.

Black, J. D. *Parity, Parity, Parity.* Cambridge: Harvard Committee on the Social Sciences, 1943.

Danhoff, Clarence H., "Agriculture." In *The Growth of the American Economy,* ed. Harold F. Williamson, chap. 8. Englewood Cliffs, N.J.: Prentice-Hall, 1951.

Davis, Lance E., Richard A. Easterlin, William N. Parker, et al. *American Economic Growth: An Economist's History of the United States,* chap. 11. New York: Harper & Row, 1972.

Hathaway, Dale E. *Government and Agriculture: Economic Policy in a Democratic Society.* New York: Macmillan, 1963.

Heady, Earl O., *Economics of Agricultural Production and Resource Use*. Englewood Cliffs, N.J.: Prentice-Hall, 1952.

Johnson, D. G. *Trade and Agriculture: A Study of Inconsistent Policies.* New York: Wiley, 1950.

Pearlberg, Don. *American Farm Policy*. New York: Wiley, 1964.

Rassmussen, Wayne David. *Readings in the History of American Agriculture*. Urbana: University of Illinois Press, 1960.

Robertson, Ross M. *History of the American Economy*. 2nd ed. New York: Harcourt, Brace & World, Inc., 1964. Ch. 11 and 18.

Ruttan, Vernon W., Arley D. Waldo, and James P. Houck. *Agricultural Policy in an Affluent Society*. New York: W. W. Norton, 1969.

Schultze, Charles L. *The Distribution of Farm Subsidies: Who Gets the Benefits?* Washington, D.C.: The Brookings Institution, 1971.

Schultz, Theodore. *The Economic Organization of Agriculture*. New York: McGraw-Hill, 1953.

Shepherd, Geoffrey S. *Agricultural Price and Income Policy*. 3rd ed. Ames: Iowa University Press, 1952.

## Commentary

In the first chapter, Professor Mercer developed the concepts of markets and of supply and demand curves to illustrate the nature of the farm problem. By introducing the concept of the production function he was able to indicate how changes in technology and investment in capital equipment and fertilizers offset attempts to limit the growth of farm output by limiting land utilization. Thus we find that simple notions turn out to be powerful tools for analysis, once they are thoroughly understood.

It is a simple matter to see how market intervention, for even the best of reasons, may lead to greater problems than existed before. In the case of American agriculture, farmers responded quite naturally to the efforts to raise prices on their behalf. With prices for output considerably higher than their costs, they found it profitable to invest in even greater output. We should have found it surprising if surpluses hadn't developed, so long as any action to support prices was maintained.

What about the reverse situation faced more recently in which we see consumers concerned about the high price of food? Can we solve the problem by policy measures designed to force down the prices farmers receive for their output? By now it should be clear that attempts to control price are very likely to be self-defeating. If we review what Professor Mercer has taught us about price elasticity of supply, we would expect that direct efforts to hold down prices will cause a decline in supply, and shortages, just as efforts to force prices upward lead to surpluses. The advantage of a competitive market is that it is largely self-correcting. Hence, market intervention is likely to be fraught with undesired consequences. Our remarks are not intended to suggest that all market intervention is bad but that it must be justified by solid evidence of market failure, and corrective measures must be ones that will correct that failure. In the case of the farm problem the market failure was created by intervention rather than resolved by it.

In Chapter 2, Walter Mead analyzes the "energy crisis" and its concomitant environmental problems. We find that he also utilizes the notions of producer supply and consumer demand to interpret the "crisis." His analysis extends the use of supply curves to take account of additional alternative sources of supply, in this case foreign as well as domestic production. This permits him to evaluate the impact of another form of market intervention, import controls.

Professor Mead goes on to an additional facet of the energy problem. We know that the impacts of energy use can lead to undesirable side effects such as environmental degradation. Economists refer to such effects as externalities. Professor Mead will suggest a way to relate such problems to the analysis of supplying our energy needs.

# 2

# Oil, Energy, and Environmental Concern

Walter J. Mead

Within the last half dozen years, oil in particular, energy in general, and the question of their impact on the environment have become major areas of public policy interest. Various subsidies and government help have made the oil industry an area of contention for many years. It was, however, the famous Santa Barbara offshore oil spill on January 28, 1969 that catapulted oil into the limelight of public policy concern. The drama of the spill and its consequences for environmental degradation brought both oil and the environment under nationwide scrutiny.

In a very real sense, the environmental issue was born in Santa Barbara on January 28, 1969. It is unlikely that the percentage depletion allowance for oil would have been reduced from 27.5 to 22 percent in 1969 in the absence of the oil spill. Since 1969, the more broadly conceived energy industry has become the subject of nationwide attention. Wide publicity has been given to fears of an emerging and inevitable "energy crisis." It is therefore both important and timely to examine oil, energy in general, and the impact of energy production and use on the environment.

## Energy Demand and Supply

It is well known that total energy consumption has been increasing rapidly in the United States and even more so in the rest of the world. From 1947 through 1971, energy consumption of coal, petroleum, and natural gas increased from 31,709 trillion to 65,786 trillion Btu's (British thermal units).[1]

1. U.S. Department of the Interior, *United States Energy through the Year 2000* (December 1972), p. 54.

This implies a compound growth rate of 3.1 percent annually. Within this 24-year period, growth rates seemed to be increasing over time. From 1965 through 1971 there was a 4.2 percent compound annual growth rate.

The underdeveloped regions of the world had an annual energy consumption growth rate of 7.7 percent in the years 1950 through 1965. This may be compared with 3.9 percent for the developed regions of the world. The energy-GNP elasticity coefficient for underdeveloped regions was 1.67. This means that for every 1 percent increase in GNP, energy consumption increased 1.67 percent. In comparison, the elasticity coefficient for developed regions was 0.85, and for the United States in particular it was 0.81.[2]

There have been a multitude of energy demand projections covering the remainder of this century. These projections all tell a story of continued growth in energy demand, perhaps because the authors read each other's reports. The National Petroleum Council, a group made up almost entirely of petroleum industry leaders serving in an advisory capacity to the Department of the Interior, projected a growth rate from 1971 through 1985 amounting to 4.2 percent annually.[3] For the thirty years 1970 through the year 2000, the U.S. Department of Interior projected an energy demand growth rate amounting to 3.5 percent compounded annually.[4]

The authors of the energy demand projections as a group are guilty of being economically naive in their method of analysis. They seldom mention price and instead implicitly assume that the demand curve for energy has an elasticity of zero (that is, a constant quantity of energy is demanded regardless of its price). Oil, gas, and coal reserves are produced only in geological time. In the human time frame, these energy sources must be considered nonreproducible resources. Consequently, if production continues each year and even grows at compound growth rates, stored energy resources must decline. Therefore, as decades pass and consumption annually increases, it is inevitable that a point will be reached when prices for new energy supplies will increase sharply. But the time-honored law of demand says that quantities demanded vary inversely with price. Thus, at higher prices people conserve on energy, and quantities demanded decline. The standard energy demand projection is silent on price. If growing scarcity causes energy prices to increase faster in the future than in the past, then it is not reasonable to project past annual growth rates of energy consumption into the future. At substantially higher prices, growth rates will be reduced.

2. Joel Darmstadter, *Energy in the World Economy* (1971), p. 37.

3. National Petroleum Council, *U.S. Energy Outlook, and Initial Appraisal, 1971–1985*, I (July 1971), p. 9.

4. U.S. Department of the Interior, *United States Energy, A Summary Review* (January 1972), p. v.

Quantities demanded of any product are subject to some manipulation through advertising. In the past, sellers of primary energy sources have actively promoted sales of their product. Furthermore, producers of electric power who in turn use primary fuels as inputs have also promoted the sale of electricity through advertising. If advertising in the future is restricted, then it is even more unreasonable to simply project past growth rates.

In 1969, fossil fuels accounted for 96 percent of all energy consumption in the United States; hydropower accounted for approximately 4 percent of energy production, leaving an insignificant remainder accounted for by nuclear power. Hydropower, which is close to full development in the United States, cannot be counted on to meet any significant part of the growing domestic demand for energy. Until controlled nuclear fusion is perfected and used in conjunction with breeder reactors, and until solar energy technology is perfected, we must rely on continued interim use of fossil fuel sources. Fossil fuels are nonrenewable resources. In effect, we are drawing on a physically fixed inventory. While the physical resource is fixed, producibility is a function of production cost and the price at which it may be sold. Thus, at higher prices, marginal resources become economically recoverable.

Energy minerals may be divided into two categories: (1) proved and recoverable reserves, and (2) resources. Energy mineral *reserves* are defined as minerals recoverable under current cost and revenue conditions, whereas *resources* are defined as minerals that cannot be considered part of current supply because recovery cost exceeds their current market value.

Table 2–1 shows 1969 U.S. production; cumulative production through 1969; proved and recoverable reserves, and resources of various energy minerals. All minerals are shown according to their Btu content. Relative to petroleum and natural gas, our reserves of coal are very large, adequate for 73 years of production at 1969 production rates. At higher prices, some of the immense coal resources would become economically operable, vastly extending the nation's coal productive potential.

Crude oil reserves in the United States are adequate for only 10.6 years' production at the 1972 rate (including Prudhoe Bay, Alaska reserves). Recent government policies, including oil import quotas, have caused domestic crude oil production to be at high levels sustainable for only a relatively short period of time. Similarly, natural gas (dry) reserves are adequate for only 12 years' production at 1971 production rates. Natural gas consumption in the United States has been stimulated by federal government policies which hold gas prices below market equilibrium levels.

The United States has 48.2 percent of the estimated world coal reserves.[5] The largest remaining proved oil reserves are in the Middle East; where 53

5. National Coal Association, *World Coal Trade* (1972 edition).

Table 2–1
Domestic Energy Reserves and Resources
(in units of $10^{15}$ Btu)

| Commodity | 1969 Domestic Production | Cumulative Production Through 1969 | Reserves Proved Recoverable at End of 1969[a] | Remaining Recoverable Resources |
|---|---|---|---|---|
| Coal | 14.951 | 1,040 | 1,087 | 64,400 |
| Petroleum (crude oil) | 18.922 | 501 | 166 | 594 |
| Natural Gas (liquid) | 2.392 | 49 | 33 | 168 |
| Natural Gas (dry) | 20.466 | 382 | 284 | 975 |
| Shale oil | Neg. | Neg. | 113 | 1,066 |
| Uranium: U235 | | | | |
| <$ 8/lb. | 5.15 | 83 | 83 | 200 |
| $ 8–10/lb. | — | — | 56 | 278 |
| $10–15/lb. | — | — | — | 687 |
| Uranium: U–238 | 710 | | | |
| <$ 8/lb. | | 11,486 | 11,504 | 27,631 |
| $ 8–10/lb. | — | — | 7,669 | 38,345 |
| $10–15/lb. | — | — | 9,022 | 56,390 |
| Thorium | NA | NA | NA | 15,025 |

[a]Does not include Prudhoe Bay, Alaska, estimated to contain 9.6 billion of crude oil or 54 X $10^{15}$ Btu's of reserves.

Source: Associated Universities, Inc. *Reference Energy Systems and Resource Data for Use in the Assessment of Energy Technologies*, (Report), April 1972, p. 29. Brookhaven National Laboratory, Upton, N. Y.

percent of the proved reserves are found. The communist countries account for a total of 15 percent of known oil reserves, and the United States accounts for 5.5 percent. The largest known natural gas reserves are held by communist countries. These amount to 35 percent of the total. The United States is second with 14.4 percent.[6]

While the United States has been well endowed with petroleum resources, its extremely high standard of living has caused it to consume about 34 percent of the world's annual energy use, although it has only 6 percent of world population.[7]

There currently is no production of synthetic oil from the nation's large oil shale reserves. Although shale oil production is currently on the threshold of profitability, it involves serious environmental consequences.

Uranium reserves, in the form of U–235 currently being used in nuclear fission, are of limited supply. As breeder reactors are perfected, the supplies

6. *Oil and Gas Journal* (December 25, 1972), pp. 82–83.

7. *Energy—The Ultimate Resource*, study submitted to the Task Force on Energy of the Subcommittee on Science, Research, and Development of the Committee on Science and Astronautics, U.S. House of Representatives, 92nd Congress, 1st session, October 1971, p. 19.

of U–238 and thorium will become available for conversion into fissionable atoms.

A net power production from controlled fusion is likely to be achieved toward the end of this century. If such a controlled fusion can be based upon a deuterium-deuterium reaction, the basic energy supply would become virtually unlimited, since deuterium is available in all normal water.

Solar energy is for all practical purposes an inexhaustible source of power. By use of currently known technology, present energy consumption requirements could be met by the collection of solar energy on a series of plates covering approximately 0.1 percent of the world's land area. However, considerable research and development will be required to collect, store, and deliver such energy.

It is evident from the foregoing discussion of energy growth rates and limited fossil fuel supplies that unless we are willing to drastically alter life styles and severely reduce future energy consumption, unconventional fuel sources must be developed in the future. Development of such fuel sources of course requires large investments for research. This research and development, like any other investment, must be judged in terms of its social rate of return. It may be helpful to distinguish applied research from basic research. Applied research, on the one hand, pays off either by reducing costs of production or by developing better or new products. The firm engaging in such research and development investments anticipates a return through cost savings or revenue expansion. Basic research, on the other hand, yields benefits to society that are external to the firm undertaking such research. Thus, a private firm is not able to capture benefits that flow from basic research and development investments. As a consequence, basic research is not likely to be undertaken by private enterprise, but its financing is instead a proper function of the federal government. Benefits accrue to the nation and costs are borne by society at large through the usual system of taxation.

Development of unconventional fuel sources appears to fall within the category of basic research. It is unlikely that any firm would be able to capture all of the benefits, particularly the environmental benefits, which flow from development of a system for collecting, storing, and distributing solar energy. If this is the case, and furthermore, if the social rate of return is attractive relative to other possible public investments, then research and development costs for unconventional energy sources would properly rest with the federal government.

## The Energy Crisis

Recently, wide publicity has been given to the energy crisis argument. This argument refers not to an environmental crisis, but rather to a condition of inadequate supplies or unsatisfied demands at existing prices.

### An Economic Interpretation

Within the context of free markets the energy crisis argument makes very little sense. If the demand for energy at existing prices is growing faster than supply, then the future price of energy will increase in turn, equating supply and demand at higher prices. In Figure 2–1 we begin with supply and de-

Figure 2–1. Effect of an increase in demand on price.

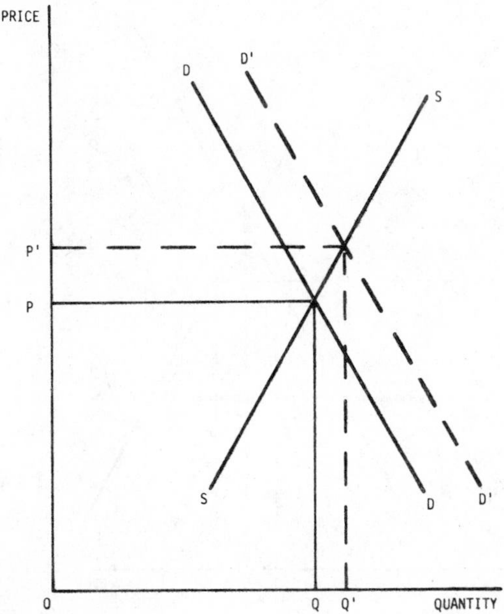


mand curves indicating a price *P* and quantity *Q*, then show a relative increase in demand from *D* to *D′*. We find that the new equilibrium price is *P′* and quantity *Q′*. There is no excess of demand over supply. Supply equals demand at a higher price. There is no energy crisis. If through continued depletion of exhaustible resources, the supply curve should shift to the left, then price would again increase. The market, however, would have performed its function of allocating an increasingly scarce resource among higher valued uses. There would still be no crisis, only a higher price.

### A Natural Gas Crisis

Man is capable of creating his crises. Currently there is an energy crisis in natural gas characterized by inability of some potential consumers to obtain gas supplies. Under political pressure from gas utilities and their customers, the Federal government, through the Federal Power Commission, has undertaken to control field prices of natural gas in interstate commerce. Figure 2–2 shows an equilibrium price at *P* and an equilibrium quantity *Q*. By

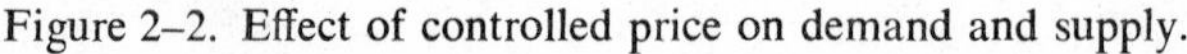
Figure 2–2. Effect of controlled price on demand and supply.

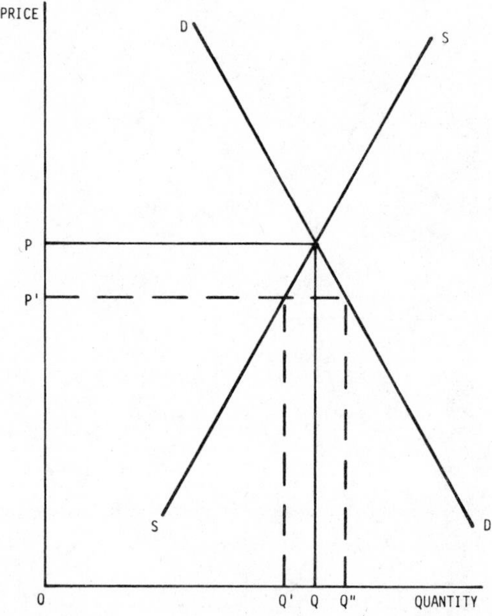


holding price below the equilibrium point, say at *P′*, we create a situation in which the quantity demanded *Q″* exceeds the quantity supplied *Q′*. By price control we have created a genuine energy crisis. We can eliminate the crisis by permitting the market to allocate scarce resources. According to the illustration, supply would equal demand at *P*.

Alternatively, we can eliminate the crisis by providing a subsidy to the producers. A producer subsidy will lower the net production costs and, in turn, bring forth an expansion of output. Because natural gas is a nonrenewable resource, such expansion is temporary and must be offset by future contractions. Thus, the subsidy creates a new problem—resource misallocation over time. In Figure 2–3 we have shown the effect of a producer subsidy. The supply curve is shifted to the right. Thus by subsidizing producers, quantity supplied can be increased to *Q″*, providing an equilibrium price at *P′*. The subsidy approach encourages lavish use of a scarce energy resource such as gas. By lowering the price from its normal equilibrium *P*

Figure 2–3. Effect of producer subsidy on supply, demand and price.

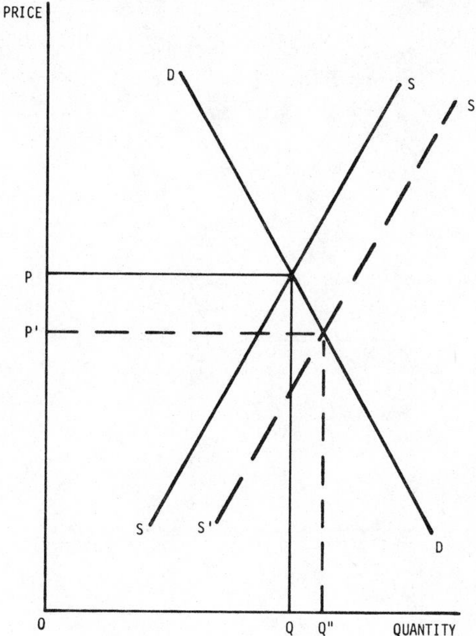


to a subsidized and therefore artificial equilibrium at *P′*, consumers are led to accelerated consumption and hence accelerated exhaustion of a nonrenewable resource.

## A Crude Oil Crisis

In addition to a natural gas crisis, much has been written and spoken about a crisis in crude oil supplies. This crisis, also, has been manufactured by public policies. Throughout most of the history of the petroleum industry in the United States, proven reserves of crude oil have increased annually. They reached a peak in 1961 when they amounted to 31.8 billion barrels, or 12.7 times annual production. Domestic reserves declined to 28.9 billion barrels of reserves in 1970, not counting the Alaskan (Prudhoe Bay) discovery. The reserve to production ratio in this year was 8.7. With the Prudhoe Bay discovery, the amount of reserves increases to 36.8 billion barrels at the end of 1972, and the reserve to production ratio becomes 10.6.[8] The

8. American Petroleum Institute, *Reserves of Crude Oil, Natural Gas Liquids and Natural Gas in the United States and Canada and United States Productive Capacity as of December 31, 1970* (May 1971), p. 25; *Oil and Gas Journal* (December 25, 1972), p. 83.

Figure 2–4. Effect of crude oil import quotas.

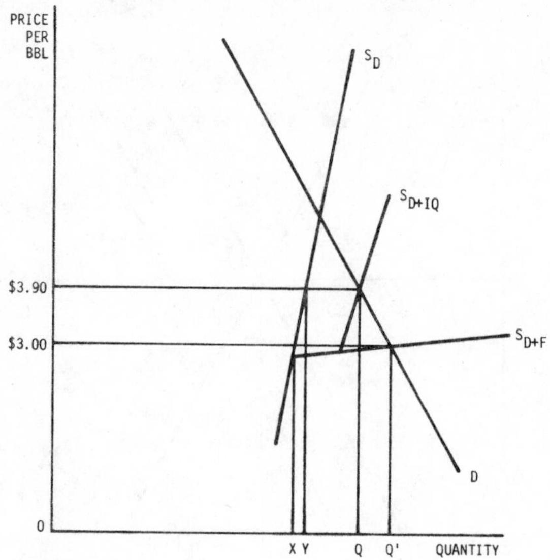


alleged crisis in petroleum supply is not one in which supply is short of the quantity demanded, but instead is one where the difference between domestic supply and demand for crude oil is compensated by increased imports from abroad. In 1960, imports accounted for 18 percent of total domestic petroleum consumption. By 1970 this percentage had increased to 23 percent. The National Petroleum Council estimates that by 1985 imports will account for 57 percent of total domestic demand.[9]

To intensify the problem, crude oil imports from abroad had been limited by an executive order issued in 1959 by President Eisenhower. (This quota system was abandoned by President Nixon in May 1973.) The effect was to cause domestic prices of crude oil to rise above world levels. Domestic production was stimulated by this high price and our favorable endowment of petroleum resources has been rapidly depleted by an artificially accelerated rate of domestic production. The predictable result is that we have no choice in the near future but to import an increasingly larger share of our crude oil from abroad.

The price and quantity effects of import quotas are illustrated in Figure 2–4. The United States' domestic demand for crude oil is shown by demand curve *D*. In the absence of import quotas (i.e., under free trade conditions),

9. National Petroleum Council, *U.S. Energy Outlook*, p. 28.

the amount supplied from domestic plus foreign sources is shown by $S_{D+F}$. The free-trade price of oil would be approximately $3 per barrel under conditions prevailing during the 1960s. However, imports from foreign sources have been restricted by U.S. import quotas. Thus, the permitted supply is shown by supply curve $S_{D+IQ}$. Since the total supply of oil is given as the horizontal distance *OQ*, the market is cleared at a price of approximately $3.90 per barrel. Thus, at this high domestic price, domestic producers supply *OY* rather than *OX* quantities of crude oil.

The rationale used by the oil industry in support of its demands for restrictions on imports is the national security rationale. According to this argument, imports from abroad must be restricted in order to avoid dependence upon unstable foreign sources, particularly Middle Eastern sources. This reasoning is designed to offer a socially acceptable basis for the policy. The real motive, however, appears to be purely economic. By restricting competition in fuel supplies, the domestic selling price of oil is automatically increased from $3 to $3.90 per barrel in our illustration. For most of the history of oil import quotas the differential has not been $.90 per barrel but more like $1.25 per barrel. Proof of this statement is the fact that the average selling price of an import quota ticket during the 1960s was around $1.25 per barrel.

The dependency argument carries a great deal of emotional weight. The Arab nations have borne the brunt of this attack. The specter of American national security being at the mercy of Arab intrigue has been a powerful emotional argument. The record of oil imports in 1970 indicates that only 16 percent of our imports came from Arab countries and these imports amounted to only 1.4 percent of our domestic consumption.[10] Our three principal crude oil suppliers in order of importance were Canada, Venezuela, and Indonesia, all non-Arab countries. These countries together supplied 76 percent of our imports in 1970.

In recent years there have been approximately 15 net oil exporting countries and the number is growing annually. Hence, diversity of supply from foreign sources provides a measure of security for the United States against concerted foreign action.

In the area of nonrenewable resources, the dependency argument loses much of its validity. If this nation lacks crude oil reserves and foreign nations in turn have plentiful reserves, then dependency on foreign sources of crude oil is a fact of life. The longer we restrict imports from abroad and thereby accelerate production from our own dwindling reserves, the more dependent we become on foreign crude sources. A system of import quotas that causes domestic prices to be higher and thereby stimulates domestic exploration, development, and production of crude oil achieves a degree of

10. American Petroleum Institute, *Annual Statistical Review* (April 1971), pp. 9–10.

self-sufficiency for the present. However, present security of supply is attained at the expense of greater future dependency.

Import quotas were instituted in 1959 without asking the obvious question—what are the alternative means of meeting the national security objective? It obviously follows that the relevant economic question also remained unasked—what are the costs of alternative means to the national security goal?

The Department of Interior studied the social cost of the mandatory oil import quota system and concluded that it developed additional domestic production at a cost of $1.04 per barrel.[11] Recent studies have indicated that foreign oil could be purchased and stored in salt domes in the United States at a cost of $.33 per barrel. Steel tanks could be constructed in the United States and oil stored in them at an annual cost of $.74 per barrel.[12]

The least-cost system of providing secure long-term oil supplies for national security is a system of shut-in national defense petroleum reserves.[13] Under this natural storage system, some existing oil fields would be fully developed and then placed on a shut-in standby condition so that production could be started on a sixty-day notice basis. There is currently one such petroleum reserve in a partially developed situation—the Elk Hills Naval Petroleum Reserve No. 1. This Reserve, located near Bakersfield, California, would be capable of producing 453 million barrels in the initial year of emergency production if it were a fully developed shut-in field. This production is currently equal to the total annual crude oil imports into the West Coast from all foreign sources, excluding Canada. Thus a fully developed Petroleum Reserve at Elk Hills would provide a high degree of national security for the West Coast. Other similar petroleum reserves could be established throughout the United States, including offshore locations, wherever a large relatively new oil field exists.

The total social cost of this form of national defense petroleum reserve is estimated to be 8.5 cents per barrel of reserves per year, or 32 cents per barrel of additional emergency oil supplies for one year.[14] This is significantly lower than the social cost of the system of oil import quotas estimated at $1.04 per barrel per year.

The solutions offered by the oil industry to solve the alleged crude oil supply crisis generally take the form of continued and strengthened restrictions on foreign competition, plus additional tax and other subsidies to the

11. U.S. Department of the Interior, "The Cost of the Oil Import Quota System," mimeographed (September 1969), table 4.

12. Testimony of Walter J. Mead before the U.S. Senate Committee on Interior and Insular Affairs, May 30, 1973, forthcoming in *Hearings*.

13. W. J. Mead and P. E. Sorensen, "A National Defense Petroleum Reserve Alternative to Oil Import Quotas," *Land Economics* (August 1971), p. 221.

14. Ibid., p. 222.

oil industry. The president of the American Petroleum Institute (an industry organization that generally reflects the views of the larger integrated oil companies) recommended to the U.S. Senate two public policies relative to crude oil supplies. After affirming that "energy needs should be met by private competitive enterprise with minimum government regulations," the API spokesman asked that "oil and uranium import controls should be continued to encourage expansion of domestic supplies. Such controls will contribute to national security and help assure consumers of adequate supplies at reasonable long-run prices." He then asked that "tax provisions appropriate to the unique characteristics of fuels and minerals should be strengthened."[15]

For the smaller producers, Mr. Robert Burch, executive director of the Rocky Mountain Oil and Gas Association testifying before the U.S. House of Representatives Interior and Insular Affairs Committee charged that government policies were needlessly leading the nation into a most critical energy supply situation. This industry spokesman called for "significantly higher prices, an increase in percentage depletion for the duration of the energy crisis, investment tax credits for domestic exploration and development, a ceiling on imports, and encouragement of maximum participation of independents in exploration and development of the public domain."[16]

The percentage depletion allowance applicable to crude oil and gas production has also contributed to our present dependence on foreign supplies. The Revenue Act of 1918 granted 100 percent tax-free income to oil producers equal to the discovery value of the oil property, independent of any discovery costs and investments in that oil property. The Revenue Act of 1924 reduced the tax-free income flow to a maximum of 50 percent of the property's net income. In 1926 a rule of thumb was established permitting 27.5 percent of the gross income (not net income) from an oil property to be free of tax up to a limit of 50 percent of the net income from that property. The 1969 tax law revision reduced the percentage depletion allowance from 27.5 percent down to 22 percent. Where the full value of the depletion allowance is used, the effect is to reduce federal income tax rates on oil income by half.

The rationale of the depletion allowance has become one of stimulating the discovery and production of domestic crude oil and gas in order to achieve national security objectives. However, the percentage depletion allowance applies equally to foreign production by U.S. companies.

If the percentage depletion allowance has in fact had the effect of increasing domestic production since 1918, then it follows that exploitation

15. Testimony of Mr. Frank N. Ikard, president, American Petroleum Institute, before the "National Goals Symposium," *Hearings Before the Committee on Interior and Insular Affairs*, U.S. Senate, 92nd Congress, 1st session, October 20, 1971, p. 115.

16. *Oil and Gas Journal* (April 24, 1972), p. 44.

of our domestic reserves has proceeded at a faster rate than would have occurred without this favorable tax treatment. It further follows that since crude oil is a nonrenewable natural resource, accelerated production from 1918 to date has caused less oil to remain in the ground. Thus we are more dependent upon foreign supplies today and in the future as a result of past stimulation of production through the depletion allowance.[17]

Some of the effects of the depletion allowance tax provision have been nullified by another interference with the market mechanism on behalf of the oil industry. Prorationing, defined as "the rules and procedures by which a regulatory agency determines the total crude-oil production from a state and allocates the total among the various reservoirs and to the producers in each reservoir"[18] consists of two parts: (1) MER (Maximum Efficient Rate) prorationing, and (2) market-demand prorationing. Under MER prorationing, attempts are made to calculate the maximum efficient rate of production. These permitted levels of production are then called allowables. The need for MER type prorationing follows from the fact of common reservoir ownership. In the absence of unitization and MER type prorationing, each owner of the common property, oil, in a given reservoir would compete to recover at least his full share before it would be drained away by other owners. The result would be vast overinvestment and inefficient utilization of the oil reservoir.

While the need for MER type prorationing is granted, the only justification for market-demand prorationing is from the point of view of the owner who would presumably prefer high prices to low prices for his crude oil. Under market-demand prorationing, the state regulatory agency determines and has restricted production to a level calculated to equal the quantity demanded at some desired price, usually the prevailing price. If market-demand prorationing is set at 30 percent, as it has been on historical occasions, then the producer is able to produce only 30 percent of his maximum efficient rate of recovery. If market-demand prorationing is set at 100 percent, then theoretically there are no restraints on output designed to attain some desired high price level. The Texas Railroad Commission, charged by Texas law with administering the prorationing system in Texas, raised the market-demand percentage to 100 percent of schedule allowables, effective in April 1972. The 100 percent level has remained in effect to date in Texas and has also been established by the counterpart regulatory commissions in other leading oil-producing states.

17. W. J. Mead, "The System of Government Subsidies to the Oil Industry," testimony before the Subcommittee on Antitrust and Monopoly, Committee on the Judiciary, U.S. Senate, 91st Congress, 1st session, March 11, 1969.

18. W. Lovejoy and P. Homan, *Economic Aspects of Oil Conservation Regulation* (1967), p. 127.

One effect of the market-demand prorationing system has been to restrict oil production in order to attain a higher price. Thus exploitation of domestic oil reserves has been at a lower rate than would have occurred in the absence of market-demand prorationing. Therefore, market demand prorationing has offset some of the effects of depletion allowance on the level of U.S. oil production.

Another effect of the market-demand prorationing system has been to maintain some reserve production capacity. However, with market-demand prorationing at 100 percent, reserve productive capacity is approximately zero. The import quota system, together with percentage depletion allowances, has presumably caused domestic production in the past to be higher than it would be otherwise, and market-demand prorationing has presumably created an excess productive potential that would otherwise not be available. The reserve productive potential has now disappeared, and the nation's present reserves have been depleted at an artificially high rate. Thus, past policy of government interference on behalf of the oil industry would appear to have been counterproductive with respect to a long-term national security goal. This conclusion should surprise no one except those who took the national security rationalization seriously. Presumably, the economic motive for depletion allowance is a tax reduction for the oil producer.

The economic motive for both import quotas and market-demand prorationing is to obtain a higher price for crude oil production. The alleged crisis in crude oil supplies, like that in natural gas, appears to be largely manufactured by privately motivated public policies.

## Environmental Issues

The production and use of energy have direct impacts on environmental quality. Coal production in particular leads to water quality degradation, and where strip-mining practices are followed, damage to the ecology and the landscape may be severe. Fossil fuel combustion is the primary source of air pollution. Economics has a major contribution to make in conceptualizing the environmental issue, analyzing and measuring the extent of the problem, and in proposing alternative solutions to it.

### Optimum Resource Allocation and "Externalities"

In a mixed free enterprise system such as prevails in the United States, resources are allocated among competing uses through a process of decentralized decision-making. Private control over capital resources leads business decision-makers to employ and allocate resources in such a manner as to maximize the difference between revenue generated from production and cost incurred in production. This is the traditional profit-maximizing objective of business management. Economic theorists have demonstrated with the apparent precision of both geometry and higher mathematics that under specific assumptions an optimum allocation of resources will occur when decisions are made on the basis outlined above. One of the primary assumptions underlying the proof is that all costs of using resources and producing products are borne by the producer and all benefits from production accrue to the producer. As an alternative expression, this assumption requires that there be no "externalities." An externality is a cost or a benefit that spills over to society and is not borne by or does not accrue to the producer who is responsible for the cost or benefit. The classic illustration of an external cost is the air pollution situation. A producer of electric power utilizing coal or oil as his primary energy may pollute society's air, and society in general, not just the producer, bears the cost. If through legislation the government imposes on the producer a cost equal to the external social cost, then that externality is said to be "internalized."

Similarly, some benefits may be external to the firm responsible for them. For example, if a firm through its research and development achieves a basic invention that would economically capture the energy of the sun as well as store and distribute such energy cheaply, relative to other fuel sources, then society would have achieved an enormous source of nonpolluting energy. But basic inventions of this type are not patentable. Even if they were subject to patenting, the history of patent experience clearly indicates that protection from inroads of competition are less than perfect. Thus the producer cannot capture the full benefit of his invention. In effect they spill over and are captured by others who have not incurred the initial research and development expenditure. If we are able to place an economic value on this externality and further, if through legislation we should confer upon the inventor a subsidy equal to the external benefit, then the externality would again have been internalized.

This phenomenon is not simply a matter of equity (distributive justice). Resources in the market system are directed by anticipated returns on an investment. Environmental pollution as we know it historically has been characterized by externalities. The individual who drives an automobile pollutes society's atmosphere. His share of the cost is given roughly by a ratio in which the numerator is 1 and the denominator is the total number of people affected by the polluted air.

The economic solution to reducing environmental pollution is (1) to evaluate externalities and,(2) to internalize them. This policy recommendation is easy to make; implementing it is extremely difficult. Scientists must identify the physical and biological effects of environmental pollution. Having these data, economists must then evaluate the impacts. The economic techniques for accomplishing this objective are still in their infancy. Nevertheless, substantial progress has been made in the decade or two in which economists have been attempting to develop tools of evaluation. If the difficulty of physical and biological identification and economic evaluation leads society to take no action, then we have in effect said that the externality has a value of zero. While tools are being perfected for identification and evaluation, rough approximations of the external cost may still be far superior to an implicit assumption of zero cost.

While economists as a general rule prefer to use the market mechanism to reduce environmental pollution through internalizing externalities, some people prefer the regulatory approach. The latter approach would charge government with the responsibility of establishing and administering standards designed to reduce environmental pollution. If the regulatory approach is to be administered correctly, it too requires identification and economic evaluation. Furthermore, the regulatory approach requires a benefit-cost analysis of the regulation itself. Administration of regulations is not costless. Regulation of the proposed trans-Alaskan pipeline, in the name of environmental protection, imposes very high resource costs on society. In fact, the cost of the regulation may well exceed the value of the environmental benefit.

The regulatory approach has yet another major fault. When a regulatory commission has been established for environmental purposes, it is normally established with considerable enthusiasm by its advocates. With the passage of time, enthusiasm wanes. After a decade or two, regulatory commissions have a way of becoming captives of the group to be regulated. The bureaucracy develops a self-sustaining life, with maintenance of itself as a prime objective. This becomes a substantial social cost.

### The Santa Barbara Oil Spill

The Santa Barbara oil spill is a case in point of environmental degradation associated with energy production. In a sense, the oil spill problem started on February 6, 1968, when the U.S. Department of the Interior held its third and largest California offshore oil and gas lease sale. The largest bid submitted for any of the 75 tracts offered was received for tract #402. The winning bid, amounting to $61,400,000, was submitted by a combine led by Union Oil Company of California and joined by Texaco, Inc., Gulf Oil Corp., and Mobil Oil Corp.

The blowout on Platform A established on this tract occurred on January 28, 1969. As a blowout, it lasted for only about 13 minutes and consisted of "heavy condensate mist" rather than black oil. By dropping the drill string down the drill hole and closing the blowout preventors, the condensate fluid became temporarily confined to the largely uncased well bore.

Shortly thereafter gas bubbles appeared on the ocean surface, and within two hours "large turbulent boiling" had started emitting both gas and abundant black oil.[19] The oil spill phase had begun. The uninhibited oil and gas flow lasted 14½ days until cementing of the bore hole was completed on February 8, and the flow was substantially reduced. On February 25, "a high though intermittent rate of oil flow resumed."[20] Further cementing corrected this situation.

Estimates of the total volume of oil spilled into the channel from Platform A vary widely. The most thorough estimates were made by A. A. Allen of General Research Corp., who estimated that in the first 100 days "over 3¼ million gallons of oil were released into the Santa Barbara Channel . . ."[21]

In order to place the Santa Barbara spill in perspective it may be compared to the Torrey Canyon incident in which about 30 million gallons of crude oil were spilled in the English Channel.[22] This is approximately ten times the volume of oil spilled to date in the Santa Barbara Channel. In the Torrey Canyon spill, about 140 miles of British and French beaches were oil-polluted, whereas about 30 miles of California beaches were oil-covered.

The Santa Barbara spill is an excellent example of the externalities problem. When oil companies calculated their bids for the oil leases in 1968, they presumably estimated probable revenues from the sale of oil likely to be discovered on each tract and subtracted the probable private costs of producing such oil to obtain a probable profit. Then with appropriate discounting and adjustments for risk, they used such estimates to calculate their bids. However, these estimates of private benefits, costs and profits, do not necessarily correspond with social benefits, costs, and profits. With the knowledge of hindsight, we now know that the flood of oil onto Santa Barbara County beaches imposed social costs on society. The probability of such a spill occurring, multiplied by the social cost of the probable spill, should have been internalized so that it would become part of the bid calculation in 1968.

Having experienced the oil spill we are now in a position to evaluate its social cost. The following effects have been identified:[23] (1) The presence

19. T. H. McCulloh, *Geologic Characteristics of the Dos Quadras Offshore Oil Field,* U.S. Geological Survey Professional Paper No. 679, p. 40.

20. Ibid., p. 43.

21. Alan A. Allen, *Hearings before the Subcommittee on Minerals, Materials, and Fuels of the Committee on Interior and Insular Affairs,* U.S. Senate, 91st Congress, 1st session, May 20, 1969, pp. 149–150.

22. Great Britain, Cabinet Office, *The Torrey Canyon, Report of the Committee of Scientists on the Scientific and Technical Aspects of the Torrey Canyon Disaster,* London, HMSO, 1967, p. vi.

23. W. J. Mead and P. E. Sorensen, "The Economic Cost of the Santa Barbara Spill," *Santa Barbara Oil Symposium,* held at the University of California, Santa Barbara, December 16–18, 1970, pp. 183–226.

of oil on the recreation beaches caused a loss of tourism to the City of Santa Barbara. Most of this tourism cost, however, was private cost to the motel and hotel operators in Santa Barbara and is not a social cost. Evidence indicates that the decline in motel–hotel occupancy following the spill was offset by a corresponding increase elsewhere. Hence, the private losses to Santa Barbara tourist facilities were offset by a gain to operators in other communities. A social cost would have occurred only if people who planned to take a vacation in Santa Barbara (a) were denied their vacation because of the spill and the lack of available accommodations elsewhere, or (b) suffered a loss of vacation utility by having to settle for an inferior location. (2) The commercial fishing industry was clearly damaged and a social cost resulted from the fact that an oil boom was placed across the mouth of the Santa Barbara harbor, effectively locking in fishing vessels. Later, oil on the surface of the water fouled some of the fish catch and rendered it unfit for sale. The fishing industry and society suffered a loss of approximately two months of fishing production due to idled fishing equipment. (3) There was a loss in real property values due to the effect of the spill on beachfront property values. (4) Damage to sea birds, wildlife and marine organisms created a social cost. To the degree that an economic resource such as fish or kelp is reduced in value, and further, that a part of nature has been destroyed and a loss of utility is felt by a large segment of society, a real social cost is incurred. (5) Loss of 3¼ million gallons of oil is a social cost as well as a private cost borne by the operating companies. In addition, the blowout and subsequent spill required the use of society's resources to control the spill, to collect some of the oil, and to clean up the beach damage. (6) Residents of Santa Barbara and visitors to the area suffered a real loss in recreational value. Use of the beach and the total marine environment was severely curtailed during the period of beach and water contamination.

An effort was made to identify, measure, and evaluate the physical, biological, and economic costs of the oil spill. Preliminary estimates shown in Table 2–2 indicate that the total social cost of the oil spill was about $16 million.[24]

Numerous suits have been filed against the operating companies, seeking compensation for private damages. It is clear that the operating companies have already incurred substantial private costs due to lost oil production, suppressing the spill, collecting oil, cleaning up the beaches, cleaning damaged property, and compensating damaged parties in some cases. However, this internalization of social cost occurred after the moment of the lease sale. Consequently, internalization had no effect on decisions made in February 1968 to cast specific bids on the oil leases. Had these costs been internalized in a probability sense prior to the point of bidding, then in some

24. Ibid., p. 225.

Table 2–2
Estimates of the Economic Cost of the Santa Barbara Oil Spill

| | | |
|---|---|---|
| Union Oil Company on behalf of itself and three partners—Gulf, Mobil and Texaco. | | |
| A— Beach cleanup | $4,887,000 | |
| B— Oil well control efforts | 3,600,000 | |
| C— Oil collection efforts | 2,000,000 | |
| | | $10,487,000 |
| U.S. Department of the Interior | | $ 382,000 |
| State of California | | 200,000 |
| County of Santa Barbara | | 57,200 |
| City of Santa Barbara | | negligible |
| Damage to tourism | | negligible |
| Damage to commercial fishing industry | | 804,250 |
| Property value loss | | 1,197,000 |
| Fish life damage | | negligible |
| Bird life damage | | 7,400 |
| Seal and sea lion damage | | negligible |
| Intertidal plant and animal damage—low estimate | | 1,000 |
| high estimate | | 25,000 |
| Value of lost oil | | 130,000 |
| Recreational value lost | | 3,150,000 |
| Low estimate | | $16,415,850 |
| High estimate | | $16,439,850 |

cases no bids would have been offered and in other cases the bids would have been reduced in amount.

So far as the future is concerned, firms in the oil industry and government agencies have learned much from the Santa Barbara oil spill. New regulations have been issued to reduce the probability in the future of similar accidents. Carrying out these regulations imposes costs on the operating firms (and society). In addition, as oil companies bid for future oil and gas leases, they are likely to calculate a potential liability for a future oil spill and include an appropriate valuation for this liability in their bid calculations. It is more likely that future costs will be appropriately internalized with the result that future oil bearing properties are more efficiently allocated.

### What Is the Optimal Level of Environmental Pollution?

Apart from new catastrophes such as the Santa Barbara oil spill, the United States, like every other nation in the world, is suffering a degree of existing environmental pollution. Public policy decisions need to be made to affect the level of pollution. The appropriate question is—What is the optimum level of pollution?

Air pollution is the result of individual action of people who are dumping their garbage into a common property resource called air. Doing so, individuals impose costs on society but not on themselves. If regulatory

Figure 2–5. Optimum level of pollution.

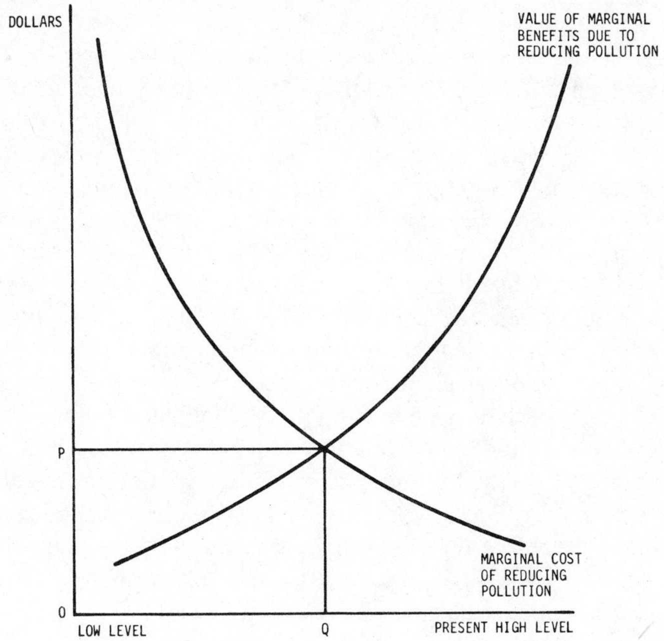


measures are adopted to reduce the existing level of air pollution, useful resources must in effect be exchanged for cleaner air. The economic problem of cleaning up the environment is illustrated in Figure 2–5.[25] If we start from a present high level of environmental pollution and move to the left toward a clean environment in this figure, we find that by attacking the easiest problems first, the marginal cost (the cost of the first identifiable effort) of reducing air pollution is rather small. Correspondingly, we find that since we have attacked the easiest problems first, the marginal benefits due to reducing this degree of pollution will be relatively high. These values are shown in the two curves of Figure 2–5. Having accomplished the first step in reducing pollution we move on to the second step. However, this next attack is the "second easiest," or the second most productive step. In this second position it is likely that the marginal cost of the attack will be slightly higher than the first and the value of the marginal benefits due to reducing pollution will be somewhat less. As long as the value of the mar-

25. For a more detailed discussion of environmental economics, see A. M. Freeman, "The Economics of Pollution Control and Environmental Quality" (General Learning Press, 1971).

ginal benefits exceeds the marginal cost of reducing air pollution, society clearly benefits by taking successive steps toward the left. However, at point *Q* the two marginal curves intersect. At this intersection we find that the cost of the last step taken to reduce pollution exactly equals the value of the reduction in pollution. This is the optimum level of pollution. If we should decide to continue a war on air pollution by moving to the left of point *Q*, then we would be incurring costs for reducing pollution greater than the value which society places on the reduction of pollution. The air is now relatively clean. We have fought all the easy battles. New steps taken to reduce air pollution make only modest and difficult-to-perceive gains in reduced pollution, while the costs in terms of other resources used up are now quite large. When one argues that the optimum level of pollution is zero pollution, one is saying that we must eliminate that last hardly noticeable level of pollution, even though it involves extremely large costs to society. That last trace of pollution cannot be eliminated so long as there is one internal combustion machine in use. Having eliminated all of the "unnecessary" use of fossil fuel burning, one must go on and eliminate the "necessary" and even the "absolutely necessary" use of fossil fuels. Point *Q* is the economic optimal level of pollution because at this point the value (price *P*) of the trade-off between increasingly clean air and increasingly costly efforts to improve air quality are exactly equal.

## Conclusion

A century of history clearly demonstrates that the demand for energy has been increasing at nearly constant compound annual rates of growth. As underdeveloped areas of the world strive for higher living standards, their rates of growth in energy use have been and are likely to continue to be in excess of that of the United States. The National Petroleum Council has estimated that from 1971 through 1985 the compound annual growth rate in the U.S. demand for energy will be about 4.2 percent. The primary energy source in the present and at least for the period through 1985 is likely to be combustion of fossil fuels. Supplies of oil, gas, and coal are physically fixed. Through new technology it is possible to more effectively utilize our existing resources. Through more exploration it is possible to find new energy reserves. However, a point in time will be reached where supply can equal demand only at substantially higher energy prices.

The so-called energy crisis appears to be a crisis created by governmental policies rationalized in terms of the public interest, but probably motivated in fact by private interests. The natural gas crisis is one in which demand exceeds supply at prevailing prices, and some potential users of natural gas are not able to have their demands satisfied. This shortage has been created by the Federal Power Commission through holding the field price of natural gas below its equilibrium level. The solution to the natural gas crisis is relatively simple, namely, abandon efforts to control gas prices and permit the market mechanism to allocate scarce resources.

Similarly, an alleged future crisis in crude oil supply has been created by public policies to restrict competition from foreign crude oil through the use of import quotas and by percentage depletion allowances which have stimulated domestic production of petroleum. Import quotas have caused domestic crude oil prices to rise substantially above world levels and accelerated the use of domestic oil reserves. The depletion allowance, as a tax subsidy, has similarly stimulated domestic production. Both measures together have created a situation of rapid depletion in U.S. crude oil reserves and have consequently made this nation more dependent upon foreign sources than it would otherwise be.

The solution to the oil supply crisis and the dependency problem is complex. Part of the solution was the recent (May 1973) elimination of import quotas. As a result, we will begin using more foreign crude supplies and less of our own. In order to meet the national security need and avoid dependence upon foreign sources, we might establish a series of National Defense Petroleum Reserves. Such reserves could consist of (1) fully developed oil fields shut-in and placed in a ready reserve status, to be used for national security purposes only, and (2) oil stored in salt domes or steel tanks. In addition, a vastly expanded research and development program might be introduced to develop new, less polluting energy sources. The demand for energy might be reduced by applying higher excise taxes on energy.

Energy production and use have severe impacts on the environment. In our mixed free enterprise economy, decisions are commonly made on the basis of expected private rates of return. However, where some costs are not borne by the enterprise in question, but instead spill over onto society and become external costs, then private rates of return diverge from social rates of return and we fail to allocate our scarce resources in an optimal manner. The primary solution to this problem is to internalize external costs and benefits. While this process involves difficult problems of measurement and evaluation, appropriate tools are now being perfected and appropriate public policy steps can be taken. However, regulation will also be necessary where the market mechanism can be shown to be inadequate or where externalities cannot be effectively internalized.

The degree of existing environmental pollution has obviously become oppressive for American society. This nation has a high standard of living and can probably afford to trade off some growth in consumer production for a cleaner environment. As society moves toward a cleaner environment it needs an answer to the question—What is the optimal level of pollution? Solutions to this difficult problem involve a high degree of cooperation between physical and biological scientists, engineers, and economists. Failure to analyze important problems of environmental protection in terms of economic values is to settle for unnecessarily lower standards of living; and environmental quality is part of that standard of living.

## Commentary

Thus far we have dealt with problems concerning price and output levels in reasonably competitive market situations. We noted that society may be able to influence price and output by market interference and that the output levels of nonmarket goods (externalities) may also be influenced by the extent of our market interference. That is, using Professor Mead's example, when we attain an optimal level of pollution we will, at the same time, have established the desired output levels for alternative forms of energy. We leave for discussion in a later chapter the practical details of alternative ways to reach such an optimum level.

In demonstrating how we reach the optimum position two of the most basic concepts of the economist are utilized: the notion of marginal cost and marginal benefit. While it is intuitively easy to grasp the principle that we should continue to use additional quantities of a resource up to the point that the added benefit from that use is just equal to the added cost, nonetheless, even where public and private decisions regarding resource use follow such a simple rule, the outcome may still not be correct for society. In other words, the rule is incomplete. We must distinquish between setting private marginal benefits and social marginal benefits equal to marginal cost.

This may, at first, not seem to have much relationship to the question of "Democratic Ideals and Economic Power," by Robert McGuckin, but in fact, the existence of corporate power and the logical use of that power by private firms may not be in the best interests of society. Firms can be expected to invoke the rule, setting private marginal costs equal to private marginal benefits and thereby maximizing their own profits. However, if true monopoly power exists, the outcome will not be the same as if social marginal benefits equalled social marginal costs. Professor McGuckin will show how the key to the problem is in the way the economy is organized. We shall see how the concentration of economic power can thwart the will of the majority. In addition, we shall be adding some new tools to our economist's tool kit.

Professor McGuckin will also be raising a question even more fundamental than simply the effect of the concentration of power, a question that will be a matter of concern to every citizen, and—unfortunately—one which does not have a simple answer. That is, is there a regulatory process which will transfer power from producers to consumers, i.e., is there any way to guarantee to consumers sovereignty over how much is produced and consumed?

# 3

# Democratic Ideals and Economic Power: An Investigation Into the Concentration of Economic Power in Large Corporations

Robert H. McGuckin

The preservation of the ultimate democratic ideal, individual freedom, requires that power be diffused among the individual members of a society. Politically, this is usually expressed as "one man, one vote." Yet, simple majority rule is not a guarantee of individual freedom. For example, in the United States, slavery was once the majority will. Thus, a free society must incorporate systems of checks and balances in order to protect minority rights and thwart the excesses of simple majorities. These checks usually require group decisions to be based on more than a simple majority.

The nature of a society's economic system is at least as important as its political organization in the maintenance of freedom.[1] For example, the right of an individual to enter into voluntary exchanges is a major component of individual freedom. Freedom to exchange includes the right of a person to choose his job; further, it implies individual rights to private property.[2]

The relationship between economic organization and freedom can also be viewed in terms of the role economic power plays in checking political

1. The relationship of economic and political power and freedom are the subject of a series of provocative essays by Milton Friedman in *Capitalism and Freedom* (University of Chicago Press, 1962). This discussion draws heavily on those essays.

2. It is important to note that individual rights or freedoms are not absolute. Where there are large external effects associated with individual actions, the rights to these actions are usually denied. For example, the exercise of free speech rights does not include yelling "Fire!" in a crowded theatre. Similarly, the right to burn one's home is restricted if the fire and smoke spread to a neighbor's property.

power. Unless an advocate can generate the resources necessary to inform the electorate of his views, his freedom of speech is an empty liberty.[3] This fact suggests that the separation of the economic system from political control lessens the possibility of coercive power in any society. Although such a distinction between economic and political power is useful analytically, the reader should not draw the conclusion that they are ever totally independent. Political power can lead to the creation of institutions and the formulation of laws that enhance the economic power of some individuals or groups, and diminish that of others. For example, monopoly power may and often does rest on special licensing laws enacted through the political system. At the same time, the market power of a monopolist may lead to political decisions which reinforce the monopolist's power. Nevertheless, the chances for preserving or creating a free society are enhanced to the extent that economic power is both diffused and separate from political power.

The foregoing remarks illustrate the fundamental proposition that the organization of property is of prime importance in the society's balance of power. Under capitalism, the individual citizen has exclusive rights of use and enjoyment of his property. While capitalism and laissez-faire doctrine place great emphasis on the right to own private property, the existence of such rights do not sufficiently differentiate capitalism from other economic systems—say feudalism—where property rights exist for some individuals. The virtues of capitalism, as preached by Adam Smith and successive generations of economists, rest on the diffusion of economic power in society. This diffusion of power requires that the control of property (the means of production) be spread among the members of society in such a way that individuals or groups are unable to coerce one another.[4]

Industrialization of American society aggravated the problem of maintaining diffusion of property control among individuals. The years following the Civil War saw a steady increase in the scope of the nation's industrial activity and a corresponding decrease in the importance of agriculture and family business as a source of employment and income. It was during this period that the concentration of economic power first became an issue of national concern. The emergence of large corporate organizations known as "trusts," as the major productive units led to widespread fear that the

3. This point is particularly relevant to discussions of democratic socialism and other systems within which large portions of a society's property come under the control of political authorities.

4. This discussion of spreading economic power is not meant to imply that property should be equally divided among the members of the society. While some readers may find the goal of perfect equality a noble one, a case for some inequality in the distribution of property and income can also be made.

economic power of a few gigantic organizations would dominate the economy. After more than a century of research, public debate, and legislative action, these fears are still a pervasive aspect of much current thinking.

A most important factor in understanding the impact of economic power on individual freedom is inequality in the control of economic resources within the economy. Even more important, indeed crucial, are the trends and underlying causes of a given index of inequality. Since most of our discussion will be concerned with large corporations, we begin with a description of the history and nature of corporate enterprises.

## The Corporate Revolution

Although the corporate form of organization did not become a dominant American force until well after the Civil War, its historical origins were much earlier. Originally, corporate charters were special royal grants which enabled groups of individuals to operate as a single person. In its modern form the corporation is a "legal individual," distinct from the individuals who own it, with rights to transfer property, incur debts, and produce and sell products. In the corporate organization each individual contributes a portion of the corporate resources in return for partial ownership, which is embodied in the stock certificate.

Organization along corporate lines has several advantages over either individual proprietorship or partnership. First, losses incurred by the individual are limited to his ownership in the corporation. By contrast, liability for losses in both proprietorship and partnership may extend to the businessman's home and personal belongings in most states. Thus organization under a corporate form can protect the businessman's family from total bankruptcy in case the business fails.

Second, the death of an owner of corporate stock does not necessitate the liquidation of the corporation. In contrast, the surviving family of a proprietor may be forced to liquidate, because there are no easily traded stock shares for them to sell. Society is thus provided with important savings in the case of corporations. Liquidation of specialized productive equipment, besides interrupting the flow of goods and services, requires the expenditure of scarce resources. This is because the organizational and planning costs are likely to be quite large, particularly for big businesses.

The foregoing were not of decisive importance at a time when the economy was organized around the family farm or a small family-owned store. Such enterprises were generally passed to the family survivor. In any event, because production was organized on a small scale, liquidation costs were not large. In fact, pre-Civil War corporations were generally restricted to such large-scale undertakings as the construction of turnpikes, bridges and canals, or the operation of banks and insurance companies.[5]

The industrial revolution and the development of railroads, with their large demands for capital resources, were the dominant forces in the emergence of the corporate form of organization. Although the transformation of the American economy was gradual, by the late 1960s more than 80 percent of the total sales in the economy was handled by corporate organizations. Manufacturing, with over one-third of the economy's total sales, had over 95 percent of its total receipts accounted for by corporations.

## Managerial Capitalism

The dominance of the corporate form is an indisputable fact of American life, and there is substantial agreement among scholars on the factors that are responsible for this position. There is far less agreement on the extent and consequences of managerial capitalism. A fundamental factor in the operation of the family farm, as well as the early trusts, was the unification of ownership and management decision-making in an individual entrepreneur. The large corporations of the late nineteenth and early twentieth centuries were associated with names such as Rockefeller, Carnegie, and Morgan, all of whom, in addition to managing large empires, had substantial ownership interest in their enterprises. However, as the twentieth century progressed, stock ownership became diffused among larger and larger numbers of individuals. Today most of the largest corporations have shareholders numbering in the tens of thousands.

The dispersion of corporate ownership among large numbers of individuals led to an increased role for the professional manager in the operation of the modern corporation. The emergence of this managerial class and the separation of the ownership and managerial functions of the firm have led many writers to conclude that there also exists a separation of ownership and control in the modern corporation; that is, ownership of corporate stock does not lead to control in large enterprises. Presumably, this separation results from an inability of the widely dispersed owners of corporate shares to control management.[6] Actually, evidence as to whether or not

5. Since the rights of due process were not completely extended to corporations until after the Civil War, when the 14th Amendment was interpreted to include corporations, there were also legal restrictions associated with the corporate form. Yet, if the advantages of this form had been decisive before the war, the matter would probably have been pursued in the courts much earlier.

6. Some writers have suggested that with widespread ownership, minority interests can maintain effective control of large corporations. Under these circumstances, an individual or family can control a large corporation with 5 to 10 percent of the voting shares. If this is true, then an individual with $50 million invested in a billion dollar corporation would have effective control over the entire billion dollars in assets.

there is a separation of ownership and control is inconclusive. Nevertheless, the existence of a widely dispersed ownership is *not* sufficient to guarantee management the discretion to pursue their own objectives independent of stockholders' desires. This is because the threat of takeovers (mergers) provides a check on managers who are inefficient. That is to say, if management follows policies not in accord with stockholder objectives, the value of the company's stock will fall and others may purchase control, thereafter replacing the existing management. Therefore, proof of managerial control requires more evidence than a mere showing that managers and shareholders are not the same individuals. Although these issues were first raised in the early thirties, they are still under extensive examination by economists and other social scientists.

While much debate still continues on the scope of managerial control (separation of ownership and control), there is little doubt that the corporate revolution is substantially complete. Yet to say that the economy is substantially organized along corporate lines and that some of these corporations are very large has little significance in itself. *Large* is a relative word, and to evaluate the economic power of corporations standards of measurement must be developed. Two commonly employed measures of economic power are discussed below.

## Economic Concentration

We define economic concentration, or the concentration ratio, as the share held by the largest organizational units (the number making up the largest organizational units is arbitrary and is usually defined in the context of the particular problem under consideration) within the sphere of economic activity in which they are engaged.

It was stated earlier that over 80 percent of the total receipts in the economy were accounted for by organizations having a corporate structure. If, instead, we had said that corporate organizations account for more than one trillion dollars in receipts per year, the informational content of that statistic would have been much less meaningful. The reason is simply that one trillion dollars in sales is much less significant for an economy where the total sales are 1,000 trillion dollars than it is for an economy where total sales are 1.5 trillion dollars.

In studying the importance and extent of economic concentration, economists have focused principally on two forms of the concentration ratio. One of these is the aggregate or economy-wide concentration of economic activity. The other deals with concentration of economic activity within particular markets or industries. Aggregate concentration measures provide information on the extent to which resources are exchanged within, rather than among, organizations; that is, the degree to which exchanges take place outside the marketplace. Thus they indicate the extent to which a few decision-making units manage the resources of the entire economy or particular sectors (e.g., manufacturing) of it. In contrast, measures of market concentration are utilized to indicate the degree of power of buyers and sellers in individual exchanges at the market level. Low levels of both buyer and seller concentration indicate that neither has significant power and that exchanges within the market are likely to be voluntary. Viewed from the seller side of the market (the primary focus of this essay), the concentration ratio provides an indication of whether the conditions in individual markets are compatible with competition on the one hand or monopoly on the other.[7]

Before turning to an examination of selected data, we note that aggregate concentration also has implications for the separation of economic and political power discussed previously. To the extent that the resources of the economy are concentrated in a small number of corporations and the ownership and/or control of these organizations is in the hands of a few individuals or family groups, the political power of these individuals may be disproportionately large in terms of their numbers. As has been stated, the links between ownership concentration, concentration of control, aggregate concentration, and political power are still the subject of considerable debate and uncertainty. While the issues raised here cut across many disciplines and cannot be handled adequately in a single essay, the figures on aggregate concentration are suggestive.[8] Evidence on aggregate concentration and its trends are considered below.

## Aggregate Concentration: Current Levels and Trends

In this section the principal focus is an examination of the extent to which economic activity in the industrial sector is concentrated in large firms. The reason for emphasizing the industrial or manufacturing sector is that the data and information for manufacturing corporations are the most complete and detailed available. This is not surprising in view of the central role of this sector in our economy. For most measures of economic activity, the manufacturing sector accounts for roughly one-third of the total value in the economy.

While a large number of variables are employed in measuring concentration (e.g., total assets, net capital assets, sales, value added, value of shipments, income, and employment), we shall concentrate on three var-

7. While our discussion is mainly concerned with corporate power, the existence of labor unions raises similar issues in the labor market.

8. Aside from questions of political power, the concentration of ownership of economic resources also relates to questions of the distribution of income in the economy.

iables: total assets, value added, and total sales. Total assets are used to measure the extent to which productive resources and financial strength are concentrated in large corporations. While there are several problems with this measure—most of them due to the fact that assets as listed on corporation balance sheets reflect book or purchase value, not current value—assets do provide a useful indicator of the magnitude of large firms' participation in the economy.

The other measures, total sales and value added, both refer to the value of goods and services that enter into final demand. Value added differs from total sales in that it eliminates double counting associated with combining several stages of production. Consider the case of a manufacturer who makes steel ingots from iron ore purchased at $100. Assume the manufacturer of the ingots sells them for $150. It is clear that the total value added by the ingot manufacturer is only $50, since the mining company that sold him the iron ore has already added $100 to the final purchase price. The $50 in value added by the ingot manufacturer, as well as the $100 in value added by the mining company, is accounted for by labor (wages), ownership (profits and depreciation), financial capital (interest), and government (tax payments). Since the sum of the value added by all organization units is equal to gross national product, value added provides an indication of large firm control of economic activity based on current market values. Total sales will be used in measuring concentration in particular markets where double counting is not a problem.

Tables 3–1, 3–2, and 3–3 and Figure 3–1 show information on both the level and trend of aggregate concentration.[9] Table 3–1, based on 1962 data, indicates that the 20 largest corporations controlled 25 percent of all manufacturing assets, while the 1,000 largest controlled 74.8 percent of the same figure. It follows that the 419,000 smallest companies (those below the thousand largest) accounted for only 25.2 percent of total manufacturing assets. Of the approximately 420,000 business units in operation at the end of 1962, roughly 43 percent were organized as corporations, and these corporate enterprises had ownership control of 98.4 percent of the total assets of manufacturing. The fact that the 20 largest companies had total assets approximately the same as the 419,000 smallest, indicates clearly the high degree of inequality that characterizes the size distribution of firms in the U.S. industrial sector.

The data in Tables 3–2, 3–3, and 3–4 and Figure 3–1 show that the share of total manufacturing assets held by the largest corporations has increased significantly in the 27 years between 1941 and 1968. For exam-

9. While data presented in this chapter refer to different years and time periods and are not always directly comparable, the percentage figures can be taken as representative of the postwar period.

Table 3–1
Concentration of Total Manufacturing Assets, 4th Quarter, 1962

| Corporate size group | Assets (millions of dollars) | Assets As A Percent Of: All manu-facturing | Corpora-tions only |
|---|---|---|---|
| 5 largest | 36,447 | 12.3% | 12.5% |
| 10 largest | 54,353 | 18.4 | 18.7 |
| 20 largest | 73,825 | 25.0 | 25.4 |
| 50 largest | 105,421 | 35.7 | 36.2 |
| 100 largest | 136,222 | 46.1 | 46.8 |
| 200 largest | 165,328 | 55.9 | 56.8 |
| 500 largest | 199,894 | 67.6 | 68.7 |
| 1,000 largest | 221,279 | 74.8 | 76.0 |
| Corporations with assets over $10 million[1] | 237,410 | 80.3 | 81.6 |
| All corporations[2] | 291,022 | 98.4 | 100.0 |
| Total manufacturing businesses[3] | 295,690 | 100.0 | — |

[1]There were 2,041 manufacturing corporations in operation during the 1st quarter of 1963.

[2]This group includes about 180,000 manufacturing corporations.

[3]Includes asset estimates for approximately 240,000 manufacturing proprietorships and partnerships. There were 420,000 enterprises in manufacturing.

Source: Testimony of Willard F. Mueller, "Economic Concentration," in hearings on *Status and Future of Small Business* before Select Committee on Small Business, U.S. Senate, 90th Congress, 1st session, March 1967. Part I.

ple, Table 3–2 shows that the 100 largest enterprises increased their share of total manufacturing assets by 11 percentage points between 1941 and 1968. Utilizing the same underlying data, we can see from Table 3–3 that in 1941, the 100 largest corporations accounted for 38 percent of manufacturing assets, but by 1968 the same 38 percent was accounted for by only the 53 largest enterprises. Figure 3–1 summarizes the data contained in Table 3–2 and 3–3. Looking at Table 3–4, we can also see that the 100

Table 3–2
Aggregate Concentration, Alternative Levels—
1941, 1964 and 1968 (Percent of corporate manufacturing assets)

| Largest | 1941 | 1964 | 1968 |
|---|---|---|---|
| 100 | 38.4 | 46.8 | 49.4 |
| 200 | 46.2 | 57.2 | 61.1 |
| 300 | 50.2 | 62.9 | 67.3 |
| 400 | 53.0 | 66.6 | 71.1 |
| 500 | 55.3 | 69.3 | 73.8 |
| 600 | 57.0 | 71.4 | 75.9 |
| 700 | 58.4 | 73.1 | 77.5 |
| 800 | 59.6 | 74.5 | 78.8 |
| 900 | 60.7 | 75.6 | 79.9 |
| 1,000 | 61.6 | 76.6 | 80.8 |

Source: U.S. Federal Trade Commission, *Economic Report on Corporate Mergers*, Washington, D.C., 1969, p. 167.

Table 3–3
Number of Companies in 1941, 1964, and 1968 Holding Identical Share of All Corporate Manufacturing Assets

| Share of assets (percent) | Number of companies holding share in: 1941 | 1964 | 1968 |
|---|---|---|---|
| 38% | 100 | 59 | 53 |
| 46 | 200 | 97 | 86 |
| 50 | 300 | 125 | 104 |
| 53 | 400 | 150 | 124 |
| 55 | 500 | 175 | 141 |
| 57 | 600 | 197 | 156 |
| 58 | 700 | 218 | 170 |
| 59 | 800 | 236 | 182 |
| 60 | 900 | 255 | 195 |
| 61 | 1,000 | 272 | 207 |

Source: FTC, *Economic Report*, p. 168.

Figure 3–1. Cumulative share of corporate manufacturing assets held by 1,000 largest corporations, 1941, 1964, and 1968.

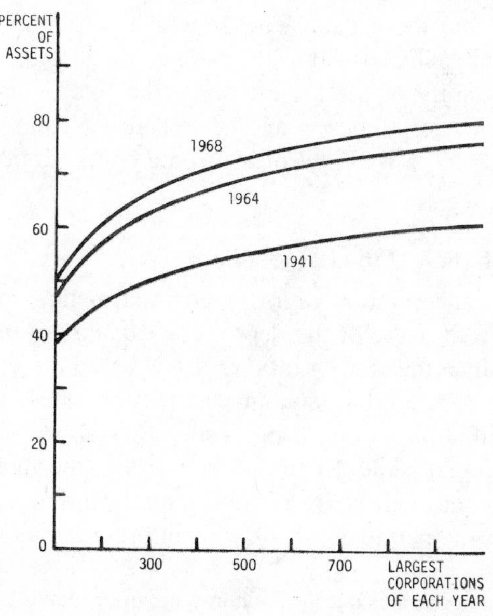


Source: Ibid., Table 3-1.

Table 3–4
Share of Total Value Added by Manufacture Accounted for by the Largest 200 Manufacturing Companies—1967 and Earlier Years*

| | Percent of total value added by manufacturer | | | | | | |
|---|---|---|---|---|---|---|---|
| Company rank group | 1967 | 1966 | 1963 | 1962 | 1958 | 1954 | 1947 |
| Largest 50 companies | 25 | 25 | 25 | 24 | 23 | 23 | 17 |
| Largest 100 companies | 33 | 33 | 33 | 32 | 30 | 30 | 23 |
| Largest 150 companies | 38 | 38 | 37 | 36 | 35 | 34 | 27 |
| Largest 200 companies | 42 | 42 | 41 | 40 | 38 | 37 | 30 |

*1962 and 1966 based on the *Annual Survey of Manufactures*, other years on the *Census of Manufactures*. "Largest companies" are those which were the largest in each of the specified years.

Source: U.S. Bureau of Census, *Census of Manufactures*, vol. 1, January, 1971.

largest manufacturing companies increased their share of value added by 10 percentage points between 1947 and 1967. Considering all evidence, there appears to be little doubt that aggregate concentration, at least for the manufacturing sector, increased substantially during the last 20 or 30 years.[10]

Although the data indicate clearly that aggregate concentration in the manufacturing sector—the largest and probably the most important—has increased in recent years, the precise interpretation of these figures is, as previously indicated, not clear. Several important factors must be considered to evaluate these data. These include such things as the size distribution of firms included within the category of largest firms, the turnover or change in identity of the largest firms, the role of merger and relative growth in determining trends in aggregate concentration, and distributional factors which underlie the level of aggregate concentration.

### The Size Distribution of the Largest Firms

The aggregate concentration ratio, or, for that matter, the market concentration ratio is a measure of the degree of inequality in the size distribution of firms. Yet, since the concentration ratio is based on an arbitrary number of firms' share of the total economic activity, it offers us no information about the distribution among firms lying either above or below the cutoff point. For example, while Table 3–2 shows that the thousand largest corporations increased their share of total manufacturing assets from 61.6 to 80.8 percent in the period 1941–68, this information alone tells us nothing

10. The trend in aggregate concentration in years prior to World War II is extremely difficult to estimate, since our data in the earlier periods is not systematic with respect to time. While many economists would probably agree that concentration did increase after 1900, there is a substantial minority view on the question. In any case, no significant decline is discernible.

Table 3–5
Size Distribution Within the 1,000 Largest Corporations,
1941, 1964, and 1968 (Percent of total assets held by 1,000 largest)

| Largest | 1941 | 1964 | 1968 |
|---|---|---|---|
| 100 | 62.3% | 61.1% | 61.1% |
| 200 | 75.0 | 74.7 | 75.6 |
| 300 | 81.5 | 82.1 | 83.3 |
| 400 | 86.0 | 86.9 | 88.0 |
| 500 | 89.8 | 90.5 | 91.4 |
| 600 | 92.5 | 93.2 | 94.0 |
| 700 | 94.8 | 95.4 | 96.0 |
| 800 | 96.8 | 97.3 | 97.5 |
| 900 | 98.5 | 98.7 | 98.9 |
| 1,000 | 100.0 | 100.0 | 100.0 |

Source: FTC, *Economic Report*, p. 708.

about the relative sizes of firms classified among the thousand largest. Evidence on this question is presented in Table 3–5.

It is readily ascertained from Table 3–5 that the distribution of firm sizes among the thousand largest corporations is practically identical in both 1941 and 1968. In fact, the distributions in each year are so similar that they can be represented on a single Lorenz curve (Figure 3–2). While the distribution among the thousand largest firms has remained remarkably stable over time, the spread in absolute size between the largest and smallest firms has declined substantially. For example, in 1955 the largest firm was 69 times as large as the firm ranked 200, but by 1965 the largest firm was only 46 times as large as the 200th largest.[11] Notwithstanding the decrease in the absolute size range among the largest firms, there was an increase in inequality for the total population of firms. That is, since the largest firms increased their share of the total assets, and at the same time the total number of firms increased, the spread between the largest and smallest firm had to increase substantially.

## Membership Turnover Among the Largest Firms

In addition to the size distribution among the largest firms, another important factor necessary for interpretation of the trend in aggregate concentration is the identity of firms included in the largest size classes. The statement that the thousand largest firms increased their share of total manufacturing assets by roughly 20 percent in the period 1941 to 1961

11. These figures were computed from the *Fortune Directory of the 500 Largest U.S. Industrial Corporations,* Annual, 1954–1970, Time, Inc. with size rankings based on total assets.

Figure 3–2. Lorenz curve representing the size distributions of assets within the 1,000 largest manufacturers, 1941, 1964, and 1968.

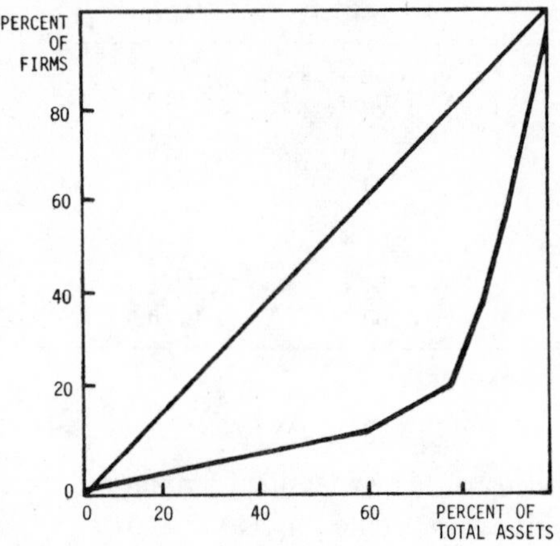


loses much of its drama in light of the fact that 66 percent of the thousand largest companies in 1941 were not among the thousand largest in 1968 (Table 3–6). This table also shows that, while there was substantially less turnover among the 200 largest corporations in 1941, this group saw 20 percent of its number excluded from the thousand largest corporations by 1968.

As indicated in Table 3–6 the two main reasons causing companies to leave the thousand largest classification were acquisitions (384) and inade-

Table 3–6
Reasons Manufacturing Corporations Ranking among the 1,000 Largest of 1941 were not among 1,000 Largest of 1968

| Reason for exclusion in 1968 | 1941 Asset rank | | | | | |
|---|---|---|---|---|---|---|
| | 1–200 | 201–400 | 401–600 | 601–800 | 801–1,000 | Total |
| Acquired during 1942–1968 | 37 | 70 | 87 | 96 | 94 | 384 |
| Liquidated, no buyer identified | 0 | 2 | 6 | 5 | 3 | 16 |
| Reclassified to nonmanufacturing | 2 | 4 | 7 | 7 | 7 | 27 |
| Still operating, but too small in 1968 | 2 | 9 | 41 | 74 | 88 | 214 |
| Unknown and "special explanations"* | 0 | 4 | 3 | 8 | 5 | 20 |
| TOTAL | 41 | 89 | 144 | 190 | 197 | 661 |

*Two of these companies were later consolidated into Castle and Cooke, which was not then predominantly a manufacturing firm. Four of these companies were confiscated by the Castro government. The remaining 14 could not be identified in 1968.

Source: FTC, *Economic Report*, p. 715.

quate growth (214). Note that the true number of liquidations may be substantially higher than the total of 16 shown. It was indicated earlier that the costs of liquidation are greater for large firms than for small. For this reason, liquidation often takes the form of changes in management and reorganization of a firm while maintaining the same corporate name. Liquidations of this nature may have significant impacts on the power of the corporation, although they will not be reflected in the figures of Table 3–6. In addition to changes in management in large enterprises, there is considerable turnover in the ownership of U.S. corporations.

### Mergers and Relative Growth in Aggregate Concentration Trends

Economists distinguish sharply between turnover resulting from the more rapid growth of small firms and that associated with merger or the acquiring of one firm by another. In fact, the Federal Trade Commission's report on corporate mergers states that "practically all of the increases in the share of industrial assets held by the 200 largest corporations were directly attributable to mergers." The FTC report attributes 15.6 of the 18.9 percentage point increase (1947–68) in the share of the 200 largest corporations in 1968 to merger activity.[12] Further, it has been estimated that the number of large firms (those with assets above $10 million) would have been 25 to 35 percent larger in 1968 in the absence of mergers during the 1948–68 period.[13] Notwithstanding these facts, FTC figures indicate there was still a substantial growth in the number of large firms. For example, during the decade 1959 through 1969, the number of corporations with assets of 25 million or more increased from 883 to 1,354. The number of corporations with assets above $10 million increased from 1,938 to 2,593 during the same time period.[14]

Considering the effects of merger activity, two basic questions arise. First, what was the role of merger growth in the total growth of those firms which are largest at a point in time? Second, what was the role of mergers in the growth of the largest firms relative to other firms in the economy? Growth due to merger activity includes both the direct effect of the acquisition of assets through the merger, and the indirect effect which is associated with the post-merger growth of the firm due to its previously acquired assets.

As we noted previously, the FTC study indicates that of the 18.5 percentage point increase in the share of total manufacturing assets held by the

12. Economic Report on Corporate Mergers, U.S. Federal Trade Commission, Washington, D.C., 1966, pp. 191–193.

13. Michael Gort and Thomas F. Hogarty, "New Evidence on Mergers." *The Journal of Law and Economics*, April, 1970, pp. 319–331.

14. It is also true that some of the increases in the number of large corporations were the result of merger activity. Increases in the price level have also increased the number of large corporations.

200 largest firms (1968) between 1947 and 1968, 15.6 percentage points were attributable to merger-acquired assets. The FTC analysis subdivides this total of merger-related growth of 15.6 percentage points as follows: 8.9 percentage points directly attributable to mergers, and 6.7 percentage points to post-merger or indirect growth. According to these figures, it would appear that merger activity was the primary force responsible for increases in aggregate concentration during the postwar period. However, the FTC conclusions are not as clear-cut as they may seem.

Tables 3–7 and 3–8 provide information on the merger activity between the years 1947 and 1968 for the largest firms, based on 1968 assets. Table 3–7 shows that, on average, the 200 largest firms of 1968 had approximately 20 percent of their direct growth accounted for by mergers during the preceding 20-year period. Although the average contribution of mergers to asset growth for the 200 largest was 20.6 percent, the relative contribution of mergers was greater for firms ranked below the largest 50 than for those ranked between 1 and 50. Table 3–8 indicates that these same 200 firms acquired almost 11 percent of all manufacturing assets in the 1948–68 period; and that almost 80 percent of this amount was acquired after 1955. The figures also demonstrate that 6.23 percentage points were accounted for in the period 1960 through 1968. Comparing these figures with those in Table 3–9 demonstrates that the time period when aggregate concentration was experiencing its greatest increases did not coincide with the time period associated with the bulk of merger activity.

Table 3–7
Total Acquisition Growth of the 200 Largest Manufacturing Corporations of 1968 as a Percent of their Total Growth, 1948–1968

| Size of Acquiring Corporation | Assets of Group 1948 ($ millions) | Assets of Group 1968 ($ millions) | Asset Growth 1948–68 ($ millions) | Value of Acquired Assets 1948–68 ($ millions) | Acquired Assets as a percent of Asset Growth 1948–68 |
|---|---|---|---|---|---|
| 5 Largest | 10,101 | 55,935 | 45,834 | 1,293 | 2.8% |
| 6–10 | 6,472 | 30,932 | 24,460 | 675 | 2.8 |
| 11–20 | 7,463 | 35,205 | 27,742 | 4,483 | 16.2 |
| 21–50 | 10,447 | 59,713 | 49,266 | 11,976 | 24.3 |
| 1–50 | 34,483 | 181,785 | 147,302 | 18,427 | 12.5 |
| 51–100 | 8,979 | 57,218 | 48,239 | 13,334 | 27.6 |
| 101–150 | 6,071 | 33,591 | 27,520 | 13,478 | 49.0 |
| 151–200 | 3,630 | 23,013 | 19,383 | 4,762 | 24.6 |
| TOTAL | 53,164* | 295,607 | 242,443* | 50,003* | 20.6 |

*Detail does not add to total due to rounding.

Source: FTC, *Economic Report*, p. 181.

Table 3–8
Assets Acquired by the 200 Largest Manufacturing Corporations of 1968 as a Percent of Total Manufacturing, 1948–1968

| Year | Value of Acquired Assets ($ millions) | Acquired Assets as a Percent of Total Manufacturing Assets of Year | Cumulative Proportion |
|---|---|---|---|
| 1948 | 151 | .12% | .12% |
| 49 | 63 | .05 | .17 |
| 50 | 101 | .07 | .24 |
| 51 | 178 | .10 | .34 |
| 52 | 320 | .18 | .53 |
| 53 | 580 | .31 | .83 |
| 54 | 1,094 | .58 | 1.41 |
| 55 | 1,438 | .70 | 2.11 |
| 56 | 1,613 | .72 | 2.83 |
| 57 | 1,027 | .43 | 3.26 |
| 58 | 855 | .35 | 3.61 |
| 59 | 1,398 | .53 | 4.14 |
| 60 | 1,080 | .39 | 4.53 |
| 61 | 1,607 | .55 | 5.08 |
| 62 | 1,233 | .40 | 5.48 |
| 63 | 1,965 | .61 | 6.09 |
| 64 | 1,452 | .42 | 6.51 |
| 65 | 2,364 | .63 | 7.14 |
| 66 | 2,226 | .53 | 7.67 |
| 67 | 6,852 | 1.51 | 9.18 |
| 68 | 7,942 | 1.58 | 10.76 |
| TOTAL | 35,539 | 10.76 | — |

Source: FTC, *Economic Report*, p. 715.

A glance at Table 3–9, which summarizes various information presented earlier, indicates three things: (1) While the bulk (approximately 60 percent) of the total assets acquired by the 200 largest firms in 1968 were acquired after 1960, the share of these 200 largest firms increased by 11.6 percentage points (roughly 60 percent of the total increase) in the period 1947 through 1960; (2) During the same period (1947–60) the aggregate concentration ratio rose 9.4 percentage points (approximately 67 percent of its total rise) while the bulk of the assets were purchased after 1960 (approximately 60 percent); and (3) Of the 12 percentage point increase in the concentration ratio based on value added, 75 percent had occurred by 1960, the bulk of it during the 1947–1954 period. Furthermore, most of this increase was attributable to the 50 largest firms (6 of the 8 percentage points) which, as shown earlier, exhibited a relatively small proportion of the total merger activity. While it is clear that mergers are an important aspect of both the level and changes in aggregate concentration, this analysis casts considerable doubt on the exceedingly strong conclusion of the FTC report regarding the central importance of mergers in explaining postwar trends in aggregate concentration.

Table 3–9
Aggregate Concentration Ratios in Manufacturing—
Levels and Changes, 1947–1968

| Period/Year | Asset Concentration (200 Largest Firms) of 1968 | Asset Concentration (200 Largest Firms) | Value Added Concentration (200 Largest Firms) | Value Added Concentration (50 Largest Firms) |
|---|---|---|---|---|
| Levels | | | | |
| 1947 | 42.5 | 47.2 | 30 | 17 |
| 1960 | 54.1 | 56.4* | 39 | 23* |
| 1968 | 60.9 | 60.9 | 42 | 25 |
| Changes | | | | |
| 1947–60 | 11.6 | 9.4 | 9.0 | 6.0 |
| 1960–68 | 6.9 | 4.3 | 3.0 | 2.0 |
| 1947–68 | 18.7 | 13.7 | 12.0 | 8.0 |

*Estimated by interpolation.

Sources: Column 1) FTC, *Economic Report*, Figs. 3–4, p. 192.
Column 2) FTC, *Economic Report*, Tables 3–4, p. 176.
Columns 3–4) Ibid., Table 4.

**Distribution Factors in Aggregate Concentration**

Our discussion has focused on factors which underlie the level and trend of statistical measures of aggregate concentration: first, the relative and absolute size differences among firms classified as the largest in the manufacturing sector; then analysis proceeded with a consideration of the role of merger activity (distributed across the time spectrum) in the trend towards increasing levels of aggregate concentration. Now to be considered is the role that the distributions or patterns of industry activities play in explaining the level of aggregate concentration in manufacturing. One aspect, the relationship between industry activity and aggregate concentration, is to be found in the relative growth rates among industries. For example, some of the largest firms in the economy are located in the automobile and aircraft industries. It has been shown that a substantial proportion of the increase in value added associated with the largest firms during the postwar period (1947–54) was the result of rapid growth in the demand for motor vehicles and aircraft following the war. That is to say, since demand for the products of already large firms grew faster than the demand for smaller firms producing in other industries, increases in aggregate concentration were attributable, in large part, to changes in the composition of output for the economy.

In addition to the importance of changes in relative demand as explanation of trends in aggregate concentration, the distribution of demand among industries is an important ingredient in explaining current levels of aggregate oncentration. Figures in Table 3–10, compiled by Fred Weston, illustrate this point. The data in Table 3–10 demonstrate that 5 industries (3.2 per-

Table 3–10
Relative Importance of Five Three-Digit Industries and Manufacturing Concentration, 1968

| SIC* | | Total Assets end of 1968 ($ billions) | Number of Firms in Largest 100 |
|---|---|---|---|
| 291 | Petroleum Refining | 75.3 | 18 |
| 331 | Primary Iron and Steel | 26.8 | 6 |
| 371 | Motor Vehicles and Equipment | 35.9 | 3 |
| 372 | Aircraft and Parts | 19.3 | 8 |
| 281 | Basic Chemicals | 26.7 | 7 |
| | Subtotal | 184.0 | 42 |
| | Total All Manufacturing | 485.9 | |
| | Percent 5 Industries to Total Value | 37.9% | |
| | (5/155) Number | 3.2% | |

*SIC industry codes are explained in a later section of the chapter.

Source: Fred Weston in *Conglomerate Mergers and Acquisitions: Opinion and Analysis*, St. Johns Law Review 44 (Spring 1970; special ed.), p. 78.

cent of the total) in manufacturing account for 37.9 percent of the total assets in manufacturing. Furthermore, 42 of the hundred largest firms, with assets approximating 29 percent of all manufacturing, are located in those five industries. These figures clearly indicate the importance of the few largest industries in explaining the degree of aggregate concentration in the economy.

To this juncture, major attention has been focused on describing the levels and trends on aggregate concentration along with some factors important in the evaluation of data. It is now time to examine competition and monopoly in individual markets and industries. At this level of analysis we are mainly concerned with power of coercion in individual transactions. The reader will recall that aggregate concentration had important implications for the separation of economic and political power. As noted earlier, it is monopoly power that economists from the time of Adam Smith have been primarily concerned about. In fact, unless large firms have monopoly power in individual markets, in the absence of political considerations they do not offer any special threat to individual freedom.

### Basic Concepts in the Theory of the Firm and Market

The economist defines a market as a place where individual buyers and sellers come together to exchange goods and services. Economic theory distinguishes among markets on the basis of various structural characteristics. At the one extreme, perfect competition requires a large number of independent buyers and sellers, none of which by their individual action can affect the price at which goods exchange. At the other extreme, when there is only one seller, that seller is called a monopolist and the market is considered devoid of competition.[15] Market structures that lie between the two extremes—competition and monopoly—are classified either as oligopolies or as monopolistically competitive industries. Of these two intermediate cases, oligopoly is by far the most important and encompasses markets in which sellers are limited in number and/or highly unequal in size. In addition to few sellers, oligopolistic markets may also be characterized by a large degree of differentiation in the products of the sellers.

While it is almost impossible to find real world markets which fit exactly the assumptions of either perfect competition or monopoly, these market models are useful guides to the study of real world markets. For example, evidence will be given below which indicates that a majority of manufacturing industries conform closely enough to the competitive mold to be called "workably" competitive. On the other hand, some oligopolistic industries can be reasonably considered as shared monopolies, with the result that many of the predictions of the theoretical model of monopoly are valid. Before turning to empirical evidence on the structure of markets in the U.S. economy, we must consider more carefully the reasons why economists prefer the competitive outcome to that which results under monopoly conditions.

Individual consumers, faced with a variety of goods and services available for purchase, different tastes, and limited budgets, must decide how to allocate their limited income among the various goods and services so as to maximize their own well-being or satisfaction. Assuming only that the individual choices among goods and services are restricted by the consumer's budget, demand curves can be derived for each individual showing quantity of any particular good or service he will purchase at various prices. The total demand for any product can be obtained by summing the quantity of the product each consumer would purchase at a particular price. Figure 3–3 illustrates a typical demand curve for a good or service. As can be seen, the demand curve ($DD$) is negatively sloped, reflecting the fact that only at lower prices will consumers increase their purchase of the product. Thus at price $P_1$, consumers will purchase $Q_1$, and if the price falls to $P_2$ they will then purchase the higher quantity $Q_2$.

It is important that the reader recognize that the analysis which follows assumes a given income distribution among the population. That is, we are not particularly concerned in this analysis with whether the individual members of the society have a "fair share" of the income. Since the society can always tax and subsidize particular elements of the population, it can

15. If there is only one buyer in the market, that buyer is said to have monopsony power. The concepts are, of course, analogous.

Figure 3–3. Market demand curve.

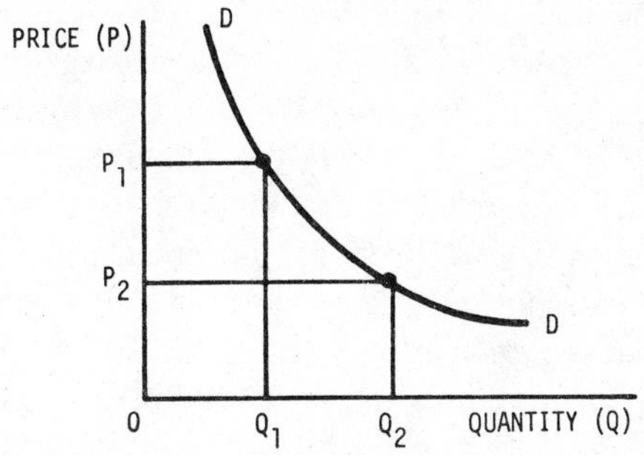


distribute purchasing power in any way desired. Note also that we are considering a society in which there are laws and enforcement against acts of physical force or violence. This assumes that the only way for an individual to obtain goods and services is by paying for them out of his limited budget. Such a legal framework is important to any society which must ration scarce goods and services to the individual consumers. In the absence of a formally enforced mechanism, those individuals with superior physical force or weapons will allocate society's resources in accordance with their own desires.

#### Theory of Monopoly and Competition

Given the market demand curve, which represents the sum of the demands of individual buyers, we now focus on the sellers' side of the market. As previously noted, individual buyers seek to maximize their satisfaction within the limit of their budget. Similarly, individual sellers or firms attempt to maximize their profits subject to constraints imposed by the demand for their products and the technology necessary to produce them. While one may argue that not all firms are organized to maximize profits (e.g., nonprofit corporations), the vast majority of business enterprise is organized in this fashion. Whether the business is a proprietorship or a large corporation, its basic resources are owned by individuals who invest (save some of their income) in order to procure a greater income in the future. Just as the individual prefers the highest possible interest rate on his savings account, so does he prefer the highest rate of return on savings he invests in business enterprises.

If we consider the market for a single product, then we may assume that the technology associated with that product is the same for all sellers in the market. While patent restrictions and other factors may mean some firms do not have access to the latest technology, inclusion of this factor would only complicate the analysis needlessly. Further, it is assumed that the technology of the industry will allow the competitive result.[16] Having abstracted from technological questions, we can now concentrate on the remaining constraint for the firm, namely the demand curve or the aggregate desires of individual consumers. Thus, the firm is viewed as a decision-maker who seeks to maximize profit by producing goods or services that have specific costs and can be sold subject to constraints imposed by the demand curve which the enterprise faces.

Since the demand curve tells the seller the price per unit of output he will receive for any quantity which it places on the market, we call the demand curve of the firm its average revenue curve. Once a firm knows its demand curve, it can calculate the total revenue associated with any level of output it produces. To see why this is so, consider a firm producing $Q_1$ units and facing the demand curve given in Figure 3–3. If the firm produces $Q_1$ units of output, then it can sell each unit at the price $P_1$ (the average revenue per unit). Therefore, its total revenue will be $P_1 \times Q_1$. Since the firm's total revenue (*TR*) can be derived from the demand curve, and the firm presumably knows how much it will cost to produce any level of output, say $Q_1$ or $Q_2$, once it knows its demand curve the firm can easily calculate its profit by taking the difference between *TR* and *TC* (total cost) at each level of output. Knowing the profit at each level of output, the firm will choose that level of output at which its total profit is a maximum.

To progress with the analysis, it is useful to develop a rule that tells us at what level of output the firm will maximize its total profit. It can be shown that the firm will maximize its profit at that level of output at which its marginal revenue (defined as the extra or additional revenue received from selling one more unit of output) is equal to its marginal cost (defined as the extra or additional cost incurred in producing one more unit of output). To see why this is so, consider the case where *MR* is greater than (less than) *MC*. If the firm gains more (less) revenue from an additional unit sold than the cost incurred in producing that extra unit, then it pays the firm to increase (decrease) its output by that extra unit. Therefore, only at that output at which $MR = MC$ will the firm have no desire to change its output since if it either increases or decreases output its total profit will

16. One of the most important factors in the determination of market power is economies of scale (lower average costs associated with large firms) connected with the technology required in production. The telephone industry is an example of an industry where the technology dictates the existence of only one firm in a given area. Notwithstanding the technological limitations to the number of firms in some industries, it is the author's belief that economies of scale are *not* of decisive importance in most industries.

decline. While the same rule is applicable to both the monopolist and the perfect competitor, the average and marginal revenue curves facing each will not be the same.[17]

By definition, the monopolist is the only seller in the market. This being so, his demand curve is identical to the industry or market demand curve shown in Figure 3–3. The monopolist therefore knows that if he is to increase his sales he must reduce the price of his product. It is important to recognize that the monopolist's power is limited by consumer demand for his product, and that the existence of monopoly power does not guarantee him excessive power. For example, the only producer of buggy whips, while being a monopolist, would have little power, since the demand for buggy whips was significantly reduced by the introduction of the automobile.[18]

In contrast to the monopolist, the perfect competitor has no control over the price he receives for his output. For a market to be perfectly competitive, there must be a large number of independent sellers so that when one seller raises his price above that of another, consumers will simply switch to another firm. The existence of a large number of sellers assures that no individual seller has any control over the price he receives for his product, and that there is complete dispersion of power in the market.[19]

The basic differences between the monopolist and the competitor can be represented on a graph. Figure 3–4 contrasts the demand curve facing the pure monopolist and the perfect competitor. As can be seen, the demand or average revenue curve ($AR$) of the monopolist slopes downward and is identical to the industry demand curve. In contrast, the demand curve facing the perfect competitor is simply a straight line at the price determined by the interaction of supply and demand in the market. The horizontal demand or average revenue curve for the perfect competitor indicates that the firm can sell all it wants at the price $P_1$, but if it raises its price to, say, $P_2$, it will not be able to sell any of its product. Figure 3–4 also shows the marginal revenue curves for both the monopolist and the perfect competitor.

17. For simplicity and ease of presentation it is assumed that the cost curves for both the competitor and the monopolists are the same. Assume that a competitively organized industry is suddenly transformed into a monopoly. We could then consider it as a firm with a large number of identical plants. In real world markets there are usually organizational costs which prevent this type of monopoly operation.

18. Technological change of this sort has always been important in undermining monopoly power. For another example, the power of railroads was undermined by the introduction of truck and plane transportation.

19. As an example of a firm operating in a competitive market, consider a farmer who grows corn. He produces his corn each year and accepts the prevailing market price, since he knows that withholding it from the market has no effect on its price. His inability to affect the market price results from his individual corn crop being an insignificant portion of the total.

Figure 3–4. Revenue curves for the monopolist and the competitive firm.

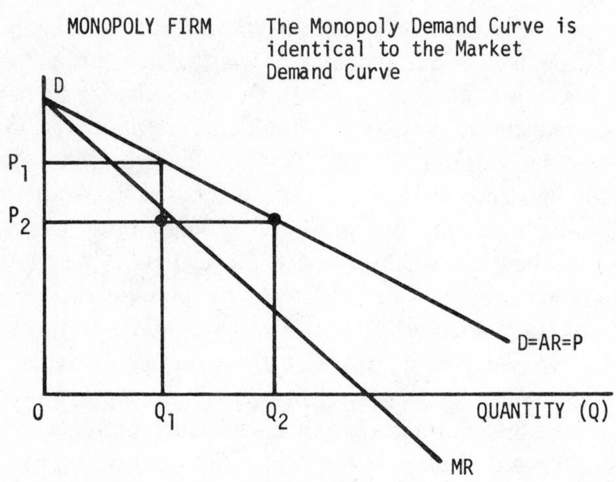


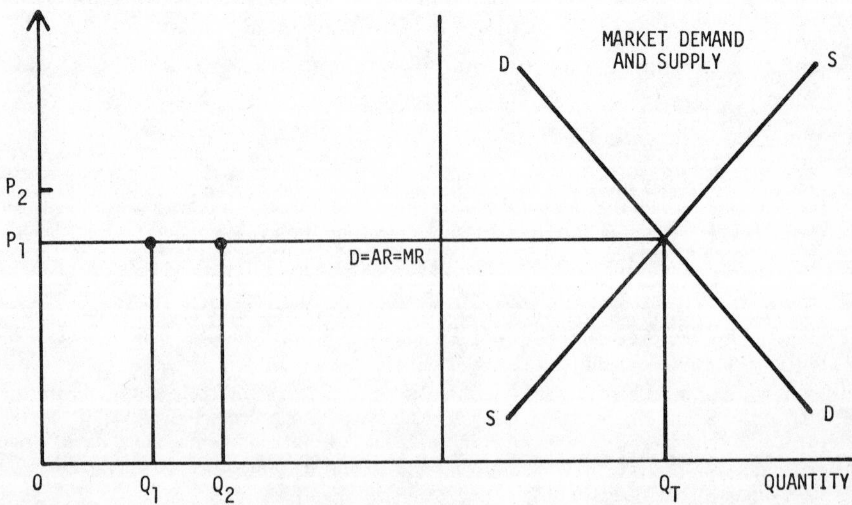

For the monopolist, the marginal revenue curve is always below the average revenue curve, while for the competitor the average and marginal revenue curves are identical. It is easy to see why the marginal revenue curves differ between the two types of firms. Consider a perfect competitor who sells one additional unit of output $(Q_2 - Q_1)$. The additional revenue he receives is $P_1$, since the price he receives for that additional unit does not change. However, for the monopolist to sell that additional unit $(Q_2 - Q_1)$, he must reduce the price of his product from $P_1$ to $P_2$, not only on the additional unit, but on every unit that he sells.

One way to view the relationship between marginal revenue and average revenue is in terms of the general relationship between an average and marginal curve. The following example will clarify the relationship. Consider a classroom in which the average student's height is 5′6″. A new student enters the class and we recalculate the average height and find it to still be 5′6″. We then know that that marginal or extra student's height was equal to the average height of the class. If after the addition of the marginal student the average height had fallen to 5′4″, we would then know the extra student (the marginal one) was shorter than the average student. Generalizing this example, we can see that if the average is falling, the marginal must then be below it; if the average is rising, then the marginal must be above it; and, finally, if the average is constant, then the marginal equals the average.

Having examined the revenue curves facing the monopolist and competitor, as well as the profit maximizing rule, we can deduce that the competitive firm will produce that level of output where price equals marginal revenue equals marginal cost $(P = MR = MC)$, while the monopolist will produce that level of output at which price is greater than marginal revenue which in turn equals marginal cost $(P > MR = MC)$. Before continuing with the comparison of the competitive vs. monopoly market structure we shall consider briefly what the economist means when he refers to costs.

The production of output by a firm requires that it purchase resources such as capital, labor, and raw materials, and that it organize them in the specific way dictated by the technology of the production process. These resources are scarce, and will have uses in the production processes of other goods and services. Therefore, the true cost to society of using resources in producing a given product is the highest value foregone by not utilizing them in another activity. If markets are perfect and there are no externalities (e.g., smoke pollution for which there is no explicit price), then the price the firm pays to hire the resources it utilizes will reflect the true value or opportunity cost of those resources.[20]

20. The proof of this statement is difficult and omitted here. Note that economists refer to foregone opportunities as opportunity costs.

Figure 3–5. Comparison of monopoly and competitive price and output. (The comparisons shown in this figure are strictly applicable only in the case of a constant cost industry in long-run equilibrium. Nevertheless, the same conclusions hold under less restrictive assumptions.)

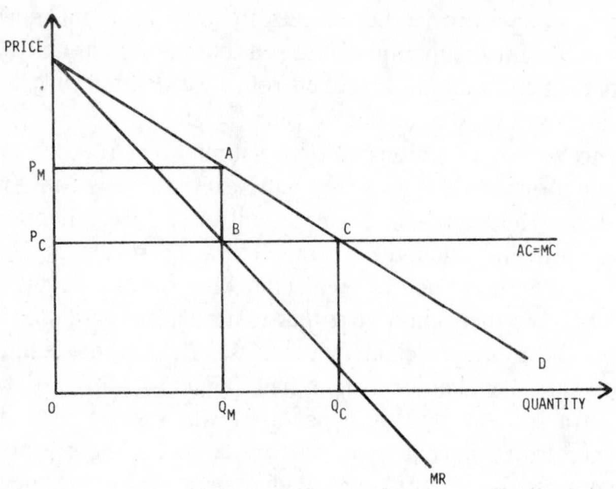


In addition to the explicit costs the firm incurs in the purchase of resources or inputs, the economist also includes the implicit or nonpurchased costs it incurs. Aside from externalities, the major element of implicit cost is normal profit or the return to the entrepreneur. The entrepreneur or owner-manager of the firm risks his invested resources and brings his organizational talents to the productive process. (An alternative to the use of resources in forming a firm is to put them in a savings account at earned interest.) Since both the entrepreneur's financial capital and organizational ability will have alternative uses, the 'normal profit' is the opportunity cost of his resources. In contrast, economic profit refers to returns above that which would be necessary to retain resources in the activity in which they are currently utilized.[21]

To keep our graphic analysis as simple as possible, let us assume that the average cost does not change with the level of output. This assumption of constant average cost means that marginal cost is equal to average cost. Both are represented by the horizontal line $P_CBC$ in Figure 3–5. The de-

21. The concept of economic profit is not restricted to operations of business enterprises. For example, if a star baseball or football player receives $100,000 per year in salary, while the best he could do in another activity is $10,000 per year, then the star athlete is making an economic profit of $90,000 per year.

mand curve ($D$) and marginal revenue curve ($MR$) for a monopoly firm are also shown in Figure 3–5. Utilizing the profit maximization rule, we can see that $MC$ equals $MR$ at the point $B$ which is associated with output $Q_M$. Thus, the profit maximizing monopolist will sell output $Q_M$ at the price $P_M$, since point A on the demand curve is associated with output $Q_M$. It is easily seen in the diagram that the distance $AB$, the difference between average revenue and average cost, is the economic profit per unit of output. Since the firm sells $Q_M$ units of output, the total economic profit of the firm is given by the area $P_MABP_C$ or $OQ_M \times AB = P_CP_M \times BP_C$.

Our previous discussion indicated that the demand curve of the monopolist was identical to that of the industry, while the demand curve facing the perfectly competitive producer was a horizontal line determined by the intersection of market supply and demand. Thus, we cannot utilize Figure 3–5 to make a direct comparison of the output in price for a competitive firm with that of a monopoly firm. However, with the use of a few simplifying assumptions, we can compare the price and output of a competitive industry with that of the monopolist.[22]

Since we know the competitive firm will produce that output for which price equals marginal revenue equals marginal cost, and since, by assumption, costs are the same for all firms, it follows that the competitive industry will produce output $Q_C$ at price $P_C = MC$. That is, since we know that $P = MC$ for the competitive firm, and that price is given by the intersection of market supply and demand, point C must be the intersection of supply and demand for the competitive industry. This analysis indicates clearly why economists prefer the competitive outcome over that associated with monopoly. Under competition the quantity produced is greater and the price is less ($Q_C$ greater than $Q_M$, and $P_C$ less than $P_M$) than under a monopoly organization.

Economists argue that from society's point of view there is a more efficient allocation of resources when markets are competitive. Because the monopolist restricts output to $Q_M$, the price he receives ($P_M$) is greater than the marginal cost of producing $Q_M$. While $MR$ reflects the value of an extra unit of output to the monopolist, the value of the output to society is given by the demand curve $D$. Thus, while the monopolist maximizes his own profit at output $Q_M$, society's welfare, as reflected by the individual preferences embodied in the demand curve, would be increased by allocating more resources to the product of the monopolist, since at the margin, the value of an extra unit of output to society is greater than the cost of that extra unit as reflected in the marginal cost curve. The loss to society which results from the inefficient allocation of resources is represented

22. Technically, we are assuming a constant cost industry in long-run equilibrium.

by the triangle *ABC* in Figure 3–5, and is often called the dead-weight loss.[23]

In calculating the dead-weight loss due to monopoly misallocation, we excluded the economic profit $P_C P_M BA$, since that amount is not lost to society, but instead is economic gain to the monopolist. Whether one views this monopoly profit as an ill-gotten gain depends on one's value judgment concerning the worthiness of the recipient. For example, while many would begrudge the large corporation making an economic profit, many would not find it objectionable if an individual fisherman had exclusive right to the sale of caviar which was only purchased by rich individuals. The reader is left to draw his own conclusions concerning the morality of economic profit in the two cases. Before turning to some empirical evidence on the prevalence of monopoly and competition, we should make clear that economic profit is not restricted to monopoly situations. Even if the economy was perfectly competitive in all industries, there would still exist economic profit in the short run. Only under long-run conditions will there be no economic profit associated with competitive industries.

To illustrate the difference between the short and the long run and indicate the important function of economic profit, let us consider the following example. Assume there is an increase in the demand for a given product because of a change in tastes of individual consumers. This increase in demand will tend to raise the price of the product. Since the individual competitor has been operating with no economic profit (price equals average cost), the increase in price will lead to an economic profit. This economic profit acts as a signal to other firms (which are earning only a normal return in their respective industries) to form a new firm (or diversify) and enter the industry with the economic profit. Since it takes time to build and organize new productive facilities, in the short run those enterprises already operating in the activity will be able to earn profits in excess of the normal rate. However, as new firms enter the industry, they will tend to increase the supply of the product and consequently lower the product price. In competitive markets, entry will continue until the product price has been lowered to the point where no firm is making an economic profit. Thus, economic profit signals entrepreneurs to move resources from one area of the economy to another.

Our discussion of traditional theory on monopoly and competition has shown that monopoly power restricts individual freedom by reducing the alternatives of individual buyers in the purchase of goods and services. The

23. In the U.S. economy, the dead-weight loss is not a trivial matter. Economists have estimated that it probably lies between 3 and 6 percent of the gross national product. If the 6 percent value figure is correct, the total dollar value of the dead-weight loss would be in the range of 60 billion dollars. For further reading see Fred M. Scherer *Industrial Structure and Economic Performance,* Rand McNally, 1970, pp. 400–411.

direct results of these restrictions are found to be an inefficient allocation of society's resources and possible undesirable influences on the distribution of income. Another effect which many economists believe to be important is called *x*-inefficiency. This type of inefficiency occurs because the monopolist lacks competition from rival producers. Consequently, he does not utilize cost-minimizing procedures. An analogy can be found in the controversy over grading. While some educators and students feel grades inhibit learning, others argue that the pressure of grades forces students to be efficient in their study habits.

There is a minority view on the desirability of economic concentration by big business and monopoly. Some economists, the best known being John Kenneth Galbraith, have argued that some degree of monopoly power is necessary to foster technical change or progress, and that the misallocation of current resources associated with monopoly power is a small price to pay for such advances. The argument, which I do not find supported by the empirical research on the subject, is summarized by Galbraith as follows.[24]

> Thus, while the incentives in the American economy do not, at any given moment, act to encourage the largest possible production at the lowest possible price, this is not the tragedy that it appears to be at first glance. The market concentration of American industry that is affirmed by the statistics and condemned by the competitive model turn out on closer examination to be favorable to technical change. To get the ideal equilibrium of price and output of the competitive model, we should almost certainly have to forego the change. Life might be simpler were we to do so, but progress, as it is called, is a wheel to which we are all bound.

### Market Concentration

Concentration ratios measure the extent to which a given number of firms control a market at a given point in time. While the probability that monopolistic practices exist is expected to be greater for higher than lower concentrated industries, the relationship is subject to numerous qualifications. Generally, these qualifications can be traced to two factors. First, the narrowness of the index itself—inequality in firms' shares—as measured by concentration, is associated with wide variations in the structure of the remaining market. Second, a large number of behavioral patterns are compatible with a given concentration index. Nevertheless, since concentration ratios are dominated by large firms, they offer a distinct advantage. By measuring the total share of the market controlled by the largest firms, con-

24. John Galbraith, "The Economics of Technical Development," in *Monopoly Power and Economic Performance,* ed. Edwin Mansfield, Norton, rev. ed, 1968.

Table 3–11

Number of Industries and Value of Shipments, by Industry Group.
Value of Shipments Concentration Ratio for 4 Largest Companies Ranked on Value of Shipments: 1963

| Code | Industry Group | Total | | Value of shipments concentration ratio for 4 largest companies (value figures in millions of dollars) 70–100 | | 50–69 | | 30–49 | | Less than 30 | | Weighted Average |
|---|---|---|---|---|---|---|---|---|---|---|---|---|
| | | Number of indus-tries | Value of ship-ments | Number of indus-tries | Value of ship-ments | Number of indus-tries | Value of ship-ments | Number of indus-tries | Value of ship-ments | Number of indus-tries | Value of ship-ments | |
| | All Industry | 417 | 415,744 | 45 | 65,158 | 72 | 73,114 | 129 | 104,657 | 171 | 172,812 | 37 |
| 20 | Food/kindred products | 44 | 68,466 | 5 | 2,386 | 9 | 9,550 | 17 | 25,139 | 13 | 31,391 | 34 |
| 21 | Tobacco manufactures | 4 | 4,520 | 2 | 4,022 | 2 | — | — | — | — | — | 75 |
| 22 | Textile mills products | 29 | 15,741 | 1 | 376 | 5 | 1,771 | 14 | 8,430 | 9 | 5,164 | 33 |
| 23 | Apparel/related products | 33 | 17,097 | — | — | 1 | 571 | 4 | 656 | 28 | 15,870 | 17 |
| 24 | Lumber/Wood | 13 | 9,200 | — | — | — | — | 4 | 443 | 9 | 8,757 | 15 |
| 25 | Furniture + Fixtures | 12 | 5,884 | — | — | — | — | 3 | 618 | 9 | 5,266 | 17 |
| 26 | Paper/allied products | 17 | 16,357 | 1 | 110 | 3 | 2,149 | 6 | 2,831 | 7 | 11,267 | 31 |
| 27 | Printing/Publishing | 15 | 16,166 | — | — | 1 | 346 | 4 | 1,372 | 10 | 14,448 | 18 |
| 28 | Chemical/allied products | 28 | 31,773 | 7. | 5,226 | 7 | 8,367 | 9 | 10,503 | 5 | 7,677 | 45 |
| 29 | Petroleum/Coal products | 5 | 17,995 | 1 | 72 | — | — | 3 | 17,496 | 1 | 427 | 34 |
| 30 | Rubber/Plastic products | 5 | 9,116 | 2 | 2,999 | 1 | 354 | — | — | 2 | 5,763 | 35 |
| 31 | Leather/leather products | 10 | 4,210 | — | — | 1 | 52 | 2 | 369 | 7 | 3,788 | 23 |
| 32 | Stone, clay, and glass | 27 | 12,289 | 2 | 974 | 8 | 3,507 | 10 | 2,161 | 7 | 5,647 | 37 |
| 33 | Primary metals | 24 | 35,621 | 5 | 3,148 | 4 | 19,300 | 7 | 6,995 | 8 | 6,178 | 46 |
| 34 | Fabricated metals | 28 | 23,065 | 2 | 2,153 | 3 | 515 | 6 | 2,918 | 17 | 17,479 | 25 |
| 35 | Machinery (excluding electrical) | 38 | 30,363 | 2 | 931 | 7 | 4,469 | 11 | 9,593 | 18 | 15,368 | 34 |
| 36 | Electrical machinery | 33 | 29,840 | 10 | 5,683 | 10 | 6,689 | 8 | 5,736 | 5 | 11,732 | 45 |
| 37 | Transportation equipment | 14 | 55,428 | 3 | 36,810 | 5 | 12,053 | 2 | 4,848 | 4 | 1,717 | 62 |
| 38 | Instruments | 11 | 6,118 | — | — | 4 | 2,685 | 5 | 1,736 | 2 | 1,697 | 46 |
| 39 | Misc. manufacturing | 27 | 6,495 | 2 | 268 | 1 | 238 | 14 | 2,813 | 10 | 3,176 | 29 |

Source: U.S. Bureau of Census, *Concentration Ratios in Manufacturing Industry 1963*, Part II, Washington, D.C., 1966, Table 5.

centration ratios enable us to ascertain the likelihood that a shared monopoly exists.

Earlier discussion suggested that a market is defined in terms of interactions between supply and demand. This means that data utilized in the analysis must be derived from relevant areas of economic activity, i.e., we must isolate carefully what sellers and products are to be included in the market. For example, the market for automobiles contains three major domestic producers. Yet can we say that they are likely to have a shared monopoly? Bicycles, trains, and airplanes also compete for the consumers' transportation dollars. The problem, of course, is that in some instances, we want to focus on the consumers' freedom to choose among various types of cars—and in other instances, to consider their alternatives with respect to all forms of transportation.

For purposes of statistical reporting, data are developed at various levels of detail and grouped according to the Standard Industrial Classification (SIC). The SIC system is based on number codes, with the number of reported digits determining the level of detail employed in the classification. For instance, major group 36 is defined to include producers of electrical equipment and supplies. This very broad category is then subdivided, for example, into SIC 363 (household appliances), which is further subdivided into SIC 3631 (electric household cooking equipment). This process is continued with, in some instances, 7-digit codes employed in the classification scheme. A majority of the concentration data is reported at the 4-digit industry level of detail, although the 5-digit product level is sometimes utilized (e.g., SIC 36311 is electric household ranges and ovens).

Although concentration data have now been compiled for 1967, preliminary analysis suggests that the 1963 data, which have been more extensively tabulated, are closely comparable. Table 3–11 distributes, for all 417 4-digit industries in manufacturing, the number and total shipments by both major industry category and 4-firm concentration ratios. Table 3–12 provides similar information distributed by size class and the concentration ratio. As we noted at an earlier point in the discussion, the vast majority (roughly 73 percent) of all industries have relatively low levels of concentration (less than 50 percent). In addition, approximately 42 percent of the industries show 4-firm concentration ratios less than 30 percent. While there are disagreements on what level of concentration constitutes a problem, most economists consider 70 percent too high and 40 or 50 percent and above to be moderate-to-high.

Considering the 45 industries (27 percent) in which concentration exceeds 70 percent, the data shown in Table 3–11 indicate that these industries account for 15.7 percent of all shipments. If we exclude motor vehicles (SIC 3717), the figure drops to roughly 7 percent. These statistics suggest that the largest industries are not the most concentrated. In fact, there ap-

Table 3–12

Number of Industries and Value of Shipments, by Size of Value of Shipments.
Value of Shipments Concentration Ratio for 4 Largest Companies Ranked on Value of Shipments: 1963

| | Size class (1963 value of shipments) | Total | | Value of shipments concentration ratio for 4 largest companies (value figures in millions of dollars) 70–100 | | 50–69 | | 30–49 | | Less than 30 | | |
|---|---|---|---|---|---|---|---|---|---|---|---|---|
| | | Number of industries | Value of shipments | Number of industries | Value of shipments | Number of industries | Value of shipments | Number of industries | Value of shipments | Number of industries | Value of shipments | Weighted average |
| | Total | 417 | 415,744 | 45 | 65,158 | 72 | 73,114 | 129 | 104,657 | 171 | 172,812 | 37 |
| 1) | $1 billion and over | 110 | 301,825 | 11 | 54,137 | 18 | 51,884 | 22 | 70,517 | 59 | 125,287 | 36 |
| 2) | $500,000,000 to $999,999,999 | 87 | 61,244 | 7 | 4,480 | 18 | 12,771 | 22 | 15,218 | 40 | 28,775 | 36 |
| 3) | $200,000,000 to $499,999,999 | 125 | 41,488 | 15 | 5,069 | 21 | 6,674 | 42 | 13,730 | 47 | 16,015 | 39 |
| 4) | $100,000,000 to $199,999,999 | 58 | 8,841 | 8 | 1,208 | 9 | 1,440 | 27 | 4,225 | 14 | 1,968 | 44 |
| 5) | $ 50,000,000 to $ 99,999,999 | 26 | 1,936 | 3 | 214 | 5 | 312 | 9 | 719 | 9 | 691 | 39 |
| 6) | Less than $50,000,000 | 11 | 408 | 1 | 49 | 1 | 34 | 7 | 246 | 2 | 79 | 43 |

Note: Detail may not add to totals because of independent rounding.

Source: Idem., Table 3–11.

pears to be a moderate trend toward lower concentration with increasing industry size. This interpretation is supported in Table 3–12, which indicates that the relative proportion of industries with concentration ratios above 70 percent is roughly equal for each size class (8–13 percent). In addition, the weighted average[25] concentration ratio tends to be lower for the two largest industry classes. In fact, if we remove automobiles from the calculations, the average for the largest class becomes .34.

Glancing again at Table 3–11, it is easily seen that concentration levels differ sharply among major groups. For example, almost half of all industries with concentration ratios above 70 percent are found in three major groups—chemicals, primary metals, and electrical equipment. In addition, differences in concentration have been found among various types of industries (e.g., consumer versus producer industries).[26]

Some of these differences result from demand and technological considerations, while others are attributable to institutional restrictions and other barriers to entry. Definitive answers require further analysis of these factors. Nevertheless, on the basis of this analysis it appears fair to conclude that roughly 75 percent of the U.S. industrial sector is workably competitive and that public policy (antitrust enforcement) should give careful attention to the remaining manufacturing industries, particularly the 10.7 percent with concentration ratios over 70 percent.

Earlier, considerable time was spent discussing the trend in aggregate concentration. For reasons similar to those already discussed, it is important to examine this question at the industry level. Clearly, the implications for competition are more severe if the extent of industry concentration is increasing over time.

On the basis of 213 essentially comparable industries[27] there appears to have been no tendency for 4-firm concentration ratio in manufacturing industries to either increase or decrease. Of the 213 comparable industries, 81 increased, 86 decreased, while 46 were constant over the period (Table 3–13). Nevertheless, it has also been shown that, while producer goods industries experienced considerably more declines than increases, the reverse was true for consumer industries. Thus, despite stable trends overall, there is substantial concern about certain groups of industries.[28]

25. Weighted averages are calculated in order to account for differences in size among the groups. That is, industry concentration figures are weighted by size of industry to arrive at the average for the total category.

26. See, for example, Collins and Preston, "Price-Cost Margins and Industry Structure," *The Review of Economics and Statistics,* 1969, pp. 271–286.

27. Industry definitions change over time and this is the largest sample available for the period. Since these industries are a good sample of the total population, conclusions based on them should be representative.

28. The FTC has recently (1972) instituted antitrust suits against firms in the cereal industry where the concentration ratio has been over 80 percent for the past 20 years.

Table 3–13
Distribution of 213 Comparable Industries by Change in 4-Firm Concentration Ratios: 1947–1963

| | Number of industries in which concentration ratios: | | |
|---|---|---|---|
| | increased | stayed the same[1] | decreased |
| 4-firm concentration ratios | 81 | 46 | 86 |
| | Percent of industries in which concentration ratios: | | |
| | increased | stayed the same[1] | decreased |
| 4-firm concentration ratios | 38 | 22 | 40 |

[1]Increases or decreases 3 percentage points or less.

Source: Idem., Table 3–1.

The theory and evidence developed in this chapter lead us to conclude that continuing public scrutiny is necessary in several areas and that concentration of power in business units, labor units, or political parties is a serious problem for a society dedicated to individual freedom. However, there is a 'Catch 22' in public policy. Simply stated, regulation of economic agents by government authorities may lead to an undesirable merger of political and economic power. Thus, before new laws and regulations are generated, we must be sure that the costs (in terms of both resources utilized and individual freedom) are not greater than the losses associated with leaving the economic agent alone. This is not meant to suggest that political or government intervention in economic affairs is undesirable per se. An example of the difficulty is the history of Interstate Commerce Commission (ICC), formed in 1887 in response to problems arising from monopoly power in railroad transportation. Today the ICC acts as the protector of an inefficient industry faced with strong competitive pressures from other forms of transportation. Although it may have been desirable to regulate railroads in the years before the development of truck and airline competition, the justifications for regulation of the sort practiced today are at the least debatable. To most observers the ICC appears to be more interested in perpetuating its own existence than in promoting efficient and equitable transportation. The ossification of the ICC and its close interrelationship with the regulated companies is particularly troublesome on grounds of both efficiency and freedom. 'Catch 22' can be avoided, but only with careful research which considers both the economic and political costs of particular actions. To focus on one factor and not the other is folly.

## Suggested Reading

Averitt, Robert T. *The Dual Economy*. Norton, 1968.

Berle, A. A. and G. C. Means. *The Modern Corporation and Private Property*. Revised ed. New York: Harcourt, Brace & World, 1967.

Bureau of Census, U.S. Department of Commerce, *Concentration Ratios in Manufacturing Industry, 1963: Parts I and II,* 1966.

Bureau of Economics, U.S. Federal Trade Commission, *Economic Report on Corporate Mergers: Staff Report to the Federal Trade Commission.* 1969.

Bureau of Economics, U.S. Federal Trade Commission. *Large Mergers in Manufacturing and Mining,* 1948–69 (Statistical Report No. 5, Publication No. R 6–15–7). February 1970.

Bureau of Economics, U.S. Federal Trade Commission, *The Influence of Market Structure on Profit Performance of Food Manufacturing Companies,* September 1969.

*Business Concentration and Price Policy*. A Conference of the Universities-National Bureau Committee for Economic Research. National Bureau of Economic Research, Princeton, N.J.: Princeton University Press, 1955.

Collins, Norman R. and Lee E. Preston. "Price-Cost Margins and Industry Structure." *The Review of Economics and Statistics* (1969): 271–286.

Collins, Norman R. and Lee E. Preston. "The Size Structure of the Largest Industrial Firms, 1909–1958." *The American Economic Review* (December 1961): 986–1003.

Gort, Michael. "An Economic Disturbance Theory of Mergers." *The Quarterly Journal of Economics* (November 1969): 624–642.

Hall, Marshall and Leonard Weiss. "Firm Size and Profitability." *The Review of Economics and Statistics* (1967): 319–331.

Hindley, Brian. "Separation of Ownership and Control in the Modern Corporation." *Journal of Law and Economics* (April 1970): 185–221.

Hymer, Stephen and Peter Pashigian. "Firm Size and Rate of Growth." *Journal of Political Economy* (December 1962): 556–569.

Larner, R. J. "Ownership and Control in the 200 Largest Non-financial Corporations 1929 and 1963." *The American Economic Review* (September 1966): 532–539.

McGuckin, Robert, "Entry, Concentration Change, and Stability of Market Shares." *Southern Economic Journal* (January 1972).

Preston, Lee, "The Industry and Enterprise Structure of the U.S. Economy." New York: General Learning Press, 1971.

Scherer, Fred M., *Industrial Structure and Economic Performance,* Chicago: Rand McNally, 1970.

Shepherd, William G. "Trends of Concentration in American Manufacturing Industry, 1947–58." *Review of Economics and Statistics.* May 1964, Pp. 200–212.

Shepherd, William G. "What Does the Survivor Technique Show About Economics of Scale?" *The Southern Economic Journal* (July 1967): 113–122.

## Commentary

In his discussion of the concentration of economic power, Professor McGuckin indicates some of the problems associated with devising a truly democratic method to achieve consumers' desires through the use of markets. Markets do transmit information on consumers' wants but we still may wish to establish a number of alternative methods to control power so that the outcomes will be the socially desired ones. We find that previous market analysis must be modified to distinguish between demand or *average revenue* (a measure of marginal benefits to consumers) and *marginal revenue* (a measure of marginal benefits to the firms having market power). In effect, the problem can be studied with the introduction of a single addition to our kit of economic tools: the marginal revenue curve.

In the following chapter by M. Bruce Johnson, other complexities emerge in the effort to achieve the most desirable allocation of output between consumers or to reach the most desirable level of total output of the product. The title, "Fair Pricing and the Economics of Congestion," might have been subtitled "Time Is Money," for, as Professor Johnson points out, the key to the correct solution to the problem of congestion is knowing how individuals value their time and properly taking advantage of that information. But, as we shall see, a more complex analysis is required than we have used thus far. The addition of the time dimension allows a consideration of shifts in demand over the day or week. Another step forward in the direction of analyzing investment decisions is the decision in this case as to how great the productive capacity for a good or service should be when demand is not steady from hour to hour or day to day.

In more practical terms we shall be dealing with the question of what size subway system do we build when we know there will be rush hour traffic and periods of only limited use; or, how many seats we should put in the theater to take care of Saturday night demand. Not surprisingly, these questions must be related to the price we expect to charge for the services. Thus, the question is more correctly stated: What price and quantity should we establish to meet peak demands for a service if we hope to best serve the social interest? Professor Johnson provides us with an answer.

# 4

# Fair Pricing and the Economics of Congestion

M. Bruce Johnson

It is frequently alleged that the pace of life in twentieth-century America has increased in tempo. From an economist's point of view, this situation can be described as one in which the real income available to individuals has increased largely because of technological advance, while the amount of time available to the individual for enjoying this higher real income is limited by the number of hours in the day. As time becomes a relatively scarce resource, individuals are less tolerant of activities that waste time. In this connection, phenomena such as waiting for long periods in registration lines, traffic congestion, and other similar nonproductive uses of time attract our attention as bottlenecks in the economic system.

Entrepreneurs who perceive ways to eliminate congestion in various activities generally reap higher rewards; consider the success of some of the fast-food franchisers. The unique success of the McDonald's and Colonel Sanders' food chains may be attributed more to the fast service than to the quality of the food purveyed.

Most consumers do not enjoy waiting in line for a good or service; alternatively stated, consumers attempt to minimize the time and expense of acquiring goods and services. Every one of us has felt the squeeze of congestion—on the freeway, at the check-out counter, on the beach, or at the campground—and each of us has thought "there must be a better way." Before investigating the nature, causes and cures of congestion and waiting lines, we must review briefly the competitive market model of demand and supply.

### A Review of the Nature of Demand Curves

Demand and supply curves are typically assumed to remain stable over the time period under discussion. For example, a demand curve which indicates that 10,000 units of a particular commodity will be demanded per week at a certain price includes the tacit assumption that the output will be sold at a constant rate per hour or per day over the interval of the week. This is not a bad approximation for a wide variety of applications of demand and supply curves. This assumption of uniformity of the rate of sales over a period of time does, however, cause considerable difficulty in another class of problems.

The demand for meals in a university cafeteria is probably stable day after day throughout the academic year. During the course of a day, however, the demand is not uniform; peaks occur during the breakfast hour, the lunch hour, and the dinner hour. A look at the cafeteria's capacity to produce meals will show idle capacity over most of the day, with peaks at the three mealtime hours, particularly the lunch hour. Clearly, then, the demand for cafeteria meals is not constant through the day but moves through a cycle that is reasonably predictable.

This phenomenon occurs in a wide variety of other products and services as well. As demand increases, the capacity of a road system is pressed and congestion eventually develops. This problem is quite common in investor-owned public utilities as well as publicly-owned supplies of goods and services. The telephone company has idle facilities during the late evening and early morning hours (i.e., they could accommodate many more telephone calls than they are called upon to produce). The gas company has a seasonal cycle as well as a daily cycle in the demand for natural gas; an industrial demand peak occurs during the day and a residential demand peak for heating purposes occurs at night. With the advent of the winter season, the residential heating demand peak will be even larger. Public utilities providing electric service formerly experienced a peak demand for electricity during the winter months because the longer hours of darkness required more electricity for lighting purposes. Since air conditioning has become widespread, the peak for electric power has shifted from the winter months to the summer months. Finally, some establishments experience a weekly cycle rather than one that is daily or seasonal. For example, movies are typically more crowded on Friday and Saturday evenings, retail stores on Saturdays, and churches on Sundays. Thus, a demand curve can shift around over a period of a day, a week, a month, or a year.

This movement of the demand curve raises some interesting problems for the manager of an economic enterprise. Assume the demand cycle is predictable as opposed to random. The latter circumstances would raise problems too sophisticated to attempt to handle here, given the limited tools and techniques at our disposal.

## Capacity of the Enterprise and Excess Demand

Assume the plant manager has a fixed plant whose equipment defines a certain maximum rate of output. Given that capacity, he can produce any output from zero up to that maximum output which is fixed in the short run. If the capacity of the plant is 1000 units per day, the enterprise can produce any output between 0 and 1000, but it cannot produce any more output without entering into an investment decision to expand the plant and equipment. This latter action requires a passage of economic time; it also results in fixed plant and equipment that may be very specialized in nature. Moreover, the expansion once begun cannot be easily reversed.

As demand shifts up and down over the course of the day, the manager will experience periods in which he is producing at less than his output capacity and other intervals in which he is producing exactly at the capacity. In fact, if he is producing at capacity for any more than a brief period of time, he probably has unsatisfied customers who cannot be served, given his existing limited capacity. When potential customers are turned away—customers who would be willing to buy the good or service at the announced price but cannot because there is not enough output capacity—economists refer to the situation as one of excess demand.

Figure 4–1. Excess demand.

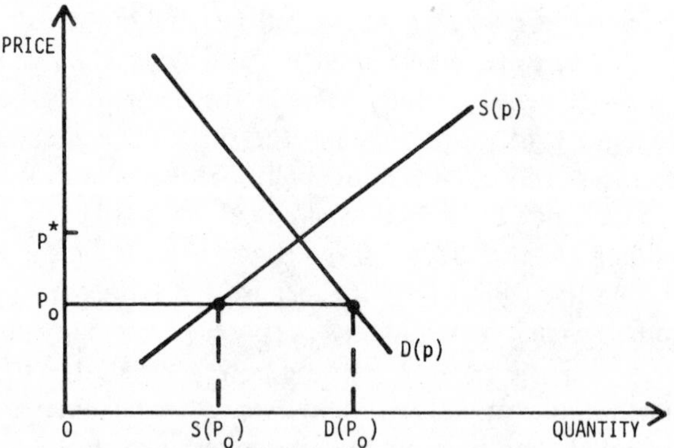


Figure 4–1 illustrates excess demand for the price $P_o$. Note that the amount of the good that consumers wish to purchase at the price $P_o$ is greater than the amount the supplier is willing to deliver at that price. With demand and supply curves that have the normal slopes, the equilibrium

price P* must be above the price $P_0$. If the price $P_0$ persists over time, so will excess demand. The existence of excess demand is a prima facie case for arguing that the price $P_0$ is too low, since if the price were raised to P* the excess demand would disappear. This is because the amount supplied would have increased and the amount demanded would have decreased at the higher price.

## Nonprice Rationing

In many circumstances legal and other constraints may operate to prevent a price from rising. In that event various devices are used in the real world to ration the limited goods among the potential demanders. When the amount individuals collectively wish to purchase is greater than the amount available for sale, waiting lines or queues may form. This essentially raises the final price of the good by imposing a time cost in addition to the money cost of acquiring the good. Individuals whose time is valuable relative to the general population will drop out of the market and not consume the good. Restaurants and supermarkets use this technique for rationing the available capacity output during peak demand times.

In some situations managers accept reservations so that demand is matched to supply and the unsatisfied demanders do not appear on the scene to attempt to secure the good or service. Supermarkets and cafeterias do not accept reservations, but elegant restaurants do. The explanation is that a customer of the cafeteria or the supermarket usually has an alternative store he can patronize with only a small expenditure of time and travel. An elegant restaurant, on the other hand, typically does not have good substitutes close at hand. Moreover, the decision to visit an elegant restaurant is probably occasioned by a greater commitment of time, distance, and expenditure on the part of the customer.

The California State Park Department until recently allocated camping sites on a first-come, first-serve basis. During the peak summer months, particularly on weekends, excess demand was experienced and potential campers were turned away at the gates of the parks. Disappointed campers frequently complained that they had spent considerable time and money traveling to the particular park, only to find that it was filled to capacity. The California Park Department now has a reservation system to alleviate this problem.

There are, however, ways to allocate scarce goods other than waiting lines or reservations systems. One method might be called a "clout" system. After a long wait for a table at a restaurant you may have noticed a new arrival walk directly to the headwaiter, whisper a few words, "shake" hands, and be seated immediately. This phenomenon occurs in nightclubs, parking lots, prestige schools, superbowl football games, opening night performances and, no doubt, in any situation where price is not allowed to increase in order to ration the scarce good.

If the solution to the scarcity of the good or service lies simply with an increase in the price, why doesn't price increase? If a free competitive market is permitted to work, price will rise and the excess demand will be eliminated by an increase in the amount supplied and a decrease in the amount demanded, as shown in Figure 4–1. Frequently, arbitrary legal prohibitions against a price rise prevent the market from equating demand and supply. Take the case of rent control in New York City. The prices of rental units are fixed at a level below the equilibrium price. Hence, the amount of housing that people want to rent at the rent controlled price is greater than the amount available. Since price cannot rise, such devices as key fees and "favors" are required of the prospective tenant if he wishes to secure an apartment.

It is obvious that legal prohibitions against price increases in such cases lead to inefficiency and inequities. A basic economic optimality condition is not met: that the price equal the marginal cost of the good or service. Hence, those individuals fortunate enough to secure an apartment will be paying a price that is less than the value to them of the good or service. Moreover, a lower regulated price puts the market on a lower position on the supply curve, meaning that fewer rental units are forthcoming at that price than would be forthcoming at the higher equilibrium price.

## Optimal Allocation of Scarce Resources

The optimality condition that price equals marginal cost is worth discussing at some length, because it is fundamental to what follows in the chapter. Assume for the moment that the economy is organized along competitive lines. In this situation, no firm will have monopoly power (single seller) in connection with the product it sells or monopsony power (single buyer) in connection with the inputs it purchases. All firms are price takers; that is, however large or small their sales or purchases, they do not affect the price of the good or the input. Given many firms in each industry, the industry supply curve will represent the marginal cost of producing output in that industry.

As the supply curve rises from left to right, it represents the locus of price—quantity points at which the firms collectively will be willing to produce. We can think of this supply curve as society's marginal cost curve of producing the particular output. The dollar figure read off the vertical axis represents the dollar value of the inputs used to produce each of the prospective levels of output. If the equilibrium price in this market is determined by the intersection of the market demand curve and this supply curve, we have the result that the price consumers pay for the amount produced is equal to the marginal cost of producing that output. Assuming this occurs in each and every industry, the equilibrium prices for all of the commodities are optimal, since any alteration of the prices would lead to a situation where price was either greater than or less than marginal cost for some goods and services.

If price is greater than marginal cost for Good A, not enough of this good is produced; as long as price is greater than marginal cost, the value that consumers put on the last unit produced is greater than the cost of producing that unit. Hence, output of this good should be increased until price and marginal cost are once again equal. If, however, price is less than marginal cost, too much of the good has been produced. With price less than marginal cost for Good B, we know that the value that consumers place on the last unit of Good B is less than the cost society incurred in producing that unit. Clearly this situation calls for a reduction in the production of Good B until a level of output is reached at which price and marginal costs are once again the same.

Although this optimality rule that price should equal marginal cost was derived under conditions of perfect competition, it has wider application. The logic extends to the case of monopoly as well. Since a monopolist does have an effect on the price of the product he sells (depending on how much he sells), he will typically produce less than the socially desired amount of output. In other words, his profit maximizing output will be at a level where price exceeds marginal cost. Although there are some exceptions to the application of this rule to the case of a monopolist (depending largely on the shape and configuration of his cost curves), the rule that price should equal marginal cost is an efficient rule. Thus, we have come to the point where we conclude that our enterprise, whether it is perfectly competitive or a monopoly, should produce a level of output where price equals marginal cost.

### Peak and Off-peak Demand

Now we must tie this notion of optimal output and price into the peak, off-peak problem posed at the outset of the discussion. To recapitulate, the manager notes that over a certain part of the day he is producing at *less* than his capacity and over another portion of the day he is producing *at* his capacity. If the firm charges the same price to both peak and off-peak customers, it will be violating the optimality condition that price equals marginal cost.

The rationale behind that conclusion proceeds as follows: When demand is in an off-peak period, the customers are taking an output that is less than the capacity of the firm. Since that capacity was necessitated not by the off-peak customers but by the peak customers, the off-peak customers should be charged a price that represents the marginal cost of producing the good exclusive of its fixed plant and equipment cost. The latter costs are justified by and occasioned by the peak users, not the off-peak users. If the off-peak users were to disappear from the market completely, the firm would still have its capacity and would maintain it presumably at that level. Hence, the marginal cost of producing another unit of the output, given that you already have a fixed plant and equipment, is merely the extra variable cost (labor and raw materials) of producing the off-peak output.

Suppose we designate the short-run marginal cost of output by the symbol $b$. Let us assume further that the short-run marginal cost is constant up to the capacity of the plant. If the off-peak users are charged $b$ per unit of output, the peak users must be charged $b$ plus a surcharge sufficient to cover the capital cost (plant and equipment costs). Suppose we designate the capital charge per unit of output per period by the symbol $\beta$. That cost, too, is assumed to be a constant over the range of output up to and beyond the capacity of the firm. The coefficient $\beta$ can be interpreted as the capital charge per unit of output over the entire period.

If our firm is to break even (i.e., cover its costs exactly), the peak period users of the product will have to bear the entire capital costs of the firm. This means, for example, that if the peak period lasted for half a day, the firm would have to charge the peak users a price equal to $b + 2\beta$ since $\beta$ is the full period capital charge per unit of output, and the peak users are only using the output of the firm for half of the day.

Figure 4–2 illustrates the foregoing analysis in detail. The off-peak de-

Figure 4–2. Peak load pricing.

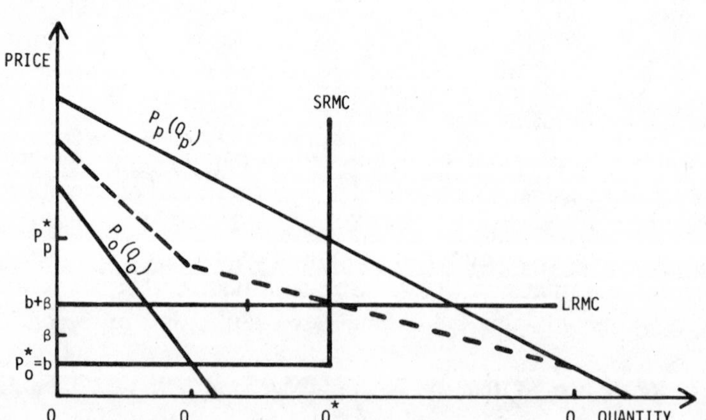

mand curve is represented by the downward-sloping demand curve labeled $P_o(Q_o)$. Notice that it is everywhere below the peak demand curve labeled $P_p(Q_p)$. The curves have different slopes as might be expected in the general case; there is no reason to believe that demand curves shift parallel to themselves over the daily cycle. Note that $b$, short-run marginal cost, is represented by a horizontal line starting from the price axis.

The long-run marginal cost, $b + \beta$, is a horizontal line above short-run marginal cost, since long-run differs from short-run marginal cost because of the capacity charge $\beta$. For the moment, ignore the kinked broken line in the diagram as well as the vertical portion of the short-run marginal cost curve. The plant manager has the information provided by the two demand curves and the two horizontal cost curves in the diagram. His problem is to decide now what level of capacity output he should produce. The manager must decide on a particular level of investment that will result in a particular plant which, in turn, will enable him to produce outputs between zero and some maximum capacity output. Furthermore, he must decide what price to charge peak users and off-peak users for their respective outputs.

One further bit of information is required before we can determine the optimal capacity output and the optimal prices. We must know what fraction of the period each of the demand curves is operative. Following our earlier assumption that the peak and off-peak demand curves were each relevant 50 percent of the time, we can assign the fraction one-half to each demand curve. This means that one-half of the time over the period of the day the demand curve $P_p$ will be the relevant demand curve and there will be no off-peak demanders. During the other half of the period, the off-peak demand curve $P_o(Q_o)$ will be in operation and the peak demand curve $P_p(Q_p)$ will "disappear."

## Demand for Capacity

Suppose now the question is how much each of the respective groups of customers would be willing to pay over and above the short-run marginal cost that they have to pay for output. In other words, we are asking how much the respective consumer groups are willing to pay for the existence of capacity in this firm. The answer can be found by computing the difference between the amount consumers are willing to pay for the product and the short-run marginal cost. Graphically, this is the vertical distance between the demand curve and the short-run marginal cost curve $b$ (as long as that distance is positive). For example, the off-peak users would have a positive demand for capacity, $P_o(Q_o) - b$, for output levels 0 up to that output $Q_o$ determined by the intersection of the off-peak demand curve and the short-run marginal cost curve. For output levels beyond that point, the amount of money off-peak users are willing to pay for extra units of output falls below the short-run marginal cost and therefore these users do not have a positive demand for capacity. A similar argument applies for the peak users except that the demand for capacity, $P_p(Q_p) - b$, is positive for output levels from 0 up to $Q_p$. At this output the value peak users place on it is just equal to short-run marginal cost $b$.

Now let us add up the willingness to pay for output on the part of both peak and off-peak users. Since each demand curve is relevant for one-half of the period, we can add the sum: $\frac{1}{2} P_p(Q_p) + \frac{1}{2} P_o(Q_o)$. Stated this way it is clear that the sum is an average of the two demand curves. The dashed line beginning on the price axis lies halfway between the two demand curves and falls until it reaches that output at which off-peak demand price equals short-run marginal cost, at $Q_o$. For outputs above $Q_o$, the off-peak people are not willing to pay any positive amount for capacity and so from this point on, the demand for capacity is simply equal to one-half the peak users' demand. The dashed line then moves directly to the intersection of the peak demand curve and the short-run marginal cost curve above $Q_p$.

We have now derived the demand for output for the firm. The supply or cost of capacity per unit output is given by the long-run marginal cost $b + \beta$. If we find the intersection of the demand for capacity curve and the long-run marginal cost curve, we shall have determined the optimal output capacity for this firm. That output occurs at the point labeled $Q^*$ in the diagram. Under our assumptions of a fixed capacity for the firm (once the investment decision is made), we can draw a vertical line above $Q^*$ through the intersection of the demand for capacity and the long-run marginal cost curves. Then, the short-run marginal cost curve for the firm is horizontal at the level $b$ from 0 output out to $Q^*$ output; beyond $Q^*$ the short-run marginal cost curve becomes vertical.

## Optimal Peak and Off-peak Prices

Having determined the optimal capacity output for the firm experiencing peak load demand, we now turn to the question of determining the optimal set of prices for the peak and off-peak users. We can let the supply and demand analysis determine this for us directly from the diagram. The off-peak demand curve intersects the short-run marginal cost curve at the output $Q_0$ and the price $b$. Hence, we charge a price equal to short-run marginal cost $b$ and we supply $Q_0$ units of output to the off-peak users. Since they do not use the plant to capacity ($Q_0$ is less than $Q^*$), we do not impose a capital charge or plant equipment charge to off-peak users. The peak users, however, do demand an output equal to the full capacity output of the plant. If we were to charge peak users the same price ($b$) as the off-peak users, we would have an excess demand of considerable magnitude.

Instead, we look for the intersection of the short-run marginal cost and the peak demand curve in order to find that price we will charge the peak users for the capacity output $Q^*$ that they demand. That price is labeled $P^*_p$.

It might appear at first that we are charging the peak users too much since the price $P^*_p$ is greater than the long-run marginal cost $b + \beta$ of supplying that output. However, remember that the peak users only demand this level of output for one-half the period. Thus, $P^*_p$ will be equal to $b + 2\beta$, but only for that portion of the period that the peak demand is relevant. For the rest of the period, $P^*_p$ is equal to 0 since the peak demand curve is not operative. The total revenue of the firm will naturally equal the collections from the peak users and the off-peak users. We have $\frac{1}{2} P^*_0 Q^*_0 + \frac{1}{2} P^*_p Q^*_p$ as our revenue. The fractions enter into the expression because each demand is relevant for only one-half of the period.

Finally, the necessity for nonprice rationing schemes of one sort or another is eliminated because prices are used to distribute the potential users between the peak and the off-peak periods. Note that no customer is forced to purchase the good or service in one period or another; the price schedule is posted and the individual consumer himself decides whether he wants to pay the higher peak-load price to have service during the peak times or whether he wishes to pay the lower price during the off-peak times. Most of us attempt to schedule our long-distance telephone calls in the evening hours in order to avoid the telephone toll surcharge that exists during the peak daytime business hours. Yet, if we wish to pay the higher price, we may place our call during peak hours. Similarly, we have a choice of paying the lower off-peak price to attend the matinee movie during the weekday, or we can pay the higher price and see the movie at prime time on Friday or Saturday evening.

Not needing to assign customers to one period or another has some important implications in addition to the obvious fact that freedom of choice is maximized. During peak demand periods the limited output is sold to those individuals who are willing to pay the most for it (those individuals with the highest valuation of the good). This arrangement has implications that may not be apparent at first glance. Suppose that a set of customers had been purchasing a commodity at a constant rate through the period over a number of periods in the past, and suppose that the capacity of the supplying curve had been sufficient to satisfy their demand. We are assuming, in other words, a situation without a peak and an off-peak, one that simply has a uniform demand through the period. Now suppose that a new set of customers enters the market with a desire to buy this good only during certain subintervals of time during the period. If the previously announced price and the previous capacity remain in force, excess demand will occur during the subinterval in which the new customers want the good or service. Hence, the manager should use the strategy developed above: He should construct a demand-for-capacity curve, find the intersection of that curve with the long-run marginal cost curve, and invest in a plant that has a capacity consistent with the intersection so described. He should then institute a two-tier pricing scheme with a higher price during the peak period so that excess demand would be eliminated.

## Special Interest Groups

A frequently heard complaint in a situation such as this goes as follows: The original users of the commodity still want to buy during the subinterval that now appears to be the peak period, and they wish to buy at the original (lower) price. They argue that the additional capacity and the commensurate additional capital cost were incurred by the firm because of the new customers, not the original customers. Therefore, the original users argue that they are entitled to pay the old price while the new peak load customers should pay a higher price for the commodity during the same subinterval of time.

Whatever intuitive appeal this argument might have, it is incorrect. The pricing scheme is efficient, equitable, and optimal when a price is charged that just clears the market during the peak subinterval. Prices are associated with particular times or subintervals during the period, not with particular individuals. The response to the original customers should be: You are in competition for this scarce good or service with other individuals. If you wish to pay the appropriate peak load price, you may continue to receive the good throughout the entire decision period. On the other hand, you have the alternative of increasing your demands during the off-peak times so as to achieve the same total consumption over the period that you previously had. This variation on the argument "we were here first and therefore we deserve special consideration," is no more valid in this situation than it is in any other.

On occasion it is alleged that peak load pricing discriminates against poor people. This argument is only valid to the extent that a price system discriminates against those people who have less income in favor of those who have more. If goods are distributed through a price system, those individuals who have higher incomes will obtain more goods and services than those who have lower incomes. The alternative to a pricing system is a rationing scheme that by no means guarantees that a "poor" person would fare any better or as well as he does under a pricing system. With a pricing system the individual has the choice of those commodities he will finally purchase, subject to his available income and the level of prices. Under a rationing scheme he would have no choice, but would be forced to consume that bundle of goods and services that the public authority considered "good for him." Note that the welfare recipient receives food stamps, furniture, medical care, legal aid, etc.—not a cash grant to be used as he sees fit.

There is no reason to believe that a peak load pricing scheme would discriminate against lower income customers. It might be argued that the working poor cannot attend movies during the matinee times when prices are lowest, but must pay the higher peak prices during the evening. On the other hand, peak load prices for telephone service are higher during the day when the working poor are theoretically working, in which case the peak-load pricing arrangement works in their favor. If the lower income individuals work the night shift as opposed to the day shift, the previous conclusions are reversed: Peak load pricing in the telephone case works to their disadvantage and in the movie case to their advantage. In sum, peak load pricing does not appear to discriminate systematically against or in favor of any particular income class.

## Congestion

To this point we have discussed examples of the application of peak load pricing. Now let us turn to cases where peak load pricing should be used, for reasons other than political. The most dramatic example is the case of urban road systems. Here is a publicly produced service (use of a road system by a private automobile) that has all of the features consistent with a peak load pricing problem. During the early hours of the morning the demand for road use has shifted toward the origin to such an extent that there is excess capacity in the system. The road could accommodate many more cars than it is called upon to service.

Two peak periods, the morning rush and the evening rush, have been identified by empirical studies of urban road systems. If we think of the short-run marginal cost curve in Figure 4–3 as associated with a given

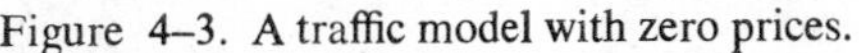

Figure 4–3. A traffic model with zero prices.

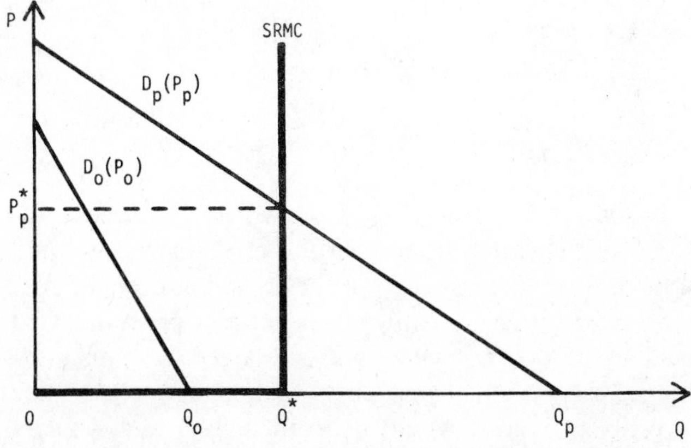

road system that has a fixed capacity for producing trips, we can analyze the effect of the absence of peak load pricing. Assume that the road system has a capacity of $Q^*$ trips per hour given the existing physical facilities and design. In the short run it is not possible to change that capacity; there is no known way to increase the number of cars that can traverse a given road short of forcing them to drive at a given speed, to refrain from passing, to stay in their own lane, etc. (the procedures followed by an army truck convoy). The short-run marginal cost curve in the first analysis coincides with the quantity axis from the zero rate of output out to $Q^*$ and then becomes vertical at $Q^*$. This curve has been drawn as a heavier line to indicate its shape in Figure 4–3.

Our working assumption is that no price at all is charged for the use of the road system, not to mention a differential peak and off-peak pricing scheme. Suppose, for the sake of illustration, that there are a simple peak and an off peak during the course of the day—only two demand functions or subintervals are relevant. By definition, the first demand curve labeled $D_o$ has its intercept on the quantity axis to the left of $Q^*$. If the price charge to the off-peak users is zero, according to the demand curve they will demand $Q_o$ trips per hour because that is the number of trips they would like to have if trips are free.

In fact, charging a zero price for the off-peak users is not significantly different from the optimal price that should be charged. The short-run marginal cost (variable cost) of using the road for another vehicle trip once the road is in place is virtually zero. The physical depreciation (wear and tear) that the road experiences because a car passes over it is so small that it can be ignored. We are saying that the short-run marginal cost for output levels between 0 and $Q^*$ is equal to zero. This was the coefficient $b$ in the earlier general analysis.

But, in practice, we charge a zero price to the peak users as well. According to the demand curve $D_p$ in Figure 4–3, customers will demand $Q_p$ trips per hour at a zero price during that interval of time. However, it is also clear from Figure 4–3 that $Q_p$ trips per hour cannot be supplied by the existing road system. The capacity of that system is $Q^*$ which is considerably less than $Q_p$. The intersection of the peak demand curve $D_p$ and the vertical portion of the short-run marginal cost curve gives the appropriate peak hour charge ($P^*_p$) per trip that would equate supply and demand.

A price of $P^*_p$ should be charged to peak users to eliminate excess demand. Notice this price has nothing to do with the wear and tear on the road as a result of the cars passing over the road. Indeed, in the short run the optimal price is not even related to the capital cost of the road system, since after the road system is built, the peak load price is levied to keep demand equal to supply, not necessarily to cover the capital cost of the system. Suppose the peak demand curve shifted upward. In this case an appropriate peak load price would be even higher, and would obviously generate an excess of revenue over cost to the road department. In the short run, then, peak load pricing simply allocates a scarce resource among the competing users but does not necessarily lead to a break-even situation for the public utility that manages the road system. If a demand-for-capacity curve were constructed and a long-run marginal cost curve introduced, the optimum size of the road could be determined. This would lead to an expansion or contraction along with an appropriate set of peak and off-peak prices (the latter still equal to zero).

In view of the current situation of road pricing in the real world, the foregoing analysis is academic. Since peak load prices are not charged, large excess demands occur during peak times. Although excess demands may mean that customers are turned away in the case of most commodities or services, it does not imply that this is so in the case of roads. If all available telephone circuits are busy during a peak time, the additional customer is not able to secure any part of the capacity to place his call. Similarly, the potential moviegoer is turned away if a theatre is filled. However, when the road system is operating at its capacity, the additional customer is not turned away; instead, he drives his car onto the ramp and into the stream of traffic. As he does so, he increases the density of cars per unit distance of the road and adds perceptibly to congestion.

Even though the capacity of the road system is $Q^*$ trips per hour, if enough additional drivers crowd into the system, density will be raised to the point where the actual number of trips per hour declines below the designed capacity $Q^*$. The effect of congestion is to raise the price above zero. This is so because as the speed of traffic slows gasoline consumption, the probability of an accident, the wear and tear on the automobile, and the amount of time the driver has to spend on the road, all increase. The net effect is to raise the effective price of a trip on the road above the apparent price of zero.

## A Freeway Congestion Model

Having introduced the effects of congestion on a road system when excess demand is positive, we should now develop a more sophisticated cost curve than the kinked short-run marginal cost curve we have been using. The first step is to construct a congestion model relevant to a freeway system. Suppose we measure the following variables for any given road or section of road: $F$ is flow (the number of vehicles that emerge from the road per minute), our measure of the quantity of output. $D$ is density (the average number of vehicles per mile along the road at any given moment). $S$ is speed (the average speed in miles per minute that a typical automobile achieves when traveling along the road). The reciprocal of speed is simply the number of minutes per mile it takes a typical driver to move along a given mile of road; define $T \equiv 1/S$.

Now assume that $T$ depends in a known way upon density. According to the results of empirical studies of traffic flows on road systems, the $T$ function in Figure 4–4 rises from the positive intercept $T_o$ at an increasing rate

Figure 4–4. Traffic density curve.

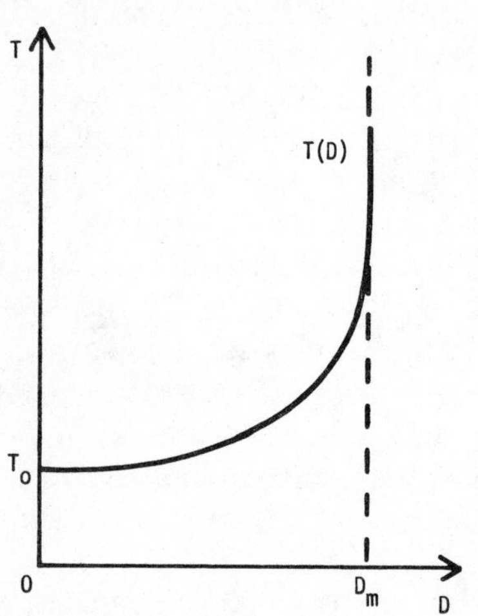


Figure 4–5. Traffic flow curve.

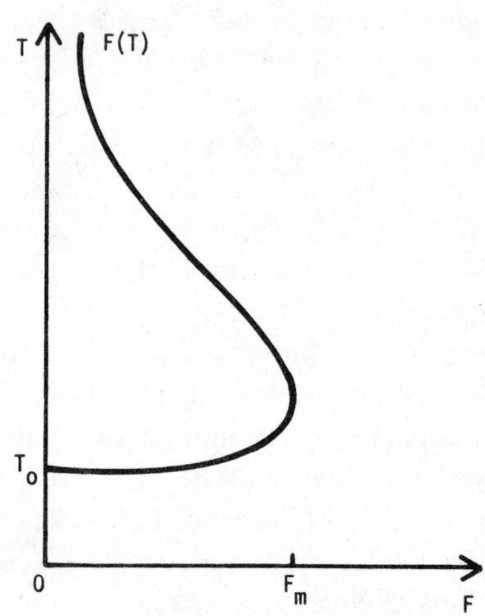


as it approaches the density level $D_M$ asymptotically. The curve is drawn for a particular design of a given road. The shape of the curve implies that the time it takes the average driver to go a given mile at low densities does not increase as density increases (alternatively, speed does not fall as density increases). A positive intercept $T_o$ indicates that there is a minimum time (or maximum speed) imposed by the speed limit relevant to the particular road segment. As density increases the speed drops, or the time increases, until density reaches the maximum that is physically possible. The latter situation occurs when the cars are packed on the road bumper to bumper and side to side.

The flow through the road (our measure of output) is simply the product of density and speed: $F = D \cdot S$ or $F = D/T$. The flow function, which is given in Figure 4–5, has a definite relationship to the density function of Figure 4–4. The intercept is at the same level $T_o$; the flow function is horizontal as long as the density function is horizontal. The flow function begins to rise as soon as the density function rises. It reaches its maximum and then bends back upon itself as indicated in Figure 4–5.

The physical interpretation of this system is as follows: For relatively low levels of density (cars per mile) the road system can produce trips without an increase in time or a decrease in speed· As density increases, however, the speed falls and the time increases per mile until a maximum flow through the system is reached. Beyond that point, higher levels of density will so congest the road that the system will actually produce fewer completed trips than it is capable of producing. The backward-bending portion of the flow curve represents the situation on most urban freeways during peak hours. Unlimited access to the road system has permitted the addition of drivers who cannot be efficiently accommodated; the presence of these drivers increases density and creates congestion, resulting in the system's actually producing fewer completed trips than would be possible if the extra motorist had not been on the road.

## Inefficiencies and Congestion Taxes

We can state categorically that those points on the backward-bending portion of the flow curve are suboptimal and inefficient points, and the system should never be permitted to move to these points. The question then remains: How can the system avoid moving beyond the maximum point on the flow curve to the backward-bending portion? Some undesirable costs would accompany one frequently suggested arrangement, that of controlled access to an urban freeway. It has been proposed (and such systems have been implemented) that traffic signs regulate the access to freeways. A motorist pulling up to a freeway on-ramp would be directed by a traffic light and his access controlled. While this would achieve the stated goal of remaining on the bottom portion of the flow curve, it does not take into account the dead-weight loss of time to individuals (and the value of that time) when they are waiting at the on-ramp.

We should keep in mind that the ultimate objective is to increase the welfare of individuals, not necessarily to run a road system in the most efficient manner that engineers can contrive. Although controlled access would lead to a superior solution as far as the physical operation of the road is concerned, it would leave those individuals waiting in line considerably worse off. The time spent waiting does have a monetary value to those individuals, and this time must be included in the total calculations of the net cost and benefits of any reorganization of the road system. The time spent waiting in line is a dead-weight loss, both to the individuals and to society. There is no way this time "tax," and that is surely what the time spent waiting in line is, can be collected and the proceeds used by society.

A superior method of allocating the scarce road space at peak periods is to charge a money price to the users. This has the advantage of allowing individuals to decide whether or not they want to travel at a peak time and pay the correspondingly higher price. Under the controlled access scheme, they do not have this option. One motorist may impute a very high value to his time and yet be forced to wait in line while someone with a considerably smaller value of time who, by chance, preceded him is permitted to travel on the road. This misallocation of the scarce resource is avoided under the pricing scheme and does not have the disadvantage of the dead-weight loss of time involved for those people forced to queue up.

## Economic Externalities

Without specifically stating it as such, we have constructed a situation that is characterized as an externality. Externalities in the economics literature refer to the effect the actions of individuals have on the situations faced by other individuals. By definition, these effects are not priced in the marketplace. In this example, if one drives his car onto the freeway, he slows the traffic and hence increases the time cost of the trip for every other individual on the road system. The impact of his action is said to be an externality because it affects other individuals and he is not forced to pay for the cost he adds to their actions. An optimal pricing system would, in fact, charge each individual for the extra cost he imposes on others.

It is generally agreed that government has a legitimate role in this situation; if possible, the government should initiate a system of tolls or taxes that will internalize the externality. In other words, the taxes that a person pays when he takes to the road will reflect the extra costs that he has by his presence imposed on fellow motorists.

The appropriate set of taxes is derived as follows: First, look at the flow curve as it rises from the positive intercept $T_o$ up to the maximum flow at $F_M$. Ignore the backward-bending portion of the curve and consider the bottom portion as the existing private marginal cost curve for highway travel. Draw in the curve that is marginal to this curve in Figure 4–6. Note that the marginal social cost curve (*MSC*) coincides with the marginal private cost curve (*MPC*) as long as the latter is horizontal. This relationship holds for all marginal and average curves; in this case the *MSC* curve is marginal to the *MPC* curve. When the *MPC* curve begins to rise, the *MSC* curve rises at a faster rate and so lies everywhere above the *MPC* curve. The *MSC* curve goes to infinity when the *MPC* curve reaches $F_m$. The difference between the two curves, measured as a vertical distance, is the amount of the tax that should be imposed on motorists at each and every level of quantity. For exam-

Figure 4–6. Congestion pricing.

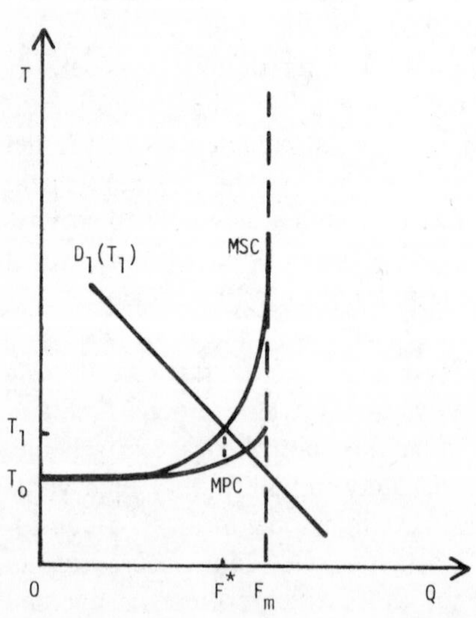

ple, if $D_1$ is the demand curve over a certain subinterval of time, $T_1$ should be the total price paid by each motorist; $T_1$ is composed of the distance from the horizontal axis up to the *MPC* curve (the actual time spent traveling) and the broken-line vertical distance between *MSC* and *MPC* (the tax).

If the tax is imposed in terms of time, as Figure 4–6 indicates, this scheme is subject to the same criticism as the controlled access arrangement, i.e., a time tax is a dead-weight loss to the individuals concerned and to society as well. Hence, the time tax should be multiplied by a value of time in terms of dollars so that the tax proceeds can be collected and used by society for other purposes, such as expansion of the road system, construction of a mass rapid transit system, and saving the redwoods.

As the demand curve shifts up and down during the course of the day, the congestion tax will vary from zero in the morning off-peak hours to a very large value during the peak hours. In any event, under a peak-load pricing scheme, the system will never move "around the corner" to the backward-bending portion on the flow curve.

## Conclusion

If scarce resources are to be efficiently allocated to their most valuable uses in society, prices must be used to inform consumers of the value of the resources. When road use is free and congestion results, that congestion could be reduced by an appropriate set of peak and off-peak prices.

One should not infer from the preceding analysis that a toll booth and the outstretched palm of the toll collector will be found at every intersection. Clearly, the cost of collecting a congestion tax must be considered in the design of an optimal urban road congestion tax scheme. Recent advances in technology eliminate the necessity of toll gates at which automobiles must stop (if cars must stop to pay a toll, congestion is exacerbated rather than reduced). Electronic devices can signal current toll rates to drivers, and can identify a particular auto and record its presence at a given time and place. The auto owner can then be billed periodically for his congestion charges. In sum, a more efficient use of resources brought about by peak load pricing will improve consumer welfare.

## Suggested Reading

Bailey, Elizabeth E. "Peak-load pricing under regulatory constraint." *Journal of Political Economy* 80, no. 4 (July/August 1972).

Boiteux, Marcel. "Peak-load pricing." *Journal of Business* 33 (April 1960).

Brown, Jr., Gardner, and M. Bruce Johnson. "Public utility pricing and output under risk." *American Economic Review* 59 (March 1969).

Dreze, J. A. "Some post-war contributions of French economists to theory and public policy." *American Economic Review* 52 (Supplement; June 1964).

Hirshleifer, Jack. "Peak-loads and efficient pricing: a comment." *Quarterly Journal of Economics* 72, no. 288 (August 1958).

Johnson, M. Bruce. "On the economics of road congestion." *Econometrica* 32, no. 1–2, (January–April 1964).

Littlechild, S. C. "Peak-pricing of telephone calls." *Bell Journal of Economics and Management Science* no. 1 (Autumn 1970).

Mohring, Herbert. "The peak-load problem with increasing returns and pricing constraints." *American Economic Review* 60 (September 1970).

Pressman, Israel. "Peak-load pricing." *Bell Journal of Economics and Management Science* 1 (Autumn 1970).

Stiner, Peter O. "Peak-loads and efficient pricing." *Quarterly Journal of Economics* 71, no. 285 (November 1957).

Turvey, Ralph. "Peak-load pricing." *Journal of Political Economy* 76, no. 1 (January/February 1968).

Walters, Alan. "Theory and measurement of private and social cost of highway congestion." *Econometrica* 29, no. 4 (October 1961).

Williamson, Oliver E. "Peak-load pricing and optimal capacity under indivisibility constraints." *American Economic Review* 56, no. 4 (September 1966).

# Commentary

Chapter 4 has expanded our understanding of the important social function that price plays as a rationing device. While at first blush it may seem paradoxical, or even unfair, that consumers should pay different prices at different times for the same good or service, a closer inspection shows it is to their advantage. Foreknowledge that price will vary as consumer demand for entertainment or public facilities varies, gives the consumer a choice. He may organize his activities to take advantage of cheaper prices, or if he wishes to consume at peak times, he will know that to obtain the service he must pay the higher price. Price is an advantageous and efficient way of transmitting information about demand and supply between consumers and producers.

Unfortunately, the advantages of peak load pricing to the consumer are not always available. Tradition or difficulty in administering peak load pricing may lead to the use of nonprice rationing schemes. Waiting is a rationing scheme very familiar to most of us. Life is too short to spend standing in line, and the option of reorganizing the timing of our consumption is lost in the queue.

In the chapter that follows, W. Douglas Morgan continues to pursue the ways that society allocates or—as is often the case for water—misallocates scarce resources. Agencies responsible for providing water often fail to recognize the importance of price in their decision-making process. When they do, they often charge the wrong price. Professor Morgan stresses once again the importance of pricing goods at their marginal cost of production so that consumers neither overvalue the good and consume too little nor undervalue it and consume lavishly.

This chapter expands upon a topic introduced by Professor Johnson in Chapter 4: How much should we invest in capacity? Investment projects that will generate benefits and incur costs in future years are evaluated and the question of choices between alternative investment possibilities is examined. The answers to these questions set forth a guide to investment in projects that will provide water for ourselves and our children in the future.

# 5

# Allocating the Elixir of Life: Water

W. Douglas Morgan

Water, water, everywhere,
Nor any drop to drink.
*Coleridge*

Although many of the problems that confront water users today are quite different from those of the Ancient Mariner, the above lines properly interpreted could describe part of the current water problem. In this chapter we shall deal, in a general manner, with the sort of condition alluded to in Coleridge's famous poem. Water appears almost everywhere, yet the crux of the water problem is that water is seldom found in the right place, at the right time, and in the right amount.

In California, for example, normal annual precipitation varies from as high as 59 inches in the northern part of the state to a little over 3 inches in the Imperial Valley in the south. About two-thirds of California's annual water runoff originates north of San Francisco, whereas two-thirds of the water use takes place in the southern portion of the state where two-thirds of the population lives. In addition, the bulk of the rainfall occurs in the winter months, whereas the greatest use of water occurs in the summer months. As observed recently by the magazine *Time,* "California has everything—usually in the wrong place."

California has recognized for some time that it has a water problem. As a remedy for the shortage of water, Los Angeles first went to the Owens Valley and then to the Colorado River for its water. More recently, in response to continuing "deficiency" of water in the southern portion and a tacit "surplus" in the north, the state embarked upon a comprehensive water plan. The first portion to be implemented was the Central Valley

Project—taking surplus water from the Sacramento Valley and transporting it primarily to the southern end of the San Joaquin Valley, a water deficit area. The second phase to be implemented was the Feather River Project, which takes the surplus in the Sacramento delta and distributes 60 percent to Southern California, 30 percent to the San Joaquin Valley, and the remainder to coastal cities from San Francisco southward.

While it appears that the water problem is primarily one of allocation, and thus amenable to economic analysis, there are other facets which complicate matters. As described previously, the answer to the alleged deficiency in the southern portion of the state has been the proposal and construction of large-scale water projects to increase the supply of water to that locale.

Much of the water problem in California can be traced to pricing policies. For example, water districts typically charge different prices to different classes of users. The largest users typically pay the lowest price. As a result of this pricing arrangement water is misallocated within the local district. But this is not all. The pricing schemes used are promotional, i.e., the more water used, the lower the price per unit of water. Coupled with promotional pricing, many districts make generous use of the tax base of the region and hide a portion of the cost in the property tax. As a consequence, the user price of water does not reflect its economic cost, and water is again misallocated within the district. The same argument holds for the allocation of water between different districts and regions.

Once water is misallocated in local districts, the quantity of water used is much higher than economically necessary, and districts tend to use up their current supply faster than economically necessary. Thus, because of the errors made in pricing, water districts typically plan for and make large unneeded additions to their water supply well before they are economically justified.

## Concepts and Practices

To understand why and how water districts get into a shortage situation requiring them to import or augment their water supply, some insight into how water managers perceive and react to water is needed.

Most water industry spokesmen appear to suffer from what might be called a "requirements mentality." As we shall see, the requirements mentality stems from considering water as a special distinct good, very different from other commodities. Although water is necessary to life, once the minimum biological needs are taken care of, water can be considered and allocated just like any other private good. However, current thinking by the water industry continues to produce the "requirements approach," that is, a certain amount of water *has* to be delivered to consumers no matter what the conditions. This type of thinking makes it difficult to initiate any rational allocation process. In fact, using the requirement approach produces no information on how to price the good correctly. Instead, the pricing decision is left open to judgment, rules of thumb, and to the designs of political-economic interest groups. Various economic analyses of the water industry clearly indicate the fallacious assumptions behind the requirements approach.

### Water as a Commodity

Why do people worry more about the availability of water than about the availability of, say, automobiles, lettuce, or Bibles? One reason is that a certain amount of water is necessary for life, even though the absolute amount may be very small. As a case in point, some regions get by with 3 gallons per capita per day, while the average per capita consumption in Southern California is 170 gallons per day. Nevertheless, the first gallon of water could, in general, be called a necessity of life, and because of this attribute people are concerned. But the same argument can be applied to a number of other goods, particularly foods such as beef, bread, or lettuce, which do not arouse the emotions as water does. In the case of foods, however, the *community* does not concern itself in the same manner when lettuce is scarce or when certain grades of beefsteak are known to be in short supply. Instead, individuals simply complain, tighten their belts, and reduce the quantity of the good purchased by substituting another similar product such as carrots for lettuce and pork or lamb (or cheese) for beef. Does the same thing happen when water becomes scarce? The answer is yes if one views the entire world, but the answer is usually no for middle-class suburbs where water is thought of as something different from lettuce, bread, or beef.

Another reason people get excited about water, compared to other things, is the misconception that water is free. Nature, in her own way, provides rain, filling the rivers and lakes and underground water basins. These natural sources are commonly thought of as being available to be tapped and used free to all. However, despite water being originally provided by nature, there are very few places where it is costless. In the simplest case, there is still the time and effort that must be spent in going down to the river to extract the "pail of water" or the cost of bringing it from its raw natural state to a location both convenient and useful to those who desire it. All of these factors make water scarce, that is, there are resources (energy, labor, machines) foregone to make nature's water available for our use.

Water also has additional characteristics that are similar to other goods. For example, after that first gallon, the more water one person consumes, the less is available for others. Certainly, considering water that is used up, as opposed to that used over and over again, this is true. However, water has two classifications of uses: consumptive and nonconsumptive. By consumptive use we mean the loss of one or more of the particular values that water has in its initial state. Water may contain a number of qualities of economic significance, such as location in time and space, temperature, and general purity. One consumptive use may or may not interfere with another use. For example, complementary uses may involve navigation and waste disposal simultaneously in the same river system. However, any use of water is consumptive for any use that is competing with it. In the economic sense, the nonconsumptive use of water usually involves some change in one or more of the qualities of water. For example, power boating often precludes swimming, and navigation use could preclude irrigation use. The problem for society is that for many of these uses, "used" water usually flows out of the region of influence and control of the users. Once the water has left one jurisdiction there is no incentive to consider measures which might permit different uses or establish appropriate charges for the current user. These extra costs or benefits (externalities) of multiple water uses are normally not found for most private goods such as lettuce, Bibles, or bread.

Nevertheless, it appears that many characteristics of beef and lettuce can be applied to water as well. Water is scarce and takes resources for its production. The more one person uses, the less is available for another. And as is the case for many food products, some water is necessary for life. Perhaps those who claim that water beyond the first gallon is priceless and should be obtained at all costs need to look at its characteristics and ask if they apply to other private goods. Perhaps the people who listen to these spokesmen should also make this comparison.

## Water Requirements and Needs

If water is thought of as something different from other goods and services, it automatically becomes immune to further analysis. Such is the case for water when requirements or needs are calculated. This water requirements view of the problem inhibits water managers from thinking in realistic terms about how water could be allocated among alternative uses. The final outcome of this approach leads to a faulty calculation of shortages, and leads to greater investment in water facilities than is necessary.

The terms "water use," "water requirement," "the need for water," recur frequently in the water literature and should be carefully defined. "Water use" is merely the total quantity of water used, and is simply the product of population times per capita water use. Similar in meaning, but used in another context, is "water requirement" and "water burden." Both terms mean quantity of water used per person, with the latter term often used when referring to a particular class of user, i.e., agriculture, or multifamily homes. "Water requirement" is primarily used in forecasts of water use. Used interchangeably with "requirement," is "water need." However, "need" is implicitly assumed to be a minimum level of water "below which it is poor strategy to fall" but is usually interpreted to be identical with current usage per capita. All of these terms assume that present income levels and rate structures will continue into the future.

By and large, this terminology is indicative of the problems in the water industry. Rarely does one hear the concepts *need, burden,* or *requirement* applied to other types of private goods. Never is a need calculated for Bibles, lettuce, or pencils (much less for postage stamps or building inspections). Instead, the term used is *demand.* There is never a burden associated with Bibles, lettuce, or pencils, nor does one hear of a requirement being calculated for most other goods that are purchased. The similar term used most for private goods is future demand in comparing the future market for a single producer, or the percent of the market (market share) available to him. Value-loaded terminology clouds any attempt to understand the nature of the economic forces behind water demand. The lack of clear understanding of the economic problems in the water industry often leads to shortages and many other maladies.

The typical water district uses a simplistic process in determining total water requirements. Let us assume there is very little heavy industry, since otherwise the problem would become more complex. Under this assumption, the primary demands for water are residential, light industrial, governmental, recreational, and commercial, called collectively the urban water requirement. Thus, if the water district delivered 1,000 gallons per year and there were ten people in the service area, the average urban consumption per person per year would be 100 gallons. This calculation can be repeated for other years, and the pattern or trend of per capita consumption can be estimated.[1] Using the requirements approach, the district first estimates the average water requirement (use) per person and projects this water requirement into the future, based on expected changes in the region's growth. The simplest assumption is that the current requirement will remain the same in the future. In this case total water requirement per year is estimated by multiplying the future population projections by the per capita requirement. Figure 5–1 plots the future water requirements ($W_R$) for the area under consideration as a function of calendar time. Any point on the

1. This analysis abstracts from the problem of meeting and measuring seasonal and daily peak load demands. The actual operation of satisfying daily demands is left to the water district. The economics of peak and seasonal use patterns is discussed in some detail in Chapter 4 of this book and is *directly* applicable to the water pricing decisions.

Figure 5–1. The requirements approach.

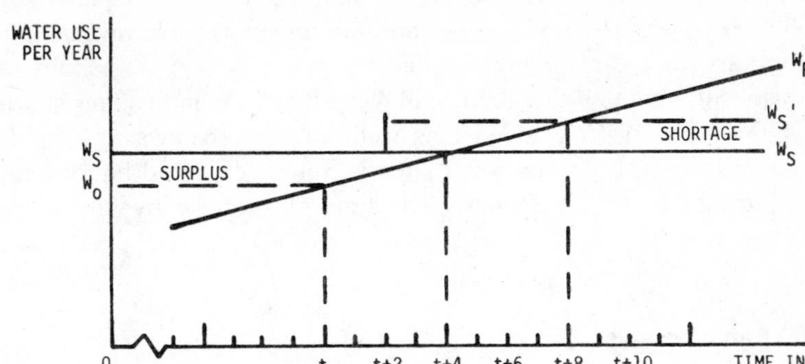


horizontal axis indicates the date ($t$), while the height to the $W_R$ line represents the projected amount of water that will be consumed in each year.

If the local district or planning commission projects high rates of population growth, there will be a high and growing requirement for water. In any analysis of this kind, population growth becomes the driving force. It is well to remember at this point that population change is not generated in a vacuum, but is the result of complex and interrelated economic, social, and environmental forces.

Included with the requirement analysis is a projection for water supply. Again, engineering studies can provide good information on water availability. For example, consider the two major sources of water: surface and ground. Surface water is captured from surface sources such as rivers and lakes. In the West, surface water projects include man-made dams which capture and store winter rain for use during the dry summer months. Engineering studies attempt to determine the capacity and storage area of such basins and to estimate the safe yield, i.e., the average amount of water which can be withdrawn annually. The safe yield coincides with the long-run annual inflow minus any other downstream use requirements. From this information the water district can calculate the average quantity of water it can obtain from surface sources. The other major water source, ground water, is found in underground aquifiers which are supplied by rain through ground and stream-bed percolation. The aquifiers hold the water which can be pumped to the surface as required. Again, if this water source is widely used, there is usually fairly good information on the safe yield.

The maximum projected yields of the major sources can be added together as illustrated by the horizontal line labeled $W_S$ in Figure 5–1. With this information it is easy to compare current and future requirements with projected supply. The solid line $W_S$ is horizontal when projected into the future because it does not include any additional water sources not already available. In Figure 5–1, at the current time, $t_o$, where use equals $W_o$ and supply is $W_S$, the water district does not face a shortage. However, if all the assumptions for the projections hold, in four years $(t + 4)$ requirements will just equal supply and there will be talk of an impending shortage. But if the water district added new wells or imported water from other sources in time $(t + 2)$, the water supply (line $W_S$) would be moved vertically upward to $W_S'$, postponing the time of shortage by four years or until time $(t + 8)$.

### Actual Requirements

While the requirements approach is not an appropriate method to establish water policy, either for water allocation or investment planning, it is useful to know the magnitude of per capita use. Besides providing a better perspective for the analysis which follows, it provides an indication of the role played by different classes of users in the water problem.

For example, over the five-year period 1960–1965, total water use in the U.S. increased from 1500 gallons per capita per day to 1600 gallons per day. From this average of 1600 gallons agriculture used 85 percent, while total urban water use accounted for the remaining 15 percent. From the urban 15 percent about 50 percent was allocated to residential, 20–30 percent commercial, 3–7 percent public, while industry used less than 5 percent.

Of course these average use figures include water from all sources, including rainfall, potable drinking water, and brackish sea water. Much of the water for agriculture and industry is used several times. Perhaps the most important aspect of the water industry to a majority of us are those thousands of agencies that collect, treat, and distribute water to the urban areas of the country. Thus, a more interesting use index would be the average urban use, incorporating primarily the residential, commercial, light industrial, and general public use. The measure used to describe urban consumption is usually gallons per capita per day (gpd). Although there are wide regional differences in per capita use, the California Department of Water Resources calculated an annual average of 172 gallons per capita per day over the period 1961–1965 for a large number of California cities. Urban water projections are often based on per capita use figures such as these. Because of increasing installation of water-using appliances and other uses stemming from affluence, many studies show an increasing per capita consumption over time. An example of this pattern is found in Table 5–1. Although the pattern of per capita consumption is rising, the reasons and rationale for such projections are not conclusive.

Industrial water use is analyzed in a similar manner, i.e., average employee use multiplied by the number of employees. Again, studies show

Table 5–1

Total and Per Capita Urban Water Requirements, South Coastal Area,* California, by Decades

| Year | Total acre-feet (in thousands) | Per capita (gal./day) |
|---|---|---|
| 1950 | 874 | 140 |
| 1960 | 1,564 | 160 |
| 1970 | 2,282 | 170 |
| 1980 | 2,978 | 176 |
| 1990 | 3,601 | 186 |
| 2000 | 4,312 | 199 |
| 2010 | 4,876 | 207 |
| 2020 | 5,289 | 210 |

*This area includes the drainage line counties to the coast extending from Ventura County to the Mexican border.

Source: Hirshleifer et al., *Water Supply: Economics, Technology, and Policy*, 2nd ed. (Chicago: University of Chicago Press, 1969), p. 313, Table 40. See also California Department of Water Resources, Bulletin 78, II, pp. 31–33.

widely differing employee use factors for different industries. For example, Table 5–2 presents a study on industrial use conducted by the California Resource Agency and modified by Leon Davidson. The study shows employee water use coefficients for California for the 1957–1959 period. Of

Table 5–2

Water Use per Employee per Annum by Industrial Subsector (1956–1959 average)

| Industrial subsector | Use per employee per annum (acre-feet) |
|---|---|
| 1. Food and kindred | 0.713019 |
| 2. Textiles | 0.190592 |
| 3. Apparel | 0.027234 |
| 4. Lumber | 0.349573 |
| 5. Furniture | 0.039699 |
| 6. Paper | 1.553275 |
| 7. Printing | 0.069461 |
| 8. Chemical | 1.082675 |
| 9. Petroleum | 4.735634 |
| 10. Rubber | 0.291075 |
| 11. Leather | 0.034440 |
| 12. Stone, clay, and glass | 0.650090 |
| 13. Primary metals | 0.381792 |
| 14. Fabricated metals | 0.349127 |
| 15. Instruments | 0.080078 |
| 16. Miscellaneous | 0.202267 |
| 17. Machinery | 0.134367 |
| 18. Electrical machinery | 0.067192 |
| 19. Transportation equipment | 0.081422 |
| 20. Weighted average | 0.335134 |

Source: L. T. Wallace, "The Economic Demand for Water in Urban Areas," in *California Water, A Study in Resource Management*, ed. David Seckler (Berkeley: University of California Press, 1971), p. 42.

the industries surveyed, apparel manufacture (with a high labor-capital ratio) shows the smallest use per employee and, as perhaps expected, petroleum (with a low labor-capital ratio) shows the greatest use per employee, requiring almost 5 acre-feet per year. It should be noted that these figures are for use, and reflect a double counting of recirculated water. Although these are not unusual unit requirements, they are valid only for the particular technological conditions that prevailed at the time of the survey. This means that any change in technology, either in the physical production process or in management's use of technology, would cause the coefficients to change.

## Demand, Supply, and Water Requirements

To develop the true meaning of the requirements approach, it is best to place the analysis in an economic framework. However, as previously noted, when the requirements approach is placed in the context of supply and demand analysis, it provides very little information. In fact, the requirements method provides absolutely no information on how water could be priced, how to measure its scarcity value, or how to reallocate for the greatest good of the community.

Figure 5–2. Requirements as a function of price.

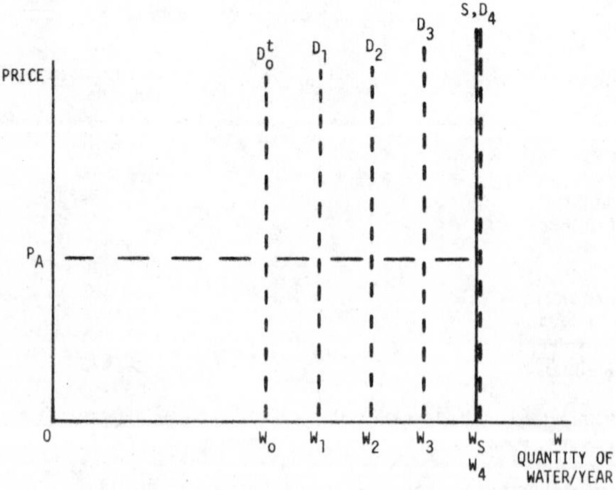


Figure 5–2 represents the requirements approach in a price-quantity framework. The supply curve (solid vertical line *S*) represents the maximum output of water available to the district in any time period. The distance along the horizontal axis from zero corresponds to the height of $W_s$

in Figure 5–1. Under the requirements approach, the demand curve can be represented by a (dashed) vertical line with current consumption at $D_o$. In the requirements case, quantity demanded is invariant with respect to price. The time dimension is represented by the subscript on each demand curve, and a different demand curve has to be drawn for each year. The curve in each year will shift to the right by the amount of population change times the unit water requirement. Notice that the combination of the demand and supply curves, based on the requirements approach, never intersect (except when they are identical or overlap at $W_S$ output). This means that there is no way to determine equilibrium price, and thus there is no indication whether too little or too much water is being supplied at the arbitrary price selected. Analogous to Figure 5–1, a surplus in Figure 5–2 is represented by the difference between *D* and *S* to the left of *S*, and a shortage is represented when *D* is to the right of *S*.

How does a water agency determine what price to set under the requirements situation? In the typical situation the price is set to cover the average cost of water, designated as $P_A$ in Figure 5–2. Note there is a tacit assumption in the requirements approach that the quantity of water demand ($W_o$, $W_1$, etc.) will not vary with price.

It was previously suggested that water has many traits that are similar to private goods (say, lettuce). Under these conditions we would classify water as a normal private good and expect that the quantity actually consumed would vary negatively with price. Thus, in the relevant range of current water usage (to avoid the problem of very small biological needs) individual demand curves (*d*) would be expected to slope down and to the right. If individual demand curves behave in such a manner, then the total demand curve for the district (the horizontal sum of each individual's demand curve indicated by the more heavily inked curve labeled *D* in Figure 5–3) would also be downward sloping.

We would suspect, however, that those individual demand curves closer to the price axis would be steeper than those further away. Also, as one moves up any individual demand curve, i.e., as the quantity demanded falls, the demand curve becomes steeper, or technically more inelastic. This means that at smaller quantities there is less responsiveness to price changes. Contrary to popular belief, there is considerable information known about the characteristics of urban demand. For example, we know that household demand should not be represented by a vertical line at the curent quantity demanded, such as illustrated by the dashed line *DR* at quantity $W_E$ in Figure 5–3. Numerous studies have been completed indicating that there is a negative price elasticity of demand. Recall that elasticity is a measure of the responsiveness of quantity consumed to a change in price, more explicitly elasticity:

$$\eta = \frac{\% \Delta Q}{\% \Delta P}.$$

Figure 5–3. The demand for water.

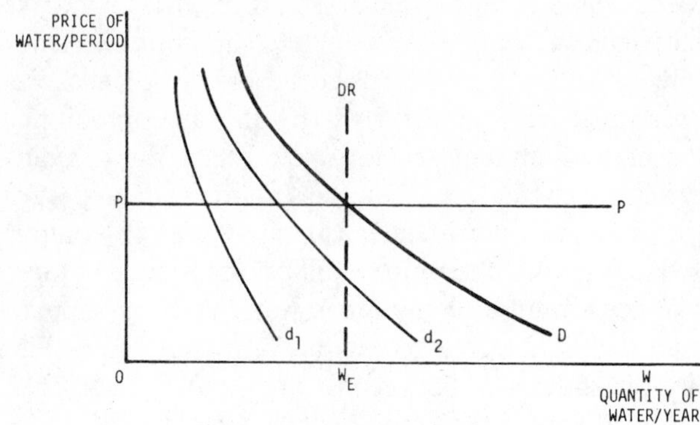


Table 5–3 summarizes the results for various studies for different parts of the United States and time periods. The evidence shows conclusively that the demand curve for urban water is *not* vertical but is downward sloping.

Table 5–3
Water Price Elasticity Estimates—Selected Geographic Areas

| | | Price-quality relationships resulting from the elasticity estimate | | |
|---|---|---|---|---|
| Location | Water use | Price elasticity estimate | Increase in price (percentage) | Decrease in quantity used (percentage) |
| United States cross-section | Residential | —.23 | 10 | 2.3 |
| California south coastal | Urban (residential commercial, and industrial) | —.31 | 10 | 3.1 |
| Georgia | Residential (all) | —.67 | 10 | 6.7 |
| California coastal | Residential (outdoor) | —.70 | 10 | 7.0 |
| California northern | Residential (all) | —1.10 | 10 | 11.0 |
| California south coastal | Residential (primarily sprinkling) | —.75 | 10 | 7.5 |

The price elasticity measurements fall within the range of −0.25 to −1.1, with a grouping around −0.4. This is strong support for the proposition that the demand is inelastic, i.e., total revenue will increase as the price rises. An elasticity equal to −0.4 means that a 10 percent *increase* in price produces a 4 percent *decrease* in the quantity demanded. Thus, the vertical demand schedules in Figure 5–2 are incorrect; that is, the demand curves slope down and to the right. Consequently, the particular price charged for water by a water agency will definitely have some effect on the quantity of water demanded. This points out that all requirement estimates are dependent upon the assumption that prices will not change in the future. Furthermore a proper rate schedule can accomplish more than raising revenue (as under the requirements approach); prices can also be used to achieve a better allocation of water.

## The Water Agency Pricing Decision

Everyone has heard of power brownouts; New York City is notorious for them. The popular suggested solution is to increase the supply of electricity. No one ever looks at the other side of the market—demand and pricing structure. Agencies that suffer from the requirements mentality think of price only as a means of obtaining revenue, not as an allocative tool. This lack of understanding of the function of price by public (and private) decision-makers brings water shortages and power brownouts.

The only way to discover how poorly water is allocated is to analyze the more common practices of water agencies. To accomplish this, criteria have to be established for evaluating alternative pricing policies. The criterion adopted by economists is to maximize the aggregate value in use. This merely means that water should be allocated in such a manner as to get the greatest value from its use. A water district or water manager should not ask for more.

## Equal Marginal Pricing

If the water district is to achieve the greatest benefits from the water it supplies, the principle of equal marginal pricing should apply. The following example will illustrate.

Consider the marginal value (demand) curves ($MV$) for the same individual for two uses, drinking and washing cars (or, if you prefer, general in-house use compared to sprinkling) as shown in Figures 5–4a and 5–4b. To make the analysis simpler, let the quantity supplied be a fixed amount. The two $MV$ curves are illustrated with the $MV_D$ (drinking) curve higher for small quantities than $MV_W$ (washing). This formulation appears intuitively correct. The two $MV$ curves are horizontally summed in Figure 5–4c to form total water demand $\Sigma MV$. If the total quantity of water is less than

Figure 5–4. The equal-marginal principle.

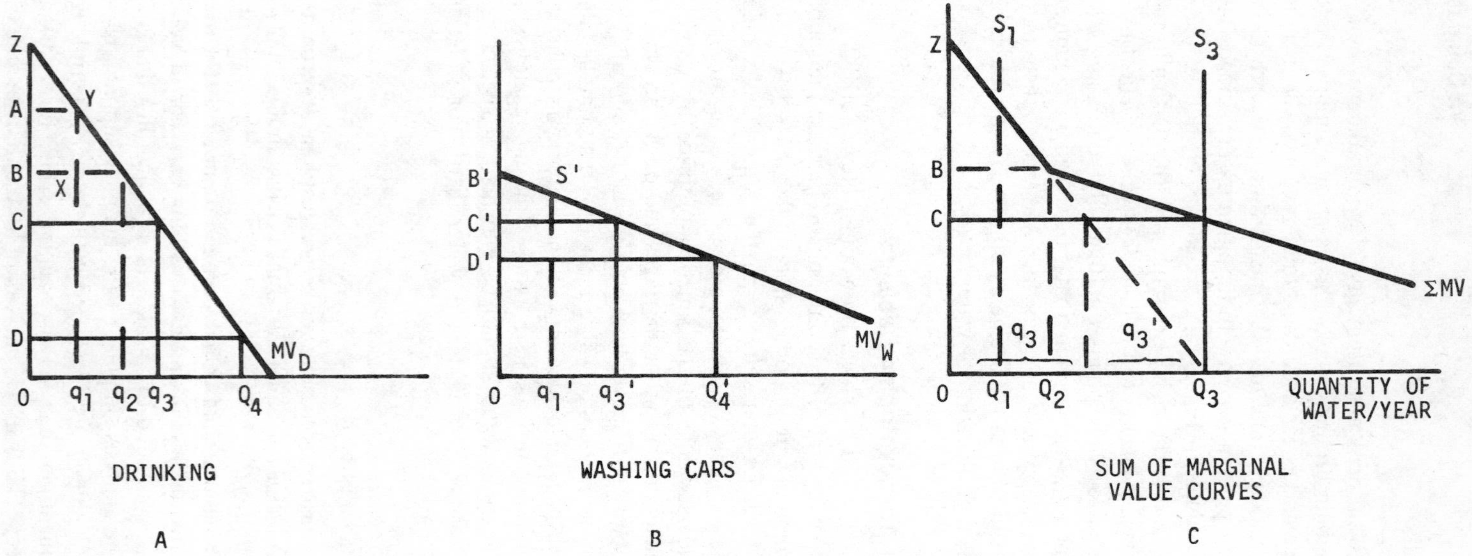

DRINKING

A

WASHING CARS

B

SUM OF MARGINAL VALUE CURVES

C

$OQ_2$, water will be allocated solely to the drinking purposes—the higher valued use. This pattern remains true for all uses up to $Q_2$ quantity. Now assume the total supply is larger, say $Q_3$; how should it be allocated between the two uses? Here the equal marginal principle comes into play. Water should be allocated so that $q_3$ amount goes to drinking and $q_3'$ goes to washing, where $q_3 + q_3' = Q_3$, and the marginal value in each use is equal to $OC$, which is identical for each water use. The best way to see that the identical price $OC$ is preferred is to ask: What if this was not true and the washing use obtained more water than the uniform rate dictates, $q_3'$? Clearly the individual would benefit by shifting resources from $W$ to $D$ because as he did so his total or *aggregate value in use* would become larger.

Total value is merely the area under the $MV$ curve, keeping changes in $q$ small. Thus, the sum of $MV$ for every $q$th unit until the given quantity is reached represents the total value in use for a given quantity of water. Consider the initial use where only $Q_1$ units of water are available. If this quantity were allocated to washing, then total value would be the area of the trapezoid $OB'S'q_1'$, or the area under the $MV$ curve up to quantity $q_1'$. However, if the same quantity were allocated to drinking, the total aggregate value would be $OZYq_1$, and there would be much *greater* aggregate value in use for drinking than for washing. (Recall the distance $OB' = OB$.) Thus, to obtain the greatest aggregate value water should be allocated so that marginal value is equal in each and every use.[2]

Another operational rule can be derived from the foregoing analysis. What if the supply were discontinuous, that is, if for some technological or institutional reason there was a fixed supply equal to $OQ_4$ (where $Q_4 = Q_4'$) and that it could be allocated to drinking or washing but *not both* uses. Figures 5–4a and 5–4b indicate that the $MV$ is lower in drinking use than washing; however, in this particular case the goal is to maximize aggregate welfare. This can be done by allocating all $Q_4$ to drinking where *total aggregate value* is greatest (measure the area of the triangles above quantity $Q_4$).

The general results are summarized in Figure 5–4c where the two $MV$ curves are horizontally summed to yield the $\Sigma MV$ curve. If quantity were fixed at $Q_1$ (vertical supply curve $S_1$) then the price would be $OA$ and water would be used only for drinking purposes. Alternatively, if the fixed supply increases to $S_3$ ($Q_3$ amount), then equilibrium price becomes $OC$ (where the $\Sigma MV$ crosses $S_3$) with $q_3$ amount being used for drinking and $q_3'$ used for washing. Any price other than $OC$ will yield an aggregate value less than the optimal one.

With this background, it is possible to evaluate aspects of pricing policies used by many water districts today.

2. This assumes no interdependence and income-compensated demand curves.

## Average Cost Pricing

One of the most common practices used by water districts is to set a price equal to the average cost per gallon of providing water. If average cost is covered, then people must be "getting what they pay for." The following analysis shows this is not the case, and that individuals under this arrangement are using too much water.

Figure 5–5. The average cost pricing rule.

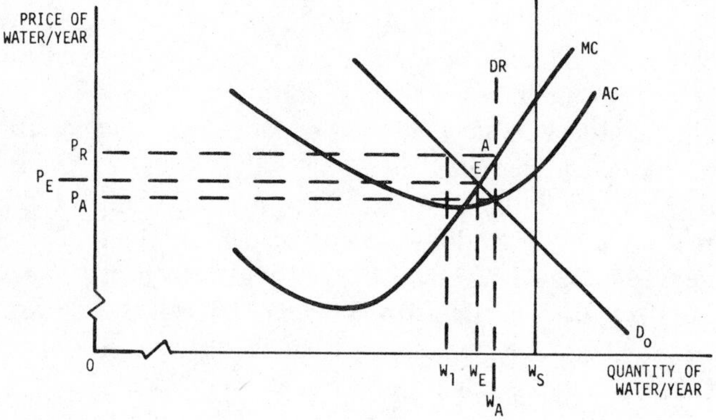


Figure 5–5 superimposes an average cost (*AC*) curve on the demand diagram previously introduced in Figure 5–3. The *AC* curve is drawn in the familiar manner, U-shaped, with the current price set to just cover *AC* at the output $W_A$. The *AC* curve is drawn U-shaped because of the law of diminishing marginal returns. As the district attempts to obtain greater quantity of water from its given system, the average cost will rise. For example, older, less efficient wells will be brought on line and most likely have a higher unit cost than those normally used. Given that the *AC* slopes upward, one thing is certain—the marginal cost curve (*MC*) is rising and *above* the *AC* curve. Thus, the cost for each *additional* (marginal) unit is higher than the unit cost (*AC*). As stated earlier, this *MC* curve is the supply curve of water for the district.

What does this say about the pricing policy where price is set equal to average cost? Assuming that all costs are correctly accounted for in the calculation of average cost (labor, raw materials, wearing out of capital equipment), and that the factors of production are purchased in reasonably competitive markets, the *MC* curve of Figure 5–5 measures the value society places on the resources used to produce the last unit of output. At price $P_A$ (the average unit price) there is a misuse of resources. The price consumers pay for the last unit of resources ($P_A$) is less than the value society places on them (the height of the $MC$ curve, $W_AA$). If the marketplace is any guide at all, perhaps these factors should be used for some alternative output such as education, controlling pollution, or printing Bibles. The correct output is $W_E$, where price $P_E$ equals $MC$.

Notice from Figure 5–5 that the requirement approach (an inelastic demand curve, $DR$) again leads to an incorrect solution, even if price is set equal to $MC$. Although the price would be equal to $MC$ (height $W_AA$) the quantity consumed would be too large because the actual demand curve is $D_o$. Thus, if price were set at $P_R = W_AA$, the quantity demanded would actually fall to $W_1$ because this is the actual quantity desired at price $P_R$. A water agency now would see that $MC$ at the quantity $W_1$ is less than price $P_R$. This is a signal to expand output until $P = MC$. Thus, there is only one efficient output, $W_E$ at price $P_E$. Average cost pricing fails to provide the correct answer in most cases.[3]

### Pricing with a Property Tax

Other complications can arise which make the current pricing decision and the existing price inappropriate for both forecasting requirements and allocating water. One of these, often found in water districts in Southern California, is the use of the property tax to defray a certain portion of water costs. The general practice is to pay for a certain portion (often 100 percent) of previously acquired capital goods by using revenue derived from the property base of the district for interest or amortization charges. Whatever the reasoning, the use of property tax charges distorts the pricing decision, misallocates water, and causes requirement forecasts to be overstated.

For instance, let us assume the extreme case in which a district is able to collect 40 percent of its revenue from a general property tax. Naturally, the user charge (price) has to cover only the remaining 60 percent of the costs. For pricing purposes, the average cost schedule has been effectively lowered to $AC_p$ in Figure 5–6.[4] Applying the average cost pricing rule, the

3. We have excluded the case where $MC$ is below $AC$ (to the left of the minimum point on $AC$). In this case applying the correct pricing rule would force the water agency to operate at a loss, i.e., $P < AC$ at the efficient level of output. While this may be important for new agencies, the bulk of water districts probably conform to the case discussed in the text.

4. The construction of $AC_p$ is similar to constructing average total cost curves from average variable cost curves. The property tax revenue for any unit of time is constant and invariant with respect to the quantity of water sold. It is a fixed amount of revenue, $\bar{R}$, which can be represented by a rectangular hyperbola, i.e., $T_p = Q/\bar{R}$ is subtracted from the $AC$ curve. Notice that at larger outputs the difference between $AC$ and $AC_p$ becomes smaller as $T_p$ decreases.

district sets price equal to $P_p$ to cover the remaining costs. Given the demand curve $D_o$, the district sells $W_p$ quantity. There are two important things to note from this analysis. First, if the practice of using property

Figure 5–6. Pricing and property taxes.

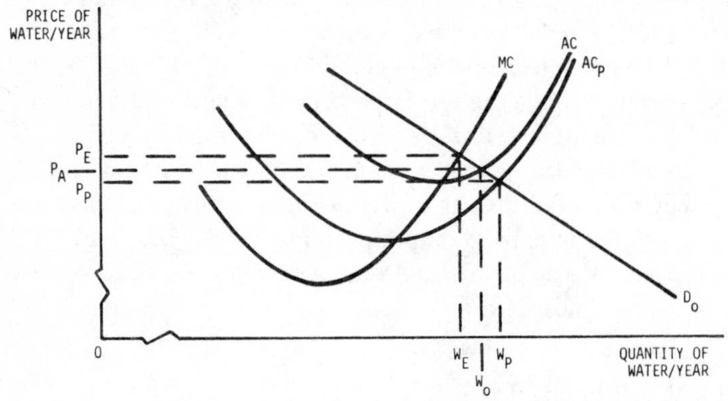


taxes has been in effect for some time, the district sees $OW_p$ quantity of water as the total "requirement," not the previous $D_R$ found in Figure 5–5. Second, the marginal pricing rule still provides the correct price and output decision for efficiency, regardless of how additional revenue is collected. Property tax revenue remains constant for each unit of time and thus is a fixed revenue, having no influence on the increase in total cost as output increases. Therefore, the correct output is $W_E$ quantity where $P = MC$.

A good example of the foregoing case is the history of the Metropolitan Water District (MWD), the main wholesaler and distributor for Southern California. During its entire history (to 1959), MWD tax collections totaled $334 million in comparison to total water revenues of only $55 million.[5] Water revenues are the user charges for water collected as a function of quantity used. It is further pointed out that the reliance on taxation results in ". . . cities with relatively large assessed valuations, but using relatively small amounts of MWD water, have tended to carry the project."[6] The example cited refers to San Diego County, which during 1958–1959 purchased 30 percent of MWD water sold, but paid only 7 percent of the taxes. In addition, during this period it was the general practice to place the MWD tax

5. Jack Hirshleifer, et al., *Water Supply*, p. 307.

6. Ibid.

levies directly on the property tax bills and not apply these tax collections to the individual water distributors' (districts') costs. The use of property taxes was an easy way to hide the costs of a unit of water from the consuming public.

## Promotional Pricing

Another complication that thwarts efficient use of resources in the water industry is the widespread use of a multipart promotional pricing system. In promotional or declining block pricing, the greater the quantity of water consumer the lower the average cost to the consumer. Figure 5–7 illustrates

Figure 5–7. Promotional pricing schedule.

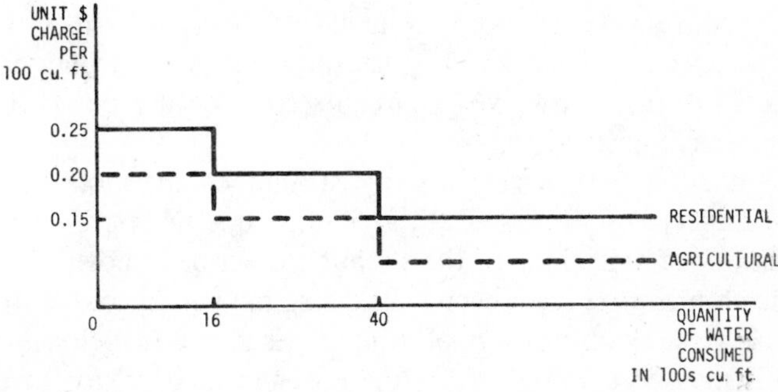


a typical block structure. The first block is usually the minimum service charge, which includes the periodic meter reading, the annual meter charge, and general account service, all of which are invariant with respect to the quantity of water used. Combined with this minimum charge is a maximum amount of water that can be consumed each billing period. In Figure 5–7, the minimum water charge is $4, and 1600 cubic feet or less can be consumed for that amount. The implicit unit price is $0.25 per hundred cu. ft. in the first block. Additional quantities of water can be purchased at decreasing marginal rates. If 5000 cu. ft. is purchased, the first 1600 cu. ft. cost $0.25 and the additional 3400 cost only $0.20 each. Under the promotional or declining block system, different classes of users are faced with different block rates. The highest charge is usually made to residential users and the lowest to agricultural or recreational users. If the additional cost of a unit of water is identical throughout the district, all users should be paying the same marginal rate, otherwise there is misallocation.[7]

An example will illustrate some of the problems characteristic of the arbitrary block rates. For many water districts, golf courses (a recreational use) obtain the lowest agricultural water rates. What is the outcome of this classification? First, there is the previously discussed efficiency argument, i.e., total value in use for the district will be increased by reallocating water to people who value it higher, residential users in particular. A transfer from lower valued to higher valued (personal use) uses would tend to reduce the fear of running out of water for personal use purposes. Of course, a uniform higher price of water will raise the price of one input factor (water) to golf courses. One would expect substitution of other inputs, especially capital, to take the place of water. Among the changes to be expected by the golf course would be: (1) a change to night watering when the evaporation rate is reduced; (2) installation of a better-designed sprinkler system which accurately senses the quantity of water to be applied for the type of soil and growth desired; (3) some redesigning of the course to reduce water runoff; and finally (4) the greens fees (club dues) would probably be increased. The last point is of particular concern because the *implicit subsidy* given golf courses has been reduced to zero with correct marginal cost pricing.

Throughout the previous discussion distributional questions have not been mentioned except in passing. But distribution questions are always present in discussions of this kind. In the situation described above, the nongolfer and nonclub members have been subsidizing the golfers and club members. Given the general impression of who plays golf and belongs to private clubs, this may be a subsidy from the lower income groups to the higher. Moreover, this sort of subsidy produces a misallocation of resources (more water than required is used on golf courses). One would expect the Chamber of Commerce and businessmen's groups to be up in arms if such a subsidy were eliminated, because they see golf courses promoting business, bringing tourists to the community, and "benefiting everyone living in the district."

Subsidies of the type just described should be brought out in the open as a separate expenditure category in the appropriate local budget. With reasonably representative legislators, the pros and cons of such a subsidy could then be discussed, evaluated, and the amount finally decided upon could

7. The only reason that the price would differ between users would be if the (properly measured) *marginal cost* for one use is different from that for another use. This exception should not be confused with an *arbitrary* classification of the different components of cost (demand, customer, capacity) to different users. It is our belief that there is no way to correctly separate total costs into one component or another. To use an overworked example, the problem is identical to dividing the total costs of producing sheep into wool, mutton and hide costs. However, the differential marginal costs can potentially be identified and paid by that marginal user.

be granted as a lump sum payment.[8] What is the advantage of a lump sum payment? First, prices (the signal to use more or less of a particular good) are not changed, thus preserving efficiency in the use of the resource. Second, the group receiving the subsidy can spend it in the way it sees fit to provide the best service (to promote tourists and benefit everyone) at the least cost. The final outcome of such a policy will be beneficial to everyone.

### Flat Rate Pricing

Other pricing policies are still used throughout the United States. Perhaps the most inefficient one in terms of water use is the flat rate or lump sum charge. In this case each water user is charged a fixed sum regardless of the quantity of water used. Of course, under this pricing policy the average fixed cost to the consumer falls as a larger quantity is used. What is important is the addition to total cost or the marginal cost to each individual consumer. In this case of flat rate pricing, the marginal cost is zero; there is no additional cost as more water is used. In terms of the individual's water use decision, each would optimally use water until its marginal value to him was zero, i.e., to the point where the demand curve just reaches the quantity axis and is thus equal to *MC*. Under this pricing system there is no economic incentive to reduce water use at all.

A good example of the effects of such a pricing policy is illustrated by the water crisis in New York City in the early 1950s.[9] While city officials were planning large-scale water development projects, a special water study committee suggested that the 25 percent of users who were then receiving unmetered water be metered. This plan offered a potential water saving of up to 200 million gallons per day for the service area, which amounted to a 25 percent decrease in current water usage. The cost of importing water from a new service was estimated to be approximately $1000 per million gallons, compared to a cost of $50 per million gallons to meter the water. The important thing to remember, as exemplified by this case, is that one of the cheapest means of obtaining water is a reallocation of the existing supplies.

A similar situation occurred in the city of Boulder, Colorado.[10] Before 1961 it had used the lump sum or flat rate pricing arrangement, with an

8. In addition, many districts often have special classes of users that receive free (zero cost) water. Although usually based on some historical arrangement, sometimes this practice is based on a transfer of income in kind, i.e., the water district will provide another level of government with water if that government lets the district use its building or computer. Arrangements of this kind should be discouraged. With marginal costs equal to zero for both the water district and the other governmental unit, inefficient use and overuse of both goods by the governments will result.

9. A full description can be found in Hirshleifer, et al., ch. 10.

10. Steve H. Hanke, "Demand for Water Under Dynamic Conditions," *Water Resources Research* (October 1970), p. 1253.

average per capita use under this arrangement of 9.2 thousand gallons per month. Universal metering was imposed the following year and the per capita monthly usage fell to 5.9 thousand gallons per month, a reduction of 36 percent. These examples illustrate that reallocation of uses by raising the marginal cost to the users (in these cases by metering) is a powerful, low-cost water conservation measure.

### Inflexible Pricing

Another factor which compounds the previously mentioned errors for rational decision-making in the water industry is the practice by most water districts of maintaining the same prices for long periods of time. For example, New York City had one single rate from 1850 to 1934, and another single rate from 1935 to 1950. The aversion to changing prices as demand or cost conditions change, means that a full marginal cost pricing technique cannot be effectively implemented. In addition, the tendency to maintain stable prices means that other growing revenue sources often need to be found to cover rising costs. This produces an incentive to use the growing property tax base to augment revenue for the particular district, compounding the problem still further.

We have argued that there is no economic basis for maintaining constant prices. Nobody expects such private goods as automobiles, lettuce, or beefsteak to have the same price for ten or more years, and the same should be true for water. In addition, the normal type of contract for the sale of water is a short-term one, i.e., from payment period to payment period. In other words, an individual's purchase of water today does not bind him in any way for purchases tomorrow.[11]

There is one situation where price flexibility is particularly important for proper water allocation. This occurs when the quantity of water provided is very close to the capacity of the water system. Figure 5–8 depicts a simplified version of such a situation. The short-run marginal cost curve $S$ is virtually horizontal until capacity is reached (point $A$), becoming vertical (zero supply elasticity) at the capacity output $W_S$. Abstracting somewhat, when the demand curve is $D_o$, the price charged (before capacity is reached) is equal to $P_o$, which is equal to $MC$. However, if the urban area continues to grow and demand shifts rightward to $D_1$ and then to $D_2$, the price rises from $P_o$ to $P_1$ to $P_2$. By adopting the correct $MC$ pricing procedure when demand is increasing, none of the shortages found in the requirements case (see pp. 123–124) are produced. The existing supply of water ($W_S$) is

11. If certain customers are averse to price fluctuation, there would be no reason why water districts could not enter into long-term contracts where price is set equal to *long-run* marginal cost.

Figure 5–8. Pricing at capacity.

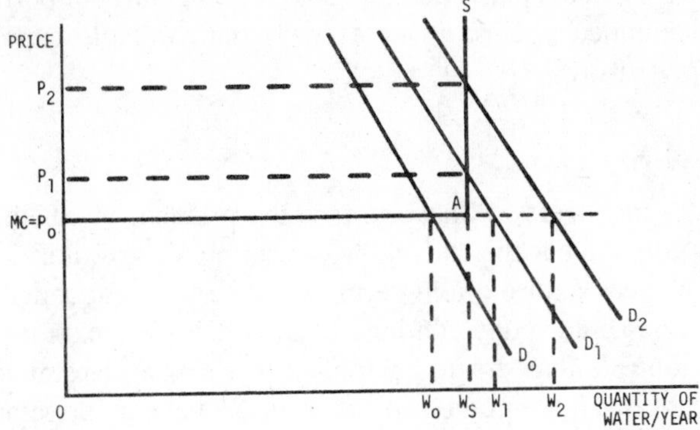


fully used and completely allocated to the highest marginal valued uses. Moreover, this is accomplished without any large administrative costs by the pricing system.[12]

The reader will recall that the requirements approach assumes price will remain at $P_0$ while demand increases from $D_0$ to $D_1$ and then to $D_2$. The quantity of water demanded would thus grow from $W_0$ to $W_1$ and $W_2$, quantities in excess of the available supply ($W_S$). In such a situation other administrative devices must be found to decide who "deserves" or gets the water. Often the allocation decision falls to the water districts' governing board. However, it sometimes passes to a high administrator or bureaucrat in the district's system. Given the potential for arbitrary outcomes, as well as its administrative costs, a far better and more efficient solution would be to let the price system work and to have the water district set (by trial and error) the price so that the existing capacity is just used up. Of course, this is merely another application of the marginal cost pricing rule recommended by economists for allocating resources.

The foregoing discussion has illustrated some of the problems associated with the allocation of a current water supply. It is shown that many of the pricing practices used in the water industry deviate from the economists' $P = MC$ rule. By and large, the misallocation permits a larger quantity of

12. Often water districts are constrained to *not* earn a profit, i.e., any revenue over its costs. In the last case the proper price $P_1$ and $P_2$ could be well above average unit costs and thus yield revenue greater than costs, i.e., a profit. There are no real problems with this situation. The extra income could be transferred to another government agency or rebated to water users on any basis other than the quantity of water used. As before, a lump sum transfer generally will not affect the marginal price and thus efficiency in water use will be maintained. Of course, the confusion lies in thinking of prices only as a revenue source, not as an allocater of scarce goods.

water to be consumed than is economically efficient. In terms of allocation, this deviation from price-equals-marginal cost is particularly important when the quantity demanded is close to or exceeds the available supply, as illustrated on pp. 138–139.

### The Investment Decision

Eventually water managers will have to face the problem of whether or not to invest funds to augment the existing water supply. The water investment decision is by its very nature a long-term one. The wells, aqueducts, reservoirs, and pipelines built today continue to deliver water years into the future. The decision rule that should be applied to a single investment project is a commonsense one—adopt the project when the benefits or gains derived from the project are equal to or greater than the costs of the investment. A common way to classify projects is by the ratio of benefits to costs, $B/C$. If $B/C$ is greater than one, then the gains of the project are larger than the costs and vice versa. Such a benefit-cost analysis is not, however, easy to apply to water projects. Many of the so-called benefits projected for such projects are typically overstated so they tend to give an upward bias to the benefit side of the argument. For example, the official economic analysis for the California Feather River Project was submitted to the legislature in 1959 with a ratio of benefits to costs ($B/C$) of 2.5. This means there would be 2.5 as many proposed benefits as proposed costs. After the first set of bonds was approved, the $B/C$ ratio was subsequently revised to 1.3. An independent study conducted in 1966 indicated a $B/C$ ratio of 0.75. This means that every dollar of costs poured into the water plan produces only 75¢ of benefits to the residents of California.

The special economic problem involved in any investment analysis is how to compare benefits and costs which occur at different periods in the future, while the decision has to be made in the present. In market economies, the presence of a rate of interest leads to the correct solution. The methodology used is called discounting.

### Discounting

Investment goods, by definition, are real goods used for the production of output in the current and future periods. Such goods are not used up in the current time period but instead continue to produce output for a long time before replacement is necessary. A water investment decision made today will provide an output of water today and into the future as well. The future values of water or other output have to be evaluated in terms of making the decision today, because this is the time when the real resources (land, labor, capital) are being allocated to water use instead of for freeways or education.

The technique of discounting allows us to calculate what a dollar that will be received next year is worth today. To put the discounting problem in a more familiar context, consider the process of *lending;* how many dollars could one get in one year by giving up a dollar today? The local savings and loan association provides an immediate answer for most of us. It will take your dollar today and pay you $1.05 at the end of one year, or 5 percent on your original dollar plus your original dollar (assuming annual compounding). This can be expressed algebraically by

$$V_0 (1 + r) = V_1 \quad \text{or} \quad \$1.00\,(1.05) = \$1.05. \tag{1}$$

where $V$ stands for value in period 0 (today) or 1 (one year from today or tomorrow) and $r$ is the annual interest rate set equal to .05 or 5 percent. The 1 in the term $(1 + r)$ merely indicates you received the original dollar back at the final period. If the interest rate ($r$) were zero, then a dollar today is worth just a dollar tomorrow. The calculation can be worked backward, too, by reasking the original question: How much is $1.05 received next year worth today? We want to find out $V_0$ (value today) of $V_1$ (value one year from today).

Solving Equation 1 for $V_0$, we obtain

$$V_0 = \frac{V_1}{(1 + r)}, \quad \text{or} \quad \$1.00 = \frac{\$1.05}{1.05} = \$1.00. \tag{2}$$

Thus, $1.05 to be received a year from today is worth only $1.00 today if the interest rate is 5 percent. If the interest rate were 10 percent the $1.05 would only be worth $\frac{\$1.05}{1.10}$ or $0.95, less than a dollar. The process of finding out what a sum received (or expended) in the future is worth in the current period (today) is called discounting or finding the present value.

Discounting is a necessary technique in any realistic benefit-cost analysis of all investment projects—public or private. The general formula for discounting is:

$$V_0 = R_0 + \frac{R_1}{(1 + r)} + \frac{R_2}{(1 + r)^2} + \frac{R_3}{(1 + r)^3} + \cdots + \frac{R_n}{(1 + r)^n}, \tag{3}$$

where $V_0$ is the present value at time zero of an income or expenditure stream $R$ (either positive or negative values) continuing into the future for $n$ periods, discounted at the annual interest rate $r$. Note that the denominator of the third term is squared, and the fourth is cubed, etc. This is so because $R_2$ dollars has to be brought back to the previous time period (period one) by dividing by $(1 + r)$, and then brought back to time zero by dividing again by $(1 + r)$. Thus,

$$R_2/(1 + r) \times (1 + r) = R_2/(1 + r)^2.$$

A similar procedure is necessary for $R_4$, $R_5$, and $R_n$.

Three important facts should be evident from this general formula. The higher the positive values of $R$, the larger will be the value of $V_0$; the larger $r$, the smaller will be $V_0$; and an $R$ occurring later in the income or expenditure stream makes a lesser contribution (for a constant $r$) than an $R$ of equal value occurring earlier or closer to the present.

**Costs, Benefits and the Decision Rule**

The public investment decision rule can be stated as follows: only adopt projects whose present value of benefits (calculated using the appropriate interest rate) is equal to or greater than the present value of costs. The present value of benefits $B_0$ calculated by adding the discounted sum of the individual benefits in each year is

$$B_0 = b_0 + \frac{b_1}{1 + r} + \frac{b_2}{(1 + r)^2} + \cdots + \frac{b_n}{(1 + r)^n}. \quad (4)$$

The $b$'s in this case are the *estimated* value of benefits in each year. The present value of costs $C_0$ is expressed by

$$C_0 = k_0 + o_0 + \frac{k_1 + o_1}{1 + r} + \frac{k_2 + o_2}{(1 + r)^2} + \cdots + \frac{k_n + o_n}{(1 + r)^n} \quad (5)$$

where $o$ designates operating costs (such as pumping, maintenance and repair) and $k$ denotes the capital (or investment) costs of the project. To calculate the present value of net benefits, $NB$, we subtract Equation 5 from Equation 4 above, or

$$B_0 - C_0 = NB.$$

If net benefits are negative, the project should be rejected.

With the definition of costs restricted to include only investment and operation, costs can be calculated from engineering studies and appropriately discounted. All other considerations affecting the net present value of the project are included in the estimation of benefits $(b)$.

The measurement of the benefits of water projects, such as California's Feather River Project, involves many problems. Economist Kenneth Boulding captures some of the flavor of the difficulties in verse:

All benefits that are dispersable
Should be, perhaps, non-reimbursible
But people should be made to pay
For benefits that come their way—
Unless we want to subsidize
The good, the needy, or the wise.
(It would be well to be quite sure
Just who *are* the deserving poor,
Or else the state-supported ditch
May serve the Undeserving Rich).[13]

The term "benefit" is used to describe the demand side of the investment decision, whereas "value" is used when the individual district pricing decision is discussed. Many large multipurpose investment projects produce several outputs, some of which can be valued by market prices and others for which no market generated prices are available. The inclusion of both types of outputs on the demand side has led to the adoption of the more inclusive term, benefits.

Benefits (positive and negative) may be classified in different ways. One procedure is to differentiate between primary and secondary benefits. Primary benefits are derived from those products or services proximate to the motivation for the project, such as water, electricity, or flood protection. Secondary benefits are values over and above those of the immediate products or services of the project. Extreme care must be exercised in their measurement.

Suppose, for example, the project consists of only the importation of an external source of water through an aqueduct system which crosses uninhabitable land. In this case, the benefits ($b$'s) are simple to calculate because they only amount to the marginal value in use ($P$) of the water ($W$) provided in each time period (i.e., the quantity of water times price: $W \times P = b$). The obvious role of price in the calculation of benefits establishes the importance of proper pricing (discussed on pp. 129–140). If the pricing scheme used is incorrect, then false signals will be transmitted to the investment decision process.

For more complex projects, additional outputs have to be measured. Externalities are a case in point. Many projects, in addition to producing a primary output, produce other goods, often not distributed through a market

13. Kenneth Boulding, "The Feather River Anthology or 'Holy Water,'" *Industrial Water Engineering* no. 12 (December 1966), pp. 22–33.

mechanism. For example, the heat produced by a desalter, the drainage problems on land near a reservoir, and value of historical sites are all examples of technological externalities. Their values should be included as (positive or negative) benefits in the calculation of $B_0$. Note that all examples of this type of externality involve a change in technological or production conditions elsewhere in the economy. What should not be included in benefit calculations are changes in money values (wage rates or land prices) which merely represent a transfer from one segment of the economy to another. As an example of such inappropriate accounting the Bureau of Reclamation in its earlier national level investment analysis often counted large quantities of secondary benefits of this nature. To the primary benefits of irrigation (water) they added the indirect or secondary benefits of the increased profits of wholesalers and retailers who handled the increased output of agricultural products, profits from the firms that sold to the new irrigated agricultural sector, and the increase in land value of residential property. So long as the national economy is fully employed, the inclusion of these items leads to an overestimate of benefits.[14]

For water projects with a large quantity of consumptive or urban use the following rule of thumb will insure a more nearly correct evaluation of benefits. The benefits of urban water in any time period cannot exceed the smaller of:

a) The marginal value in use, or
b) The cost of the next cheapest alternative source.

The rule follows from the common sense of opportunity cost. For example, if the marginal value in use is $15 per acre foot, but the opportunity cost is $10 from an alternative source, the benefits per unit of additional water could not be greater than $10. This rule always chooses the least cost combination of resources.

A further difficulty in measuring the benefits (positive and negative) of a project occurs because some of the by-products are intangible in terms of dollar value. While it is relatively easy to calculate the tangible benefits which motivated the investment, such as output of water and electricity, it is more difficult (but not impossible) to estimate the quantity and value of activities such as recreation, flood control, or the preservation of historical sites, since no market transaction is involved. Economic research is improving our understanding of these problems.

### Choosing a Discount Rate

Once benefits and costs are established, the remaining task is to determine then present value so net benefits can be calculated. As discussed on pp.

14. The effects of secondary benefits or other income transfers can be presented as a supplement to the efficiency benefit cost tabulation.

141–144, the calculation of present value involves discounting. The problem is to choose the appropriate discount rate. If the discount rate is too low, the project will look more favorable than it really is. For an apt summary of the effects of discounting, we again turn to Kenneth Boulding:

> Around the mysteries of finance
> We must perform a ritual dance
> Because the long-term interest rate
> Determines any project's fate:
>
> At 3 percent the case is clear
> At 4, some searching doubts appear
> At 5, it draws its final breath
> While 6 percent is certain death.[15]

A wide range of interest rates exists in the economy today. The government borrows for a short period at 5 percent, but pays 6¾ percent for periods of more than ten years. Municipalities borrow for 4¾ percent, while it costs the individual homeowner 7¼ percent for his home mortgage. His stockbroker suggests a return of 15 percent at the time he pays 18 percent on his credit-card purchases. All evidence indicates that the interest rate is positive, meaning that discounting has to be used to properly reflect time preference and productivity. But which positive interest rate should be used? Although the argument over the exact discount rate is not completely settled, economists can offer a few guidelines which will quickly narrow the range of rates to use. First, all rates on government bonds have special attributes which make the rates paid lower than corresponding rates found elsewhere in the private sector. The particular characteristic of government bonds is that they are virtually risk-free, being backed by the taxing power of the government. Second, when analyzing a water investment project, we are evaluating forward up to 50 years, so we should be looking at long-term rates, not short-term government bills. Tax-free municipal bonds should be excluded from consideration because their rate is governed by the highest marginal personal income tax rate. So far in this discussion the lowest rate that would be acceptable is the rate on a long-term (30-year) government bond. Turning to the private sector, the yield on good long-term corporate bonds (Aaa) generally runs higher than long-term government bonds, and as the quality of bonds (from Aaa to Bb) goes down (or risk goes up), the difference in rates rises even further.

It would be foolish not to admit there is some risk involved in public projects, which means the rate on corporate long-term bonds would be even more appropriate than the riskless government long-term bond rate.

15. Kenneth Boulding, "The Economist and the Engineer," in *Economics and Public Policy in Water Resource Development,* eds. Steven C. Smith and Emery Castle, (Ames, Iowa: Iowa State University Press, 1964), pp. 82–92.

Approximately the same interest rate level is found in the rate that private homeowners pay on their mortgages, i.e., anywhere from 7 to 8 percent today (1972). The mortgage rate is by far the best rate that homeowners get for long-term funds, but their marginal rate must be slightly higher because individuals can be found borrowing at 12 percent, i.e., receiving a dollar's worth of goods today in payment for $1.12 tomorrow. Essentially, any discount rate less than 6 to 7 percent is pure economic nonsense.

Finally, the problem can be viewed in another way. Assume there exists a riskless rate of interest of *r* percent (for example, 5 percent), and that resources in this hypothetical economy are used by both the corporate and household sectors. To simplify, further assume that households can earn the riskless rate percent and pay no tax, whereas corporations pay a tax of 50 percent (not far from the corporate tax rate). In this case the resources (capital equipment) used by the corporate sector *must* earn a minimum of 10 percent (5 percent for the stockholders and 5 percent for taxes). The central point is that the actual return on resources in the corporate sector is 10 percent in order that the corporation can pay 5 percent, the going riskless rate to stockholders. Also, if households use resources (buy goods) instead of loaning, the implicit interest rate is at least 5 percent on the households' use of resources. Presume a water district now comes along and desires to use resources (the same resources earning 10 percent in the corporate sector and at least 5 percent in the household) to augment its water supply. Assume for simplicity that 50 percent of the resources will come from the corporate and the remainder from the household sector. What is the opportunity cost of these resources? The answer is that 50 percent at 0.10, and 50 percent at 0.05 means $(.5(.10) + .5(.05) = .075)$—at least 7.5 percent—or 2½ percent higher than the riskless rate. Although this example is oversimplified to a large degree, it points out real-world facts that cannot be overlooked in the choice of a discount rate. Once resources are taken away from the corporate sector, the discount rate will be higher than the riskless rate *r*, approaching $2r$ (10 percent in the example) if all the resources are derived from the private corporate sector. Also the casual evidence presented earlier indicates that very few households are able to use resources at the riskless rate, but a minimum long-term rate is that available on home mortgages. The conclusion reached from this discussion about the marginal opportunity cost for resources used in the economy is that it is probably well above the riskless rate, and at least in the range of 7–12 percent (in 1972) depending on tax rates and particular source of resources.

To illustrate the impact of higher interest rates on the investment decision, note that a benefit of $1 occurring 50 years from now has a present value of:

$0.37 discounted at 2%
0.14 discounted at 4%
0.03 discounted at 7%

Thus, we can see that fewer but more productive investment projects will be generated if the discount rate upon which decisions are based is representative of the true opportunity cost for resources rather than being some arbitrary riskless rate.

### Benefit-Cost Summary

The foregoing considerations are all a part of benefit-cost analysis. The required information is generally compiled in a summary table. The left-hand side of the summary table presents estimates of the benefits (in present value terms) divided into two groups. The first group contains the benefits that have been quantified in dollar terms, such as the value of irrigation water, or electric power sales. Below this the (currently) nonquantifiable benefits—the intangibles—are listed without a dollar value attached. For the intangibles a physical change and its order of magnitude can easily be incorporated. An example could include the project's effect on historical sites, the increase in recreational use, or other items where market generated information is scarce or nonexistent. All benefits presented in the summary tables for the particular project must have detailed analyses of their derivation and the particular values attached to physical outputs.

Similarly, on the right-hand side of the summary table the estimates of costs are presented. A useful classification is to divide the quantifiable costs between capital and operating expenditures. The lower portion of the cost presentation would include a tabulation of the intangible economic costs of the project with physical changes if known.

A summary exhibit of this type goes a long way in aiding decision-making for any investment project. First, the actual decision-making body (legislature, local council or water board) has the economic effects presented to them in a clear, well-organized fashion. The actual quantifiable economic benefits and costs are separated from the (more often political) intangibles. Second, the decision-making body, by comparing listings of this sort for several alternative projects (or variations on a particular project), can obtain greater information on the trade-offs generated by choosing one project over another. For example, assume a regional water agency is considering two alternative water supply projects, A and B, having comparable costs. Further, assume that project A has quantifiable net benefits (discounted benefits minus discounted costs) of 100 and has the intangible effect of destroying a particular historical site. On the other hand, project B has a quantifiable net present value of 90 and has no intangible effects. If the decision-making body chooses project B over project A, it is implicitly placing a value of 10 on the intangible effects induced by project A. Thus, the implicit trade-offs made in public decisions are spelled out more effectively using a benefit-cost framework. The end result would be that decisions made on investment projects will be more efficient and more consistent with the preferences of the governed.

## Conclusion

The ease with which water managers think in terms of requirement instead of demand is one of the most fundamental misconceptions of public decision-makers. The deficiency of the requirements approach is not that it has failed to forecast future "needs," but that it fosters an approach to water management that results in excessive costs. As a result of this thinking, managers within the water industry ignore the effects on demand of current pricing policy. In addition, average cost pricing, flat rate pricing, and the use of property taxes to defray costs are all practices that should be eliminated. Changes in pricing schedules and metering are often omitted from consideration, leading to gross misallocations, inefficient uses and water shortages well in advance of a true economic shortage.

Similar problems arise when the decision to invest in additional supplies is made. The measurement of the economic gains or benefits, while difficult, can be simplified by keeping in mind the concept of opportunity cost. This is especially true for the supply of urban water. It is usually the communities' misfortune that those responsible for water-supply decisions tend to regard themselves not as mere purveyors of a commodity, but instead as crusaders for the cause of ample water.

## Suggested Reading

Bain, Joe S., Richard E. Caves, and Julius Margolis. *Northern California's Water Industry: The Comparative Efficiency of Public Enterprise in Developing a Scarce Natural Resource.* Baltimore: The Johns Hopkins Press, 1966.

Hanke, Steven H. "Pricing Urban Water." In *Public Prices for Public Products,* ed. Selma Mushkin. The Urban Institute. Washington, D.C., 1972.

Kneese, A. V., and B. T. Bower. *Managing Water Quality: Economics, Technology, Institutions.* Baltimore: The Johns Hopkins Press, 1968.

Maass, A., et al. *Design of Water Resource Systems.* Cambridge, Mass.: Harvard University Press, 1962.

# Commentary

The foregoing illustrations of various pricing schemes for water reinforce the notion of the importance of marginal cost pricing to society. When the price the consumer pays for water is equal to the value of resources used in producing the last unit for consumption, water is neither being undervalued nor overvalued, and the quantity consumed is neither too little nor too large.

When a government agency steps in and a competitive market is no longer the means for facilitating exchange between producers and consumers, the efficient allocation of resources is no longer assured, and the price paid for a resource is likely not to be its marginal cost of production. The capacity of water agencies for devising pricing schemes which will misallocate water seems virtually unlimited. Average cost pricing with or without the added feature of covering a fraction of costs from property taxes, promotional pricing, flat rate pricing, and the maintenance of inflexible prices are some of the uneconomic water allocation schemes discussed by Professor Morgan.

The public should be concerned not only with current demand, but with the choice of investment projects to deliver water in the future. Morgan notes that there are many public demands for limited investment resources and, hence, we should choose projects wisely. Since different investments have different time horizons and different patterns of costs and benefits over time, these sums must be discounted to current dollars to permit a comparison of the net present value of various investment projects The rate of return at which future dollars are discounted should accurately reflect the returns which could be realized from investing the public's dollar. Professor Morgan notes that since many projects involve a stream of benefits which extend into the future while the bulk of the costs are incurred in the initial phases, the lower the discount rate used to evaluate the project, the higher will be the benefit/cost ratio. The difficulty of identifying and estimating all of the benefits and costs associated with a project adds to the uncertainty in choosing between projects competing for funds.

Although water is often distributed by a governmental agency and, hence, could be thought of as a public rather than a private good, individuals could be excluded from consumption. Considered in the next chapter by Robert Deacon are environmental goods, such as air quality, from which an individual cannot be excluded. If supply is left to private markets, a suboptimal quantity will be supplied. If a public agency supplies the good, problems arise in calculating the appropriate price to charge, which—along with consumer demand—will in turn determine the appropriate quantity to supply.

# 6

# Environmental Quality: A View from the Marketplace

Robert Deacon

We have met the enemy and he is us—Pogo

With ecological crises and predictions of impending environmental disasters established as a major perturbation in the American life-style by the close of the 1960s, it would be difficult as we move into the 1970s to find a person who does not have rather firm notions regarding the causes of environmental pollution and how it should be dealt with. That individuals and groups representing every segment of the society are deeply concerned with the problem is understandable; the ecological damage is observable, many of the alarming projections theoretically defensible. That each person readily assumes a certain expertise with regard to the problem is also somewhat understandable; in gross outline the causes seem to be easily identifiable, the solutions dramatically simple. This apparent simplicity has led people to believe that the problem would be solved if only we could set up model bureaucratic agencies, devise an ideal antipollution device, or spend a large enough sum of money. Others anxiously await some elusive change in human values and behavior. All such approaches fail to realize the complexity of the problem and are fated for only partial success at best.

That our environmental problems are primarily a consequence of economic behavior and must therefore be analyzed and approached in economic terms is the central thesis of this chapter. The problems arise out of a basic conflict between the environment and man's desire to promote his material well-being. This conflict exists in all areas of human activity and it makes little sense to attribute blame to any particular segment of society. Consumers and producers alike weigh the private costs and benefits of alternative courses of action and, most often, decide against the environment. Coal mining strips away landscapes, and power plants befoul the air to produce the cheap electric power demanded by households hundreds of miles away. Industrial wastes turn rivers into sewers and even fire hazards.

The pulp and paper industry slashes down forests, leaving eroded soil and polluted streams in its wake, to satisfy consumers' demands for convenient throwaway packaging that, in turn, adds to a growing solid waste disposal problem. There are, of course, noneconomic dimensions to the problem, but these are secondary to the basic forces which motivate human activity in the marketplace.

The economic factors behind our present environmental problems need sorting out. Analyzing the task of environmental protection from the economist's viewpoint, we can examine alternative strategies for controlling pollution and explore some special problems encountered in managing particular natural assets.

## Economic Values and Environmental Standards

The economist has been described as "one who knows the price of everything and the value of nothing." The statement is, of course, false, since no economist could possibly know the price of everything and, more importantly, economists are not concerned with price per se, but with the complex factors that regulate value. It is suspected, however, that many people would agree with this indictment, particularly when economists insist on pricing nature's resources. To those unfamiliar with the basic facts of economics this must seem blasphemous. Indeed, questions like "What is the minimum bribe you would accept to let me degrade the environment?" or "How much would you be willing to pay to prevent a forest from being cut clear?" are naturally repugnant.

While reluctance to put a price on nature may seem puzzling to those trained in economics, one often finds that even economists feel uncomfortable with such questions. People who are totally at ease discussing the prices of bread, water, and such necessities of life, suddenly clam up when prices for such amenities as greenbelts and smokeless skies are mentioned. It may be that these attitudes stem from the fact that the latter commodities are traditionally not traded among individuals in markets, whereas the former are; thus prices for environmental goods are never observed.

Although many economists would hesitate to use responses to the hypothetical questions mentioned above as a basis for decision-making, the inquiries themselves have relevance. Since man must inevitably choose between levels of environmental quality and material comfort, a comparison of their relative values must be made. It is an important task of the economist to point out that none of ". . . the best things in life are free . . . ," although many have zero price. All of the earth's resources are limited in supply and all have alternative uses. For example, homes cannot be built from trees that are left standing for recreational enjoyment. Also, labor, capital, and other resources used to treat industrial sewage cannot be employed in the production of food and clothing. The inescapable fact that all actions have an opportunity cost is of fundamental importance for all decision-making problems, and has some interesting implications.

The legislation of environmental standards must, in fact, be premised on placing a price on nature. The notion that any set of standards or constraints on activity implies a dual set of imputed prices, while not obvious, follows from opportunity cost and the maximizing behavior of individuals. To illustrate this, consider the plight of a dictator governing a town through which a river runs. Although the river has great recreational and aesthetic potential, it is currently being used as a municipal sewer. Seeking to correct the situation, he proposes that sewage emissions (measured in terms of biochemical oxygen demand, or some other appropriate unit) should not exceed a certain level ($Q^*$)—where this is some nonnegative level below the current rate of discharge. Sewage treatment will, of course, be costly and will divert some of the town's resources away from the production of other goods, but in his judgment, these resources are well spent.

Since the dictator is benign, he will attempt to set the standard at the correct level, one that will increase the welfare of the citizenry as much as possible. There will, however, be those who argue that the standard is overly stringent and should be relaxed a bit. Now if the dictator truly believes that he has chosen the best standard, he must reply that any such move would make the community worse off, i.e., that it would involve aesthetic losses that outweigh the value of the resources that could be saved from lowering treatment levels. Correspondingly, to those who contend the standard is too lax, the response must be that the incremental gains to stream quality achieved by tightening emission control would not be worth the added treatment costs. At the margin (for the last unit of effluent reduced to meet the standard) the incremental gain in aesthetic or recreational value must be exactly matched by the marginal cost of treatment. This leads to a curious conclusion. Since the marginal cost of treatment can be calculated in monetary terms, the dictator has unwittingly attached an implicit dollar value to stream quality; he has measured the seemingly unmeasurable. Unless he is omniscient as well as benign, the choice of $Q^*$ may, in fact, be suboptimal. Yet the point of our illustration remains; once one chooses a standard or constraint and defends it, an implicit price has been attached to the regulated resource.[1]

This relationship between standards and imputed prices can be depicted graphically. Consider the hypothetical production possibilities curve in Figure 6–1. The set of points contained by the boundary of the curve depicts the options available to our hypothetical community, given its

1. For a more advanced discussion of this topic see Harold A. Thomas, Jr., "The Animal Farm: A Mathematical Model for the Discussion of Social Standards for Control of the Environment," *Quarterly Journal of Economics* (February 1963).

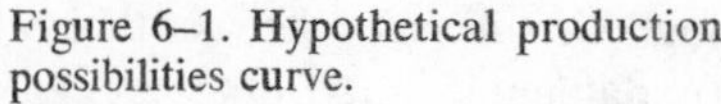
Figure 6–1. Hypothetical production possibilities curve.

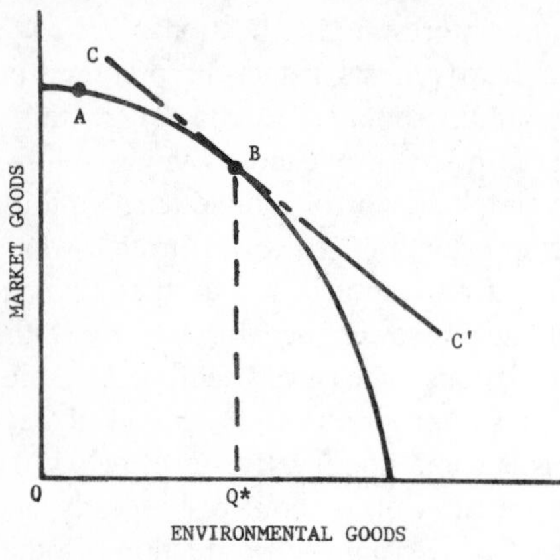


resource constraints and the existing level of technology. Since both environmental goods and market goods are desirable, any movement to the northeast makes the community better off. Suppose the community starts off at point *A* producing a high level of market goods at the expense of the environment. If an environmental quality standard is adopted (at $Q^*$) and is attained efficiently, this will move the community to point *B* on the production possibilities curve. The slope of the production possibilities curve is the marginal rate of transformation for the two goods, and the slope of the tangent line *CC′* passing through point *B* shows society's marginal cost of providing the last increment of environmental quality in terms of market goods. If one believes that the standard $Q^*$ is optimal, the argument must be that the slope of the line *CC′* also measures the rate at which society is willing to trade off the two goods; the marginal rate of transformation must equal society's marginal rate of substitution. If the two were not equal, community welfare could be enhanced by moving to a point on the curve where they were equated.

A concrete example of the relationship between pollution standards and imputed prices for environmental resources is provided by recent studies of air pollution control in the St. Louis airshed. Analyzing air pollution abatement in the context of a linear programming model, Robert Kohn[2] estimated *shadow prices* for concentrations of various pollutants, which are implied by statutory air quality goals. These shadow prices (displayed in Table 6–1) show the cost that would be incurred if standards were tightened by an incremental amount. Thus, for example, if the allowable level for particulates were decreased by one unit (from 75 to 74 $\mu g/m^3$), the implied benefit must be at least $239,100 for the standard to be worth maintaining.

Realizing the intimate connection between optimal standards and imputed prices, one may choose not to defend standards in terms of community welfare. While such a course avoids implicit pricing, it also exposes one to the charge that the decisions reached are capricious. Even with the minimal standards in force today, this argument is being made. In the future as stan-

2. Robert E. Kohn, "Air Quality, the Cost of Capital and the Multi-Product Production Function," *Southern Economic Journal* (October 1971), pp. 156–160.

Table 6–1

Air Quality Goals and Shadow Prices for St. Louis Airshed

| | Carbon Monoxide | Total Hydro-Carbons | Oxides of Nitrogen | Sulfur Dioxide | Particulates |
|---|---|---|---|---|---|
| Projected Concentration without Abatement | 9.0 ppm | 3.94 ppm | .0944 ppm | .0690 ppm | 128.0 $\mu g/m^3$ |
| Statutory or Related Goal | 5.0 ppm | 3.10 ppm | .069 ppm | .020 ppm | 75.0 $\mu g/m^3$ |
| Shadow Price of Goal* | $2,000,000 | $15,388,000 | $1,435,800,000 | $439,100,000 | $239,100 |

*Figures show the imputed value of changing each goal by one full unit and may be misleading at first glance. For example, the figure for hydrocarbons shows that the shadow price of changing the goal from 3.10 to 2.10 ppm is $15,388,000, which implies that the shadow price of going from a goal of 3.10 to 3.09 ppm is $153,880.

Source: R. Kohn, "Air Quality," p. 158.

dards are tightened and control costs rise, the claim that environmental and aesthetic values cannot be measured or compared will offer cold comfort to the decision-maker who must take his case to consumers and taxpayers.

If aesthetics can be gained only at the expense of mundane material goods, then choosing the proper mix of the two necessitates comparing relative values; this is the central point. In practice, we may find it difficult to accurately estimate the value of environmental resources. Yet merely realizing that such values exist is crucial to an analysis of environmental problems and policy.

## Economic Roots of the Problem

At least since the time of Adam Smith, economists have extolled the virtues of the unfettered market as a device for efficiently allocating society's scarce resources among competing uses. While cases of market failure have long been acknowledged and analyzed, such instances were in the past considered to be rare and isolated phenomena. Unfortunately, such occurrences are becoming more commonplace.[3] Restoration of the market's allocative efficiency necessitates finding out why markets malfunction. Analyzing the concepts of *property rights* and *public goods* provides insight into areas where markets fail.

3. For a detailed discussion of the pervasiveness of "externalities" and implications of the law of conservation of energy and matter for economic activity, see Ayres, Kneese, and D'Arge, *Economics and the Environment: A Materials Balance Approach* (Baltimore: Johns Hopkins U. Press, 1970).

## Property Rights

In rather broad terms economic activity may be thought of as a process of exchange among individual agents; consumers exchange goods and services (or claims to them) with firms and other consumers by buying and selling final products and factors of production. In order that these exchanges be beneficial to the community, societies design rules to govern how they may take place. Perhaps the most obvious of these is that exchange should be voluntary. Involuntary exchange, commonly called extortion, is not allowed under society's rules of the game. There are also rules which specify how a particular good or service may or may not be used. One may not hire labor to murder one's enemies nor use one's automobile as a weapon. In fact, the notion that goods are exchanged is a bit misleading; rather, it is the *right* to use an asset or service in particular ways that is exchanged. Thus, when a fruit grower hires a farm laborer, he is exchanging a wage for the right to use so many hours of the laborer's time for cultivating and harvesting his crops. Likewise, when purchasing an automobile, the buyer exchanges money for the right to use the auto for transportation, subject to speed limits and a variety of other rules of the road. With each such property right comes the obligation not to use the asset or service in a disallowed fashion.

Besides specifying rules for use, rights to property are generally vested exclusively in a specific party. In order to exercise this right it must be possible to exclude other parties from using the asset. For example, when one purchases a home, he receives the right to exclude others from occupying it. Rights which cannot be enforced in this manner are seldom valuable. Finally, property rights generally specify how assets and services may be transferred between individuals, i.e., how and between whom the property may be exchanged.

In cases where the above-mentioned rules of property can be carefully spelled out and enforced, the self-interested behavior of individuals tends to allocate resources tolerably well. Where such rights are not well-defined or not enforceable, private market allocations are generally inefficient. With respect to environmental resources, exclusivity is probably the most important dimension of property rights. Assets for which exclusive rights are not defined and enforced are generally called common property. To see how markets fail in such instances, consider the historical case of such a resource: the beaver.[4] During the eighteenth century the beaver hat came into fashion in Europe, creating a huge demand for beaver pelts. Due to the fugitive nature of the resource, property rights to the population were not

4. An excellent discussion of the same problem in a slightly different context is H. Scott Gordon, "The Economic Theory of a Common Property Resource: The Fishery," *Journal of Political Economy* (April 1954).

assigned to individual trappers;[5] anyone with requisite skills and equipment was allowed to take the animals in any number. Even if exclusive rights had been assigned to an individual, the act would have been meaningless because enforcement of exclusion would have been virtually impossible.

A resource such as the beaver has at least two alternative and mutually exclusive uses. The animal can be trapped to produce beaver hats today, or it can be left undisturbed to produce more beaver and hence more hats next spring; the social opportunity cost of harvesting today is the foregone return in future periods. While it would have been eminently sensible for all trappers as a group to restrict current harvests and ensure a future supply, it was not rational for any individual trapper to do so. The trapper who left an animal to reproduce had no guarantee that it would not be taken by someone else. Thus, the future value disappeared as a private opportunity cost of present harvest. In this particular case, the outcome was that "future beaver" were not provided; the populations were hunted to the point of virtual extinction.

All resources can yield value in several alternative pursuits. However, when the value accruing to one or more of these uses cannot be captured by a specific party, the resource will be misallocated. The institutions in a market-oriented economy do not provide incentives for furnishing such common property resources or commodities or for using them efficiently if they occur naturally. It is no coincidence that the "tragedy of the commons"[6] has been documented in the exploitation of virtually all common property resources: ocean fisheries, game resources, communal pasture lands, subsurface water, and petroleum are but a few examples.

Most environmental resources (e.g., clean air and pure water) fall into this common property category. By their very nature exclusive rights cannot be assigned, so the problem cannot be solved by trying to make these resources private property. The privately rational decisions of individuals lead to a socially irrational misallocation of valuable resources. In such cases we cannot depend upon the market mechanism and must turn to our political institutions for a rational policy.[7]

5. There is sparse evidence to suggest that this fact was not universally true. Evidently the Indians living around Quebec instituted a system of tribal property rights by assigning hunting lands to individual families. For an interesting discussion of this see H. Demsetz, "Toward a Theory of Property Rights," *American Economic Review* (May 1966) and references cited therein.

6. Although this particular phrase was popularized by Garret Hardin's famous article "The Tragedy of the Commons," *Science* 162, 1253 (1968), economists have been studying the same phenomenon for a number of years. See, for example, footnote 4.

7. This does not mean that *all* cases of market failure ought to be treated with government intervention. The costs of making political decisions and maintaining the bureaucratic machinery needed to implement policy may be substantial and should be weighed against the magnitude of market misallocations before we opt for government intervention.

## Public Goods

Closely related to nonexclusive or common property resources is a class of commodities and services which economists call public goods. Many of these goods do not occur naturally, but must be deliberately produced. Public goods frequently display the communal attribute that once provided, they are available for all to consume. Traditional examples include flood control dams and lighthouses. The communal aspect of such goods is, however, often a matter of choice rather than a physical imperative. Public goods frequently exhibit enormous economies of joint consumption by several individuals simultaneously, as with fire protection and highways, so that it is generally economical to provide such goods for the entire community rather than have each individual supply his own. This is also the case with most environmental goods and services. In polar cases joint consumption economies are perfect in that "each individual's consumption of such a [public] good leads to no subtraction from any other individual's consumption of that good."[8] The extent of joint consumption economies in public goods is largely a matter of degree. While such economies are nearly perfect for lighthouses and flood control dams, they are only partially present in fire protection and highways. Although extreme cases may be hard to find, the concept of a pure public good provides a sharp contrast to private goods, where one person's consumption necessarily reduces the amount available to others.

There is no problem distributing public goods once they are produced, since the total amount supplied is automatically made available for all members of the community to share. The problem lies in providing the goods at the appropriate rates of output. Once again private markets cannot generally be relied upon. To encourage a supplier to provide any good and to defray his expenses of provision, the supplier must be able to enforce a charge for his services. If, however, the good in question is public, such charges cannot be enforced since nonpaying individuals cannot be excluded from consuming. Each individual will therefore withhold payment, realizing that if the payments of others are sufficient to provide the good, he will obtain a free ride. When all potential consumers follow this individually rational policy, the outcome is socially irrational, i.e., a service which could yield value in excess of cost will not be provided at all. It is no accident that police and fire protection, national defense, highways, and lighthouses are not generally supplied by the private sector.

8. Paul A. Samuelson, "The Pure Theory of Public Expenditure," *Review of Economics and Statistics* (November 1954). This is the classic article on the economics of public goods.

**Provision of a Public Good: Environmental Quality**

Economists have developed a rather complete theory of the provision of public goods. Since environmental assets exhibit the same essential features, it follows that environmental problems can be examined as an application of the theory of public goods. To illustrate this theory consider a community of individuals inhabiting the banks of a polluted stream. The recreational potential of the river is diminished for each person in the community and each would be willing to pay for an improvement in water quality. In general each individual's willingness-to-pay for incremental improvements of stream quality diminishes as the amount of effluent discharged is reduced and stream quality improves. The willingness-to-pay schedule for individual $i$ is plotted as $W_i$ in Figure 6–2. It closely resembles a demand curve for a private good and slopes downward to the right for the same reasons.

Although little evidence has been gathered to support the notion of willingness-to-pay for improved water quality, Ronald Ridker[9] has estimated individuals' willingness-to-pay for reduced levels of air pollution in Philadelphia. Ridker used the results of interviews conducted among six hundred housewives residing in three different areas of the city. The areas were chosen in such a fashion that the socioeconomic backgrounds of persons interviewed were similar, but air pollution levels experienced varied widely between households. A variety of questions was asked concerning expenditure of time and money on air pollution-related activities such as painting, cleaning, laundering, etc. In addition, respondents were asked to state how much they would be willing to pay for pollution abatement. In particular, housewives were asked how much they would be willing to pay for the following three solutions:

1) A complete and total solution to the problem.
2) A device which would remove all soot and dirt from the air in and around your own house.
3) A community solution in which citizens band together, each paying the same amount, to keep the entire neighborhood free of air pollution.

The responses, separated by the level of air pollution experienced by the respondent, are summarized in Table 6–2.

Because answers to hypothetical questions are also hypothetical, one encounters problems in interpreting such responses. However, the evidence in Table 6–2 lends support to the notion that consumers are willing to pay

9. Ronald G. Ridker, *Economic Costs of Air Pollution* (New York: Praeger, 1967), ch. 3.

for environmental quality. More importantly, these data support the contention that willingness-to-pay schedules slope downward to the right. Although the questions did not refer directly to incremental improvements in air quality, the fact that persons in low pollution areas are on average less willing to pay for a total solution than those in high pollution areas indirectly implies that "marginal" willingness-to-pay diminishes.

Figure 6–2. Community "demand" for water quality.

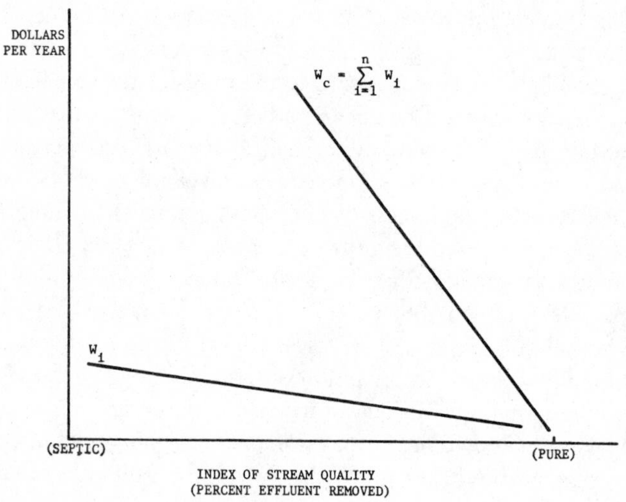


Returning to our illustrative example of a polluted watershed, each of the *n* individuals in the community has a downward sloping willingness-to-

Table 6–2
Willingness-to-Pay Per Month
for Pollution Control

| | High Pollution Area | | Low Pollution Area | | |
|---|---|---|---|---|---|
| Type of Solution | Mean | Variance | Mean | Variance | *P** |
| 1) Complete solution | $0.62 | $0.43 | $0.43 | $0.07 | .80 |
| 2) Private solution | 0.55 | 0.37 | 0.45 | 0.15 | .80 |
| 3) Neighborhood solution | 0.62 | 0.28 | 0.46 | 0.46 | .95 |

**P* is the probability that the observed difference in mean responses is significant, that is, not due to chance.

Source: Ridker, *Economic Costs*, p. 82.

pay schedule ($W_i$ in Figure 6–2) which measures his marginal evaluation of improved water quality in terms of money (i.e., claims to other goods). To compute the entire community's marginal evaluation for clean water, one must sum the individual $W_i$ curves vertically; this summation is labelled $W_c$ in Figure 6–2. Notice that the curves are summed vertically for this public good in contrast to the usual horizontal summation carried out to aggregate demand for a private good. Since a single level of the public good (clean water) can be simultaneously enjoyed by all individuals, the community's marginal evaluation for any particular level of stream quality is found by adding up the marginal evaluations of each individual; hence the vertical summation.[10] Suppose that the public good in question, stream quality, can be provided only by reducing the rate of effluent discharged from a factory upstream. In general, emissions may be reduced by a variety of methods such as direct treatment, changes in production processes, substitution among inputs, etc., all of which are costly. Figure 6–3 shows the marginal cost of reducing waste emissions measured in biochemical oxygen demand (BOD) from a beet sugar plant. Notice that marginal costs rise as the rate of discharge approaches zero (100 percent removal). Sharply rising marginal costs seem to be a phenomenon encountered in all areas of pollution control.

The appropriate level of pollution control activity is found by combining the community's marginal evaluation schedule and the marginal cost curve as shown in Figure 6–4. The point where the two curves cross has, of course, a special significance. At that point the marginal evaluation of an incremental improvement in stream quality is identical to the cost of providing it. It is easy to show that $Q^*$ is the appropriate level of provision for this public good; any increase in stream quality above $Q^*$ would involve costs that outweigh benefits, while reduction to a level below $Q^*$ would forego benefits that are greater than the costs saved.

The failure of private market incentives to allocate an optimal amount of resources for provision of this public good is also shown in Figure 6–4. Since $W_i$ represents an individual's willingness to pay for stream quality, it can be seen that a private individual acting alone would provide no more than $Q_i$ units of stream quality. This is the point where marginal private benefit is equated to marginal cost. Once this level is provided, there is no incentive for other individuals to enhance stream quality, since all can freely enjoy $Q_i$, and any increase in pollution abatement will involve costs that outweigh private benefits. Since the good in question is public, joint consumption by the community is indicated and the amount provided will

10. Simple vertical summation implies that the good is purely public, i.e., that the economies from joint consumption are complete.

Figure 6–3. Incremental costs of reducing biochemical oxygen-demanding (BOD) content of lime, flume, and condenser water wastes from 2700-ton-per-day beet sugar plant.

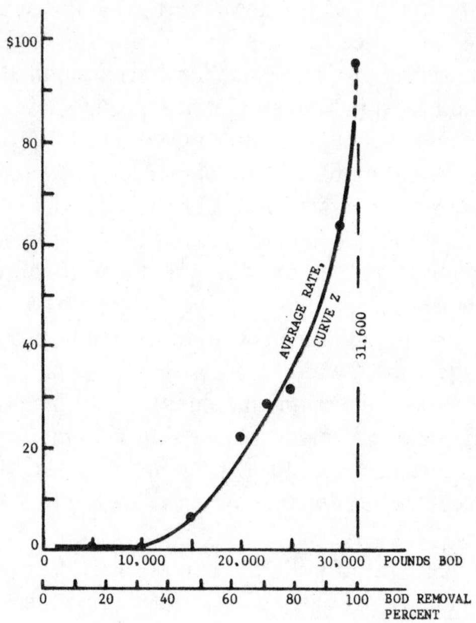


Source: *Second Annual Report of the Council on Environmental Quality* (Washington, D.C.: U.S. Government Printing Office, 1972), p. 119.

be the same to each citizen. The decision on how much to supply and how to finance its provision must, therefore, be a collective one.

## Policy Options

The foregoing discussion shows that private markets react only to private costs and benefits, i.e., those which are borne or captured by individuals. In cases where the benefit gained (or cost borne) by an individual is only a fraction of that accruing to society at large, the incentives in private markets fail to allocate resources efficiently. Collective action by the community to equate marginal social costs and benefits is needed to reach an optimal outcome.

Characterizing the solution is only part of the battle, and problems of implementing it remain. Any comprehensive strategy to control environmental pollution will reallocate a substantial portion of the nation's re-

Figure 6–4. Determination of the optimal level of stream quality.

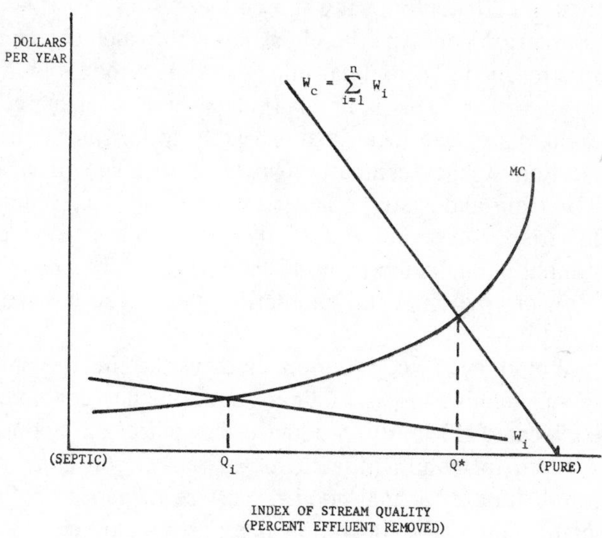


sources. However, some policies may accomplish the task more efficiently than others. In order to weigh the merits of alternative policy options, criteria or goals for an optimal policy are needed.

## Criteria for Policy Selection

A minimum feasibility requirement is that a policy be capable of meeting society's stated environmental quality goal. This is a criterion which any acceptable policy must be able to attain. However, even this initial goal is not as straightforward as it may seem. So far, we have implicitly assumed that levels of environmental quality are uniquely related to rates of discharge. In fact, the effect of waste emission upon stream or airshed quality depends upon a variety of climatic, meteorological and hydrological conditions. For example, the life-sustaining capacity of a river depends upon the level of dissolved oxygen present (as well as toxic concentrations, acidity and other factors). When organic waste is added to the water, oxygen-consuming bacteria begin to decompose the waste, reducing it to its chemical constituents, and lowering the river's level of dissolved oxygen in the process. But oxygen levels in the river also depend upon the rate at which new oxygen is absorbed from the atmosphere; this is a function of the depth of the water, its temperature, turbidity, rate of flow, and surface area. Thus, the effect of a particular rate of discharge upon the stream's life-support capacity depends upon a variety of water conditions. From this it follows that a policy which attempts to meet a given stream quality goal must be able to tailor regional emission patterns to local water conditions.

A second criterion concerns the efficiency with which the environmental quality goal is reached. An optimal policy will meet that goal at the lowest possible cost to society. This is crucial, since the cost of merely satisfying existing federal, state, and local goals is likely to be substantial. Environmental Protection Agency estimates (however reliable) place the cost of attaining stated air and water quality standards at $62 billion over the 1970–1975 period.[11] Expenditures of this magnitude can be expected to create substantial public reaction, and it is likely that the public will be less opposed to tough environmental standards than to the costs of achieving them.

A third and often neglected criterion concerns the effect of environmental policy upon the relative prices of final goods in the economy. When resources are allocated efficiently, product prices reflect the opportunity costs of resources used to manufacture them as well as consumer preferences. When the production of a final good or service degrades or "uses up" an environmental resource, the foregone value of this resource should show up through costs of production in the price of the final product. Thus, an efficient policy will readjust relative prices for final consumption items in the economy and will induce consumers to substitute away from those goods which produce pollution as a by-product.

## Evaluation of Alternative Policy Options

The four alternative implementation strategies most often proposed are: pollution standards, taxes on the emission of effluent, subsidies to emitters for pollution abatement, and institution of markets in "rights to pollute." As we have seen, environmental problems arise because the incentives in private markets, as presently instituted, fail to use the environment wisely. Accordingly, the four policies listed above can be viewed as attempts to either circumvent the market, simulate an efficient market solution, or set up a "new" market directly.

### Effluent Standards

The most straightforward of these four policies and the easiest understood is the effluent standard. In its ideal form, it is a legal maximum on the amount of a particular type of waste which may be discharged into the

11. *Second Annual Report of the Council on Environmental Quality* (Washington, D.C.: U.S. Government Printing Office, 1972), p. 111.

environment per time period. To see how it works, examine the case of a single firm polluting a watershed. In order to correct the situation, the local water pollution control agency estimates the marginal social cost and benefit functions, arrives at an optimal goal ($Q^*$) for stream quality and translates this into a legal standard on emissions. Setting and enforcing this standard thus attains the feasibility requirement for an optimal policy.

One can see how this policy fares in terms of the other two criteria of performance by examining how the firm would react to such a standard. Since the firm is pursuing profits, it will attempt to minimize the effect of the standard upon its rate of profit, i.e., it will seek to meet the standard at the lowest possible cost. This will probably be accomplished by a variety of actions such as on-site treatment, changes in production processes or substitution among inputs. Combining such measures in a cost-minimizing fashion would attain the second goal. While waste emissions would be reduced efficiently, the activity would raise the firm's costs of doing business. Its marginal cost schedule for producing output would shift up and, if other competing firms face similar standards, the price of the final product would rise.

Under ideal conditions, a pollution standard can, therefore, achieve all three policy goals. However, careful examination of the conditions needed for this result shed light on areas where problems may arise. First of all, the emitter is faced with an effluent standard and allowed to meet it in any fashion he chooses. In practice, however, this is seldom the case. Typically, the control agency will specify that a particular treatment device must be installed or that a particular grade of fuel must be used. For example:

> In one of the major U.S. industrial cities, current regulations in regard to sulfur content in fuel call for a limit of 1 percent sulfur in oil, which will be reduced to 0.5 percent in 1972 and 0.3 percent in 1973. In coal, this limitation is now 2 percent and is scheduled for reduction to 1 percent in 1971 and 0.3 percent in 1972. It is significant that sulfur in fuel, which hurts no one until it is converted to sulfur dioxide, is sharply limited, whereas in the state in which this industrial city is located, there is no regulation on sulfur dioxide emission.[12]

While such a policy can attain the desired rate of reduction, it does not permit the emitter to meet the standard in the least costly fashion. In fairness it should be noted that at present the technology available for monitoring emissions is in its infancy; thus, monitoring inputs or overseeing production processes may, for the time being, be the only feasible way of

12. P. Sporn, "Possible Impacts of Environmental Standards on Electric Power Availability and Costs," in *Energy, Economic Growth and the Environment,* S. H. Schurr, ed. (Baltimore: Johns Hopkins U. Press, 1972), p. 73.

enforcing a standard. Still, the heavy emphasis placed on monitoring inputs seems unjustified.

Another possible shortcoming can be identified by noting that the example was framed in terms of a single firm polluting a watershed. More often several firms will be involved, producing a variety of products and employing a wide variety of technologies and inputs. The problem then becomes the allocation of the allowable effluent among the several emitters. Of course, one could insist on proportional reductions by all emitters and still attain the first policy goal ($Q^*$), but the second and third goals are in doubt.

In order to efficiently allocate the permitted waste load among emitters, detailed information must be available on the technological opportunities of each firm. For example, suppose there are two firms with marginal cost functions for waste reduction as shown in Figure 6–5. The adopted standard

Figure 6–5. Allocating pollution standards.

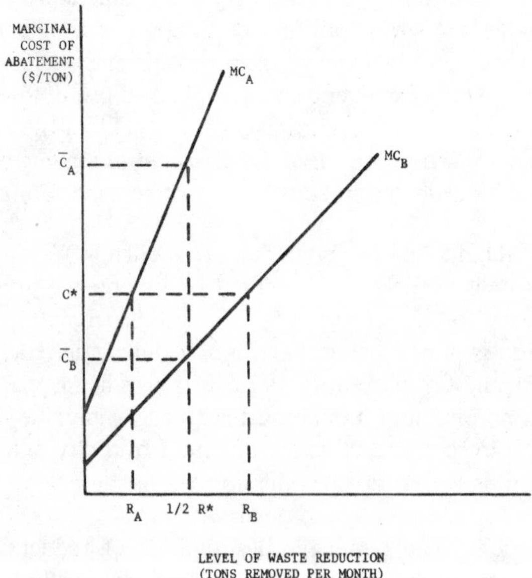


requires removal of $R^*$ tons of waste per month. Suppose this standard is allocated to the two emitters in an "equitable" fashion, requiring each to reduce wastes by ½$R^*$. From the diagram it is apparent that with this policy, the cost to firm $A$ from reducing waste by an incremental amount ($\bar{C}A$ is substantially above $B$'s marginal cost ($\bar{C}B$). Since it is more costly at the margin for *A* to treat his waste than it is for *B*, the total cost of attaining $R^*$ could be reduced by relaxing *A*'s standard and tightening *B*'s. It is always possible to reduce costs by shifting treatment activity to that firm that can remove waste most efficiently (i.e., at lowest marginal cost). When the marginal cost of removal is equal for both firms, no further changes in the allocation of the quota can reduce cost. This situation occurs where *A*'s level of removal is $R^*_A$ and *B*'s is $R^*_B$ (of course, $R^*_A + R^*_B = R^*$) and the marginal cost of further abatement is $C^*$ for both firms.

In order to achieve such a result via standards, one needs detailed information on the technological opportunities (i.e., marginal cost curves) for each firm. In the two-firm case, this may not be an insurmountable problem. But when it is noted that there are often dozens of firms polluting a given watershed, generally producing dissimilar outputs, and using a variety of technologies, the dimensions of the problem grow rapidly. Furthermore, it would probably be necessary to go to the individual emitters in order to obtain detailed knowledge of the abatement costs of each firm. However, it is in the economic interest of each firm to misrepresent its treatment cost function, since overestimation of costs will reduce the firm's required level of abatement.

In summary, an effluent standard can meet the first goal, reducing pollution to the desired level, but it falls short of the second and third. As currently practiced, standards will not allocate resources efficiently and provide a least cost solution. Further, although prices of final products will rise, they will not do so in an optimal fashion; i.e., there will still be (positive or negative) discrepancies between marginal social costs and prices.

### Effluent Taxes

The most widely proposed alternative to the standard is the effluent tax. This method relies upon the profit motive and impersonal market forces to produce the desired result. The higher the tax, the greater the incentive for polluters to reduce emissions. In principle any given level of pollution control can be attained by a tax set equal to the marginal benefit of waste reduction. As noted earlier the optimum occurs where the marginal social cost and benefits from control are equated. Thus, choosing an optimal standard implicitly requires estimating the optimal tax.

The tax works by internalizing the presently neglected external costs of economic activity and making these costs a normal part of doing business. If a manufacturer wants to use the waste assimilative capacity of a natural resource, he must pay for it. It is, therefore, in his own best interest to economize on its use. Any action to reduce his level of emissions, whether by on-site treatment, recycling, process changes, or modification of or substitution among inputs, will reduce his tax bill and increase profits. It will be profitable to reduce emissions up to the level where the marginal cost of reduction is equal to the tax rate.

Since all firms in the same watershed or airshed will face the same tax,[13] it follows that the tax will cause the marginal cost of further treatment to be equal for all. Of course, the actual levels of reduction will vary among firms as treatment costs vary. Those firms which can reduce emissions with relative efficiency, i.e., have a relatively low marginal cost of reduction, will undertake a relatively larger share of pollution control and will have lower tax bills. Going back to Figure 6–5, it can be seen that this is the least-cost solution. Furthermore, since the external costs of production have been internalized by a tax, this new cost will show up as an increased price for final products. As noted previously, when relative prices in the economy change, consumers will be induced to substitute away from those goods whose production degrades environmental resources and toward cleaner products. Notice also that the effluent tax does not require the control agency to obtain detailed information on the technologies of individual emitters as the standards system does. Hence, there is no incentive for the polluter to consciously misrepresent his costs of reduction.

In terms of the goals considered, effluent taxes clearly dominate a policy of individual pollution control standards. Most importantly, effluent taxes can reduce the real resource cost of attaining any given level of environmental quality. Equivalently, for any given expenditure of resources, a system of charges will provide a greater degree of environmental protection.

The importance of this point cannot be overemphasized. In detailed studies of pollution control in the Delaware Estuary,[14] researchers estimated the economic costs of reducing wasteloads under alternative abatement schemes. The goals to be met were "stream standards" expressed in terms of dissolved oxygen (DO) levels for the estuary. The policy options considered were:

*Uniform treatment:* A scheme representative of conventional water pollution control programs whereby all dischargers must remove a specified equal proportion of their respective wasteloads before discharging into the water body.

*Least cost:* A policy which intensively examines each discharger's technological options for waste reduction, compares these options with the specific water conditions at each outfall, and specifies the allowable waste-

13. This assumes, of course, that water or atmospheric conditions are uniform throughout the controlled region.

14. The information in this section was taken from Edwin L. Johnson, "A Study in the Economics of Water Quality Management," *Water Resources Research,* (April 1967), pp. 291–305.

load for each individual emitter in such a way that total costs of abatement are minimized.

*Single effluent charge:* A uniform price per unit of oxygen demanding material discharged applied to each waste source.

*Zone effluent charge:* An effluent charge which varies with the geographical location of the waste discharger and depends upon local stream conditions.

Since the assimilative capacities of a stream will differ by location (according to local water conditions as noted earlier), an efficient policy would vary allowable emission levels accordingly. The least-cost policy takes this consideration into full account by tailoring effluent standards to water conditions existing at each individual discharger's outfall. The uniform treatment and single effluent charge policies made no such attempt; thus, under these schemes waste treatment will be overly extensive in areas where the assimilative capacities of the water are relatively high. The zone effluent charge system partially accounts for differing stream conditions by dividing the estuary into a number of regions which have similar water characteristics and levying different charges in different zones. By increasing the number of zones, costs under this system approach those for the least-cost policy.

The figures in Table 6–3 show estimated abatement costs under alternative control policies. Despite the fact that these figures do not include administrative and information costs, they do help corroborate the hypothesis that effluent standards, as presently administered, allocate waste reduction resources in a less efficient manner than would (single or zoned) effluent charges. For water quality goals in the range below 4 mg DO/litre, expenditure of resources for uniform treatment is in the range of 25 to 100 percent higher than that required under single or zone effluent charges. Cost

Table 6–3
Typical Economic Costs of Treatment to Achieve Specified DO* Goals

| | | Treatment Costs (millions of dollars per year) | | |
|---|---|---|---|---|
| DO Goal | Uniform Treatment | Single Effluent Charge | Zone Effluent Charge | Least Cost |
| 2 | 5.0 | 2.4 | 2.4 | 1.6 |
| 2—3 | 8.4 | 7.7 | 6.3 | 5.8 |
| 3 | 11.2 | 7.7 | 7.4 | 6.9 |
| 3—4 | 20.0 | 12.0 | 8.6 | 7.0 |
| 4 | 23.3 | 23.0 | 23.0 | 16.0 |

*Dissolved oxygen in mg/litre.
Source: Johnson, "A Study," p. 297.

differences are most marked in the range of 3–4 mg DO/litre. Since attainment of the 4 mg/litre goal requires almost 100 percent removal of all wastes, the costs of the three policies tend to converge at this level.

If administrative and setup costs were included, the total cost figures would, no doubt, change significantly. Due to the obviously large data requirements for the least-cost and zone effluent charge systems, these two policies would be the most costly to administer. In all likelihood, the uniform treatment scheme would require the smallest administrative outlay. Furthermore, the present technology for monitoring emissions on a continuous basis is not well developed. To the extent that a system of charges requires more accurate information than effluent standards, this factor may further mitigate in favor of legal standards. Little is known about the magnitudes of these effects and a detailed investigation is beyond the scope of this chapter. The political feasibility of alternative policies is briefly analyzed on pp. 174–176.

### Pollution Control Subsidies

Pollution abatement subsidies or "bribes" provide incentives to decrease waste emissions in the same way that effluent taxes do. A subsidy presents the entrepreneur with a new source of revenue, and since it is tied directly to effluent reductions, the entrepreneur will reduce emissions up to the point where the marginal revenue (subsidy) per unit of abatement is equal to the marginal cost of abatement. If one views this policy as a lump-sum grant to emitters which is then taxed away as wastes are discharged, the symmetry of the tax and subsidy policies becomes more apparent. In principle, a subsidy of $10 per ton of emission reduced will bring forth the same level of abatement as a tax of $10 per ton on waste discharges.

Since bribes and charges operate in a similar fashion, the allocative efficiencies of effluent charges carry over to the policy of paying abatement subsidies. All firms will find it profitable to reduce emissions in the least costly (most economically efficient) manner. Further, since all firms face the same subsidy rate (if environmental conditions are homogeneous), abatement resources will be allocated among firms in an efficient manner. Finally, the various measures undertaken to reduce emissions will raise the marginal costs of producing final products. These rising costs will be reflected in higher prices for final products, thus rearranging consumption patterns in an optimal fashion. Although there has been some controversy over an alleged asymmetry between bribes (or subsidies) and charges, if both policies are administered in a symmetric fashion the outcomes will be identical.

The subsidy scheme does, however, involve substantial problems in implementation. In current practice, subsidies are generally not offered for effluent control as such, but rather are tied to the installation of a particular type of pollution control equipment. Thus other, possibly more efficient means of control such as process changes are not undertaken. For example, federal grants to municipalities for construction of waste treatment plants do not provide an incentive for commercial and industrial firms to reduce their discharges. In fact, to the extent that these subsidies are passed along in the form of reduced sewer charges, the incentive may be perverse.

Even if subsidies are tied directly to discharge reductions, as they should be, this policy still encounters difficulties. Since the amount of the subsidy depends upon waste reduction, a logical question is "reduction from what level?" Ideally the answer would be "from that level which would have prevailed without the subsidy"; but how is one to determine what that is? The recipient of the subsidy has an incentive to overestimate his presubsidy rate of discharge.

Assuming that this latter dilemma could be reconciled, there is still an important long-run problem with this policy. Suppose that the firm affected by a subsidy is in a competitive industry and that emissions are a direct function of the rate of output so that abatement can be accomplished only by reducing production. Although a system of bribes will raise the firm's marginal cost of production, it will lower average costs (as shown in Figure 6–6) and yield positive economic profits. The curves labeled *MC* and *AC*

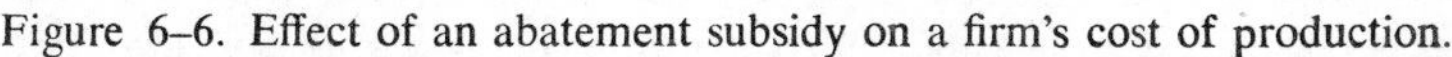
Figure 6–6. Effect of an abatement subsidy on a firm's cost of production.

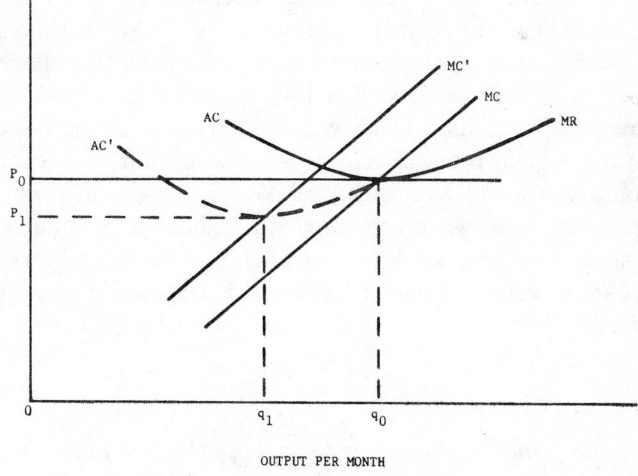


depict the marginal and average cost functions for the firm before the subsidy, while *MC′* and *AC′* show the situation after subsidy is instituted.[15] In

15. In Figure 6–6 the subsidy for abatement is viewed as a reduction in the firm's cost of producing output. One could view it as an addition to the firm's revenue function instead. The outcome reached will be the same whichever approach is taken.

Figure 6–6 the average cost curve has shifted down to $AC'$ as a result of the subsidy. Notice that the two $AC$ curves coincide at the presubsidy rate of output. This must be true if subsidies are paid only for reductions from the old profit maximizing rate of output.[16]

If all firms in the industry receive the subsidy, the marginal cost curves of all will shift up, causing the industry's short-run supply curve to shift up. In the short run, the price of the final product rises and quantity demanded falls. However, the reduction in each firm's average costs and the rise in market price both act to increase profits in the industry. In the long run, competitive industries abhor profits in much the same way that nature is said to abhor a vacuum. Without a conscious government policy to restrict entry, new firms will flock to the industry, driving down price until economic profits are eliminated. The result would be each firm producing at the minimum point on its new average cost curve $(AC')$. Prices would therefore fall to $P_1$, quantity demanded in the market would increase, and the resulting amount of waste emission would be nonoptimal. In the long run, government action would be needed to restrict the number of firms in the industry. Over time, however, as cost conditions and demand conditions in the industry change, such a policy would restrict the market from reacting to these changes.

Note that the effluent tax encounters none of these problems, and it has another less obvious advantage as well. In order to pay a subsidy, the government must obtain revenues from somewhere, which means raising taxes. In markets which are not characterized by external costs, private decisions allocate resources efficiently, and excise taxes will distort this allocation. To pay the subsidy, resources must therefore be misallocated elsewhere. An effluent charge, on the other hand, generates revenue at the same time it corrects a disparity in resource allocation. The resulting pollution charge revenue could be used to reduce excise taxes elsewhere, thus providing an added benefit. In short, when compared with other policy options such as taxes, the subsidy scheme has little to recommend it. Possibly its only advantage is that it would encounter less political opposition from industries being regulated.

## Marketing Rights to Pollute

The most recent policy proposal, and perhaps the most interesting from a conceptual standpoint, is institution of an actual market to allocate pollu-

16. The subsidy can be expressed in simple terms as $s(d_o - d)$ where $s$ is the rate paid per unit of abatement and $d_o$ and $d$ are, respectively, the presubsidy and postsubsidy rates of waste discharge. Notice that the subsidy "dries up" completely if the firm returns to its presubsidy rate of discharge (i.e., $d = d_o$). Since discharges of $d_o$ correspond to the old profit maximizing rate of output $q_o$, it follows that the firm's total and average costs are the same with or without the subsidy at this rate of production.

tion control resources, suggested by J. H. Dales.[17] Unlike other schemes, it does not seek to bypass or imitate a market solution, but rather aims at creating markets where none previously existed. Because Dales's idea is a fairly novel one, it is difficult to assess the administrative and political difficulties such a scheme may encounter, but, theoretically, it combines many of the advantages of both the effluent standard and effluent tax policies.

One of the often cited advantages of a system of effluent standards is that our present institutional and technological constraints make such a system easier to administer than a system of effluent charges. The straightforward and easily understood effect of a standard accounts for much of the support this approach has in bureaucratic circles. Furthermore, the tradition of legislative precedent is much stronger for standards than for taxes. However, as noted earlier, standards as presently applied fail to allocate activities efficiently among dischargers and thus, on efficiency grounds, charges are preferable.

The policy proposed by Dales essentially opts for a standard on total emissions but employs market forces to efficiently allocate the total allowable wasteload among dischargers. This is accomplished by selling units of the total standard to individual emitters. Take, for example, the case of a hypothetical water quality control agency, seeking to manage stream quality. Initially, via the political process or through direct estimation of costs and benefits, the agency would adopt some standard for stream quality (perhaps expressed in terms of dissolved oxygen levels). Examining water conditions at various reaches on the river, the "stream standards" would be transformed into a system of zoned effluent standards, essentially a set of limits on the maximum amount of effluent that could be discharged into each reach of the river. Having established the policy that during a specified time period no more than $Y$ tons of effluent could be discharged into a certain region on the river, the public agency could issue $Y$ pollution rights and auction them to individuals. Law would specify that anyone emitting $Z$ tons of waste during the time period must hold $Z$ pollution rights. Presumably, the standard would be set below the present rate of discharge, so that pollution rights would be economically scarce and would command a positive price. Profit maximizing firms would find it to their advantage to undertake waste reduction up to the point where the marginal cost of treating an extra ton of waste is equal to the market price of a right to discharge. Those firms which could reduce waste efficiently would be induced to do so and avoid the cost of purchasing pollution rights.

The market price for rights to pollute would act in the same fashion as an effluent tax to bring about an efficient allocation of resources. The external costs of production would be internalized, through the purchase price

17. J. H. Dales, "Land, Water, and Ownership," *Canadian Journal of Economics,* (November 1968).

of discharge rights, and become a part of the cost of doing business. As these new costs show up in the prices of final products, consumers would be induced to change consumption patterns, substituting away from goods whose production damages the environment and toward cleaner products. Furthermore, like the tax, the market solution does not require detailed information on the abatement technologies of individual emitters.

A further advantage of this policy is that it attacks the pollution problem at its very heart. As shown earlier, mismanagement of environmental resources is a direct result of the fact that exclusive property rights for the use of such resources presently do not exist. Instituting such rights and making them fully transferrable among users allows market forces to allocate the resource efficiently. Since the pollution rights can be purchased by anyone, environmental groups would be able to buy rights and not exercise them. Also, this system would automatically allow for regional growth. As Dales points out, "If the region experiences demographic or industrial growth the price of rights will automatically rise and induce existing dischargers to reduce their wastes in order to make room for newcomers."[18] It should be noted that the "market" proposed in this policy is not a natural market in the sense in which we think of markets for ordinary goods and services. In a natural market the amount of a good provided is determined by impersonal economic forces. In the present context the amount of environmental quality to be supplied is specified via political process. Only after the level of supply has been established are market forces allowed to provide it in an efficient manner.

The effluent tax and "market" solutions dominate the other policies considered on grounds of economic efficiency. While all policies considered could satisfy the feasibility requirement of attaining stated environmental quality goals, difficulties in implementing abatement subsidies and effluent standards make it unlikely that either of these strategies could allocate pollution control resources optimally.

## Political Realities and Economic Possibilities

Because environmental quality is inherently a public or collective goal, the forces which will determine the extent of its provision (via standards, charges, etc.) are political. Any discussion of rational alternatives for environmental protection must face up to the existence of political as well as economic constraints.

A well-known principle in politics is that "the cards are stacked against the innovator" and in favor of the status quo. Curiously enough, the inertia

18. Ibid.

and rigidity in the public sector seem to come not so much from rigidities in specific programs and policies, but rather from a rigidity in the political process which programs must navigate before being implemented. Such obstacles as separation of powers, vetoes, two-thirds majority requirements, and other checks and balances woven through our political fabric make radical change a rare phenomenon.

The result is a system in which decisions are made in a disjointed incremental fashion. This process, which considers only incremental or limited changes built closely upon past experience, has been formally described and defended as a process of "muddling through." It must be pointed out that this description of decision-making by small changes presupposes that current policies are producing generally satisfactory results and that problems and the means for dealing with them arise in a sort of continuous or incremental fashion. Where either of these conditions is absent, innovative policies may be adopted. The Torrey Canyon and Santa Barbara oil spills are cases in point of problems which arose in a dramatic, noncontinuous fashion and, in the latter case, the response was a reassessment of government policy toward offshore drilling.

Despite a few notable counterexamples, however, political inertia and a tendency to maintain the status quo are forces to be reckoned with when formulating policy. In light of this, it is important to recognize that government appears committed to direct regulation via legislated standards as a means to protect the environment. Political tradition and legislative precedent are much more firmly established for standards than for any of the other policies discussed. Furthermore, precedent frequently is useful as a guideline for settling disputes, and it often facilitates bargaining among parties whose interests conflict. When unprecedented changes in approach to dealing with problems are attempted, negotiations among conflicting groups frequently break down. Constitutional issues may be raised and the matter may be handed to the courts for arbitration. Due to the length process (and often capricious outcomes) of court settlements, this route is to be avoided.

For all the foregoing reasons it appears inevitable that direct regulation will continue to play an important role in environmental policy. Within this context, however, it may still be possible to incorporate some of the economic advantages of alternative policies such as effluent taxes and pollution rights. For instance, as presently formulated, standards generally set a maximum on emission rates and specify fines to be paid when these limits are exceeded. If the magnitude of these fines were directly related to the rate of discharge (so many dollars per ton), they would take on the nature of an effluent tax for excessive discharge. The resulting policy would be a hybrid of standards and charges; those emitters who could reduce waste efficiently would operate within the standard, while others would find it advantageous to pay the fines. The possibility for another hybrid policy emerges when one considers "variances" to adopted standards. As an example, a local air or water quality control agency could impose a set of severe standards with the intention of granting a certain prespecified number of variances to exceed these limits. Firms could then be allowed to bid competitively among one another to acquire these variances with the result that a degree of efficiency in the allocation of abatement resources would be achieved.

In summary, existing political institutions and established practices will constrain the range of policy choice and may not allow the selection of policies on grounds of economic efficiency alone. The fact that these constraints are political and social rather than technological or physical in nature does not imply that they are any less real or binding.

## Dynamic Extensions of Environmental Control

So far we have dealt with the "pollution problem" in its simplest form. In reality the field of environmental economics is much more fertile than the description herein may lead one to believe. The tasks of estimating the benefits of cleaner air or allocating pollution control resources over time, problems which arise when hydrological or atmospheric conditions vary seasonally, and the special considerations encountered with nondegradable wastes are but a few directions in which the analysis could be extended. The latter two areas are explored briefly in the pages which follow.

## Peak Loading and Low Stream Flow

In an earlier discussion it was noted that the assimilative capacities of a stream will vary regionally with water conditions. In simple terms, if the goal to be attained is some uniform level of stream quality, the appropriate limitations on discharges will be more stringent in areas where the assimilative capacity of the stream is relatively low. Thus, if a policy of taxing emissions is followed, the tax rate will vary according to local water conditions.

The same sort of conclusions apply when one allows for the possibility that stream conditions at any particular location may vary over time. This is an important phenomenon which is encountered frequently in both air and water pollution. For example, the rate of stream flow often varies dramatically over the hydrological cycle. Low stream flow occurring during the drought season reduces the stream's capacity at each location on the stream to assimilate oxygen-demanding waste.

To see exactly how these considerations affect the analysis, examine the two diagrams in Figure 6–7. The *DD* schedule in Figure 6–7a shows the marginal social value of stream quality. For any particular set of stream conditions, stream quality can be directly related to effluent emissions or,

Figure 6–7. Variable stream flow and the benefits of abatement.

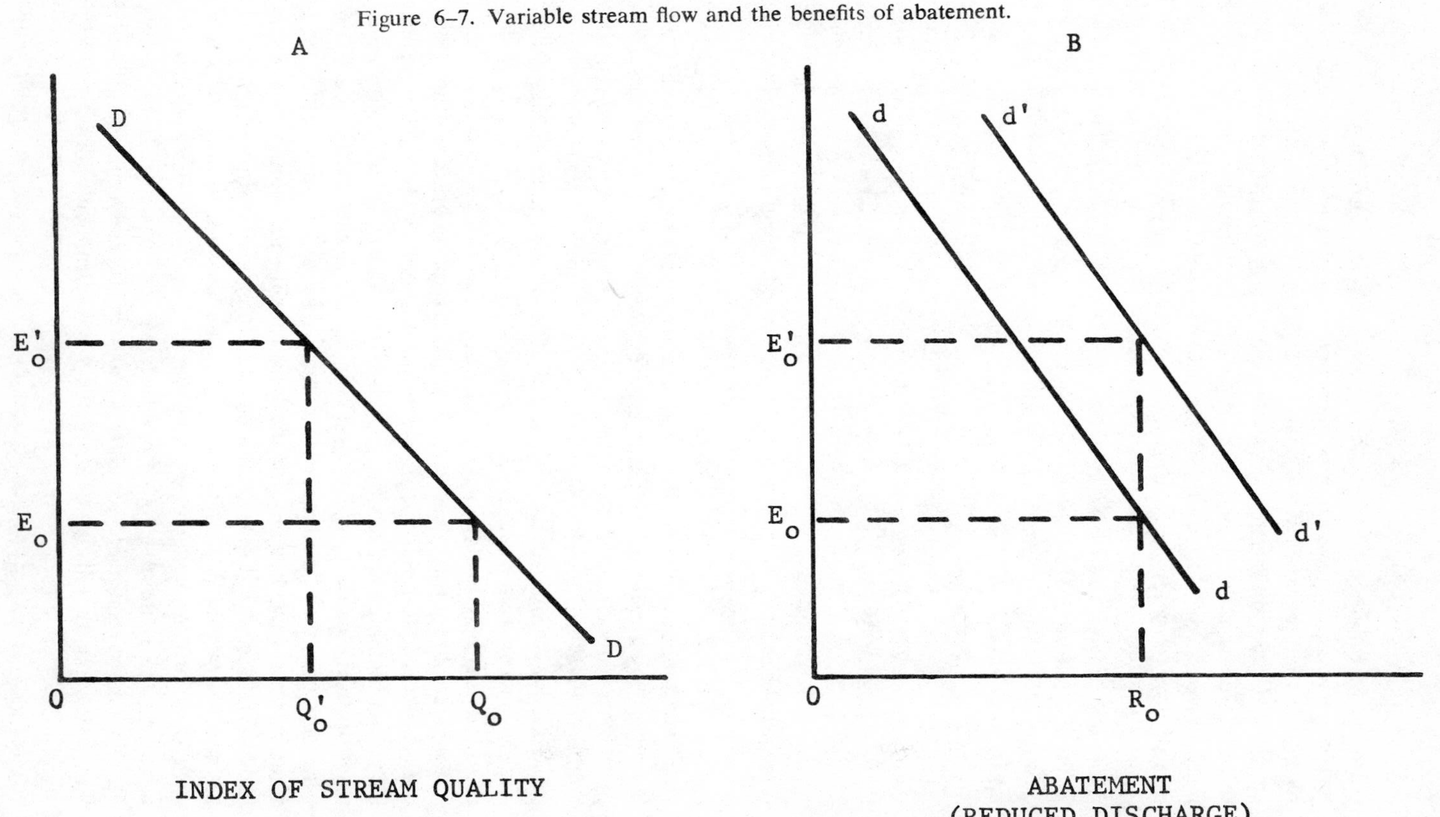

equivalently, to reductions from a specified level of discharge. For example, point $R_o$ in Figure 6–7b denotes a particular level of emissions, and, in turn, a particular level of stream quality $Q_o$ in Figure 6–7a. This can be seen by noting that the marginal social value of $R_o$ units of abatement is $E_o$, which is also the marginal social value of $Q_o$ units of stream quality. Thus, the entire curve *dd* is drawn with respect to specific water conditions. Suppose, however, that stream conditions change; specifically, assume that the rate of flow of water drops drastically. Since reduced flow diminishes the natural capacity of the stream to handle wastes, a given level of effluent reduction, say $R_o$, will now produce a lower level of stream quality $Q_o'$. Thus, the marginal social value of $R_o$ units of abatement rises from $E_o$ to $E_o'$. In fact, the entire marginal evaluation curve for waste reduction shifts up from *dd* to *dd'*. The water quality manager is now faced with a classic problem of peak demand.[19]

If there were no crucial fixed factors of production to determine a maximum capacity for reducing wasteloads, the appropriate solution would be fairly straightforward. By sketching a marginal treatment cost function in Figure 6–7b the reader can see that the appropriate rate of effluent reduction would vary between time periods. During periods of low flow, waste reduction should be more extensive; equivalently if an effluent tax is being levied, the tax rate should be higher during periods of low stream flow (assuming that marginal cost of abatement rises).

In fact, there may be a variety of ways to maintain stream quality during periods of low natural flow. Reducing rates of discharge by increased waste treatment, reduced production, process changes, or by storing effluent in holding ponds to be released when water conditions improve is one approach. In addition, the natural rate of stream flow may be augmented by releasing water from storage reservoirs upstream, or the assimilative capacity of the existing flow may be enhanced by artificial aeration or other means.

An interesting problem arises when fixed factors are important parts of the waste reduction or flow augmentation technology. For many processes it may be the case that marginal costs of improving water quality are constant up to the capacity of existing equipment. It may further be true that waste treatment or flow enhancement capacity can be augmented at constant costs as well, but only in the long run; in the short run, capacity is fixed and effectively limits the range for water quality improvement. Such assumptions are fairly descriptive of municipal waste treatment plants. In such situations the water plant manager is faced with the problem of determining the optimal level of waste treatment capacity. If the manager installs capacity sufficient to sharply curb emissions during periods of low flow, this capacity will be underutilized when stream conditions are normal.

19. See Chapter 4 in this volume.

The decision-maker must balance the cost of degrading stream quality by emitting during brief periods of low flow against the cost of letting valuable resources stand idle at other times when extensive treatment is not needed.

This type of problem was first analyzed in the context of a firm (usually a public utility) facing a demand curve which fluctuates between time periods. The two situations are, of course, analogous. Although a specific solution to this problem will not be developed here, it turns out that the optimal level of capacity depends upon the form of the short- and long-run cost functions, the shapes of the peak and off-peak marginal evaluation functions (for abatement), and the proportion of peak-demand time.

## Nondegradable Wastes

A nondegradable pollutant is one which is not readily degraded by natural forces when released into the environment. Since in the short run the substance can at best only be diluted, any positive rate of emissions of such substances tends to add to the existing stock. Obvious examples are certain pesticides (particularly chlorinated hydrocarbons which have a half life of more than ten years) and mercury. Another example is the one-way beverage containers which now litter our roadsides and beaches; oddly enough the "disposable" bottle may be one of the most durable objects yet invented. Not all pollutants occur as stocks; both water and air have remarkable capacities to cleanse themselves of many types of wastes. In these latter cases, the flow concept of pollution is probably more relevant.[20] For example, oxygen-demanding wastes when introduced into a stream at certain levels will damage water quality for a relatively short period and then disappear, as bacteria in the water reduce the waste to its natural constituents. Perhaps the best example of a pollutant which occurs as a flow is noise; upon emission it has an immediate effect and then disappears.

Effluents which occur as flows reduce social welfare by degrading the environment when they appear, but their effects are transitory. Based upon this hypothesis, the social benefits and costs of abatement were compared earlier in this essay to identify an optimal rate of discharge. Because the marginal costs of abatement rise and marginal social benefits diminish, it was found that the appropriate rate will generally be positive. However, when one considers the case where pollutants do not dissipate rapidly, the outcome may change dramatically. Emission of such a persistent substance

20. Actually the distinction between pollutants which occur as stocks versus flows is somewhat artificial. In a sense, all pollutants are stocks in that the condition of the receiving environment depends upon ambient concentrations. A decision to discharge today impairs the environment until the waste is assimilated. The difference between stock and flow pollutants is, therefore, a matter of degree and depends upon the amount of time required to assimilate the waste.

diminishes welfare not only in the present period but for all future periods until the substance eventually decays (consider, for example, the no-return beverage container). Likewise, the current condition of the environment is a function not only of the present rate of discharge, but of all previous emissions as well. If the substance does not decay at all, and if it is not technologically possible to reduce existing concentrations (as with DDT), a total ban on all emissions of the substance would not improve environmental quality, but would merely maintain it at its current level.

It follows that the condition of the environment, at any point in time, depends upon all previous emissions of persistent pollutants, i.e., upon the total stock of these substances in existence. In such a context, the term "optimal rate" of emission may make little sense, since any decision to discharge today will affect the state of nature in all future periods.

The problem is a dynamic one and a thorough analysis is beyond our present scope. However, it is at least possible that an optimal policy would call for an eventual ban on all emissions of such substances. If one believes that there exists an optimal level of environmental quality (however measured) and if the state of the environment is uniquely related to stocks of various substances, it follows that there are optimal stocks of persistent pollutants. When the optimal level is reached, it must be maintained, not increased, i.e., there must be no *net* additions to the stock, which in the context of a nondecaying substance implies a total ban on new emissions. In summary, the problems posed by nondegradable waste are complex, and the conclusions reached by careful research may be quite novel.

## Conclusion

As we have seen, incentives in private markets do not motivate man to manage his environmental resources wisely. Environmental pollution, a socially wasteful activity, is unfortunately privately profitable. Public intervention is, therefore, needed to redirect and reshape individual behavior in the marketplace. The problem is a complex one and there are no simple solutions. The road to environmental protection must be carefully planned to avoid economic inefficiencies and overcome political obstacles. A necessary first step is realizing the problem for what it is, an economic one which will require all of the analytical tools at our disposal.

Although the task ahead is difficult, the payoff is potentially very high. The social reward for better management of scarce resources rises with the degree of scarcity because any given improvement in decision-making produces greater social benefit. By the measure of any observant person, environmental quality is becoming increasingly and, perhaps, dangerously scarce. It is, therefore, high time to begin the task of searching for solutions in a well-reasoned, dispassionate manner.

## Commentary

Professor Deacon has examined the policy options for determining environmental quality. Environmental quality is a public good, consumed or enjoyed equally by all, i.e., it is common property and your enjoyment leaves no less for your neighbor. Consequently, it is difficult to exclude consumption and difficult to charge for its provision. Hence, left to its own devices, the private market system will fail to provide the optimal amount of environmental quality, i.e., the level which equates the marginal social benefits enjoyed by the public to the marginal cost of attainment. Environmental quality indeed has a cost, since other resources must be foregone to achieve clean air and pollution-free streams and rivers.

Chapter 6 pointed out several alternative policy options which would involve governmental action to remedy the failure of the private market. Setting effluent standards is a procedure which circumvents market forces. However, unless the governmental agency tailors the standards to account for both variations in environmental conditions and differences between industrial polluters in the costs of abatement, the effluent standard option will not achieve the optimal level of environmental quality. To obtain information necessary to this goal (which the market normally transmits), the regulating agency would incur large administrative costs and hence lose the main advantage of low administrative cost which recommends this policy in the case of a single effluent standard.

One option—the taxing of effluents—avoids the disadvantages of the regulatory standards approach or the subsidy scheme. The appropriate information is transmitted to polluters through the market by simulating the price which "internalizes" the social costs of pollution. In the absence of the effluent tax, these social costs of pollution are external to the private costs of the producers and hence ignored in their profit calculations and their output determination. An additional advantage of the effluent tax is that the higher costs of production are passed on to the consumer in terms of higher prices, and consumer demand is reallocated to commodities that involve less pollution. Professor Deacon sums it up in an insightful quote from Pogo, the swamp philosopher, "We have met the enemy and he is us."

In the next chapter on international monetary crises, John Pippenger turns from the case of public goods, where the private market is inadequate and public intervention is necessary, to a situation where most of the difficulties have been caused by inconsistent governmental policies designed to thwart natural market forces.

# 7

# What's All This Jazz About Gold? or Why the International Monetary System Fails to Work

John Pippenger

During the past few years international money markets have staggered from crisis to crisis. For example, in August 1971, the president of the United States threw the trading nations of the world into near panic by actions that were intended to correct a number of alleged crisis conditions. One act was to "unpeg the dollar" and to allow its value to fall relative to that of other currencies. The purpose of this was to help to correct a recurring "imbalance of payments." In addition, general restrictions were placed on trade in the form of a "tariff surcharge," an act that angered virtually all our trading partners. Trade restrictions were modified later, but the value of the dollar remained lower than previously. Our travelers abroad have felt the impact of this in virtually every purchase they have made while importers pay more for almost all foreign goods.

The terms quoted above have appeared in all the country's newspapers. Attempts by the press to explain what is going on have left people more confused than enlightened. It seems reasonable to ask why our president should take actions that anger other nations, invite retaliation, and appear to leave us worse off than before in terms of purchasing power abroad. Yet the final results were approved by monetary authorities of many nations so that future crises would either be prevented or controlled.

## Basic Concepts

To understand the system and how it operates, we need at least a basic understanding of how the money supply of a country is determined, the relation between the money supply and price level, and, finally, the relation between price levels and exchange rates. Some analytical tools are needed to understand these ideas (see glossary of terms, pp. 204–205).

### Money Supply

Commercial banks such as the Bank of America play an important role in determining the stock of money. By law such banks must hold a certain proportion of the money deposited in checking and savings accounts in the form of legal reserves. In most cases legal reserves are currency held by the bank plus the commerical bank's deposit at a central bank such as the U.S. Federal Reserve or the Bank of England.

Suppose, for example, a commercial bank has $1 million in demand deposits and $100,000 in savings deposits, and the law stipulates a 20 percent reserve requirement for demand deposits and a 5 percent reserve requirement for savings deposits. The bank under these conditions would be obligated to hold $205,000 in the form of legal reserves, i.e., cash on hand or deposits at a Federal Reserve Bank. If legal reserves fall below this amount, the bank may be subject to a penalty. In addition to these legal or "required" reserves, commercial banks want or desire additional reserves in order to protect themselves against adverse clearings or cash drains.

Cash on hand and deposits at a Federal Reserve Bank are the most liquid asset of a commercial bank and are used by commercial banks in much the same way ordinary businesses use money. Just as businesses as part of their profit maximizing activities hold some proportion of their assets in the form of money, so commercial banks in their search for profit hold some additional reserves over and above that required by law. Reserve requirements and desired additional reserves play a big role in determining the money supply.

#### Money Creation

Desired reserves ($DR$) are defined as the sum of the reserves the bank must hold by law plus the amount of additional reserves the bank wants to hold. Actual reserves ($AR$) are the total amount of cash (coin plus currency) the bank holds plus the amount of the commercial bank's deposits at Federal Reserve Banks. Surplus reserves ($SR$) are defined as actual reserves minus desired reserves, i.e., $SR = AR - DR$.

We can simplify the analysis greatly at this point with little distortion by assuming all commercial banks in the country are combined into one large bank. Given this assumption, consider the following scenario. The president of Amalgamated Commercial Banks, Inc. arrives at his office Monday morning to discover that the bank has actual reserves of $300,000 in the form of cash and deposits at Federal Reserve banks, but, given its current liabilities in the form of demand and savings deposits, the bank desires to hold only \$250,000; so the bank finds itself holding \$50,000 in the form of surplus reserves. That is, the bank is holding \$50,000 more in reserves than it wants to hold.

How can these surplus reserves be eliminated and the actual and desired level of reserves be made equal? The president of Amalgamated could donate the \$50,000 to charity, but this would only partly solve his problem and would probably make him rather unpopular with the stockholders. What the bank can do is to begin to make loans to businessmen and to buy securities such as government bonds. Suppose the bank buys \$50,000 in government bonds. The bank pays for these bonds with a check written on the bank. (A bank normally makes a business loan by crediting the amount of the loan to the checking account of the business.) Since Amalgamated is the only commercial bank in the country, whoever receives the check must deposit it in an Amalgamated bank. If the legal reserve requirement against demand deposits is 20 percent and the bank wants to hold an additional 5 percent in reserves, then desired reserves ($DR$) increase by \$12,500 so that surplus reserves ($SR$) fall by \$12,500. Remember $SR = AR - DR$, and desired reserves rise by \$12,500 while actual reserves remain unchanged.

The human computers among us will realize instantly that all the bank has to do to eliminate its surplus reserves is buy \$200,000 worth of bonds (or make loans worth \$200,000). With \$200,000 more in demand deposits, required reserves increase by \$40,000 ($200{,}000 \times 0.2$), and the amount of additional reserves the bank wants to hold rises by \$10,000 ($200{,}000 \times 0.5$), so that desired reserves increase by \$50,000, reducing surplus reserves to zero. At this point the bank would stop buying bonds or making loans. Note that at this point the bank has *created* \$200,000 in money by increasing demand deposits by \$200,000.

In order to be more realistic, the above scenario needs at least two major modifications. First, whoever sold the first \$50,000 worth of bonds might have chosen to deposit his check in his savings account rather than his checking account, in which case there would have been a smaller increase in the bank's desired reserves since the legal reserve requirement is smaller for savings than for demand deposits and also because banks generally want to hold fewer additional reserves for a dollar in a savings account than they do for a dollar in a checking account. To the extent that those who sell the bonds to the bank put part of the check they receive into their savings account, the bank would have to buy more than \$200,000 worth of bonds to eliminate \$50,000 in surplus reserves. As an extreme example, suppose all checks received by bond sellers are deposited in savings accounts, the legal reserve requirement against savings deposits is 5 percent and the bank wants to hold 3 percent of savings deposits in the form of additional reserves. Under these assumptions, for each dollar in savings deposits the bank wants to hold eight cents (8 percent) in the form of legal reserves. In that case the bank would have to buy $625,000 worth of bonds to eliminate $50,000 in surplus reserves ($50,000 = 0.08 × $625,000). Note that in this case the money supply defined as currency plus demand deposits is unchanged.

A second major modification is needed because as the public's demand deposits rise, there is normally also an increased demand for cash. Suppose the public wants to hold 20 percent of the money supply in cash. To keep things simple, let us ignore savings deposits. Beginning Monday morning with $50,000 in surplus reserves, the bank buys $50,000 in bonds. The public deposits $40,000 in its checking accounts and takes $10,000 in cash. As a result, actual reserves fall by $10,000 and desired reserves rise by $10,000 (25 percent of $40,000) so that surplus reserves decrease by $20,000 rather than $12,500 as they did when there was no cash drain. In this case the bank can eliminate its surplus reserves by buying only $125,000 worth of bonds. This generates a cash drain of $25,000 and a $25,000 increase in desired reserves.

Without resorting to tedious numerical examples, a little reflection (perhaps with pencil and paper) should reveal that the bank is going to make fewer loans and increase the money supply by less for a given amount of surplus reserves (a) the larger the cash drain, i.e., the more people want to hold money in the form of currency, (b) the larger is the reserve requirement, and (c) the more reserves banks want to hold per dollar of deposits. On the other hand, the more the public wants to hold savings deposits relative to demand deposits, the more bonds banks buy (or the more loans they make) for a given amount of surplus reserves, but the smaller the increase in the money supply. (The whole discussion, of course, applies in reverse if surplus reserves are negative.)

If what you have just read leaves you a little bewildered, relax. It was written to drive home only one point. When banks hold surplus reserves, that is, when they hold more cash and deposits at the Federal Reserve than they want to hold, they make loans, buy bonds, and increase the money supply. When banks hold fewer reserves than they want to hold, they call in loans and sell bonds, thereby decreasing the money supply.

An important point that was not considered in the above discussion is that as banks make loans and buy bonds in the process of reducing their surplus reserves, they increase the supply of credit, which tends to lower interest rates and increase bond prices. If surplus reserves are negative, then the money supply contracts as banks sell bonds and call in loans. Selling bonds and calling in loans tend to restrict the supply of credit and to drive up interest rates and drive down bond prices. But once the money supply stops expanding or contracting, this pressure to lower or raise interest rates disappears.

### Reserve Creation

Many factors, of course, affect the stock of money in the U.S. and other countries, but in almost every case the single most important factor is the amount of legal reserves held by commercial banks. Although the amount of legal reserves held by commercial banks in turn is affected by many factors, the amount of legal reserves can be effectively controlled by governments through the operations of central banks. The most important of these operations in practice is open market operations, i.e., the purchase or sale of government bonds by the central bank.

In the United States, the system of banks known as the Federal Reserve functions as the central bank. When the Federal Reserve buys government bonds, it pays for them with a check written on the Federal Reserve. The person or firm selling the bonds deposits the check in their commercial bank. The commercial bank in turn sends the check to the Federal Reserve for payment and is paid by having its checking account at a Federal Reserve bank increased by the amount of the check.

This means that if the Federal Reserve System buys $100,000 worth of government bonds, then commercial bank reserves rise by $100,000 (somewhat less if there is a cash drain). If commercial banks initially are holding no surplus reserves, they now find themselves with surplus reserves and begin the process of money and credit expansion described above, with the result that the money supply increases and interest rates tend to fall. A sale of government bonds by the central bank, of course, works in reverse, generating negative surplus reserves, contracting the money supply, and reducing the supply of credit, which tends to raise interest rates.

### How the Price Level Is Determined

After gaining at least a general idea about how the size of a country's stock of money is determined, let us turn to the relation between the stock of money and the price level. The natural place to begin is the classical quantity theory of money,

$$MV = PQ, \tag{1}$$

where $M$ is the stock of money, $V$ represents "velocity," the rapidity with which money changes hands, $P$ is some index of the price of goods and services, and $Q$ is a measure of the real output of goods and services in the country. In its crude form, $V$ and $Q$ are assumed constant so that a given percentage increase in the money stock generates an equal percentage increase in the price level. No assumption is made here that $V$ and $Q$ are constant. The only assumption required is that there are no systematic forces at work which tend, in the long run, to cause $V$ to rise by as much as $M$

falls, or vice versa. This is sufficient to guarantee that, in the long run at least, if the money stock rises significantly more rapidly than real output, then prices of goods and services rise.

As simple as this proposition is, it is very powerful and well supported by empirical evidence. There appears to be no historical period in which the stock of money rose significantly more rapidly than output for a substantial period of time, i.e., years—not days—and prices failed to rise. Conversely, there is no historical evidence that the stock of money ever fell significantly faster than output over a substantial period of time and prices failed to fall. Some historical events that support this interpretation of the quantity theory are the experience of the Black Plague in medieval Europe when output apparently fell with little change in the money supply and prices rose, the American experience after the Civil War when output rose faster than the money stock and prices fell, and recent inflationary episodes in Latin America. (The recent inflation in the United States is, from an historical point of view, neither very large nor very prolonged, but there is certainly no question that beginning about 1967 the money stock began to rise more rapidly than real output.)

### The Theory of Purchasing Power Parity

Our discussion has covered two of the three tools or theories needed to understand how the international monetary system operates or, perhaps more accurately, to understand the flaws in its operation that generate worldwide headlines. The final theory in this discussion is known as the theory of purchasing power parity. This implies that if prices rise in the United States by say 10 percent, over a given period, say two years, while prices in foreign countries remain unchanged, then the dollar price of foreign currencies will rise by 10 percent over the given two years.

Of course many factors play an important role in the determination of the price of one currency in terms of another on a day-to-day, month-to-month, or even a year-to-year basis. For example, Brazil's exports are dominated by coffee, and a severe drop in the world price of coffee normally would be reflected in a fall in the dollar price of the Brazilian cruzero. Fortunately, our purposes do not require a rigid form of the theory of purchasing power parity; all that is needed is the recognition that if prices rise (or fall) significantly faster in a given country than in other countries over a substantial period of time, then the price of other countries' currencies in terms of the given country's currency will tend to rise.

The basic rationale behind the theory of purchasing power parity is straightforward. Suppose the United States experiences a severe inflation. Prices double in one year, i.e., the purchasing power of the dollar falls by one half. Before the inflation, Americans were willing to pay $50 for a certain amount of Scotch whisky and English beer that sold for £50 in

Great Britain. Since British money must be bought before British goods can be purchased, this means Americans were willing to pay $50 for £50. If $50 bought £50, then the exchange rate between the dollar and pound was one dollar per pound.

After the price level doubles in the United States, Americans are willing to pay $100 for that bundle of Scotch whisky and English beer that still costs only £50 in Great Britain. This means Americans are now willing to pay $100 for £50. If £50 now sells for $100, then the exchange rate has also doubled from one dollar to two dollars per pound.

To take a concrete historical case: Both the United States and Great Britain experienced substantial inflation during and just after World War I. Inflation peaked in both countries in May 1920, at which time the exchange rate was $3.84 per pound sterling. In that month the index of U.S. wholesale prices stood at 269 and the U.K. wholesale price index at 340. During the next year there was a sharp decline in prices in both countries, after which prices recovered somewhat in the United States but continued to fall slowly with occasional small recoveries in the United Kingdom. By the end of 1925, the price of the British pound had risen to $4.85 and the wholesale price index in the United Kingdom had fallen to 155, while the U.S. wholesale index stood at 164. Although prices fell in both countries, they fell more rapidly in the United Kingdom than the United States, so that U.S. prices rose relative to British prices by approximately 25 percent from May, 1920 to December, 1925. During this same period the dollar price of the British pound rose approximately 30 percent from $3.84/£1.00 to $4.85/£1.00.

This is not an isolated incident. There seems to be no historical record of a case in which one country's price level rose (fell) significantly, relative to another's over a substantial period of time, and the price of the second country's currency fell (rose) in terms of the first country's. In addition, large changes in exchange rates over substantial periods of time have taken place only when there have been substantial changes in relative price levels.

### Institutions of the International Monetary System

The three basic ideas or theories needed to examine the international monetary system have now been discussed. The next step is to describe the institutional framework under which the present international monetary system operates and to consider two alternative institutional arrangements that have existed.

### Flexible Exchange Rates

Flexible exchange rates constitute the simplest international monetary system. Under a system of flexible rates, the exchange rate is determined by supply and demand in essentially the same way as the price of a stock such as General Motors is determined on the New York Stock Exchange.

There exists, at least conceptually, a demand and supply schedule for each currency in terms of every other currency. For example, a demand for and supply of British money in terms of U.S. dollars is shown in Figure 7–1. Assuming the demand and supply curves are linear simplifies the discussion without materially altering the analysis.

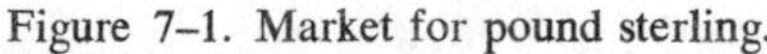
Figure 7–1. Market for pound sterling.

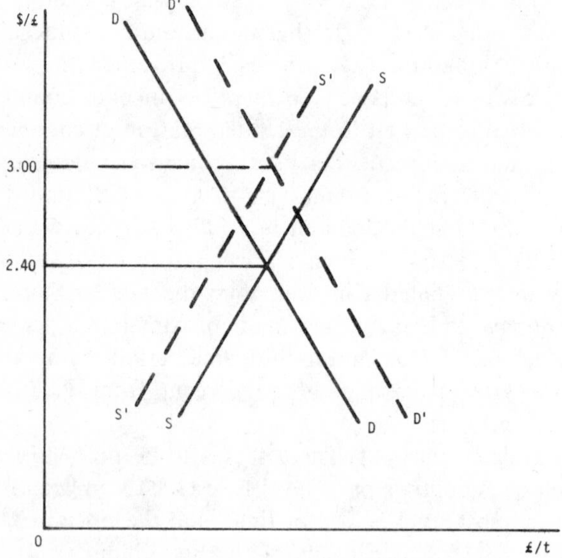


Under a system of completely flexible exchange rates, there is no government intervention in the market, and total demand and supply reflect only private demand and supply. Under these conditions the observed market price is determined by the intersection of the demand and supply curves as in Figure 7–1. As the demand and supply conditions shift under a system of flexible rates, the observed market price shifts.

Many influences, of course, can cause the demand and supply for foreign exchange to change, thereby changing exchange rates. For example, strikes, bad harvests, and changes in tastes all can affect the demand for and supply of foreign exchange. Our adoption of a weak version of purchasing power parity does not deny the existence of these other influences; rather it reflects the opinion that these other influences either are essentially temporary, e.g., strikes and bad harvests, or that while they might be important under some circumstances, these other influences do not appear historically to have been nearly as important as changes in relative price levels for determining long-run movements in exchange rates.

As a review, let's consider the effect of an increase in U.S. prices relative to British prices on the demand for and supply of pound sterling in Figure 7–1. Suppose initially one pound sterling costs \$2.40, as shown, and a Ford costs \$3,000, while an MG sells for £1,000 in Great Britain. Given the exchange rate, an American can either buy a Ford for \$3,000 or an MG for \$2,400 (£1,000 × \$2.40/£1.00). In Great Britain, on the other hand, a Ford costs £1,250 while an MG costs £1,000.

If, to take an extreme example, U.S. prices now rise by 25 percent, then the price of a Ford rises to \$3,750. In the absence of any change in exchange rates, Fords would become relatively more expensive as compared to MGs. Indeed, American goods in general would become more expensive as compared to British goods. Americans would then tend to buy more of the relatively cheaper U.K. products, thereby demanding more pound sterling in the foreign exchange market and shifting the demand curve for pounds in Figure 7–1 to the right from $D$ to $D'$.

From the British point of view, the price of British goods in terms of British money would tend to remain constant, while, at the original exchange rate, the British price of American goods would tend to rise. As a result, British residents would tend to buy fewer American goods and services and the quantity of pounds supplied in the foreign exchange market at each alternative exchange rate would tend to decline, shifting the supply curve in Figure 7–1 to the left from $S$ to $S'$.

Given a 25 percent increase in U.S. prices, and a 25 percent increase in the dollar price of the pound, the price of American goods relative to British goods will be the same as before the inflation, and the incentive for both American and British residents to shift from American to British goods will disappear. For example, before the U.S. inflation the price of a Ford relative to the price of an MG is \$3,000/\$2,400 or 1.25, while after the inflation and change in the exchange rate, the relative price is \$3,750/\$3,000 or 1.25.

To summarize, under a system of flexible exchange rates the price of foreign currency is determined by the private demand for and supply of foreign exchange. Although many influences affect the demand for and supply of foreign exchange in the short run, changes in relative price levels tend to dominate long-run changes in exchange rates.

### Adjustable Peg

The International Monetary Fund (IMF) need not concern us because of its minor role in the operation of the international monetary system, even though it is, in principle, the institution upon which the present system is built. The system is in practice run by the central banks of major countries over whom the IMF has very little control.

Most governments, in practice, choose an "official" price of the U.S. dollar in terms of their own currency. The United States in turn has an "official" price for gold. Until the summer of 1971 the Federal Reserve, acting for the U.S. Treasury, bought gold from and sold gold to other central banks reasonably freely at the then official price of $35 per ounce. The current "price" is now (1973) about $42 an ounce, but purchases and sales, especially sales, apparently are by negotiation rather than on demand.

Foreign central banks choose their official exchange rates largely on the basis of recent experience, but with a good deal of navel contemplation and consultation with the oracle at Delphi. Once an official rate is chosen, it usually is not altered until a crisis develops and the central bank believes it can no longer defend the official rate or that it soon will become impossible to defend the official rate.

Until that moment of truth arrives, the foreign central bank is obligated to keep the dollar price of the domestic currency within a narrow band around the official rate. Under the agreement reached in Washington in December 1971, each country is obligated to keep the market rate of exchange within plus or minus 2.25 percent of the official rate (before December it was plus or minus one percent).

### How the System Operates

The following example illustrates how this is done. In December 1971 the official price of the West German mark was set at approximately 31 cents per mark. Since the German central bank is obligated to keep the market rate within plus or minus 2.25 percent of this figure, there is an upper limit for the market rate of about 31.73 cents and a lower limit of about 30.33 cents as shown in Figures 7–2a and 7–2b.

There exists, at least conceptually, a demand for and supply of German marks in the foreign exchange market just as there exists a demand for and supply of any economic good in the appropriate market. If demand and supply curves intersect within the upper and lower limits as indicated in Figure 7–2a, then the rate determined by market forces alone, which is given by the intersection of private demand and supply, lies within the upper and lower limits, and the German central bank does not have to take any action to maintain the market rate within the agreed band around the official rate. If, however, private demand and supply intersect outside the band as they do in Figure 7–2b, then the exchange rate determined by private demand and supply conditions alone would lie above the upper limit.

The central bank can prevent the rate from rising above the upper limit by selling a sufficient number of marks. In the situation depicted in Figure 7–2b the dollar price of the mark would be 31.73 cents per mark if the

Figure 7–2a. Market for German marks.

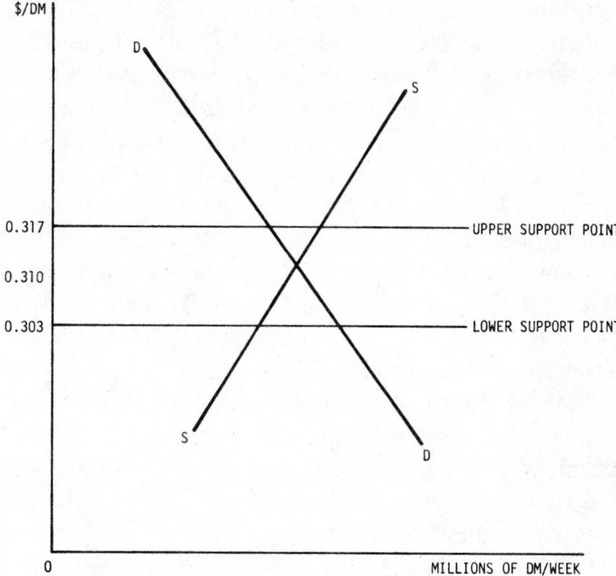


Figure 7–2b. Market for German marks.

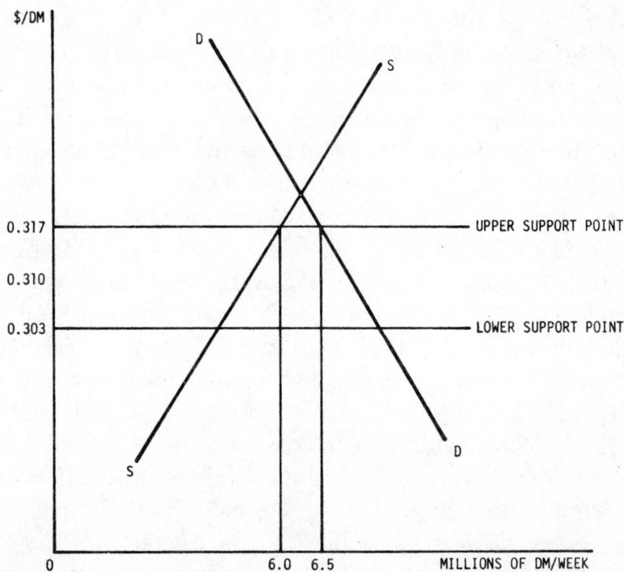

German central bank sold 500,000 marks per week. Of course, if the bank sold more marks per week, the exchange rate would be even lower.

A further illustration is shown in Figures 7–3a and 7–3b. In December 1971 Great Britain adopted approximately \$2.60 per pound as the official rate. Given the plus or minus 2.25 percent rule, this meant the Bank of England was obligated to keep the dollar price of the pound within a band whose upper limit was \$2.66 and whose lower limit was \$2.54.

If the exchange rate in the absence of central bank purchases or sales does not lie outside the agreed band, as shown in Figure 7–3a, then the Bank of England is under no obligation to either buy or sell pounds in the foreign exchange market. If, however, the private demand and supply curves intersect below the lower limit so that the market rate would lie below the agreed-upon band, then the Bank of England is obligated to buy enough pound sterling to at least bring the market rate up to the lower limit. In Figure 7–3b, if the Bank of England buys 125,000 pounds per week, which is just the difference between the quantity supplied and demanded privately at the lower limit, then the market price of pounds will be just at the lower limit. If the Bank buys more pounds per week, it can, of course, raise the market price above the lower limit.

To understand how the system operates, we must examine the effects of a purchase of pounds by the Bank of England. When the Bank of England buys pounds, it normally receives the pounds in the form of a check on a U.K. bank. The Bank of England normally "collects" the check by taking the amount of the check out of the account of the commercial bank on which the check is written. (The Bank of England is the central bank of Great Britain and every British commercial bank has an account there.) Since deposits at the Bank of England are part of the reserves of British banks, commercial bank reserves contract, the money supply tends to contract, credit conditions tighten and there is upward pressure on interest rates. Small intermittent purchases of pounds by the Bank of England of course have little impact, but if purchases each week are large or are repeated for many weeks, then the cumulative effects become important.

By contrast, the purchase of pounds by the Bank of England tends to expand the U.S. money supply and lower U.S. interest rates. When the foreign exchange dealer receives the dollar check from the Bank of England, he normally deposits it in his account in a U.S. commercial bank. If, as is often the case, the Bank of England check is written on a Federal Reserve Bank, then the U.S. commercial bank forwards the check to the Federal Reserve for collection and the commercial bank is paid by having its account at the Federal Reserve increased. This means commercial bank reserves in the United States increase, the money supply tends to increase, and there is downward pressure on U.S. interest rates.

If central banks operated in the purely passive fashion discussed up to

Figure 7–3a. Market for pound sterling.

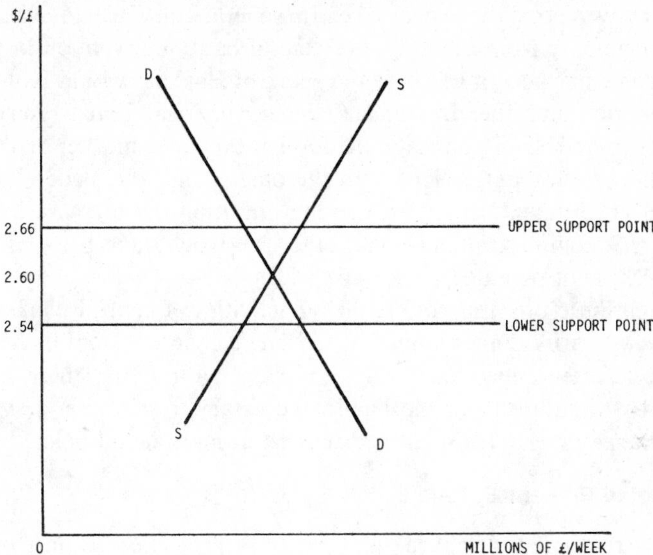


Figure 7–3b. Market for pound sterling.

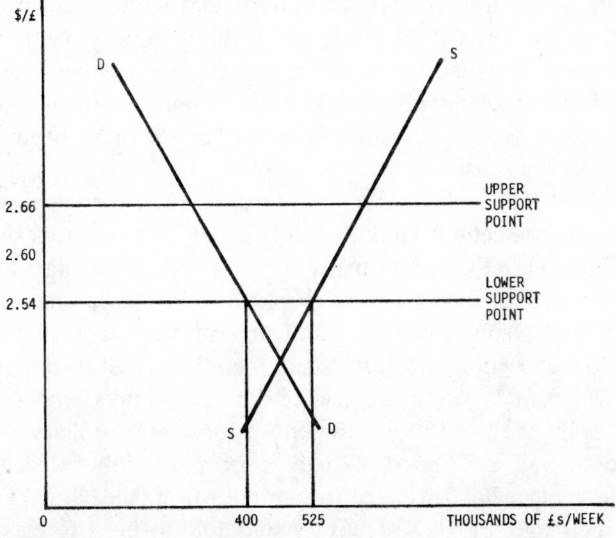

this point, then the present international monetary system would function very much like a gold standard (see pp. 197–200). Central banks, however, are very active, possibly hyperactive. In general, they try to insulate the domestic economy from the effects of central bank intervention in the foreign exchange market. In this case the Bank of England would buy government securities and thereby replace the commercial bank reserves lost through the purchase of pounds in the foreign exchange market by the Bank of England. In the United States, on the other hand, the Federal Reserve would sell government securities, thereby offsetting the increase in the reserves of U.S. commercial banks that otherwise would take place as a result of the purchase of pounds by the Bank of England.

Although these offsetting or sterilizing activities of central banks tend to insulate temporarily domestic money and credit markets from the effects of central bank intervention in the foreign exchange market, these activities also destroy the adjustment mechanism necessary to maintain a system of fixed exchange rates. This point is discussed in more detail below.

### Gold in the Present System

Partly as a result of cultural lag and partly as protection against inflation, central banks hold gold as part of their "international reserves." When a central bank buys its own currency, as the Bank of England did in the example given above, it normally pays for the purchase with a check denominated in dollars. As a result, each time it intervenes in the foreign exchange market to buy its own currency (sell dollars), the central bank's holdings of dollars declines; eventually it begins to run out of money in its checking account at the Federal Reserve. As a central bank's purchase of its own currency continues, it must rebuild its dollar checking account in order to pay for the domestic currency it purchases in the foreign exchange market. At first it may transfer funds from savings accounts it holds in the United States to its checking account, or sell U.S. government bonds it holds, but as these alternative sources are depleted, the central bank begins to sell gold to the U. S. Treasury.

When a central bank sells rather than buys its own currency, as in the German example, the central bank normally is paid with a check on a U.S. bank, which the central bank normally deposits in a checking account in the United States. If the central bank is forced to sell large amounts of its own currency over a substantial period of time in order to prevent the exchange rate from exceeding the upper limit, then the size of its dollar checking account will start to rise beyond what the bank thinks is a reasonable level. At this point the bank begins to deposit some of its dollars in savings accounts and to buy U.S. bonds. As the process of dollar accumulation continues, the central bank will try to buy gold from the U. S. Treasury. Until a few years ago the U. S. Treasury sold gold to most foreign central banks when they requested it. Today purchases and sales of gold by the

U. S. Treasury to foreign central banks appear to be by negotiation, with the Treasury selling gold only when it finds it convenient to do so.

A good deal of attention is paid to gold today. Changes in its official price take place with great fanfare and substantial declines in the U.S. stock of gold are viewed by many as a minor national disaster. Nevertheless, gold plays no essential role in the operation of the present international monetary system. Gold could be completely eliminated from the present system, and the fundamental operation of the foreign exchange market and other international markets essentially would be unaffected.

### The Gold Standard

There was a time, before World War I, when gold played a very important role in the international monetary system. From the late nineteenth century until WW I, most major western countries defined their currency as being equivalent to a certain amount of gold. This established an official price of gold. For example, the official U.S. price of gold at that time was approximately $20.67 per ounce, and the official British price of gold was approximately £4.25 per ounce.

Before WW I, a country's treasury or central bank bought and sold gold at the official price to anyone, not just to other central banks or treasuries as today. This fact, plus the existence of transportation costs, set an upper and lower limit to the market rate of exchange under a gold standard. Suppose it costs ten cents to ship one ounce of gold between the United States and United Kingdom. Under these conditions no one would pay more than $4.89 for pound sterling in the foreign exchange market because a purchase of 100 ounces of gold from the U. S. Treasury at $20.67 per ounce would cost $2,067, plus $10 to ship the gold to the U.K., for a total cost of $2,077. Since the 100 ounces of gold are worth £425.00, the cost per pound sterling comes out to about $4.89 per pound. Inasmuch as anyone could obtain pounds in this way, no one would pay over $4.89 per pound sterling.

A similar mechanism also established a minimum price for the pound. If someone in the United States were trying to sell pounds, he would never accept less than $4.84 per pound because he could always use the pounds to buy gold at the Bank of England, ship it back to the United States and sell it to the U. S. Treasury at $20.67 per ounce. Thus, the possibility of buying gold in one country at a fixed price and selling it in another at a fixed price sets an upper and lower limit to the exchange rate under a gold standard.

There were international financial crises before WW I, but even after we try to adjust for the softening effect of the passage of time, international monetary crises for major western countries before WW I do not appear to have been either as frequent or as severe as the crises that have plagued us since the end of WW II.

### Adjustment Mechanisms

Earlier it was stated that the present system has no automatic adjustment mechanism because central banks sterilize the effects of their intervention in the foreign exchange market. One crisis out of the series of recent crises between the U.S. dollar and German mark illustrates the problem. This particular crisis probably began in the fall of 1970 and culminated in the spring of 1971, when the German central bank was no longer able to keep the dollar price of the mark within the proscribed limits and was forced to let the mark find its own value in the market with only sporadic intervention by the central bank. First, a hypothetical gold standard mechanism under the conditions that existed in the spring of 1970 between the dollar and mark will be examined. Second, what actually took place under the present system will be detailed.

#### Gold Standard Mechanism

Consider the following hypothetical scenario. In the fall of 1970 the demand for and supply of marks is such that there is a tendency for the market price to rise above the upper limit determined by the gold content of the two currencies and the cost of shipping gold (see Figure 7–4). Given the gold content of the two currencies and the costs of shipping gold from the United States to Germany, no one will pay over \$0.28 per mark. At that price the

Figure 7–4. Market for German marks.

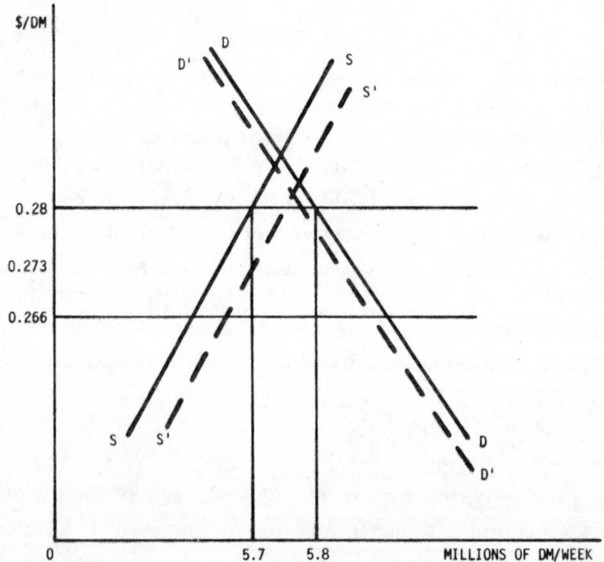

demand for marks in Figure 7–4 exceeds the supply by *DM* 1,000. Under a gold standard those who want the additional 1,000 marks at this price (or others acting for them) buy gold in the United States and ship it to Germany. The German central bank buys *DM* 1,000 worth of gold and the U. S. Federal Reserve, acting for the U. S. Treasury, sells about $280 worth of gold. (The Federal Reserve, of course, did not exist before 1913, but at this point we are considering what would have happened in 1970–1971 if the United States and Germany had been on a gold standard.)

Those who purchase gold pay for it by a check on their commercial bank in the United States. The Federal Reserve collects the check by taking the amount out of that bank's account with the Federal Reserve. Consequently, the reserves of commercial banks decline in the United States, and, as a result, the money supply tends to contract, credit conditions begin to grow tighter, and interest rates tend to rise.

The opposite chain of events takes place in Germany. There the purchase of gold by the central bank is paid for by a check on the central bank. Whoever sold the gold deposits the check in his commercial bank in Germany. That bank then forwards the check to the central bank for collection and receives an increase in its deposits at the central bank. As a result, commercial bank reserves in Germany tend to rise, the money supply tends to expand, credit conditions tend to loosen, and interest rates tend to fall.

A moderate gold flow from the United States to Germany that lasted a day, or a week, probably would have little effect on the position of the demand and supply curves shown in Figure 7–4, but as the gold flow persists two things begin to happen. First, German interest rates tend to decline as a result of the additional loans made and bonds bought by German banks, while American interest rates tend to rise as American banks call in loans and sell bonds. Second, the increase in the money supply in Germany and the decrease in the U.S. money supply tends to raise the German price level relative to the U.S. price level. It should be pointed out that the tendency for German interest rates to fall relative to U.S. rates disappears once the gold flow stops and the expansionary pressure on the German money supply and contractionary pressure on the U.S money supply disappear, while the shift in relative price levels remains after the gold flow stops.

The tendency for U.S. interest rates to rise relative to German rates as gold flows from the United States to Germany acts as a temporary or short-run adjustment mechanism. As U.S. interest rates rise relative to German rates, German investments, e.g., German stocks and bonds, become less attractive to American investors. As a result the demand for German marks, which must be used to buy these assets, declines. The alteration in relative interest rates makes American stocks and bonds more attractive to Germans, so the demand for dollars by Germans increases because American assets must be purchased with dollars, not marks.

As long as the gold continues to flow, there is pressure for U.S. interest rates to rise relative to German interest rates, and this shifts the demand for marks in Figure 7–4 to the left to $D'$ and the supply of marks to the right to $S'$ The supply curve shifts to the right because as Germans buy more dollars in order to buy more American assets, they sell more marks to foreign exchange dealers. The rightward shift in the supply of marks and leftward shift in the demand as a result of the alteration in credit conditions in the two countries, tend to shift the intersection of the demand and supply curves down toward the upper limit.

Although this adjustment mechanism is temporary, remember credit conditions eventually return to "normal" once the gold stops flowing. It is reinforced by another mechanism that is permanent, but tends to operate more slowly. As gold flows from the United States to Germany, commercial bank reserves decline in the United States and increase in Germany. As a result the U.S. money supply tends to contract and the German money supply tends to expand. Unlike interest rates, when the gold flow stops the U.S. money supply tends to remain in its reduced state, and the increase in the German money supply tends to persist.

If the gold flow is "large" or lasts for a substantial period of time, then there is a significant change in the money supplies in the two countries. As a result, German prices tend to rise and American prices tend to fall. This tends to make American goods cheaper relative to German goods, and German goods more expensive to Americans. Germans, therefore, buy more American goods. In order to buy American goods they must first buy American money with marks, and the supply of marks tends to increase. Americans on the other hand buy fewer German goods and tend to demand fewer marks. The result is that the demand for marks shifts to the left and the supply of marks shifts to the right. As long as gold continues to flow and the U.S. money supply continues to contract while the German money supply expands, U.S. interest rates tend to rise relative to German interest rates, the U.S. price level tends to fall relative to the German price level, and the intersection between demand and supply in Figure 7–4 moves down until it hits the upper gold point, and then the gold flow stops.

#### No Adjustment Mechanism under a Pegged Rate

The above description of what would have happened between the mark and dollar beginning in the fall of 1970 was hypothetical—what the historians would call an "historical counterfactual." This is a fancy way of saying it did not happen that way. What did happen was quite different. In the fall of 1970 the demand for marks did exceed the supply of marks as seen in Figure 7–4. In order to prevent the exchange rate from rising above the upper limit of about 28 cents per mark, the German central bank sold marks for dollars. If the Federal Reserve and German central banks had remained passive, the official sale of marks would have tended to increase the reserves of German commercial banks and reduce the reserves of U.S. commercial banks, and the system would have functioned in essentially the same way as a gold standard.

Central banks, however, were not passive. They were, if anything, hyperactive. The contractionary effects of official sales of marks on the reserves of U.S. commercial banks were swamped by Federal Reserve purchases of securities, while the expansionary effects of the official sale of marks on the reserves of German commercial banks were deliberately offset by the sale of government bonds and other actions taken by the German central bank in order to prevent "imported inflation."

With no tendency for the reserves of German commercial banks to increase and those of U.S. commercial banks to decrease, there were no forces at work that tended to raise U.S. interest rates relative to German interest rates or to lower U.S. prices relative to German prices. In short, no automatic adjustment mechanism was operating. As a result, the German central bank found itself faced with what appeared to be a perpetual sale of marks.

It gradually became clear to businessmen and speculators alike that the dollar price of the mark could only rise; it couldn't possibly fall by any significant amount in the foreseeable future. Consider what would happen at a racetrack if the crowd slowly began to realize that one horse for all practical purposes could not lose the race. That, indeed, is what happened in the foreign exchange market. Gradually people began to realize that it was not a question of whether the dollar price of the mark was going to rise, it was only a question of when—tomorrow, next week, or next month.

In order to avoid a loss on their dollar holdings, international corporations began to move their liquid assets out of the United States into Germany, which, of course, further aggravated the central bank's problem of holding the exchange rate by shifting the demand for marks to the right. In addition, speculators who saw a chance to make a nice gain with very little risk began to lend a hand.

The combined motives of protection against losses due to revaluation and speculation eventually generated a tidal wave of U.S. dollars into Germany. This tidal wave crested early in May 1971. The *Federal Reserve Bulletin* for October 1971 described what occurred:

> . . . in late March and early April, the German Federal Bank initiated a new program of forward mark sales in Frankfurt, with the objective of reassuring the market on the stability of the mark parity. This operation succeeded in temporarily restoring a fragile measure of confidence, but

> the German government remained confronted with the dilemma of how to make its restrictive credit policy effective while simultaneously allowing its business corporations unfettered access to the Euro-dollar market.
>
> Early in May, a report by the main German economic research institutes, recommending either a floating of the mark rate or revaluation as the best solution to this and other policy dilemmas, was greeted sympathetically by certain high-ranking German officials. The market seized on this apparent shift of policy, and speculative funds flooded into Germany. The German central bank was forced to buy dollars in mounting volume: more than $1 billion on May 3 and 4 and a further $1 billion in the first 40 minutes of trading on May 5, at which point it withdrew from the market.

With the German central bank no longer intervening systematically in the foreign exchange market, the dollar price of the mark came to be determined essentially by the private demand for and supply of marks.

Situations similar to the one for the German mark described above appeared for other major currencies in the spring of 1971. The developing international monetary crisis of the spring and early summer of 1971 undoubtedly was one of the major considerations that forced President Nixon to make his famous speech of August 15 announcing price and wage control and also announcing that the United States no longer felt obligated to buy and sell gold to other central banks and treasuries at $35 an ounce.

## An Alternative System

The system of pegged rates that existed from the end of WW II until the summer of 1971 and was revived in a modified form in December of that year appears to be doomed to failure. This is because it lacks an automatic adjustment mechanism that will absorb some of the shock from short-run blows to the system and permit the system to make the fundamental long-run adjustments necessary to maintain a system of fixed exchange rates. If we are going to build a viable international monetary system for the future, the present system needs to be modified in at least one of two directions. The first is to build institutional arrangements guaranteeing that price levels in the major industrial nations essentially move together, at least in the long run. A major step in that direction would be to prevent central banks from completely offsetting the effects of official intervention in foreign exchange markets so that countries losing international reserves would be forced, in the long run, into a "tight money" policy, while those acquiring international reserves would experience an expansionary monetary policy. The second possible modification is to abandon pegged rates and let the exchange rate be determined in the market by the forces of supply and demand.

Given the political realities of today, neither of these solutions is feasible. Central banks are not about to surrender their control over money markets to balance-of-payments considerations; and a country losing reserves and faced with a high level of unemployment in this day and age cannot be expected to follow a tight monetary policy when such a policy is generally believed to aggravate the unemployment problem. Many economists, including this writer, believe that a system in which exchange rates are determined in the marketplace by private demand and supply with no government intervention is a viable alternative to the present system. For good or ill, that opinion is not widely held outside the ranks of professional economists.

If both of these alternatives are ruled out by political considerations, what then can be done? Compromise! A system can be built in which central banks are strongly discouraged from following extremely different policies, thereby reducing at least short-run changes in relative price levels while at the same time instituting techniques to permit gradual changes in exchange rates over longer periods of time.

Several plans have been proposed for introducing long-run flexibility into exchange rates while at the same time maintaining a system that behaves very much like a system of pegged exchange rates in the short run. There are several ways to do this, but they all operate in essentially the same way. When the market rate is at or near the upper (lower) support point, the official rate is raised (lowered) slightly.

How this system would work might be illustrated by another historical counterfactual. Let's return to the market for German marks in the fall of 1970. As shown in Figure 7–4, the private demand for and supply of marks intersect above the upper support point and sales of marks by the German central bank are required to keep the rate within the proscribed limits. Under a compromise system the U.S. and German central banks would, at the very least, be encouraged not to completely offset the effects of official intervention, but far more important, under the compromise the official rate would gradually rise. Since the upper and lower support points are established by adding and subtracting a certain amount to the official rate, the upper and lower support points also rise. The system now has an automatic adjustment mechanism as long as the intersection of the private demand and supply curves does not rise faster than the official rate.

There are trade-offs possible in this compromise solution. The slower the official rate is allowed to rise when the market rate is at or near the upper support point, the more central banks must gear their policies to seeing that the intersection of the private demand and supply curves either falls or does not rise as fast as the official rate is permitted to rise. At one extreme, if the official rate is not permitted to rise at all, then central banks must surrender long-run control over the country's money supply in order to obtain an automatic adjustment mechanism. At the other extreme is the situation in which the official rate is always raised fast enough to keep the intersection of the private demand and supply curves either within or very close to the upper and lower support points. In that case, the system operates essentially like a free market, and central banks can effectively ignore what is happening to international reserves when making decisions about monetary policy.

## The Future Outlook

Some sort of compromise between a gold standard and flexible exchange rates is being widely discussed among academic economists and those outside the ivory tower who are concerned with the international monetary system. Unfortunately, there is at present little evidence to suggest that the present system of pegged rates is likely to be systematically modified along the lines of the compromise discussed above. Events have forced and will continue to force certain modifications. In December 1971 the width of the band around the official rate was widened from ± 1.0 percent to ± 2.25 percent. Several countries recently have been forced off a pegged rate, letting the market find its own level and then repegging. This is an ad hoc, as opposed to a systematic, compromise. Most discouraging of all is the apparent tendency for countries to try to maintain fixed exchange rates through the use of various controls such as tariffs, quotas, interest equalization taxes, and a whole host of bureaucratic regulations designed to force the intersection of the demand and supply curves within the upper and lower support points.

Most economists view the increase of governmental controls in this area with about the same relish they would view an outbreak of bubonic plague. The primary rationale and justification for a system of pegged exchange rates is that stable exchange rates promote international trade and capital flows. For governments to then adopt controls such as tariffs and quotas that choke off world trade and capital flows in order to maintain a system of pegged exchange rates is ludicrous.

## Glossary of Terms

*Actual reserves*
: Currency plus demand deposits at the central bank.

*Commercial banks*
: Banks with checking accounts held by private citizens and corporations.

*Desired reserves*
: Required reserves plus the legal reserves commercial banks want to hold in addition to required reserves.

*Exchange rate*

The price of foreign money in terms of the U.S. dollar, e.g., the dollar price of pound sterling, \$/£.

*Flexible exchange rates*

A system in which exchange rates are determined by private demand and supply.

*International reserves*

The gold and foreign exchange held by central banks and treasuries.

*Legal reserves*

Currency plus demand deposits at the central bank.

*Open market operation*

Purchases or sales of bonds by a central bank.

*Required reserves*

The amount of legal reserves banks are required to hold by law.

*Reserve requirement*

The proportion of a dollar in checking or savings accounts that banks must hold in the form of legal reserves.

*Stock of money*

Currency plus demand deposits at commercial banks that are held by the public. Interbank deposits are excluded.

*Surplus reserves*

Actual reserves minus desired reserves.

## Commentary

International monetary crises add another example to the list of markets (such as farm products, oil, gas) that suffer from government intervention. Chapter 7 notes that long-run changes in the relative price levels of different countries will tend to be equilibrated by changes in the rate of exchange between these countries' currencies. Intervention by governments in an attempt to stabilize the rate of exchange will tend to exhaust currency reserves and precipitate an international monetary crisis in the absence of a mechanism operating to affect relative price levels, the original source of the problem.

As Professor Pippenger elaborated, mechanisms are available that will maintain stable exchange rates and adjust domestic price levels until relative prices in trading countries balance the demand and supply of foreign exchange at the pegged exchange rate. However, these price adjustment mechanisms require domestic monetary expansion and contraction to be linked to international transactions. In contrast to the pre-World War I gold standard era, governments today are committed to policies of full employment and economic growth. Governments are no longer willing to let their country's monetary policies, price levels, interest rates, and credit conditions be dictated by international trade. Thus, the monetary policies which would adjust domestic price levels and permit a fixed exchange rate are no longer politically feasible. Nonetheless, governments and central banks are reluctant to relinquish their role of intervention in international currency markets and thus permit these markets to function as the adjustment mechanism in response to changing price levels.

The chapter that follows returns to a situation where some government intervention is justified, but the case is complicated by the fact that higher education has the attributes of both a private and a public good. Donald Winkler examines the question of who benefits the most from investment in higher education—the individual or the public. The answer to this question should help us to determine who ought to pay.

# 8

# Higher Education: Should Students Pay Their Way?

Donald R. Winkler

Higher education is in a state of financial crisis. Unprecedented growth in college enrollments and increases in costs have forced private colleges and universities in recent years to dip into endowment funds in order to make up current operating deficits. Furthermore, public colleges are encountering increasing resistance to their budget requests from state legislators, who also face a multitude of other pressing social problems. If institutions of higher learning are to continue in their efforts to provide equality of educational opportunity, revenue must be increased. The major question facing policy-makers is how this revenue should be raised. Should the government increase its subsidy to higher education, or should students be required to pay a larger share of the costs through increased tuition? Some policy-makers have even suggested that students should be made to pay the full costs of their education.

The magnitude of the problem is reflected in enrollment trends in this country over the past century. In 1870 less than 2 percent of the college-age population was enrolled in degree programs in higher education. This figure increased to 8 percent by 1920 and 15 percent by 1940, but the greatest jump occurred in the post-World War II era. The enrollment ratio increased from 18 percent in 1945 to 30 percent in 1955, and the most recent figures indicate that total college enrollment includes almost half the college-age population. Rising enrollment ratios, combined with the impact of children born during the postwar baby boom reaching college age, has resulted in enrollment more than doubling between 1958 and 1968.

Expanding enrollments, of course, result in increasing costs. In the late 1960s universities began to feel a cost-revenue squeeze.[1] Private institutions

1. The financial crisis in higher education is described in detail in Earl F. Cheit, *The New Depression in Higher Education,* Carnegie Commission on Higher Education (San Francisco: McGraw-Hill, 1971).

had to use endowment funds to meet current operating expenses, and public institutions encountered increased legislative resistance to increased budgets, even though enrollment was continuing to expand. Three options are open to colleges and universities: (1) stabilize or cut enrollment, (2) decrease costs per student enrolled, and/or (3) increase revenue from benefactors, governments, or student tuition. None of these alternatives is easy to implement.

To reduce enrollment at existing tuition levels may deny equality of educational opportunity to those minority groups just now beginning to enroll in larger numbers. To decrease costs by increasing class sizes or by eliminating expensive laboratory courses may diminish the quality of education. To attempt to decrease costs through heavier teaching loads or lower faculty salaries may lead to heavy faculty resistance and catalyze faculty unionization in addition to lowering the quality of education. It appears that while costs could be cut slightly, if we are in favor of high quality educational opportunities for all those who qualify, the only alternative is an increase in revenues.

Since endowment contributions from individuals are voluntary and not directly amenable to social control, we shall concentrate our discussion on a question of major current interest—should the government or students pay? The proponents of higher tuition sometimes argue that all the benefits of education are captured by the individual; hence, the student should pay the full costs of his education.

In this chapter we use the economic notion of investment in *human capital* to investigate the size and nature of the *private benefits* of higher education and to demonstrate how increasing tuition might affect the individual's decision to invest in himself.

The opponents of higher tuition argue that higher education generates substantial benefits to society which will not be provided in socially optimal amounts in the absence of public subsidy. They argue that the existence of these externalities dictates that society should continue to highly subsidize higher education. That is, society should meet increased enrollments with increased public budgets. We attempt to evaluate this argument by identifying and examining rough measures of the *social benefits* resulting from public and private investments in human capital.

## The Notion of Human Capital

Human capital is broadly defined as the productive talent, skills and knowledge embodied in an individual. Since all individuals do not have identical amounts of these characteristics, they do not, of course, embody equal amounts of such capital.

When an individual attempts to develop himself in order to increase his future earning power or enjoyment from life, economists interpret this as investment in his own human capital. Undertaking a course of study at an institution of higher education is one means of improving one's skills and knowledge and, hence, is one form of investment in human capital.

Benefits from investment in human capital include both future monetary and psychic income. Since psychic income is difficult if not impossible to evaluate in money terms, economists usually focus on the monetary benefits (i.e., wages and salaries) in establishing a measure for the value of human capital. The measure of human capital used throughout this paper is the money income which an individual may expect to receive in the future.

How a student who invests in his human capital by attending a college or university in order to obtain a degree can expect to earn a higher income in the future is illustrated in Figure 8–1. If a student terminates his educa-

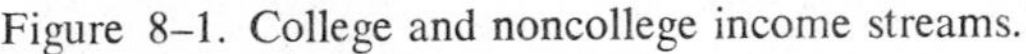

Figure 8–1. College and noncollege income streams.

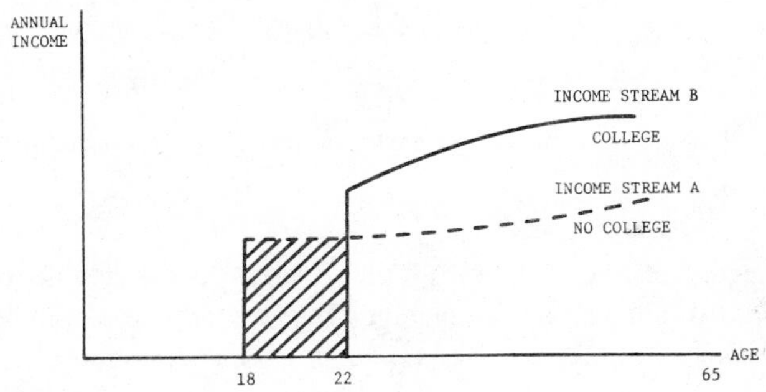


tion with the completion of high school, he can expect a stream of future income depicted by the broken line, *A*. If he decides to attend college and after four years obtains a degree, he can expect a higher stream of future income depicted by the solid line, *B*. However, it should be noted that the total income received by this person between the ages of 18 and 65 *could be smaller* if he attends college than if he does not! One reason is that while in college a student must forego the income he could have earned if he had worked instead of studied. The total income foregone by a student who has no part-time employment is given by the shaded area in the figure.

Empirical evidence suggests, however, that, in general, students need not worry that their total lifetime incomes might be lower as a result of attending college. Figure 8–2 exhibits the relationship between educational attain-

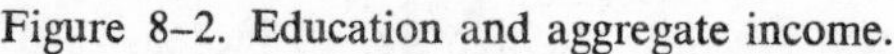


Figure 8–2. Education and aggregate income.

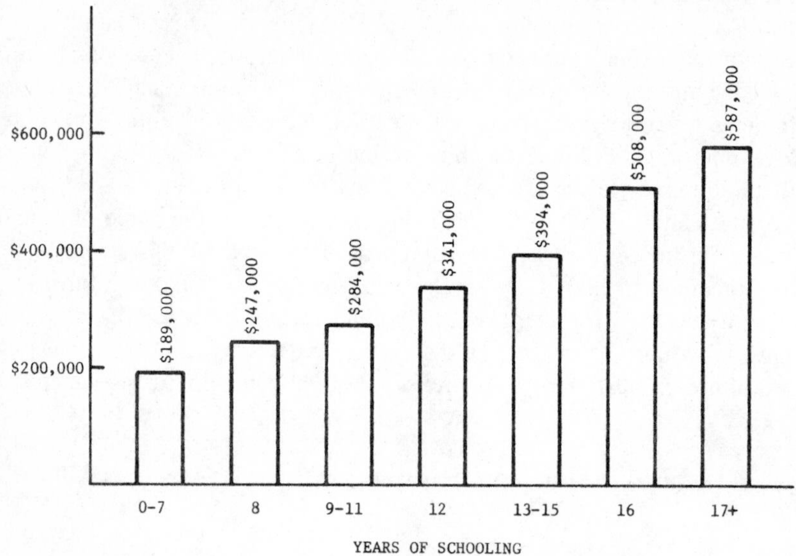


Source: U.S. Office of Education, National Center for Educational Statistics, *Digest of Educational Statistics, 1968* (Washingon, D.C.: U.S. Government Printing Office), p. 16.

ment and aggregate undiscounted lifetime income for males in the United States in 1966. It shows that an average college graduate can expect to receive half again as much income as a high school graduate who does not enter college.

The amount of human capital embodied in an individual is not determined solely by investment in education, however. The amount of human capital is also affected by one's innate ability, social background, and family business contacts. Two individuals graduating from college at the same time certainly do not expect to earn identical future incomes if one has a father who sells used cars and the other has a father who is president of General Motors. Table 8–1 shows there is great variation in terms of incomes received by high school and college graduates. Of the college graduates 21.6 percent actually earn below the median annual income of persons who have high school educations only.

The important aspect of educational investment from the point of view of the individual is how that investment increases his or her human capital. The son of a used-car salesman may find that a college education greatly enhances his future earning power, even though he has no valuable family contacts in business. In making the decision whether to invest in a college

Table 8–1
Percentage Distribution of Incomes of Males 25 and Over in 1970

| Income Class | High School Ed. (4 yrs.) | College Ed. (4 yrs.) |
|---|---|---|
| under $4000 | 1.4% | 3.7% |
| 4000–4499 | 3.4 | 1.6 |
| 5000–5999 | 5.1 | 2.2 |
| 6000–6999 | 5.7 | 2.7 |
| 7000–7999 | 6.6 | 2.7 |
| 8000–8999 | 7.6 | 3.5 |
| 9000–9999 | 7.5 | 5.3 |
| 10,000–11,999 | 15.8 | 11.7 |
| 12,000–14,999 | 17.8 | 18.5 |
| 15,000–24,999 | 19.7 | 35.1 |
| 25,000–49,999 | 3.2 | 12.0 |
| 50,000 and over | 0.3 | 1.1 |
| median income | $10,165 | $14,722 |
| mean income | 11,397 | 16,335 |

Source: U.S. Bureau of the Census, *Current Population Reports: Consumer Income*, Series P-60, No. 80 (Washington, D.C.: 1971), p. 67.

education an individual may wish to compare the expected resulting change in the value of his human capital with the expected costs of obtaining that college degree.

### The Price of Educational Investment to the Student

If asked the price or cost of educational investment, a student would probably respond that it was the amount of tuition and fees and the cost of living adjacent to a campus. Indeed, tuition and fees are an important part of his costs; in 1967–1968, students in public and private colleges spent almost $3.4 billion on these categories.[2] While students in public junior colleges on the average paid $121 per academic year in order to enroll in those institutions, students in public four-year universities paid $360 per academic year, and students in private four-year colleges paid $1,456 per academic year on the average.[3] The costs of a college education clearly depend on the type of institution that a student has chosen to attend.

The cost of living near a campus is not really a cost of higher education, since living costs must be paid whether an individual attends school or not. Of course, the cost of living may be higher than normal because books and supplies must be purchased, or apartment rents may be very high. Thus,

2. *Digest of Education Statistics, 1970,* Office of Education, National Center for Education Statistics, Washington, D.C., p. 92.

3. Students also paid an average $259 in tuition and fees at public four-year colleges (not universities) and $1162 at private four-year colleges.

the increase in the cost of living attributable to college attendance is correctly labeled an educational cost to the student.

The largest private cost item is one the student would probably not usually consider to be a cost. This is the income foregone while attending college and is usually referred to as the "opportunity cost" of education. The dollar value of this opportunity cost (assuming the student does not work while attending college) is depicted by the shaded area in Figure 8–1.

Looking at income received by institutions of higher education, one observes that the student contribution through tuition and fees is relatively small. In 1967–1968, students contributed 41.7 percent of the budget for private institutions of higher education and 13.0 percent of the budget for public institutions of higher education.[4] However, the opportunity cost is a real cost of education to both the individual and to society. If, instead of attending college, the student engaged in productive pursuit, society would have a larger total output. When one considers the total costs of higher education inclusive of opportunity costs, students contribute well over half of that total.

The price of educational investment to the individual student is summarized in Figure 8–3. The total costs of attending college are given by the shaded areas. As before, the opportunity cost is represented by the part of the shaded area lying above the horizontal axis. The direct costs, tuition and fees are given by the bar graph extending below the horizontal axis. The further down the bar extends, the larger the dollar amount of tuition and fees.

To illustrate this, let us consider the specific example of a hypothetical Mary Jones. Mary is in her senior year of high school and is trying to decide whether or not to attend college. That is, she is trying to decide whether or not to invest in her human capital to increase future earning power. Let us assume she applies for admission at State College and is accepted.

In making her decision Mary, of course, wants to know both the costs and benefits of attending college. The price of educational investment to Mary is the tuition and fees at State College and the income she foregoes while in attendance. The college catalogue informs her that tuition and fees are $500 for each academic year. She estimates that purchases of books and supplies will add an additional $100 for a total of $600. The cost of living, she estimates, will be no different in her case whether she attends college or not. Hence, she does not include any part of the usual costs of living as part of the price of educational investment.

Mary also knows that if she does not attend college, the best job she can get is a position as a secretary with the local paper mill, which pays $5000

4. *Digest of Educational Statistics, 1970,* p. 92. Federal research funds were not included as part of the budget in these calculations.

Figure 8–3. Private costs and benefits of higher education.

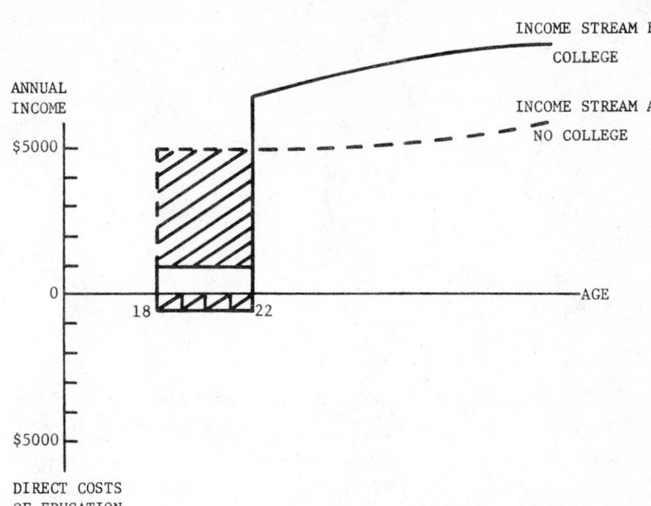


per year with no raises the first four years. This is illustrated in Figure 8–3 by income stream A, which represents the stream of future income she can expect if she does not attend college. However, like most college students, Mary expects to work during the summer months. If she can earn $1000 each summer working as a part-time secretary with the paper mill, the opportunity costs of attending college are then given by the difference between the maximum salary she could be earning if she did not attend college ($5000 per year) and her part-time earnings while attending college ($1000 per year). Her net opportunity costs of $4000 per year are depicted by the shaded area above the horizontal line.

Using Figure 8–3, Mary can quickly estimate the overall costs she must incur by attending college four years. The total direct costs are $600 × 4 = $2400, and the total opportunity costs are $4000 × 4 = $16,000. The undiscounted price of her investment is then $18,400.

### The Price of Educational Investment to Society

As noted previously, college students do not pay the full costs of their education. They receive sizable subsidies which are equal to the difference between the total cost of providing the instructional services and the costs paid by the student in the form of tuition and fees. Part of the higher education subsidy is provided by the public through local, state, and federal governmental aid. In 1967–1968 all levels of government combined contrib-

Table 8–2
Public Higher Education Subsidies by Type of Institution and Years of College Completed—1965

| Type of Institution | | Year of College 1 | 2 | 3 | 4 |
|---|---|---|---|---|---|
| University of California | Per year cost | $1,460 | $1,460 | $2,110 | $2,110 |
| 4 years | Cumulative cost | 1,460 | 2,920 | 5,030 | 7,140 |
| State colleges | Per year cost | 1,350 | 1,350 | 1,550 | 1,550 |
| 4 years | Cumulative cost | 1,350 | 2,700 | 4,250 | 5,800 |
| Junior colleges | Per year cost | 720 | 720 | — | — |
| 2 years | Cumulative cost | 720 | 1,440 | — | — |

Source: W. Lee Hansen and Burton A. Weisbrod, "The Distribution of Costs and Direct Benefits of Public Higher Education: The Case of California," *Journal of Human Resources* IV, no. 4 (Spring 1969), p. 178.

uted 35.2 percent of the total revenues of private colleges and universities and 78.2 percent of the total revenues of public colleges and universities.[5]

Although the direct contribution of government to the operations of private institutions of higher education appears small, both public and private institutions receive large indirect governmental aid. For example, colleges and universities are usually exempted from paying local and state property and income taxes. Furthermore, individuals are encouraged by the federal income tax code to contribute to the endowment funds of universities. This is an indirect government subsidy equal to the taxes the benefactor would have to pay on the gift were it not tax deductible.

What is the dollar value of the public higher education subsidy received by individual students? In a study of public higher education in California, economists estimated the figures given in Table 8–2. The size of the subsidy ranges from $720 per year in the junior colleges to $2,110 for juniors and seniors at the University of California. The cumulative public subsidy for four years at the University of California is $7,140. That is, the undiscounted price to society of investing in the college education of a student at the University of California is $7,140.

The primary source of the social or government investment in higher education is, of course, the direct and indirect taxes paid by individuals and businesses. This usually includes some combination of property, sales, personal income, corporation income, and gift and inheritance taxes.

In the case of Mary Jones, the state college she is considering entering is a public institution. Hence, in addition to student tuition and fees, its only source of revenue is government aid that comes from tax payments. The per student cost of instruction at State College is $1600 for freshmen and sophomores, and $2100 for juniors and seniors. Costs are higher for upper-classmen because of smaller class sizes and the use of more sophisti-

5. Ibid.

cated equipment. Thus the total public investment in the higher education of Mary will be the costs of instruction ($7400) less tuition ($2400), or an undiscounted sum of $5000.

### Private Returns from Investment in Higher Education

There exists abundant evidence that obtaining a college diploma increases one's future earning power; that is, it increases one's human capital. Table 8–3 shows estimated streams of income associated with high school and college graduates, based on the 1960 census. For whites, earnings at every age level are higher for college graduates than high school graduates. The same does not, however, hold true for blacks. Racial discrimination may account for the fact that having a college education does not appear to have had as large a payoff for blacks as for whites.

If, as stated earlier, a measure of the value of human capital is the money income an individual may expect to receive in the future, one way of measuring the value of human capital is to look at future income streams (see Table 8–3). However, economists usually combine all the information contained in the stream of future income into one summary statistic referred to as the present value of the future income stream.

Table 8–3
Expected Annual Earnings at Selected Ages
by Level of Schooling and Race for the Northern United States

| | Years of School Completed | | | |
|---|---|---|---|---|
| Age | 8 | 12 | 16 | 17+ |
| | Annual Earnings—Whites | | | |
| 14 | | | | |
| 18 | $1,174 | | | |
| 22 | 2,301 | $2,930 | | |
| 27 | 3,498 | 4,461 | $ 5,602 | |
| 37 | 4,809 | 6,052 | 8,713 | $ 9,578 |
| 47 | 4,967 | 6,281 | 10,109 | 12,138 |
| 57 | 4,506 | 6,023 | 9,677 | 11,398 |
| | Annual Earnings—Nonwhites | | | |
| 14 | | | | |
| 18 | $ 646 | | | |
| 22 | 1,529 | $2,122 | | |
| 27 | 2,337 | 3,201 | $3,249 | |
| 37 | 3,197 | 3,989 | 5,146 | $7,834 |
| 47 | 3,412 | 3,205 | 4,480 | 9,129 |
| 57 | 3,674 | 3,361 | 2,543 | 6,561 |

Source: Giora Hanoch, "An Economic Analysis of Earnings and Schooling," *Journal of Human Resources*, II, no. 3 (Summer 1967), pp. 316–317.

Chapter 5 contains an exposition of the notion of present value. The concept, in brief, is that \$1 today is worth more than \$1 a year from today because of interest that can be earned on a dollar placed in a savings account. Conversely, \$1 a year from today is worth less than \$1 today. If the rate of interest is 5 percent, we know that putting \$1 in the savings account today will result in \$1.05 in the account one year from today. In Chapter 5 this was expressed algebraically as

$$V_0 (1 + r) = V_1. \tag{1}$$

The general formula for computing the present value of a stream of income ($R$) was given by the expression

$$V_0 = R_0 + \frac{R_1}{(1+r)} + \frac{R_2}{(1+r)^2} + \frac{R_3}{(1+r)^3} + \cdots + \frac{R_n}{(1+r)^n}. \tag{2}$$

This expression is even more simply stated as

$$V_0 = \sum_{t=0}^{n} \frac{R_t}{(1+r)^t}, \tag{3}$$

where the $\Sigma$ notation simply indicates a sum of the present values of the incomes received between year 0 and year $n$.

It should be noted that the present value of an income stream depends in part on the rate of discount ($r$) which is chosen, and the length of the income stream. The higher the rate of discount, the lower is the present value of \$1 received $t$ years from today. For a given aggregate undiscounted income stream ( $\sum_{t=0}^{n} R_t$), the present value is higher if the higher annual incomes occur in the early years of the stream rather than the later years.

Saying that a college diploma increases one's future earning power is the same as saying it increases the value of one's human capital as measured by the present value of the income stream. A college education does not result in the same level of income for all graduates; this was shown in Table 8–1. In Table 8–4 we observe that the present value of the income stream (computed using a 3 percent rate of discount) varies according to the student's major subject area. For example, college graduates with economics degrees on the average embody human capital valued at \$339,482, while those with sociology degrees on the average embody human capital valued at \$213,590.

Another factor which must be considered is that the value of the human capital of college graduates varies greatly depending on the quality or pres-

Table 8–4
Present Values of Earnings for Students with Bachelors' Degrees

| | Sample Mean | Sample Standard Deviation |
|---|---|---|
| Economics | $339,482 | $20,236 |
| Sociology | 213,590 | 13,063 |
| Political science | 300,000 | 21,194 |
| Psychology | 262,127 | 11,300 |
| Mathematics | 342,068 | 19,713 |
| Physics | 282,758 | 13,998 |
| Statistics | 318,421 | 13,314 |
| Computer science | 306,733 | 10,751 |
| Biological sciences | 215,691 | 10,802 |
| Agricultural sciences | 225,118 | 9,325 |

Source: Assaf Razin and James D. Campbell, "Internal Allocation of University Resources," *Western Economic Journal*, X, no. 3 (September 1972), p. 315.

tige of the college and the ability or aptitude of the student as measured by his rank in class. A study of a sample of male employees of a large American corporation produced the results given in Table 8–5. As can be seen, the value of the human capital of employees who ranked in the middle one-third of their graduating class at the highest quality colleges was $146,800 (using a 5 percent rate of discount), which was greater than that for employees who ranked in the top tenth of their graduating classes at average or below-average quality colleges.

The private returns from a college education are not solely in the form of an increase in the present value of the income stream. Students may (or may not) find the process of obtaining a college education an enjoyable experience; if it is more enjoyable than the option of working, it, too, should be considered as a private benefit resulting from higher education. Benefits of this nature might be labeled current consumption benefits.

Table 8–5
Present Value of Earnings by College Quality and Class Rank, 5 Percent Discount Rate

| | College Quality | | | |
|---|---|---|---|---|
| Class Rank | Best | Above Average | Average | Below Average |
| Top 1/10 | $167,400 | $159,800 | $146,300 | $145,000 |
| Rest of top 1/3 | 158,000 | 146,400 | 140,000 | 140,200 |
| Middle 1/3 | 146,800 | 139,200 | 134,200 | 132,600 |
| Lowest 1/3 | 135,800 | 136,200 | 128,200 | 125,100 |
| Mean (all ranks) | 152,000 | 145,400 | 137,200 | 136,000 |

Source: Burton A. Weisbrod and Peter Karpoff, "Monetary Returns to College Education, Student Ability, and College Quality," *Review of Economics and Statistics*, L, no. 4 (November 1968), p. 497.

A college education may also generate a stream of future consumption benefits. For example, a college course in English literature may give a student lifelong appreciation and enjoyment of the works of Shakespeare. A more visible benefit of higher education may be employment in pleasant surroundings, nonalienating work, and other occupational fringe benefits. Another private benefit is that college-educated parents have been shown to have a strong positive influence on the scholastic achievement of their children. Indeed, part of the future income stream of their children may be attributable to this.

Presumably, a student takes these nonmonetary private benefits of a college education into account when deciding whether or not to obtain a college degree. Since it is difficult to attach a dollar value to these benefits, and in some cases even impossible to measure their size, we shall largely ignore them in the remainder of this analysis. In making decisions in the real world, however, some of these benefits may loom very large in the minds of students.

### The Private Investment Decision

In deciding whether or not to attend college, the wise student acts in much the same manner as the public enterprise discussed in Chapter 5. He compares the benefits and costs of the investment and makes the investment if benefits exceed costs. If he has several investment alternatives such as attending a vocational school, attending college and majoring in Spanish, or attending college and majoring in economics, he logically undertakes that investment for which he receives the largest net benefits. In making these decisions the student would include consumption benefits discussed above as well as income benefits. For illustrative purposes, however, we shall consider only the income benefits.

What are the private benefits of investing in higher education? They are not equal to the present value of the future income stream. Rather, they equal the difference between the present value of the income stream associated with a high school education only and the present value of the income stream associated with a college education. The present value of the income benefits of higher education, $B_0$, is given by

$$B_0 = \sum_{t=0}^{n} \frac{b_t}{(1+r)^t} \tag{4}$$

where $b_t$ represents the difference (positive or negative) between the income level associated with a high school education and that associated with a college education in year $t$ beyond college. This is a simplification of Equation 4 in Chapter 5.

The price of higher education was defined on pp. 211–213. The present value of the private costs of higher education, $C_0$, is given by

$$C_0 = \sum_{t=0}^{3} \frac{c_t}{(1 + r)^t} \tag{5}$$

where $c_t$ are the costs of the $t$th year of college. This is equivalent to Equation 5 in Chapter 5.

In making his investment decision, the student then compares the present value of the benefits with the present value of the costs. If the benefits exceed the costs and this difference is larger than that for alternative investments, he will decide to invest in higher education. On the other hand, if the costs exceed the benefits he will decide not to attend college and may work or choose some alternative investment instead.

Although there are many similarities between public and private investment decisions as discussed here, there are also some important differences. One has to do with the availability of investment funds. Public enterprises either have investment funds which are part of general tax revenues, or they can borrow funds for investment in business. However, unless repayment is guaranteed by the state or federal government, individuals are not usually able to borrow for the purpose of investing in their human capital. The primary reason for this imperfection in the capital market is that human capital, unlike physical capital, cannot be used as collateral on a loan. The use of human capital as collateral could result in human indenture, a notion rejected by most societies.

The limited availability of funds for investment in higher education means that students have to rely upon their own financial resources or those of their family. This situation has the most adverse consequences for the poor, who are not only unable to borrow for investment in their human capital, but also do not have family resources.

Limited investment funds mean that the market rate of interest may not be the factor used to discount future costs and benefits. This is a second important difference between decision-making by public enterprise and individuals concerned with investment in their human capital. In studying public investment alternatives, the decision-maker chooses a rate of discount which appears to have some relationship to the rates of interest charged in the financial markets. The individual investing in his own human capital, however, may use a discount rate which is quite different from the market interest rate. His discount rate is commonly referred to as his rate of time preference and simply indicates the value he puts on a dollar received in the future. The rate of time preference may, of course, vary greatly between individuals. It is usually assumed that the rate of time preference is low for those with high income and high for those with low income. The argument is that since the poor have little money, they have a strong preference for having an extra dollar today instead of next year. Unfortunately, a higher rate of time preference means that the poor will value the future higher education benefits, many of which occur in the distant future, much less highly than will high income individuals. As a result, the poor will also be less likely than the rich to invest in their own human capital. The variation in time preference between individuals results in no two individuals arriving at the same estimates of the benefits and costs of higher education. Consequently, they may also make different investment decisions.

The third difference between investments by public enterprises and investments in human capital by individuals is that college students do not pay the full costs of their education. Since their education is heavily subsidized, the present value of costs to them is less than the present value of costs to society as a whole. Consequently, students are more likely to undertake such an investment than would otherwise be the case.

To illustrate this, let us return to the case of Mary Jones. First, she decides that $1 received one year from now is worth 94¢ today. That is, her rate of time preference, the factor used to discount streams of future costs and benefits, is 6 percent.

Next, she determines the present value of the direct and opportunity costs she will incur in obtaining a college education. The present values of these costs are computed as follows:

$$\text{direct costs} = \$600 + \frac{\$600}{(1.06)} + \frac{\$600}{(1.06)^2} + \frac{\$600}{(1.06)^3}$$

$$= \$600 + \frac{\$600}{1.06} + \frac{\$600}{1.12} + \frac{\$600}{1.19}$$

$$= \$600 + \$566 + \$536 + \$504 = \$\ 2{,}206$$

$$\text{opportunity costs} = \$4000 + \frac{\$4000}{(1.06)} + \frac{\$4000}{(1.06)^2} + \frac{\$4000}{(1.06)^3} = \$14{,}705$$

The present value of all costs is the sum of the present values of the direct and the opportunity costs: $16,911.

To decide whether to undertake this investment in her human capital, Mary must compare the present value of the costs with the present value of the benefits of the investment. To do this she determines what her streams of future income look like with and without a college education (see Table 8–6). The differences between the income streams measure the pecuniary benefits of higher education. To make our example less complicated, Mary states that she intends to work only ten years after receiving her college diploma; at the end of that time she expects to quit working and raise a family.

Table 8–6
Mary Jone's Income Streams, by Level of Education

| | Years Beyond College | | | | | | | | | |
|---|---|---|---|---|---|---|---|---|---|---|
| | 1 | 2 | 3 | 4 | 5 | 6 | 7 | 8 | 9 | 10 |
| Income stream with high school education only | $4200 | $4400 | $4600 | $4800 | $5000 | $5100 | $5200 | $5200 | $5200 | $5200 |
| Income stream with college education | 6500 | 6700 | 7000 | 7500 | 7800 | 8100 | 8700 | 9000 | 9200 | 9700 |
| Annual difference between income streams | 2300 | 2300 | 2400 | 2700 | 2800 | 3000 | 3500 | 3800 | 4000 | 4500 |

Since we have included income Mary could have earned while attending college as an explicit component of the costs of education, we avoid double-counting that income by simply considering differences in the income stream after graduation from college. Because the first year's income after college is four years in the future, the difference between the income streams must be discounted to reflect this. With a 6 percent rate of discount (Mary's rate of time preference) $1 received four years from now is worth only 79¢ today. The present value of her income benefits is computed as follows:

$$B_0 = \frac{\$2300}{(1.06)^4} + \frac{\$2300}{(1.06)^5} + \frac{\$2400}{(1.06)^6} + \cdots + \frac{\$4500}{(1.06)^{13}} = \$19{,}780. \quad (6)$$

The present value of the differences in the income streams is $19,780.

Mary compares the costs and benefits to her of higher education and discovers that the benefits ($19,780) exceed the costs ($16,911). On the basis of this she decides the investment would be a wise one.

We have assumed Mary's rate of time preference to be 6 percent. Would her investment decision change if her rate of time preference were 10 percent? At 10 percent she would value $1 received one year from today at 90¢ today. If we again compute the present values of the costs and benefits of a college education, we find that at a 10 percent rate of discount Mary will decide not to undertake the investment. The present value of her costs ($16,041) exceeds the present value of her benefits ($14,916).

## Why Subsidize Higher Education?

As noted earlier, society makes sizable investments in the human capital of persons attending both public and private institutions of higher education. But a large number of people would obtain college educations in the absence of any public subsidy whatsoever. Why then should the public subsidize such investments in human capital?

### Capital Market Imperfections

One argument for public subsidies has to do with capital market imperfections. As we have seen, human capital differs from physical capital in that it cannot be used as collateral for borrowed funds. One important result of this market imperfection is that low-income students will find it very difficult to obtain the funds required for attending college. Students from high-income families can, of course, rely upon their families as a source of funds. This situation denies equality of educational opportunity to low-income students.

Another result of the imperfect capital market is that many individuals will be deterred from making the college investment, even though the rate of return to them would be higher than the rate of return they could obtain from investing in physical capital. From the point of view of society, this is an inefficient allocation of resources.

These deleterious results suggest that society should act to remove the imperfections in the capital market. One way of doing so is to highly subsidize higher education. However, this benefits the rich as much as it does the poor. Also, it only covers the direct costs of education; the largest part of the private costs of higher education, opportunity costs, is not subsidized. Imperfections in the capital market could be better removed through government guarantee of student loans, which would cover all the private costs of education. Such loans could be repaid over the student's lifetime.

Suppose society decided to discontinue subsidizing higher education and began to charge students the full costs of their education. In our example of Mary Jones, tuition and fees would increase at State College from $500 to $1600 for freshmen and sophomores and to $2100 for juniors and seniors. The present value of this increase in costs is exactly equal to the present value of the previous state subsidy received by Mary Jones. That sum is $6749 at a 6 percent rate of discount. If Mary had to pay the total costs of her education, the present value of the costs would exceed the benefits, and she would not undertake the investment.

### Income Redistribution

Another argument for public subsidization of higher education is that it serves to prevent an unfavorable distribution of income. One way to accomplish this would be to grant larger education subsidies to poor families than they currently pay in taxes for the purposes of higher education. Economists studying the system of higher education in California have concluded that the distribution of higher education subsidies and the 1965 distribution of the tax burden taken together may actually produce a redistribution of income from low-income to high-income families.[6] Since 1965, important changes have resulted in a more progressive state tax structure; nevertheless, it appears that the income redistribution between low-income and high-income families is not very large or significant, regardless of the direction.

Another way in which public subsidies could equalize incomes is by generating a more equal distribution of human capital. However, there is little empirical evidence that subsidizing higher education will redistribute income in favor of the poor.[7]

The arguments that imperfect capital markets or income redistribution warrants higher education subsidies are far from convincing. Public support of higher education must, instead, rest upon the assertion that there are sizable social or external benefits associated with higher education. This argument says that even if there were perfect capital markets (students could obtain loans for investment in human capital), people would still underinvest in college education because they cannot themselves capture all the benefits of their education. External benefits are defined as benefits which accrue to society from an individual's investment in education. The individual, however, has no way of charging society for those benefits. On the other hand, if society gives the student a subsidy approximately equal in size to its dollar valuation of the benefits generated by his higher education, the student may find that his private benefits will then exceed his private subsidized costs and undertake the investment. Now let us consider some possible social benefits from higher education.

### Economic Growth

One of the most commonly cited social benefits of higher education is a higher rate of economic growth. A famous study concluded that 23 percent of the nation's growth in the period 1929–1957 was attributable to increases in the human capital of its population.[8] Since college enrollment was rapidly expanding during much of this period, some portion of this 23 percent is attributable to higher education. Studies by other economists have obtained similar results. Of course, in these days of environmental awareness, the claim that economic growth is a social benefit does not go un-

6. W. Lee Hansen, and Burton A. Weisbrod, "The Distribution of Costs and Direct Benefits of Public Higher Education: The Case of California," *Journal of Human Resources* (Spring 1969), pp. 176–191. See also the critique of that study by Joseph A. Pechman, "The Distributional Effects of Public Higher Education in California," *Journal of Human Resources* (Summer 1970), pp. 361–370.

7. Lester C. Thurow, "Education and Economic Equality," *The Public Interest* (Summer 1972), pp. 66–81.

8. Edward F. Denison, *The Sources of Economic Growth in the United States and the Alternatives Before Us* (New York: Committee for Economic Development, 1962).

challenged. Economic growth may entail social costs such as pollution or congestion, as well as social benefits such as higher incomes and increased social mobility.

### Reduced Crime Rate

Another possible social benefit of increased education is a lower crime rate. People who embody large amounts of human capital tend to earn high incomes. As a result the opportunity costs of committing crimes are high, and such individuals are less likely to commit the kind of crime that may result in prison sentences. For example, while 9.6 percent of the American population in 1960 had at least four years of college, less than 1 percent of the nation's criminal population had obtained that much education.[9] One social benefit of higher education would then appear to be a lower probability of committing crime.

The costs of crime to society are very great indeed. The President's Commission on Law Enforcement and Administration of Justice estimated the costs of crime for 1965 to be about $4.2 billion for law enforcement, while the private costs of prevention and insurance amounted to $1.9 billion. If a larger number of citizens were college graduates in 1965, these costs might have been lower. Such a change in the costs of crime could then be viewed as a social benefit attributable to higher education.

### Improved Learning Environment

There is evidence that students of families where the head of household is college-educated and employed in a middle-class occupation not only do better in schools themselves, but also have a beneficial impact on the learning of their peers.[10] College-educated parents, however, receive no reimbursement for their children's productive contributions from either the school district or the parents of the children who are benefited. This externality is a social benefit which is indirectly attributable to higher education.

### Better Citizenship

Higher education may also provide better citizens and leaders. The 1968 national election study by the Survey Research Center at the University of

9. The source of these data is the U.S. Census Bureau, *U.S. Census of Population 1960,* Volume 1, "Characteristics of the Population," Part 1, U.S. Summary, and "Inmates of Institutions," PC(2)8A.

10. Several studies have concluded that students of high socioeconomic status have a beneficial effect on their peers while students of low socioeconomic status may have an adverse effect. For example, see Donald R. Winkler, *The Production of Human Capital: A Study of Minority Achievement,* unpublished Ph.D. dissertation, University of California, Berkeley, 1972, or James S. Coleman et al., *Equality of Educational Opportunity,* Office of Education, National Center for Educational Statistics (Washington, D.C.: U.S. Government Printing Office, 1966).

Michigan found for its sample of respondents that 47 percent of college graduates had at one time written to a public official, compared to 13 percent of respondents having no college education. They also found that 21 percent of college graduates compared with 6 percent of non-college graduates had given money for political campaigns, and 89 percent of college graduates compared with 72 percent of non-college graduates reported voting in the 1968 elections. Finally, 10 percent of college graduates versus 5 percent of non-college graduates reported having worked for a political party or candidate.[11] It was found that college graduates are also more likely than non-college graduates to assume positions of leadership in community affairs. Although it is impossible to put a dollar figure on the value of good citizenship as reflected in terms of voting and other political involvement, the effective working of a democracy is dependent on the active political participation of the nation's citizens.

### Career Orientation

In addition to providing instructional services to students, colleges and universities also perform a sorting and labeling function. This function is sometimes called certification and consists of sorting and directing students into activities in accordance with their interests and abilities. For example, Mary Jones may be interested in majoring in Spanish, but she does poorly in such courses and her advisor counsels her to major in some other subject area. As a result, Mary majors in electrical engineering and graduates in the top quarter of her class. Mary then graduates from college certified in terms of school attended, major field, and rank in class.

Certification is of benefit to society if it brings about a more efficient use of highly skilled manpower. If Mary did not have this certification, a prospective employer would have to go to considerable expense to determine her interests and aptitudes; in short, her suitability for a job. If Mary applied for employment at several different firms or government agencies, each of them would have to undertake the same task and incur the same expense. Certification may be more efficiently carried on in a university.

### Higher Tax Returns and Lower Transfer Payments

Lastly, higher education may affect the welfare of society through its redistributive effects. We shall consider two such effects here—first, the higher tax payments of college-educated persons, and, second, the lower transfer payments to such individuals. In a study prepared for the Joint Economic Committee of the U.S. Congress, one researcher found that, compared to

11. Stephen B. Withey, *A Degree and What Else?* Carnegie Commission on Higher Education (San Francisco: McGraw-Hill, 1971).

noncollege educated persons, college graduates paid higher taxes. This difference in the annual federal income tax revenue was $406 for northern whites, age 47, and $314 for southern whites of the same age.[12]

While college-educated persons in general contribute more in terms of tax revenue, they require less in terms of some kinds of government transfer payments. Transfer payments are money transfers between the government and citizens. One such transfer payment is aid to families with dependent children (AFDC). While 17 percent of women aged 20–54 in the general population had some college education in 1971, less than 2 percent of women of that age in AFDC families had attended college. If more AFDC women had college educations, their earning power would be higher and they would be less likely to be on welfare.[13]

### Summary

Social benefits of higher education such as those discussed above are not the same size for every student. Some individuals would exhibit a high degree of participation in community affairs in the absence of such education. Others may earn high incomes and therefore have lower probabilities of committing crimes and pay higher taxes in the absence of a college education. In general, one can make the statement that low-income students are likely to exhibit the largest social benefits. It is their incomes and their tax payments, political participation, etc. that increase the most, relative to what would have been the case in the absence of a college education.

## Who Should Pay?

The size and value of the social benefits of higher education should determine the size of the public subsidy of higher education. Research on the social benefits of higher education indicates that students of low-income families may generate larger benefits than students of high-income families. If society wishes to maximize the benefits it receives from its investment in higher education, this finding argues for larger subsidies for low-income students than for high-income students. Of course, if student demand for higher education is very price-elastic, the result of raising the subsidy and lowering the price of the educational investment to low-income students will be an increase in the enrollment of low-income students. Similarly, low-

12. David S. Mundel, "Federal Aid to Higher Education: An Analysis of Federal Subsidies to Undergraduate Education," *The Economics of Federal Subsidy Programs, Part 4—Higher Education and Manpower Subsidies,* Joint Economic Committee (Washington, D.C.: U.S. Government Printing Office, 1972), pp. 407–464.

13. Robert H. Mugge, "Education and AFDC," *Welfare in Review,* U.S. Department of Health, Education, and Welfare, Vol. 2, No. 1 (Washington, D.C.: January 1964), pp. 1–14.

ering the subsidy and raising the price of the educational investment to high-income students should result in a decrease in the enrollment of such students.

Figures 8–4 and 8–5 illustrate the relationship between price of education and enrollment of students. Figure 8–4 depicts the demand for higher education by low-income students. The present price (tuition + fees + opportunity costs) is $P_o$; at that price the aggregate demand by low-income students for higher education is represented by $Q_o$, the number of low-income students enrolled in institutions of higher education. Increasing the public subsidy lowers the price the student faces to $P_1$; at $P_1$ some larger number of low-income students, $Q_1$, demand the instructional services of higher education.

Figure 8–5 depicts the demand for higher education by high-income students. The present price is again $P_o$, the same price as that faced by low-income students. Decreasing the public subsidy to high-income students raises the price they face to $P_1'$ and decreases the enrollment of high-income students from $Q_o'$ to $Q_1'$.

At present society appears to regard the social benefits of higher education as being large enough to warrant low tuition rates (large public subsidies) for public universities. However, students of private colleges are likely to generate approximately the same amount of social benefits as students of public colleges. They should therefore receive a public subsidy equal to that received by students of public colleges. One proposal that has been made along these lines is that college students receive a direct public

Figure 8–4. Demand for higher education by low-income students.

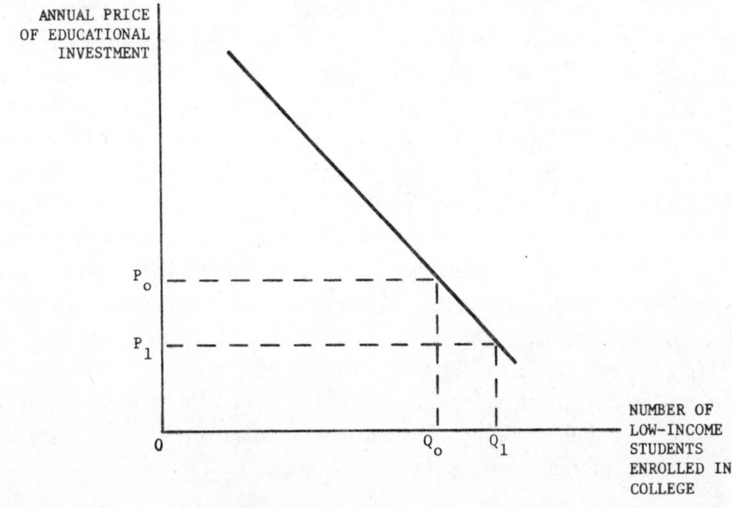

Figure 8–5. Demand for higher education by high-income students.

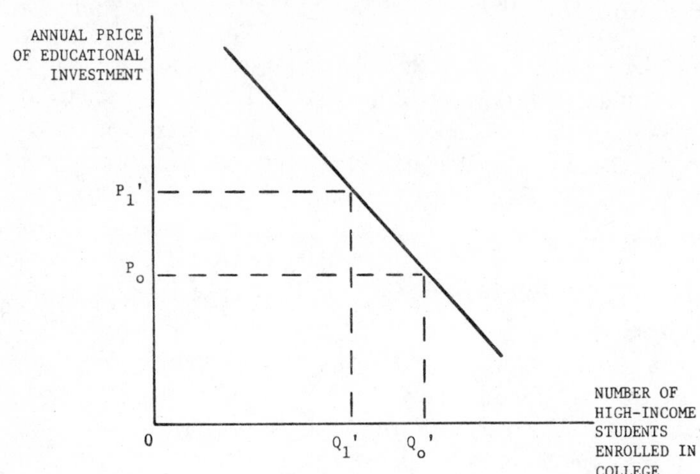


subsidy or "voucher" from the government. They could then use that voucher to purchase educational services from any educational institution of their choice, be it public or private, academic or vocational. If the costs of operating a private college are substantially more than the costs of operating a public one, the student would still end up paying higher tuition at the private college. It has been suggested that this subsidy or voucher should be a flat dollar amount and, in general, should not vary according to the institution attended.

At present, institutions of higher education charge all students approximately the same tuition and fees, irrespective of year in school. Freshmen and sophomores, juniors and seniors, and graduate students pay approximately the same tuition. Yet the costs of higher education increase with the level of training. As a result, the subsidy received by freshmen and sophomores is less than that received by juniors and seniors, which in turn is less than that received by graduate students. Society should grant subsidies in accordance with the social benefits generated by each of these groups of students. Yet, one should question whether graduate students generate more social benefits than do freshmen and sophomores. Indeed, one could argue that the size of social benefits diminishes with additional years in college. However, in the absence of better information we might assume that social benefits are equal for each year of education, which implies equal subsidies for each educational level. This in turn would mean that the level of tuition and fees would increase with educational level.

Should students pay the full costs of their education? Society cannot put a precise dollar value on the social benefits of higher education. Hence, this question must continue to be answered in the political sphere. However, economic research designed to estimate the size of education's social benefits can provide political and educational decision-makers with more accurate information in making their policies.

The evidence to date would appear to indicate that students should receive some public subsidy, with students from low-income families receiving larger subsidies than students from high-income families, and with students at private institutions receiving the same subsidy as students at public institutions. The size of the subsidy should be equal for all years of higher education. However, as the reader has probably realized by now, the evidence underlying these policy prescriptions is far from satisfactory. There is a great need for continued research into the social benefits of higher education in order to arrive at more sensible and efficient pricing policies.

## Conclusion

Unprecedented growth in college enrollments and subsequent increases in costs have resulted in a state of financial crisis for many colleges and universities. In response to this crisis, some policy-makers have argued that, since the benefits of higher education are largely private, students should pay a much larger share of the costs. That is to say, tuition should be increased, possibly to cover the full costs of education. Others have argued that higher education generates sizable social benefits and thereby warrants continued, and possibly increased, public subsidies.

Individuals invest in their human capital in order to obtain larger future incomes and other private benefits. The price of investing in higher education consists largely of foregone income and tuition and fees. In deciding whether or not to attend institutions of higher education, individuals evaluate and compare the present values of costs and benefits resulting from that investment. Therefore, reducing the price of investment through reductions in tuitions and fees will result in more individuals finding the investment worthwhile.

In addition to private returns, benefits may accrue to the public at large from investments in higher education. If these externalities are ignored by society and no subsidy is offered to investors in the form of reduced tuition levels, a less than optimal amount of investment is likely to result.

The social benefits of higher education, as defined and measured here, appear to justify continued public subsidization of higher education, although determination of the appropriate level of subsidy is very complex. Furthermore, improvements in the present distribution of public subsidies are required to maximize social benefits.

# Commentary

Professor Winkler's study on who should pay for higher education, and how much, combined two aspects of analysis from several earlier chapters: the economics of public goods and the evaluation of investment projects. Viewing investment in higher education from the standpoint of the individual making a private decision, the analysis is analogous to evaluating investment projects for water delivery, as discussed in Chapter 5. The individual determining whether or not to pursue higher education has to estimate (over the appropriate time span) the increment in earnings and other benefits attributable to further education, and calculate this stream's present value by discounting at the appropriate rate. The present value of benefits is then compared to the estimate of the present value of costs incurred to determine whether or not the benefit-cost ratio is favorable.

The difficulties encountered in calculating the benefits and costs relevant to this private decision typify those encountered in evaluating any investment project. The pecuniary benefits are most readily quantifiable, but these vary with the individual, his major subject area, and his school. The nonpecuniary or psychic benefits were much less easily reduced to dollars. The calculation of costs must include the direct costs of education and the opportunity costs of foregoing income while attending school. The difficulties do not end there. As Winkler points out, human capital is a special kind of capital which is not bought or sold in the marketplace, only rented; thus, no market price exists. Markets for financing investment in this type of capital are not perfect, and as a consequence of the invester's inability to borrow, much of the private investment in human capital is financed from current income. This, of course, is to the disadvantage of those with low current incomes. Furthermore, these same people must pay attention to current pressing needs; hence, they tend to prefer income now to income in the future. Their rate of discount is high and, as a result, investment in higher education appears much less favorable to them than to higher income individuals, ceteris paribus. To the extent that higher education is necessary to economic success and upward social mobility, imperfections in the private market financing of investment in higher education misallocate resources and perpetuate the class status of families.

Professor Winkler indicates that capital market imperfections would be sufficient grounds for governmental remedy, but the intervention for this purpose could be limited to the guaranteeing of loans for the education of individuals. The argument for government subsidy of education rests on the perception that some of the benefits of higher education accrue to the public and hence will be external to the benefit-cost calculations of the individual. To the extent that benefits are public, there will be insufficient investment in higher education if the decision is left to individuals. The difficulty with the public good hypothesis is in identifying the benefits, and even more, in measuring them. Thus, as Professor Winkler concluded, the policy prescriptions in this area are at present largely qualitative.

Chapter 9 reminds us that there is more to life than money. William Kennedy, pursuing a topic raised in the previous chapter, ponders the importance of psychic benefits in the life activity that occupies so much of our time, namely, work. Work can be fulfilling, but so often in modern industrial society it proves to be one of the less attractive aspects of life. Let us consider next whether or not work can be organized in a better way.

# 9

# Work and Dissatisfaction: Is Money Enough?

William Kennedy

Students of industrial organization and management point out that growing hostility to work is becoming a major problem in the United States and other industrial nations.[1] Although the frustration of the laborer with the mechanization process was dramatized as far back as Charlie Chaplin's movie "Modern Times," which appeared in 1936, it was not until recently that this problem became a hot item in the press and other media. In 1971, educational television ran a documentary called "The Factory," which dramatized the lack of work satisfaction in the smaller-scale production of jewelry. More recently, in the summer of 1972, NBC showed a television documentary called "Blue Collar Trap" based on the disenchanted lives of four young production workers in the Ford plant at Milpitas, California. Even more recently *Life,* in the September 1, 1972 issue featured this growing problem as its cover story.

Although common sense suggests to the ordinary man that work is the primary and dominating feature of his economic life, the index of Paul Samuelson's *Principles,* the leading economics textbook of our time, does not show a listing for the topic "work." This does not mean that economists have no interest in the problem but that, as in other sciences, the scope and method of economics dictate a special viewpoint and approach and the inevitable consequent limitations.

As Alfred Marshall pointed out in his *Principles of Economics,* economics has an advantage of precision over all the other social sciences because its main tool or instrument is the measuring rod "money." Economics deals with man's wants and the activities which he undertakes to satisfy those

1. See Chris Argyris, "We Must Make Work Worthwhile," *Life,* May 5, 1967.

wants. The quality of their outward manifestations can be observed and measured in terms of money. For example, it is common to think in terms of how much we must pay a man to do another hour of work, or how much money a man will pay for another cigar a week.

To illustrate this, consider a production worker on the automobile assembly line. Economic analysis of the assembly line worker takes place in the context of the market for his labor services. The facts gathered culminate in a supply and demand curve for his services, with the intersection indicating the price and quantity taken at the point of equilibrium. If the disagreeableness of assembly line work is a fact, what should the economist expect from his analysis? Long ago Adam Smith pointed out in his *Wealth of Nations* that if two jobs are in other respects the same, the more disagreeable one will have a premium in its wage as compensation to match the disagreeableness. Statistics show that production workers in the motor vehicle industry receive an average wage that is nearly 30 percent more than the average received in all manufacturing industries. Even if economics could establish that the 30 percent differential was payment for disagreeableness and that the wage was adequate to assure required amounts of labor in the industry, we could not be certain that our economic solutions had taken care of all the problems associated with this kind of work and worker.

The reader should note that the method proposed here differs from the method generally employed in preceding chapters. The earlier discussions were confined to the contribution of economic analyses to particular problems. If that general method were used in our analysis of work, the result would be a showing that market forces, given sufficient time, bring about an equilibrium with appropriate compensations for the disagreeableness of each occupation; the analysis ends at that point. We shall go beyond that to a more evolutionary approach which assumes that the environment changes economic behavior, and the changed behavior in turn influences the environment. Alfred Marshall made a similar point when he argued that, from a dynamic or historical perspective, a good economy must produce good men, and in turn the good men will assure continuance of the good economy. This analysis will deal with what kind of work is needed to produce an unending Marshallian chain of good men who bring about the good economy, which in turn brings about more good men.

Economics has made a valuable contribution by advancing scientific solutions to society's problems, but economic science has limitations. The real problems of economic life are not confined to the neat boundaries set by economic theory. We must therefore deal with the problem of work as an activity that spreads beyond scientific economics. As expressed by Frank H.

Knight, "economics is a branch of aesthetics and ethics to a larger extent than [it is] of mechanics."[2]

Ethics attempts to answer the question: "What is fair?" In economic life, ethics means social justice, i.e., a just resolution of economic conflicts among the members of the society. Work dissatisfaction is a problem of conflict of interests of workers and management. To the extent that the parties can resolve the conflict by fair bargaining, the requirement of ethics is largely met. This brings up the question of who is responsible: labor leaders, shop foremen, plant superintendents, or the workers themselves? Power to do something about work dissatisfaction in a complex economy is distributed in various ways throughout the social structure, so that the more difficult ethical problem is one of locating and assigning responsibility. The chief ethical principle to keep in mind here is that responsibility is in proportion to power.

Work satisfaction is much more a problem of aesthetics than of ethics. In terms of the aesthetics of work, the central question in the economic sphere is the self-realization or fulfillment of the worker. In other words, how can economic life be made not only morally good, but beautiful? The enhancement of life, as ultimate value, requires as attributes meaning, coherence, creativity and delight. The aesthetic viewpoint requires the ethical for its own coherence, but goes far beyond strictly ethical considerations. Abraham Maslow, in his *Toward a Psychology of Being,* lists the values associated with healthy psychological growth under fourteen categories including wholeness, aliveness, richness, effortlessness, playfulness, and uniqueness.[3] These and other desirable qualities furnish the criteria for aesthetic judgments on the kind of life afforded by a particular economy or economic activity.

The term aesthetic is somewhat misleading in that the aesthetic questions raised by economic life are more often studied by the science of psychology, as the title of Knight's article suggests, than by the science of aesthetics. The present school of psychology most concerned with these kinds of questions has been called Humanistic Psychology.[4] Aesthetic is, however, an appropriate term inasmuch as the ultimate end of inquiry is the art of life.

Before considering the economic, the ethical, and the aesthetic aspects of work, and their interrelationships, it will be helpful to gain some historical perspective on the concepts of work that men have held in the past.

2. Frank H. Knight, "Economic Psychology and the Value Problem," *The Ethics of Competition* (London: Allen & Unwin, 1935), p. 97. Reprinted from *The Quarterly Journal of Economics,* 39, 1925.

3. Abraham H. Maslow, *Toward a Psychology of Being* (Princeton, N.J.: 2nd ed. Van Nostrand, 1968), p. 83.

4. For good bibliographies of this school see Maslow, ibid.

## History of the Work Idea

Concepts of the work idea have been remarkably persistent. The Judeo-Christian biblical view of work as expiation for sin, which appears in the book of Genesis is an example. Adam, as a consequence of his sin, was driven from Paradise to earn his bread by the sweat of his brow. This idea, when later confronted with the claim that the contemplative life is superior to the active life, exercised a powerful influence on the concept of work. Several centuries before Christ, the Greek philosophers Socrates, Plato and Aristotle suggested that the contemplation of the good, the true and the beautiful led to a higher form of life than did active pursuits. The Greeks disdained labor because it made man unfit to exercise his capacity for contemplation. Men bound to labor became less than human. Thus the philosophers could justify slavery; it was not man, but a subhuman species, that suffered this fate. By the same argument, a slave once freed from this necessity could become human. Aristotle freed his slaves at his death.

Early Christianity appealed to the mass of men in part because it restored them to human status even if it did not break the chains of slavery. Paul, himself a tent-maker, offered a new form of contemplative life open to all—Jew and Gentile, male and female, slave and free. But the later Christian philosophers of greatest influence, Augustine and Aquinas, agreed wholeheartedly with the Greeks and could reinforce pagan philosophy with the New Testament account of Jesus's decision in favor of Mary, the contemplative, over Martha, the active.

The concept of work went through a great phase of development beginning about the year 1000 A.D. Scholars generally date the Renaissance in the 15th, 16th and 17th centuries when referring to literature and art. But an economic renaissance can be claimed for the 11th century, because at that time Europe came out of the doldrums of the Dark Ages with an unusual outburst of economic activity. This renaissance is marked by the founding of the free cities with subsequent great economic and political success. Their contributions to free economic enterprise and political democracy were hailed by Alfred Marshall in the 19th century as of great significance even to his time.

The free cities of Europe brought together the more venturesome, innovative and skilled. Unlike the Greek city-states, these free cities remained favorable to trade and industry because they had secured their prosperity, and that, in turn, ensured freedom from surrounding feudal warlords. Economic prosperity provided a surplus, not only for military defense, but for civic enterprises and imposing public buildings also. These were men of great civic pride, and through self-government they learned progressively how to tax and spend public monies to good advantage, and to make their economic activities contribute to a good social life. Self-education in economics and politics was mutually reinforcing.

The best brief characterization of the medieval economy is the "contained economy."[5] The highest social ideal was social harmony, according to which the dynamic forces of rapid capital growth and economic change had to be contained, lest they set off social changes that would disrupt society and repeat for medieval man the spectacular fall of Rome. Social harmony and social justice put emphasis upon questions of just wages and just prices to forestall economic discontent. Guild regulations attempted to meet the interests of both consumers and producers with prescriptions of quality of the product and working conditions. The term "masterpiece," which is still in current use, derived from the work presented to a reviewing board deciding on the qualifications of a craftsman to be accepted as a master of his craft. The origins of this pride in workmanship are obscure; they are not to be found in Greece or Rome, where the whole idea of ordinary labor was despised. John Ruskin characterized the work produced by the ordinary workmen on the medieval cathedrals as one of the high points of human achievement. Although the cathedral had a unity of conception, he said, each workman was given free rein to bring his imagination and fancy into play in expressing himself, so that close inspection reveals individual variations in every minor part. As a historian of art he claimed that the prior social condition of all such fine work is the possession by the community of a sound ethic.

The modern idea of work for work's sake was foreign to the medieval mind, which was more inclined to the Genesis explanation of work as expiation for sin. In this view, work is a natural and necessary part of the human condition, but if one must work, one may as well do it wholeheartedly. This was far from the vigorous gospel of work preached by Thomas Carlyle, or the therapeutic idea of Karl Marx that work was the link from man to nature whereby he overcame his alienation. The medieval mind, disbelieving in work for the sake of work, saw no contradiction in permitting beggars—refugees from work—to collect alms at the doors of cathedrals which were masterpieces of work. Luther and Calvin later argued so effectively against medieval beggary that even Catholics, who are proudest of their medieval heritage, now repudiate the beggary aspect of that heritage.

As remotely distant as the medieval mentality may be from our own, it made a contribution that still continues—the ethical ideal of social harmony among all members of the community to be achieved by social justice for all participants in economic activity, including the workers.

The image of the contained economy consists of two elements: the container and the contents that require containing. The dangerous part of the contents was newly awakened economic vigor, and eventually it proved too powerful to be contained. The next period of European economic thought

5. The title of a study by Werner Stark (London: Blackfriars, 1956).

and policy was, if anything, even more vigorous. This was the time of the rise of the modern nation-states, discovery of the New World, the greatest influx of precious metals the world's economy had ever experienced, the Renaissance, and the rise of science. The period from the 15th to the 18th Century was the opposite of the contained economy; so diverse, powerful, and often conflicting were the forces present that it is difficult to conceive of anything comprehensive enough to contain them all. As for the concept of work, there were two conflicting ideas most prominently presented: one extolling the nobility of the worker, the other condemning his bad habits of life and work.

The nobility of the worker was part of the new image of man created by the Renaissance. Intellectual interest swung away from the grand metaphysical system of the Scholastics to more concrete concerns at a time when the ideas of the ancients about humanity were rediscovered in ancient manuscripts, long buried in monastic libraries. Out of this arose a new vision of man and his powers and potentialities. Renaissance thinkers saw man as godlike, a creator here on earth. While the ideal was generally centered on the well-rounded gentleman who had perfected his powers of mind, body, and soul, some writers saw potential for human perfection in the humblest tasks. Campanella extols work in his *City of the Sun,* ". . . makes all classes of society equal; all are workers, joyful because each has work suitable to his character, nor does anyone work more than four hours a day. After that all are free to play or study as they will."[6]

In a sociological analysis of *The Tempest,* Leo Lowenthal shows that Shakespeare contrasts the competence and social value of the working class with the uselessness of the declining feudal class. This is demonstrated in the shipwreck scene where the seamen act with coolness and skill in an emergency, while the feudal lords only succeed in getting in the way and are told by the boatswain, "You mar our labor; keep your cabins; you do assist the storm." Lowenthal's analysis concludes: "The feudal lords emerge as stupid; they do not know what the relations of science, work, technology, and human skill really are. While the boat, so to speak, sails to the new world, the old lords are suffocating in an outmoded and completely senseless state of mind."[7]

Renaissance thinkers were the first to have insight into the possibilities of self-realization in all forms of work, an aesthetic ideal we still strive to attain.

Not the least trace of this noble conception of the worker appears in the contemporary writings of the economists of the period. On the contrary, no

6. Adriano Tilgher, *Homo Faber* (Chicago: Henry Regnery, 1958), p. 76.

7. Leo Lowenthal, *Literature, Popular Culture, and Society* (Englewood Cliffs, N.J.: Prentice-Hall, 1961), pp. 149–150.

set of economists before or since has had so low an estimate of the worker. This low vision expressed the narrow self-interest of the writers, and their intense anxiety over nationalism. The general view was that the workmen of one's own nation were a worthless lot, but those of rival nations were markedly more efficient. Thomas Mun (1571–1641), one of the more enlightened economists of the time, nevertheless indulged in the common practice of condemning the workers.

> For him, the Dutch were morally the good boys of Europe. In contrast with them 'we [English] leave our wonted exercises and studies, following our pleasures, and of late years besotting ourselves with pipe and pot, in a beastly manner sucking smoak, and drinking healths, until death stares many in the face.'[8]

One of Adam Smith's most welcome contributions to the literature was to put an end to this kind of condemnation of the worker. Contrary to much popular opinion, Smith was not an advocate of the big capitalist; he condemned the large corporation and the machinations of powerful merchants and manufacturers. The economic hero of the *Wealth of Nations* is the hardworking, thrifty artisan. A shoemaker, for example, through hard work and thrift saves enough to expand his shop and to hire another man. The shoemaker continues the process of adding others. Furthermore, each of the hired men may do likewise, so that Smith was highly optimistic about the potentialities of the workers and the individual prosperity and overall economic growth that would result from their efforts.

Adam Smith contributed the most persuasive rationale for the incipient Industrial Revolution that was to make the greatest changes in the nature of work in the history of mankind. If we examine man's first attempt at civilization, the Sumerian civilization of about 3000 B.C., we find the basic pattern of economic activity not much different from that engaged in by most men in 1776. The Sumerians found fertile land in the Tigris-Euphrates basin, set up irrigation works and controls, produced an agricultural surplus, and used it to build a city. There they specialized in other economic activities so that in an amazingly short time they invented the wheel for both potter's use and for transportation, invented writing, improved metal working, and traveled and traded to get metals and other wanted materials.

The two great institutions of the Industrial Revolution affecting the nature of work were the factory system and the market for labor. Even Smith was worried that the relatively small factories of his day would, through the division of labor, render its workmen "stupid." In the next century the pre-Marxian socialists became concerned with the problem of work, and the

8. Alexander Gray, *The Development of Economic Doctrine* (New York: Longmans, Green, 1931), p. 89.

French social reformer Fourier particularly gave it long and serious study. He felt work could and should be made pleasant; that men should whistle on their way to work. He made many ingenious suggestions; for example, he observed that young boys delighted in playing in filth, so for the benefit of all they should be society's garbage collectors.

The significance of the creation of markets for labor is an insight contributed by Karl Polanyi. He points out that prior to the Industrial Revolution and adoption of a laissez-faire policy, labor had not been treated as marketable. Labor and land were always treated as special parts of the organic structure of society with their own governing laws, traditions and customs. The market economy of the Classical School assumed that men had to be driven to work by hunger; hence the policy of making the alternatives to work so unattractive as to be accepted only under the direst circumstances. The Poor Law of 1834 was based on these assumptions. Polanyi argues that this is unusual in the history of mankind. The researches of economic anthropologists show that primitive tribes never starve members of their community; a man who does not produce does not lose his place by the campfire. We have been so thoroughly conditioned by the market mentality of the past two hundred years that we assume man is primarily economic man. Not so, says Polanyi; this is a brief episode in the total sweep of history. Aristotle was more nearly right in calling man a social being; man wants mainly social goodwill and status. "Man's economy is, as a rule, submerged in his social relations."[9]

Hannah Arendt, in one of the most profound philosophical studies of work in recent times, complains that the modern age is the first to raise the active life above the contemplative, and, what is worse, to raise labor, the lowest form of active life, to the highest place.[10] She conceives of three forms of active life in an ascending order of value: labor, work and action. Labor is defined as production for consumption, while work is distinguished from it as the creation of something permanent in the human world, an example being a work of art. Action, the highest form of activity, is the ancient idea of politics, of human relationships where men come together in society. While she sees the close correlation between labor and consumption ideals, in this writer's view she places them in wrong sequence. Modern society primarily honors consumption, and only incidentally labor. Even in Marxist societies, labor as such is not honored. Managers have higher social status and greater economic privileges than the managed. In free societies, the idle rich are not without honor; their high consumption levels

9. Karl Polanyi, "Our Obsolete Market Mentality," *Commentary,* February 1947. Reprinted in *The Economic Problem,* MacEwan and Weisskopf, eds. (Englewood Cliffs, N.J.: Prentice-Hall, 1970), p. 180.

10. Hannah Arendt, *The Human Condition* (Chicago: University of Chicago Press, 1958).

assure equally high social status, even if they contribute nothing productive to society. Modern societies have a consumer, not producer, orientation; this is why the meaning of labor and its psychological and spiritual aspects fail to get sufficient attention.

A similar criticism applies to the significance Polanyi gives the market for labor. The drive to make a market for labor was not a primary social aim; it was derived from the aim of consumption. The consumption ideal has had undesirable effects but these were unintended. Its original purpose was to achieve noble ideals. The Renaissance ideal of self-realization in work was severely limited in practice to a very few elite. To extend this and other rights and privileges to all was the aim of the 18th century Enlightenment, a movement which included among others, Adam Smith and the American founding fathers. The ideal of better things in life for more people has a material and economic dimension, and this dictates more production and consumption. This was the aim of a growing wealth of nations, an aim that had a broad-based and continuing appeal, for it promised all men an opportunity to get the economic means required for a life of self-realization that in all times past was the privilege of only a few. Noble purposes often have effects that were not intended: in this case, dissatisfaction with work.

## Contemporary Organization of Work

Chris Argyris has put forth a program for reorganization of work that is pragmatic rather than idealistic.[11] He proposes to raise the ethical and aesthetic plane of the work process within the framework of the existing rules of the economic game. Each innovation he cites is either as profitable or more profitable than the procedure it replaces. He has been able to sell his services in the marketplace to business firms in a competitive world. This implies that the drive to maximize profits by minimizing costs is not in itself of sufficient force to bring about the most efficient form of work.

Innovation in the organization of work is hedged with such obstacles as tradition and custom, the overcoming of which provide the economic opportunities and consulting fees of the organizational specialists. These facts have ethical implications. Who has the social responsibility of ensuring that society obtains the potential benefits of new work processes where the ethical, aesthetic, and economic are all mutually reinforcing instead of conflicting? Management has the chief responsibility of keeping informed on new and better ways of managing work, of securing appropriate consultation, and of exercising leadership in overcoming traditional resistances. Union leaders, government, and organizational consultants also have responsibilities.

A more interesting ethical speculation is to carry the question further and

11. Argyris, "Make Work Worthwhile."

ask whether management has social responsibility for ethical and aesthetic improvements even at an economic sacrifice. Long-run ethics differ from short-run ethics in that the former will accept immediate economic sacrifice in the expectation of long-run economic gains. In other words, the belief is that good ethics is good business in the long run. Large corporations have some leeway in the discretionary use of funds to express their ideas on leadership in policy. For example, beginning at the time of the New Deal and extending into the 1950s, General Electric spent large sums of money on education and propaganda trying to ensure that its concept of labor relations would prevail over the union concept. In the long run, General Electric failed to get its paternalistic concept adopted, and now has to live with the concept adopted by public opinion and the law. The money spent in fighting this trend damaged General Electric stockholders in comparison with those of competitors who foresaw long-run trends more clearly and accurately.

We are now at a juncture somewhat like that of labor relations in the thirties. A new production ethic is emerging, and the General Electric experience suggests that corporate management would be better advised to adopt a cooperative approach than to put up a last-ditch battle of resistance. The new production ethic is attractive, directly and personally, to a large and influential body of corporate managers. This is demonstrated in a recent statement by the Committee for Economic Development entitled *Social Responsibilities of Business Corporations.*[12] The statement indicates that the new managerial class wants broader psychological and spiritual satisfactions for itself and for its workers. Salary and career achievements are not enough. The successful executive wants also to feel the satisfaction of helping solve some of society's pressing problems as well as those of the corporation; the worker wants to feel the satisfaction of having produced something more meaningful than a weekly paycheck.

## Production and Consumption Ethics

We are concerned here with the problem of work, but this can be seen as one aspect of a broader production ethic already well advanced and solidly accepted in our economic and political life in its ecological aspects. Success on the ecological front helps advance a new work ethic, for both question the emphasis of our established consumption ethic. The consumption ethic so emphasizes the total quantity and the rate of growth of gross national product (GNP) as to leave in obscurity ramifications and side effects upon nature. Just as the ecological approach illuminates the abuses and misuses of natural resources, the new work ethic puts light on human resources.

12. Committee for Economic Development, *Social Responsibilities of Business Corporations,* New York, 1971, ch. 2.

One of the reasons we need a new production ethic is to restore a just balance. In the recent past so much attention has been given the consumption ethic as to leave the production ethic in the dark. But a swing to the other extreme with the neglect of the consumption ethic which contains principles vital to a good society should be avoided. The classical statement of the consumption ethic was made by the British Socialist economist, R. H. Tawney, in connection with an early argument for the nationalization of mines. Tawney argued that any organization for economic production is ". . . a body of men associated, in various degrees of competition and co-operation, to win their living by providing the community with some service which it requires."[13] From the most primitive to the most sophisticated economy, from the purest capitalistic to the purest socialistic community, there are two basic principles of the organization of production: ". . . its function is service, its method is association."[14] Society grants the right of association and in return demands service. Association is highly productive, a fact known to primitive men who discovered that two men working together could move heavy logs better than singly. The obvious danger of the productiveness of the group is that the producers get together to victimize the consumers. Hence the need for the ethical principle: the function is service to society.

The consumption ethic in its purest form holds that the producers are to use all resources in the most economical and efficient way to produce what society wants; this is humanly unacceptable. In 1842 a Royal Commission reported on working conditions of women and children in the mines of England. So shocking were the facts that Parliament immediately adopted legislation prohibiting employment of any woman or child in the mines. The report showed that little girls had worked stripped naked, harnessed to hundred-weight loads of coal which they dragged through tunnels as small as twenty-eight inches in height. Donkeys would have required higher passages and much greater expense. Mine operators were making a pure application of the consumption ethic: children were more economical and efficient than donkeys and should be employed to bring coal to society at the lowest possible cost. The state interfered with this pure exercise in social ethics and said in effect that humanity in some aspects is above the interests of society. In other words, there must be a production ethic offsetting the consumption ethic in order to protect human fundamentals.

The great outburst in implementation of the production ethic in this country occurred under the New Deal, particularly after the Supreme Court, spurred on by the threat of Franklin Roosevelt to "pack the court," found

13. R. H. Tawney, *The Acquisitive Society* (New York: Harvest Book, Harcourt, Brace & World, 1920), p. 6.

14. Ibid.

social legislation constitutional. The New Deal production ethic had a decided slant or bias reflecting the Great Depression mentality under which it took form. The strongest preoccupation of this depression slant was unemployment, which was perceived as the first and greatest evil. The generation of workers who endured, with only sporadic relief, massive and persistent unemployment right up until World War II saw billowing black smoke from factories and deafening noise within as happy indices of full employment. The present generation sees in the same things a dangerous deterioration of environmental quality necessary to sustain life. The differences in the two positions are comparable to the differences of two reporters describing the same mountain, one from a position to the north, the other from the south. This 180-degree difference can be exemplified in the question: what is a job and how does it enhance my art of living? The depression view was: why should I worry about the *art* of living when I can't even *make* a living? The job comes first; its compensation makes all the other things possible—first, physical needs, then psychological and spiritual satisfactions.

The current view, within a society of greater affluence and fuller employment, is that a job is much more than a means to other ends. It is *the* great determinant. More than anything else, it fixes one's place, not only in economic life, but in politics and society. It greatly influences one's circle of friendships and associations, one's marriage and family, and even the kinds of recreation one will come to enjoy. In our society the job is the central feature of life, the activity that shapes all the other activities constituting the art of living.

Economic affluence and security, as well as other social forces which cannot be examined here, are changing man's conception of himself and hence bringing reexamination of the art of living. One of the broadest interpretations of these developments is that formulated by Philip Rieff.[15] He sees psychological man replacing economic man. Man wants self-fulfillment; Freud's argument that civilization calls for self-renunciation and sublimation is no longer acceptable. The new creed of psychological man is that whatever enhances one's sense of well-being is good. The therapeutic replaces the economic. Hence, each man is to live "an experimental life."

## Affluence and a New Psychology of Living

Robert Jay Lifton has examined the experimental life from another angle.[16] He has observed, in studies of both Asiatic and American youth, the emer-

15. Philip Rieff, *The Triumph of the Therapeutic* (New York: Harper Torchbook, 1966), p. 26.

16. Robert J. Lifton, *Boundaries* (New York: Random House, 1969), pp. 37–63.

gence of a new life style of exploration, experiments and fluidity. The new man is designated "protean" man after Proteus of Greek mythology, who changed his shape with ease from boar to lion, to fire, to flood. He was reluctant to keep his own shape of prophet unless seized and chained. Protean man is in sharp contrast to the rational, economic man typical of advanced industrial societies. That a radically new life style is emerging in advanced societies is not a singular interpretation. Books reaching similar conclusions such as William Thompson's *At the Edge of History*[17] and Charles Reich's *Greening of America*,[18] have had a popular reception indicating considerable acceptance of the new views. If these interpretations are substantially correct, what are the implications for future organization of work?

Details of reorganization will have to come from the play of imagination upon the various facts of existing processes to bring them into concord with new life requirements. Organization of work should reflect the characteristics of the new man, that is, become much more experimental, flexible and fluid. One area of experiment clearly called for is the work-leisure pattern. The routine of 8:00 to 5:00 each day, five days a week, is deadly to protean man. Experiments in flexibility are already under way. Popular reception of the idea of the four-day week should be no surprise if protean man has already appeared on the scene.

Can these new, experimental life styles succeed against the old, ingrained habits and customs of the present system of work? The present system of work is neither an eternal verity nor a natural pattern of human behavior. Quite the contrary—the highly disciplined, mechanical pattern of contemporary factory work is but a recent, brief episode, and in sharp contrast to behavior patterns observed through the long development of man. Nor have any of his close animal relatives behaved in such a manner. Highly disciplined work is a phenomenon of the Industrial Revolution. The assembly lines of Henry Ford and the "scientific management" of Frederick Taylor, which made men's work motions as machine-like as possible, are twentieth-century innovations. If the new life styles fade away, it will not be because the older, more familiar life style has the backing of natural laws of biological or social development, but because it produces a larger flow of goods and services.

A new production ethic is a first priority because consumption-oriented societies lack integrative force, or as the sociologist might say, their symbolic universe is weak and unconvincing. Gabriel Marcel in *Being and*

17. William I. Thompson, *At the Edge of History* (New York: Harper and Row, 1970).

18. Charles Reich, *Greening of America* (New York: Random House, 1970).

*Having* has emphasized that for authentic existence, "being" is superior to "having."[19] Applying this to economic life, we might say our productive role is being, and our consuming role is having. For an economy to possess symbolic significance for man, there must be a place of dignity for him in a productive role. As Argyris points out, no amount of education or propaganda will convince a man of his dignity by demonstrations, however true and conclusive, that tightening bolt number #78 is vital to the safe operation of the vehicle, because the worker knows it is an unskilled, boring task and he feels his worth as a person is only that of the task. Sad to say, the high point of aesthetic experience for many a factory worker goes back to his high school days when he played on the football or basketball team. Then he occupied a place recognized by his fellows, to which he could make his unique contribution, and he often did so at great personal sacrifice. Argyris points to similar occurrences in economic life; for example, when utility workers are called on in an emergency. The organization of factory production for efficiency is usually on so large a scale that each worker becomes one of many replaceable parts. His unique contribution and the personal touch are the last things wanted; rather, each stroke of work should be done exactly alike.

Economic analysis correctly suggests that, in the market, extra compensation will be forthcoming to overcome the aesthetic loss, but we should be cautious in rushing to the conclusion that this provides the basis for good social policy. Some economists are too prone to think it enough to establish freedom to buy and sell in a good market and thus bring everything into a fair exchange. There is a question of priorities here: are the economic and the aesthetic equal and thus fairly exchangeable, or is one to be given priority?

John Ruskin set the priorities straight with the axiom: "There is no wealth but life." He did not mean life in the biological sense, but life in the philosophical or spiritual sense of pursuit of the highest values. Ruskin was the first to develop comprehensive aesthetics of economic life. This he did by taking as the model for economic life the production and consumption of fine art. Great artists have shown the way in which all good work is done. Good work is self-sustaining and life-enhancing, so that great artists have remained happy and productive to old age. All work, even the humblest task of everyday life, can partake of these life-giving qualities if properly done. Similarly, economic consumption should follow the lines of appreciation of art. This takes discipline and training of the senses in both the world of art and of economics. People have to be given not only the material good, but a sense of appreciation and understanding of its proper use. Ac-

19. Gabriel Marcel, *Being and Having* (New York: Harper Torchbooks, 1965).

cording to this integrated theory of art and economics, every man, no matter how humble his station, is called upon to make his economic life a work of art.

The economic and the aesthetic are not subject to fair exchange, one for the other, in the market. The economic aspects of life should be subordinate to its aesthetic aspects. Whether a worker has struck a good occupational bargain cannot be definitively judged by the economic qualities of the market and by whether he has received appropriate compensation for each disutility of the occupation. Judgment has to be made on his whole biography with primary attention to the effects of his occupation upon his aesthetic fulfillment. What is needed is an aesthetic balance sheet showing psychological and spiritual debits and credits. The main items of the balance sheet can be taken from Maslow's "values of being" (see footnote 3): wholeness, aliveness, richness, effortlessness, playfulness, and uniqueness. Most reports on factory workers' lives use words that are polar opposites to Maslow's: alienation, deadness, barrenness, strain, monotony, and routine. One of the great social questions about work is what kinds should not be allowed at all; where a society draws this line is a good indicator of the ethical and aesthetic sensitivities of its members. Aesthetic balance sheets would contribute to a program for raising the aesthetic plane of work by pointing out the worst spots, thus permitting their progressive elimination through innovation or legislation.

Even if the behavior of most people should show that they have reversed Ruskin's axiom and put money ahead of aesthetic life, this does not mean they think it good—as witness their characterization of "blue collar trap." They complain that those who run things—the Establishment—should not allow such traps. They are right according to the ethical principle that responsibility is in proportion to power, and those with most power to improve the organization of work are the leaders of business, government, and labor unions. But the ultimate decision on one of life's most vital issues must still remain a personal responsibility in large degree.

## Convergence of the Humanistic and Economic Viewpoint

The advocate of greater work satisfaction should proceed with two chief cautions or warnings: one is humanistic, the other economic. The humanistic caution is that self-reform is prior to, and superior to, social reform. In other words, social reform, no matter what its quantity or quality, cannot replace the need for self-reform. Aldous Huxley identified one of the illusions of our time as the false belief that we only have to find and adopt some new scheme of organization and all our private and social ills will vanish.[20] The best possible system of work organization will leave much for the individual to do. The common human failing is to project our psychological troubles on other persons and exterior things. The traps thought to be "out there" are often signs of traps within, and no amount of social reform or skilled direction can protect people from falling into their own traps while blaming others. Even if an ideal system of work were instituted, its final success would depend upon the qualities of self-direction and self-discipline of the individual workers. An ideal work system, an ideal society, and an ideal "civil religion," all together, will not constitute Paradise. Man will not find his Final End in them. The failure of the apotheosis of the consumption ethic should not be forgotten. One of the troubles disclosed in a study of "The Troubled American," is the disillusionment of many after arrival in the consumers' paradise of the affluent society.[21]

The science of economics makes a valuable social contribution through the insight it gives into economizing. The whole of microeconomic theory is founded on this insight, yet it is so obvious and so familiar as to be often overlooked. Philip Wicksteed described it as the administering of resources, a process we were all familiar with before we heard of economics.[22] Everyone has had to administer the resources of time. Each has but twenty-four hours per day. If one decides to get more sleep, the time must come from something else. Similarly, society has at any one instant a fixed budget of resources. A thing used for one end is lost to another. We have advocated the more aesthetic way of work even where the more efficient way must be given up. The social cost is the goods and services that the more efficient way could have produced. Substantial aesthetic uplift of the present system of factory production would entail costs that public opinion would not now accept. The consumption ethic, along with its results of high and rising levels of income, is still held in higher esteem than the proposed production ethic.

History shows that man has changed his conception of work, and sometimes sharply, as when Christianity gave dignity to manual labor and converted a culture from the Greek idea of disdain for all but agricultural work. The new production ethic proposed here involves a far less radical shift in the concept of work. It is not the introduction of a new concept of work but the raising of existing ethical and aesthetic planes of work. Nevertheless, the reform has substantial costs and, hence, substantial resistance. Among

20. Aldous Huxley, *The Perennial Philosophy* (London: Chatto and Windus, Ltd., 1946), p. 288.

21. *Newsweek,* Oct. 6, 1969.

22. Phillip Wicksteed, *The Common Sense of Political Economy* (London: Routledge and Kegan Paul, 1933), Vol. 1, ch. 1.

the foreseeable forces that may reduce the resistance are diminishing interest in evergrowing consumption and increasing interest in psychological and spiritual well-being. In an advanced society a large part of additional consumption can be designated "conspicuous," to use Veblen's term, or "unproductive," to use the term of the classical economists. If the contemporary psychological diagnoses that we have cited are correct, then future social judgments of correct balance will tend to favor a higher level of the ethics and aesthetics of production over additions to consumption. This development would represent a convergence of the two cautions earlier cited: the humanistic qualification on self-reform and the economic one on economizing. These two are not so far apart as they may have first seemed. Ultimately the social choice of economizing by shifting resources from luxuries of consumption to aesthetically better ways of producing has to be effectuated by individuals reforming themselves to submit to the required acts of abstinence.

## Commentary

Professor Kennedy underscores the fact that the conventional economic view of consumption and production tends to ignore the aesthetic values of production. The consumption ethic dominates in this perspective. Individuals gain pleasure or utility from the consumption of goods and services and leisure, but regard work as subtracting from leisure and hence diminishing their pleasure. In such a conventional framework it is not surprising that the utility obtained from the dignity and meaningfulness of work tends to be obscured.

With the consumption ethic exalted at the expense of the production ethic, concern with the organization of work and production tends to center on efficiency. A great deal is said about the increase in productivity to be gained by specialization of tasks in which the worker conserves time and concentrates on perfecting a specific skill. The measure of success is output per worker or man-hour, for this will increase consumption. Little attention is paid to the fact that grinding the head of a pin or tightening a bolt may be less rewarding to the worker than making the entire pin or assembling a meaningful component of a machine. In conventional economics there is no attempt to question whether or not the gain in utility from the consumption of more goods and services made possible by an increase in efficiency is offset by the loss in utility as a consequence of work now having less meaning or dignity.

One can question why economics has not been more concerned with work and the production ethic in the past. To a large degree it may be a problem of measurement. As Professor Kennedy points out, economics tends to be a precise social science because it uses "money" as a measuring rod. But as we recall from Chapter 8, it is difficult to measure psychic benefits. Thus, the ease of measuring the value of goods and services in contrast to the difficulty of measuring the value of aesthetics of work tends to force a preoccupation with the consumption ethic.

In the chapter that follows, we return to an examination of the decision-making process in which a community must choose between environmental quality and income. While this decision is rendered politically through the ballot box, the authors demonstrate that economic considerations may determine the vote.

# 10

# Political Choice and Environmental Quality

Perry Shapiro and Anthony Barkume

Traditionally, a property owner in the United States has held broad rights over the use of his land. As long as he did not violate the restrictions placed on the property by local zoning ordinances, an individual could develop his property any way he chose to do. In reality, zoning restrictions were not absolute. Since land-use restrictions were generally matters of local jurisdiction, it was often possible for a locally influential developer to receive a zoning variance if existing restrictions interfered with his plans. Within this system land uses were determined by the market—a piece of land was developed to generate the largest profit.

There are a number of advantages to the market allocative system; but in the case of land-use allocations the market system has a serious shortcoming. Often, if unrestricted, a developer would use his property in a way that seriously damaged the local environment. By seeking his own profit, he would diminish the welfare of others in the community. To exploit subterranean mineral deposits, landowners eroded soil, spoiled watersheds, and polluted streams. Some developers built residential areas with sufficient density to deplete existing water supplies and to cause extreme traffic congestion.

Increasingly, in recent years, the detrimental effects of land development have become matters of public concern. The 1969 Santa Barbara oil spill dramatized the damage that man does to his environment, and precipitated considerable public controversy and political action.

Recognizing that privately directed land development can lead to undesirable environmental effects, the government has assumed more rigid controls over land use. For instance, the government now requires that for many

**The authors thank Barry Stockwell, who collected the original data.**

types of use the developer prove that his proposed development will not result in serious environmental degradation. The strength and quantity of land-use legislation is rising. The government is assuming greater and more wide-ranging controls than ever before.

If one recognizes the damage caused by unrestricted land exploitation, it seems beneficial to convert land-use decisions from a private to a public process. However, publicly taken decisions are not faultless. With the unrestricted market process, the developer imposed his choice on the community. With the political process, the majority imposes its choice on the minority; or those with power impose their choices on those without power. The El Capitan referendum, as described below, demonstrates the complexities of moving the land-use process from the marketplace to the polling place.

## The El Capitan Issue

In 1970 the voters of Santa Barbara County, California, were asked to decide on "Proposition A," an ordinance allowing a large-scale (1500 housing units) residential development in a rural area. The ordinance was approved by the County Board of Supervisors, but it was challenged by local environmental groups and put to a general vote through a spirited referendum effort. The resulting election campaign generated considerable local controversy and wide public attention. Essentially, the choices were retaining local environmental amenities (open space in a rural atmosphere) or increasing community income through the construction activity generated by the development.

The object of the referendum was El Capitan Ranch on the southern coastal corridor of Santa Barbara County, twenty miles northwest of the center of the city of Santa Barbara and six miles northwest of the fringe of residential development on this corridor. The 3638-acre ranch borders the Pacific Ocean for two miles, and its hilly terrain extends east to the edge of the Los Padres National Forest at the base of the Santa Ynez Mountains. Farming for crops such as beans and tomatoes and cattle grazing constituted its agricultural uses. In 1947 the Gila Land Company purchased the property for $293,500. They farmed it for a number of years and sold it in 1966 for $3,525,000 to Jules Berman, the present owner.[1]

Since 1958 El Capitan Ranch has been designated as part of a "U" district (a zoning code restricts primary use to agriculture or grazing), in which 10 acres is the minimum allowable building site area.[2] In 1965 the County adopted a general plan designed to provide guidelines for land-use policy

1. *Santa Barbara News Press,* November 26, 1967, pp. A-1 and A-18.

2. Santa Barbara County Planning Staff, *Staff Report,* March 19, 1970, Section VII, "Zoning and Development History."

for the following twenty years. It was recommended in the plan that the "U" designation be retained for the Ranch and surrounding area until 1985 in order to "preserve the natural beauty of the area [so] that its ultimate residential and tourist value [would] be realized."[3]

In 1967 Berman first publicly proposed a large-scale residential development on El Capitan, with over 1500 parcels to be offered as homesites over a 15-year period. Of the total area of the Ranch, 2500 acres were designated for three distinct uses: summer homes (440 parcels on 440 acres); a residential cluster (195 parcels on 78 acres); and single family residential estates.[4] The "ranchos" in this third area were to range from 2 to 10 acres, with a minimum lot price of $50,000. These estates were to be provided with such extensive amenities as landscaped greenbelts interspersing the homes, a tennis club, golf course, and a private beach, and the character of the community was to be established with the development of major equestrian facilities.

Berman initially invested in the construction of a polo field, stables and pastures, and 35 miles of riding trails. He planned to have breeding facilities, riding schools, and an arena for horse shows. To enhance the prestige of the Ranch as an equestrian center, the owner acquired a large stock of Arabian horses, and imported 14 Lippanzers from Austria. To maintain the desired character of the community, deed restrictions and controls were established, these to be supplanted by a homeowners' association, similar in design to those of existing exclusive upper-income communities in Santa Barbara.

Between 1967 and 1969 Berman received conditional use permits within "U" zoning designation to allow the nonresidential development on the Ranch.[5] However, because the residential development entailed the subdivision of sites below the 10 acres allowed under the zoning, in February 1970 Berman applied for a change in the zoning from "U" to "PR," a zoning designation for a planned residential community.

A change in the zoning of the property from "U" to "PR" required a public hearing by the county planning commission, and with its approval a subsequent hearing by the county board of supervisors for final approval of a rezoning ordinance. It was within this sequence of hearings that the question of El Capitan's proposed development evolved into a major environmental issue—the object of a referendum movement and a political campaign which would bring it to a decision by the voters of Santa Barbara County in the election of that year.

3. Ibid.

4. *General Development Plan for El Capitan Ranch,* received by the Santa Barbara County Planning Staff, February 13, 1970, pp. 6–9.

5. Santa Barbara County Planning Staff, *Staff Report,* Section VIII.

With notice of a public hearing on the adoption of an ordinance permitting the rezoning to planned residential, over 50 letters, pro and con, were received by the planning commission. The letters in opposition to the rezoning all stressed the environmental issue, that an urban pattern was being established in a rural area. These were particularly conveyed by such conservation groups as the local chapter of the Sierra Club, Scenic Shoreline Preservation Conference, and "Save Our City." The latter felt that the commission's approval would mean that the citizens' "environmental well-being and quality of life would certainly be subordinated to the wishes of the developer."[6] The Citizens' Planning Association felt the action would "serve as a bellweather for the eventual development of vast areas of the south coast."[7] The Sierra Club spokesman stressed the "natural amenities" of the area and concluded that the "erosion of natural beauty starts with urbanization."[8]

The public hearing was held in April 1970, with pro and con testimony following the themes established by the letters to the Commission. Prior to the hearing the planning staff recommended that the rezoning be denied because the proposed land use conflicted with the guidelines established in the general plan. The planning commission overrode this recommendation and approved the zoning change by a 6 to 2 vote.

Following this action, opposition to the rezoning increased. On the day of the public hearing before the county supervisors, two local environmental groups (Scenic Shoreline Preservation Conference and Western Citizens for Environmental Defense) called for additional hearings to determine the suitability of the development in relation to the general plan. They claimed that if the rezoning were approved it ". . . would open the floodgate for urbanization for all the coastal rural areas of the county."[9] The hearing also received two petitions with a combined total of 500 signatures offered in testimony to deny the rezoning. Support for the El Capitan development also extended with testimony being offered in favor of the project by the secretary of the county building and trades council. The labor official cited the boost to local employment that would come with residential construction at El Capitan, which would counteract a local downturn in home building in the first half of 1970. The supervisors concluded the hearing by approving the rezoning by a vote of 4 to 1.

Opposition to the rezoning ordinance then took the form of a referendum campaign. The objective was to circulate a petition and obtain enough signatures so that the board of supervisors would be required to either repeal the ordinance or have it placed as a proposition on the November ballot.

6. Excerpted from letters received by the Santa Barbara Planning Commission.

7. Ibid.

8. Ibid.

9. Excerpted from the minutes of testimony presented at the Commission hearing.

Eleven-hundred signatures were obtained in time for filing the petition, and after a short legal contest by Berman, the rezoning ordinance was placed on the ballot as "Proposition A." More than $30,000 was expended by both sides to bring the issue to the public, and on November 3, 1970, 33,822 votes were received for the proposition (approving the rezoning) and 46,861 against.[10] Thus, by a margin of more than 13,000 votes, development of El Capitan was turned down.

During the campaign the opponents of the proposition painted a graphic scenario in campaign ads of "what was to come after El Capitan." Appealing to the land-use policy prescribed for the area by the General Plan, they emphasized: "Five years ago the citizens of Santa Barbara County decided to resist the trend that is ravaging California, the trend toward smog, highway strangulation, and reckless exploitation of natural charms . . . So they adopted . . . a General Plan."[11]

Thus the general plan prescription was perceived as saving "our real natural amenities"[12]—those of the undeveloped shoreline. As it was put in the closing paragraph of a statement made late in the campaign, "The question before Santa Barbara voters is whether to self-destruct. . . . This is essentially our last chance to preserve a balanced environment in Santa Barbara County."[13]

The owner of El Capitan and supporters of Proposition A (which included the Chamber of Commerce and organized labor) presented a different concept of environmental quality to the voters in arguing for acceptance of the development. It was claimed that El Capitan would follow the character of existing exclusive high-income communities with low-density settlement, and controls on building construction. But, more strongly, it was emphasized that the development would provide a "much-needed boost to jobs"[14] and income for the county at a time when unemployment was running 8 percent in the area. The defeat of the project was presented as the initial point in a further downward slide in the economic conditions as in the following: "If development of this kind is harassed, every worker in this county, blue collar and white, will be hurt by steadily increasing taxes and steadily decreasing employment and business volume."[15]

## A Model for Analysis of the El Capitan Issue

The analysis of the election issue begins with an outline of the technological relation between environmental quality and the production of economic

10. *Santa Barbara News Press,* November 4, 1970, p. A-1.
11. *Santa Barbara News Press,* October 18, 1970 (political advertisement), p. A-18.
12. Ibid., October 30, 1970, p. A-10.
13. Ibid., p. A-7.
14. Ibid., p. A-19.
15. Ibid., November 1, 1970, p. A-4.

goods. Economists note that the material things that make up environmental quality, such as open land, pure air and water, while desired in themselves, can serve as factors in the production of economic goods as well; for example, housing construction uses land and factory production consumes pure air and water. The trade-off between the level of economic or market activity and environmental quality for a hypothetical community is represented in Figure 10–1. The symbols *C* on the vertical axis and *E* on the

Figure 10–1. The community transformation schedule between income and environmental quality (*C* and *E*).

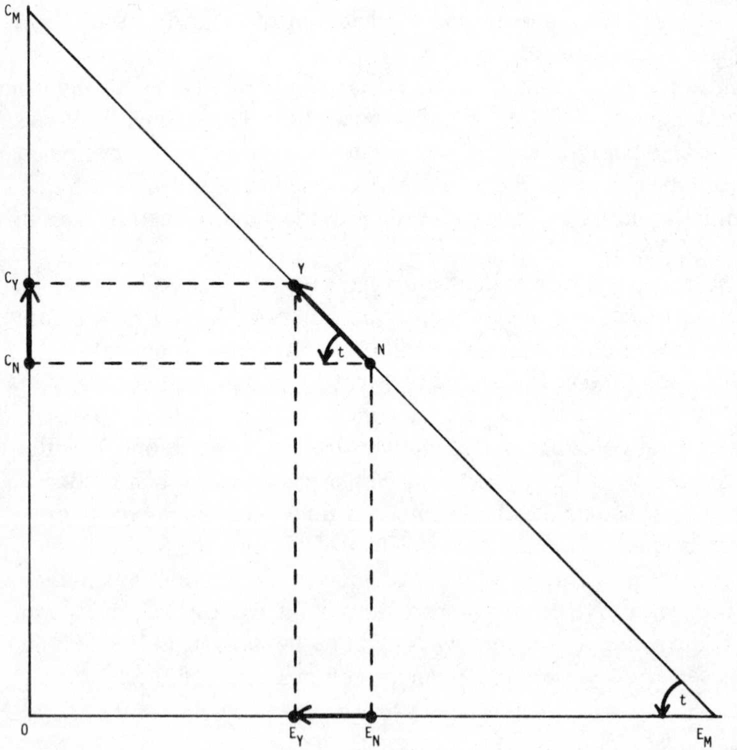


horizontal axis denote indexes of the output of economic goods (community income) and of the community's environmental quality, respectively.

Figure 10–1 summarizes several important technological relations between *C* and *E*. The line connecting points $C_M$ and $E_M$ represents the alternative combinations of $C$ and $E$ attainable to the community at a given time and level of technological knowledge. The symbols $C_M$ and $E_M$ are the two "extreme" positions on the schedule, $C_M$ being the maximum level of production which can be achieved at the cost of complete environmental destruction ($E$ is zero at that point) and $E_M$ being nature unscathed, but with consequent absence of any economic activity. The slope of the schedule, given by the letter $t$, can be interpreted in the following way. If the community decides to increase the level of environmental quality by one unit, $t$ is the amount of community income foregone with the institution of this policy: it is essentially the *price* for the improvement of environmental quality. The intermediate positions $Y$ and $N$ on the graph both represent positive levels of both $E$ and $C$. As the arrows indicate, the social policy of a move from $N$ to $Y$ implies a reduction in the level of environmental quality from $E_N$ to $E_Y$, but allows an increase in community income from $C_N$ to $C_Y$. An immediate parallel can be drawn between this illustration of transformation and the issue for the voter's decision on "Proposition A." Approval of the El Capitan project would have meant a reduction in the open space on the coastal area, that is, a reduction in the level of environmental quality of the South Coast area. However, aside from the direct economic benefit of an increased housing supply, the injection of the investment funds for the project would increase employment and, therefore, the level of community income. The first step in applying the model to the El Capitan referendum is to associate position $N$ with the consequences of rejecting "Proposition A" (that is, the status quo in the community), and the position $Y$ with the consequences of approving "Proposition A."

Figure 10–1 illustrates the alternatives open to the community as a whole. The community, however, makes a final choice ($Y$ or $N$) on the basis of the number of votes cast $Y$ and the number cast $N$, and each of these votes will depend on each citizen's preferences. Understanding each voter's decision is aided by understanding his behavior in the marketplace.

What a person can buy in the market depends on what he can earn in the market through wages, rent, interest, and profits, that is, his level of earning ability in the economy. A simple way to express his earning ability relative to others in the community is to identify his share or proportion of income. Suppose we made an arbitrarily arranged list of all income-earning members in the community, and let the symbol $\bar{C}$ be the level of community income and $C_i$ be the level of income for the $i$th individual on the list. Then

$$a_i = \frac{C_i}{\bar{C}}$$

defines his share of the total income.

Figure 10–2 depicts an individual's consumption possibilities of $C$ and $E$ in relation to the community transformation schedule. The lower his share

Figure 10–2. The relationship between the community transformation schedule and the individuals' consumption possibilities.

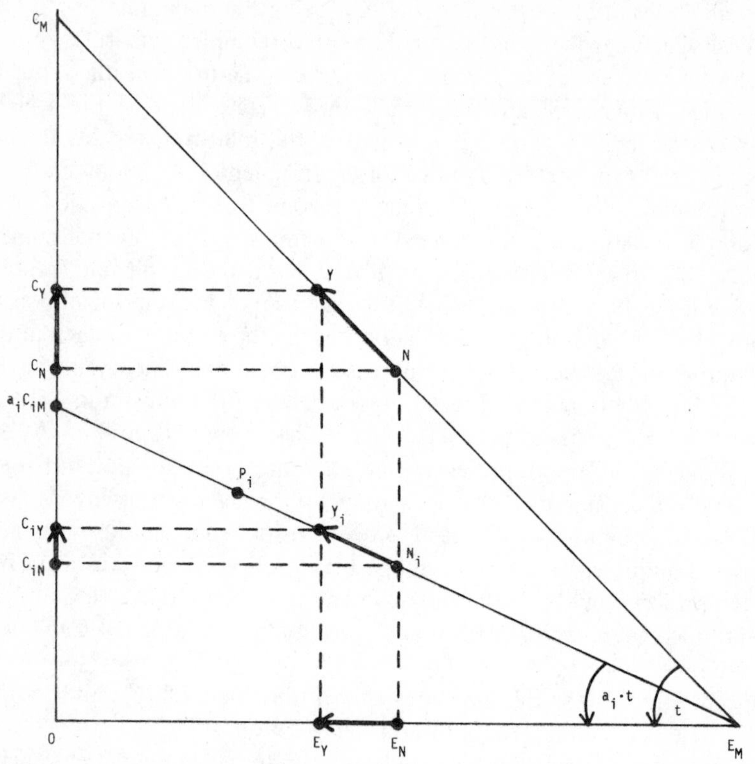


of income, the lower are his possibilities for consumption, since his highest possible consumption of economic goods $C_{iM}$ is simply defined as equal to $a_iC_M$. However, an individual's consumption possibilities for the enjoyment of the level of $E$ do not vary with his income share in that most of the things that make up environmental quality are really shared equally; we all breathe the same air, or if living in the same city, experience the same congestion traveling to work. For simplicity economists define environmental quality as a *public good*—something which all members of the community share equally.

It is reasonable to assume that the individual prefers some combinations of $C$ and $E$ to others, and, furthermore, that one combination is most preferred among those attainable, i.e., all those combinations along the schedule $a_iC_ME_M$. Then if we know his most preferred point, we could locate it on his consumption possibilities schedule. In Figure 10–2 such a point is identified by the point $P_i$. In this particular case the person prefers a higher level of income and a lower level of environmental quality than under the social policies $Y$ and $N$, which would give him combinations $Y_i$ and $N_i$, respectively.

Consider again the adoption of a social policy that dictates a move from the position $N$ to the position $Y$. Can we relate this policy to the person's individual welfare? Examine the effect of this social policy upon the individual's consumption possibilities. He moves from $N_i$ to $Y_i$, in a sense closer to his most preferred position $P_i$. Intuitively, one would say that, according to the person's preferences, combination $Y_i$ is preferred to $N_i$, since the former is closer to $P_i$. This intuition is supported by the usual convention economists make about the structure of people's preferences for combinations of goods.[16] This assumption allows us to hypothetically measure a person's welfare loss in relative terms; for example, in the case depicted in Figure 10–2, position $Y_i$ is preferred to $N_i$; therefore the person's welfare loss is greater at $N_i$ than at $Y_i$, relative to his preferred position $P_i$.[17]

Although a criterion for identifying welfare losses and gains from changes in social policy for an individual is established, why would the combination determined by social policy, even a democratic policy through majority voting, differ from any individual preferred position? The answer is that, in general, different people would have different preferred combinations, and a social compromise must therefore be made, since the social choice will determine a single level of environmental quality.

One reason for different preferred combinations is that people will have different shares of the community income. This is because consumption possibilities are greater for an individual the higher his income share. Even if everyone in the community had the same preference ranking (and they certainly do not), the most preferred alternatives would not be the same between income classes. An individual can attain more of both goods the higher his position in the income distribution scale, i.e., the higher a person's income the larger his selection of alternatives. Thus, even if the rich man and poor man were to feel the same about every alternative, the rich man could pick a better one.

Figure 10–3 depicts the consumption possibilities for a hypothetical community of only three people. Note that person 1 can be identified as the "low" income one in the community because his share, $a_1$, is the lowest. We have also plotted the pattern of preference in the community, the line of

16. The technical term for this convention is *convexity of preferences.*

17. Note we are not interested in *how much* greater is the welfare loss. We shall show a method of identifying gains and losses of different individuals in a community, but because of the subjectivity of individual satisfaction, we cannot "total up" *different* people's gains and losses.

Figure 10–3. Consumption possibilities and the distribution of income.

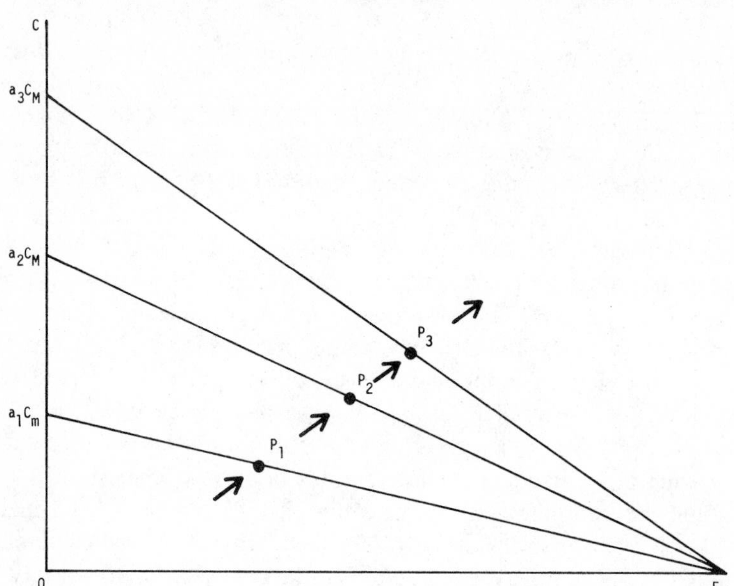


arrows through $P_1$, $P_2$ and $P_3$ indicating the direction of preference with increased income share. This particular pattern, which we shall call Case 1, shows that those with higher income shares prefer a higher level of income *and* a higher level of environmental quality in the community. This pattern of preference for environmental quality would mean that even if everyone in the community ranked alternative combinations of $C$ and $E$ in the same manner, as one's share of income increased, he would prefer an accompanying increase in environmental quality. For commodities sold in the market, economists usually denote those that assume a greater proportion of one's budget with increases in income as "luxury" goods. This hypothesis about preference for environmental quality is substantiated from other evidence in social research. Among environmental protection groups it is well known that ". . . the group most willing to pay the price of stopping air and water pollution are suburbanites, young adults, the well-educated and the affluent."[18] And even though it is generally accepted that "the quality of environment is proportional to socioeconomic status,"[19] invariably studies

18. "New Conservation Poll," *National Wildlife* 8, no. 1 (1970), p. 18.

19. "Human Ecology, Technology and the Need for Social Planning," Paul H. Ray, *American Behavioral Scientist* 11 (July–August 1968), p. 17.

of the perception of, and concern about, environmental hazards show that the poor rank environmental quality far down on their list of concerns. Air purity, for instance, is considered important only after employment and other uncertainties more related to immediate subsistence.

Although other patterns of consumption are possible (and these will be compared with Case 1 later), let us examine the establishment of a particular social policy determining the level of $E$ and corresponding level of $C$. Figure 10–4 illustrated the establishment of a social policy offering the

Figure 10–4. Illustration of "social compromise" at social policy $A$.

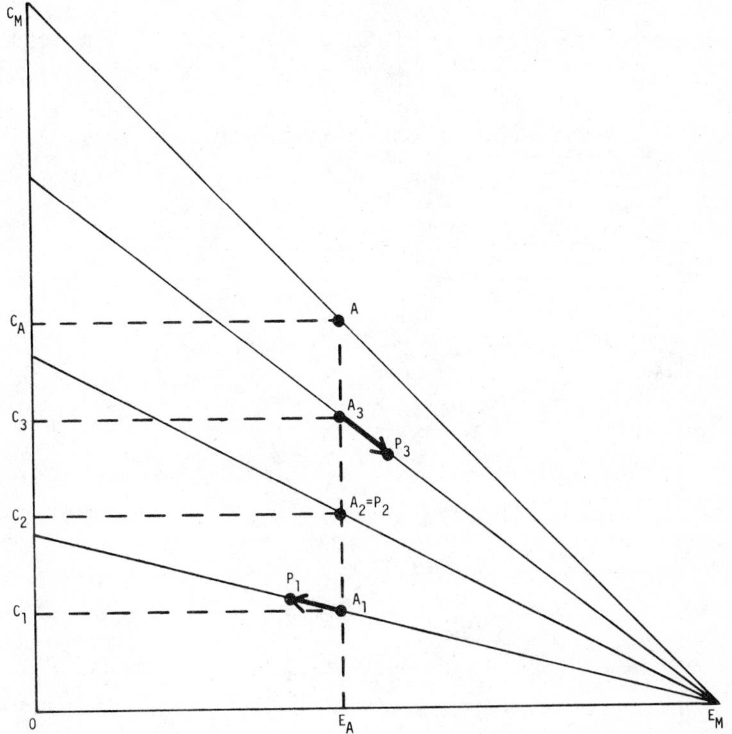


combination of $E_A$ and $C_A$. Each of the three people, therefore, enjoy the same level of environmental quality, namely $E_A$, as a public good. Two's actual level of $C$ and $E$, determined by the social policy (point $A_2$), exactly corresponds to his preferred point $P_2$, but One's and Three's preferred positions differ from their actual positions. Three would prefer *more E* and *less C,* while One would prefer *less E* and *more C;* therefore, One and Three incur some welfare loss in effecting the social compromise. If in this hypothetical community of three, social policy were decided by majority voting, an income level above that preferred by One would never be chosen, for if it were put to a vote, Two and Three would vote against the policy, since *both* would be moving away from their preferred positions $P_1$, $P_2$.

This example brings us to a more general theory of voting. Most issues of social policy presented to the voters for decision are choices between status quo and a particular change in policy. For example, the Clean Environment initiative presented to California voters in the 1972 primary did not ask how much reduction in pollution each preferred, but rather presented a specific set of pollution controls for the voter to either accept or reject.

This type of public choice is depicted in Figure 10–5. The voters have

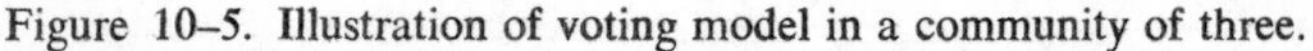

Figure 10–5. Illustration of voting model in a community of three.

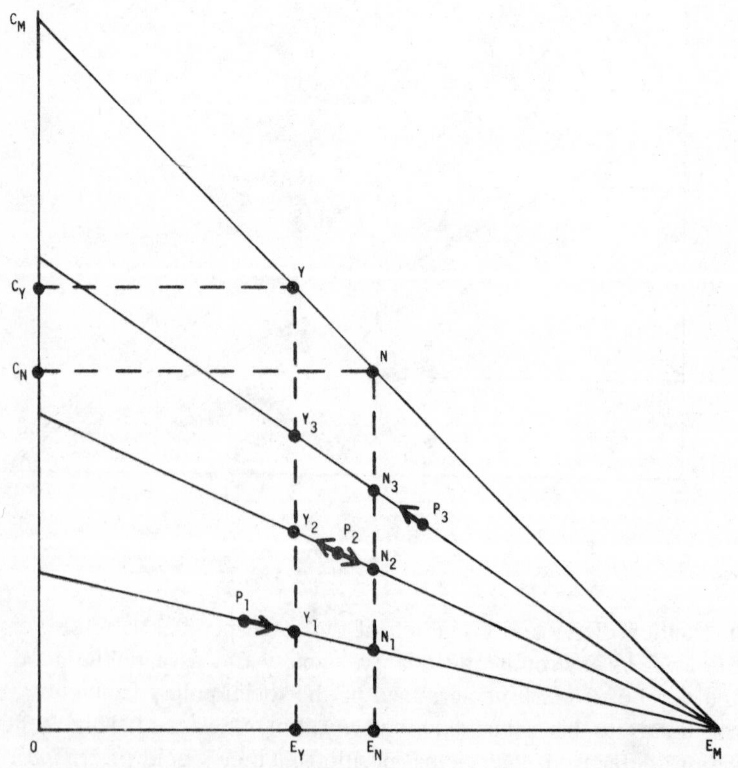

the pattern of preferences as given before with position $N$ on the community transformation schedule as the status quo. They are asked to approve a social policy calling for more $C$ and less $E$ (a move to $Y$) by a "yes" vote in an election. If they vote "no," social policy will dictate remaining at $N$—the status quo.

To determine how each citizen will vote on this issue, examine the impact of the two policies on individual welfare. For voter Three, the change in policy, if implemented, would dictate a move from $N_3$ to $Y_3$; away from his preferred position $P_3$. It therefore follows that voter Three would vote "no" (or against the policy change) since the change would dictate a loss in the estimation of his welfare. Voter One, on the other hand, would benefit from the policy change because he would move from $N_1$ to $Y_1$, closer to his preferred position $P_1$. What about voter Two? His preferred position is *between* the two alternatives, and without more specific information on his comparison of $Y_2$ and $N_2$, his vote cannot be predicted.

In summary, the basic assumption underlying this model of voting is simply that a person votes for a social policy that he feels improves his individual welfare and votes against those policies that reduce it. Based on this assumption, postulating that the higher one's share of community income, the higher level of income *and* environmental quality is preferred, the theory then predicts that the higher the income the greater the tendency to oppose (vote against) a social policy that would raise the community's level of income at the cost of lowering the level of environmental quality.

The issue presented to the Santa Barbara voters for decision on the El Capitan referendum conforms well to the type of public choice framed in the voting model. Opponents of "Proposition A" represented it as leading to an "erosion of natural beauty," while its supporters agreed it would give "a boost to jobs" available in the community. Therefore, examination of the relationship between voting patterns and income provides an opportunity to test the hypothesis that there is a positive relationship between income and the demand for environmental quality. This will shed some light on the impact of a change in public policy.

Rarely does the establishment of a new public policy make everyone better off; the usual case is that some gain and some lose as a consequence of the policy. In these cases it is even theoretically difficult to say whether or not the adoption of the social policy has increased community welfare, that is, whether or not the welfare gains enjoyed by some citizens total up to more than the losses suffered by others. However, it is important to try to establish the *incidence* of a policy change, that is, to employ some criteria to identify who loses.

In the situation given in Figure 10–5, the community's acceptance of the policy represented by position $N$ over that for $Y$ would imply that voter Three, who has the highest income share, becomes better off in his own estimation of welfare. Voter One, who has the lowest share, similarly becomes worse off. Given our hypothesis of increased preference for environmental quality with a larger share of the community's income, the incidence of a social policy, which increases the level of *E* at the cost of foregone *C*, will be borne by those with lower income shares.

Since the test of the hypothesis has important implications, a remark on the need for the possibility of refuting an hypothesis is in order before analyzing the election results. The case has been made that if a community's preferred consumption follows a certain pattern, then given the assumptions of the model, voting on issues of environmental policy will also follow a certain pattern. Examine the graph in Figure 10–6, which shows another

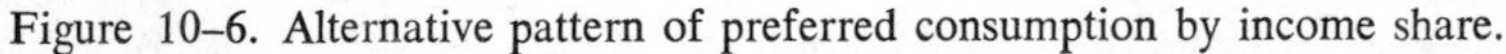
Figure 10–6. Alternative pattern of preferred consumption by income share.

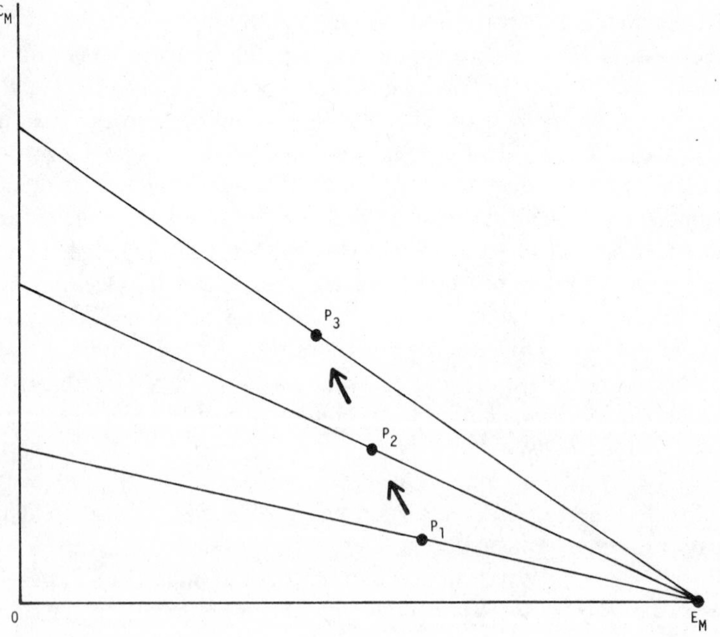


possible pattern of preference by income share in the community. In this case, the higher the income share, the lower the level of environmental quality preferred. What would the model predict about individual voting behavior on an issue such as "Proposition A"? It would predict that those with higher income shares would vote for the development, while those with lower income shares would vote again the development. Thus, if this result is observed, the hypothesis about the direction of preferred combinations of $C$ and $E$ would be refuted. This possibility that it can be proved wrong is essential if the hypothesis is to be treated empirically.

## Testing the Model

Since more than 80,000 Santa Barbara County voters participated in the decision on "Proposition A," it is impossible to get the details of information strictly required by the voting model. Identifying every voter's income share and how he voted (as was done in the hypothetical community of three) would violate the anonymity of the ballot box. The greatest detail possible was obtained from the voting records of 156 individual precincts (each of which contains between two and four hundred voters) supplied by the Santa Barbara County Registrar. Special estimates of median income for each precinct were prepared especially for the study by the county planning staff. These income estimates were used to approximate the average income share by precinct. Figure 10–7 illustrates the distribution of negative votes and income class by voting precinct in Santa Barbara.

Since the raw data obtained were in terms of group averages (e.g., median income, total "no" votes cast in precinct #121), the best way to describe the tendency to vote a certain way is to calculate the ratio of votes cast either "yes" or "no" to the total votes cast by precinct. In this study the ratio

$$P_N = \frac{\text{“No” Votes}}{\text{Total Votes}}$$

was computed for each precinct. Note that $P_N$ can range from zero to one, and in a rough way can be interpreted as the *probability* that an individual would oppose "Proposition A." With these probabilities assigned, it is possible to test the hypothesis that $P_N$ varies positively with the income levels, that is, an increase in an individual's income increases the probability of opposing the El Capitan development.

Two types of analyses were made with the data. The first was a test of the null hypothesis, which is a statistical examination of whether there is any relationship between the proportion voting "no" and the median income for each precinct. The second was an estimation of a quantitative relationship between voting and income.[20]

The null hypothesis that the computed voting ratios and respective income levels have no relationship other than a random one was tested by a

20. A variety of tests performed in each stage confirmed the hypothesis. Therefore, only the results for the simple tests will be given for illustration.

Figure 10–7. Distribution of negative votes and income class by voting precinct, City of Santa Barbara.

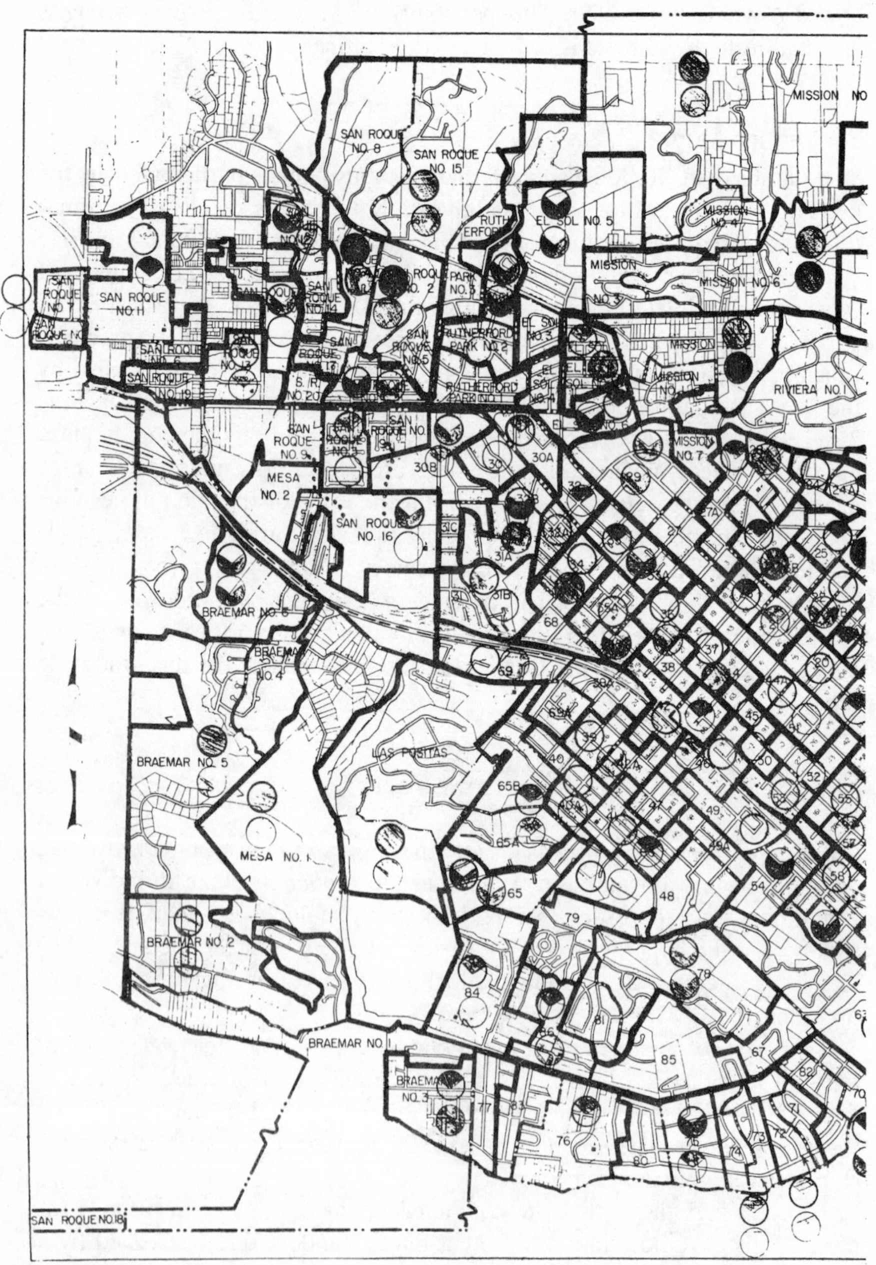

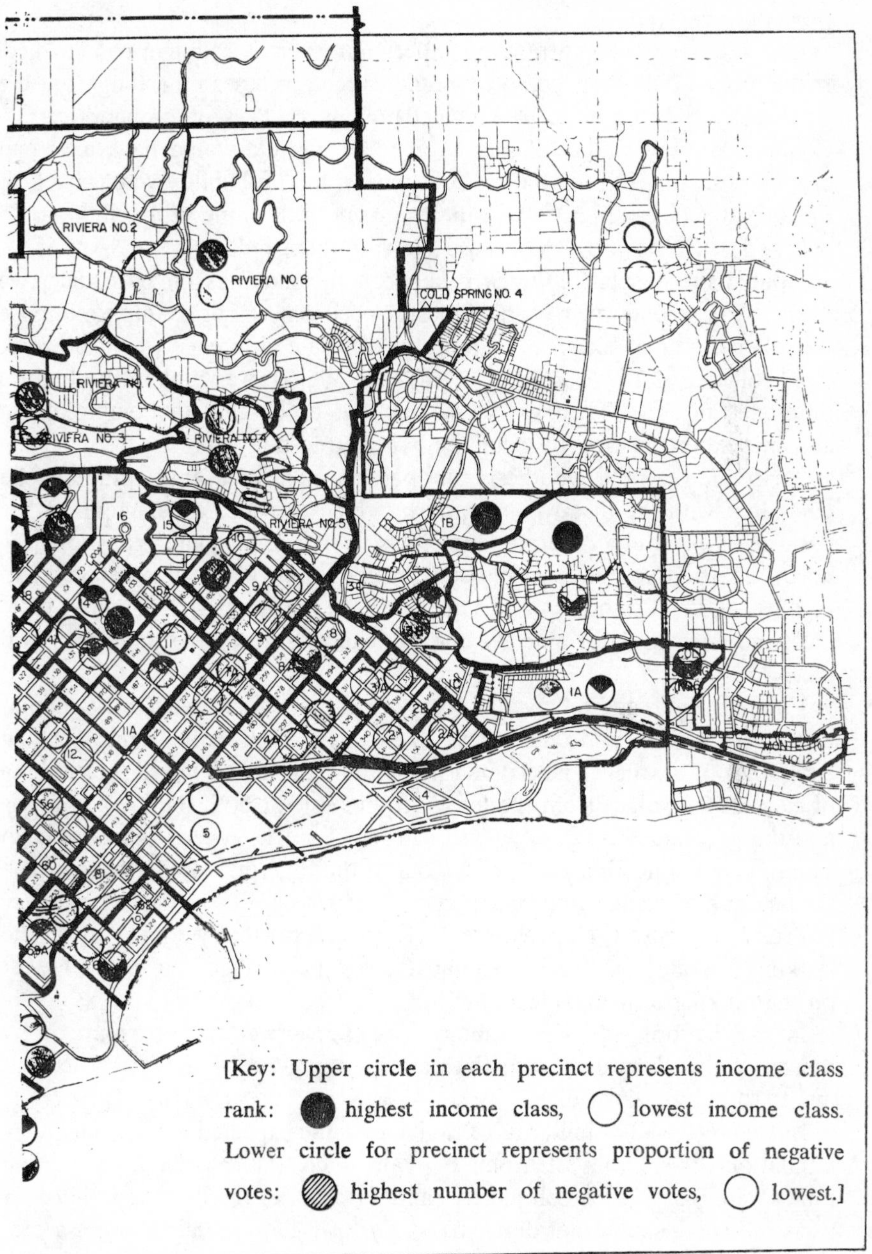


[Key: Upper circle in each precinct represents income class rank: ● highest income class, ○ lowest income class. Lower circle for precinct represents proportion of negative votes: ◍ highest number of negative votes, ○ lowest.]

Source: Santa Barbara County Registrar and Planning Staff, 1967.

routine application of the Chi-square statistic.[21] However, before giving the results, a simple conceptual experiment illustrating the logic of the testing procedure is given.

Consider conducting a random experiment such as rolling a pair of dice. If the dice weren't "loaded," you would expect, in repeated rolling, that the outcomes would be close to expected under the laws of probability. For example, the probability of any number on one die would have an equal chance of resting face up on any roll, that is, the probability would be 1/6. For any two faces appearing on the roll of both dice, the probability would be (1/6) • (1/6) = 1/36 because they are independent events. And if we computed the absolute *difference* between the numbers on both dice, we could also compute their probabilities of occurrence. For example, suppose we rolled a pair of sixes (6,6); then the absolute difference would be zero; if we rolled a (1,1), (2,2), (3,3), (4,4), or (5,5), we would also obtain a difference of zero. Then we know that the probability of computing an absolute difference of zero would be expected to be 6/36.

To frame the null hypothesis, the pattern of income and voting can be compared with the dice-rolling pattern, which provides an example of the pattern of perfectly random events. Using the Chi-square statistic, it is necessary to group or cross-classify the values of voting percentages and income, and test whether or not the resulting pattern is significantly different from one that is completely due to chance, such as the pattern of two dice.

Figures 10–8b and 8d give the resulting pattern of one such cross-tabulation of the income and voting data by grouping each variable into 6 equal categories or sextiles. The Roman numerals I through VI give the ranking of each of the values from the lowest to highest for both the income levels and the percentage of votes against "Proposition A." The numbers in each square give the number of precincts out of the total of 156 that have a particular rank of income and a certain rank of voting. For example, the entry for column 1, row 1, gives the total (10 precincts) that were lowest on the ranking of voting against El Capitan (lowest percentage "no") and lowest on the ranking of income level.

Is this pattern simply a random one? To answer this, compare it by means of the chi-square with the pattern generated by a random experiment: rolling a pair of dice.

In Figure 10–8a a similar table is given for the expected values in a cross-tabulation of 144 rolls of a pair of "fair" dice. If the income and voting ranks were paired by a completely random process, the observed values in each cell entry should not differ markedly from those obtained from a die-

21. For an illustrative use of the chi-square hypothesis for testing, see Ya-Lun Chou, *Statistical Analysis,* Ch. 14.

Figure 10–8. Number of expected dice combinations with 144 rolls; number of expected income-voting combinations.

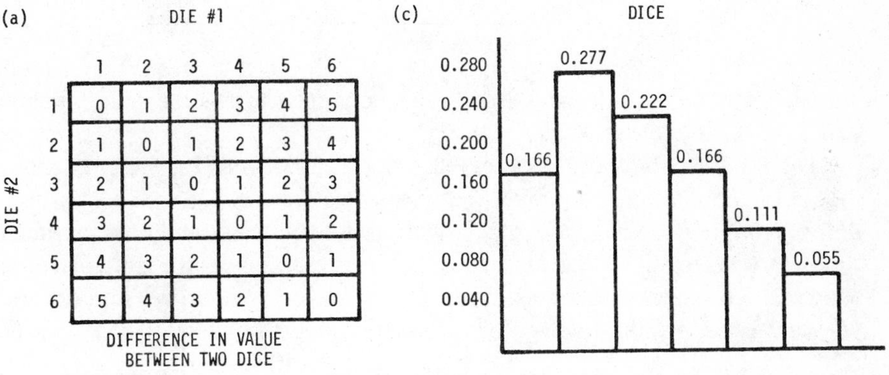


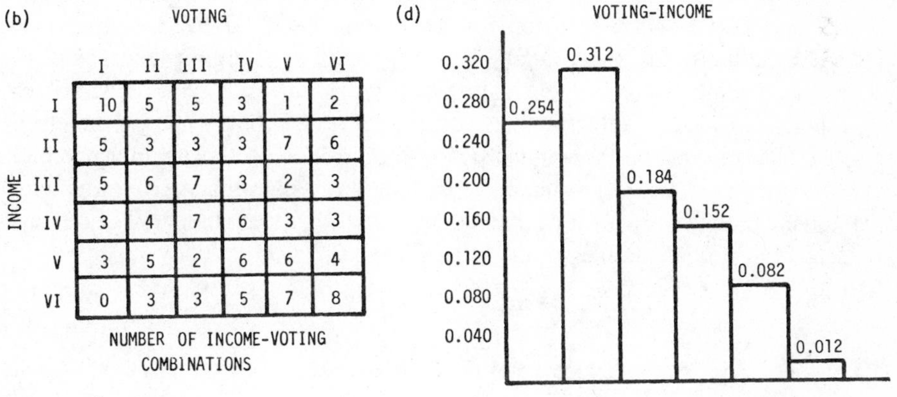

Table 10–1
Observed Difference Between Hypothesized and Actual Voting Pattern

| D (Absolute Difference) | Observed Proportion | Expected Proportion |
|---|---|---|
| 0 | 0.254 | 0.166 |
| 1 | 0.312 | 0.277 |
| 2 | 0.184 | 0.222 |
| 3 | 0.152 | 0.166 |
| 4 | 0.082 | 0.111 |
| 5 | 0.012 | 0.055 |

tossing experiment, nor should the values obtained for the absolute differences between their ranks.

Table 10–1 compares the observed proportions of rolls for each possible value of the difference between the ranks (signified as $D$, where $D = 0, 1, \cdots 5$) of income and voting, with those expected under a random process. These proportions for each value of $D$ are plotted in Figures 10–8c and 8d. To explain how these proportions are computed, the proportion $D = 0$ is simply the total of observations along the main diagonal, i.e., $\frac{24}{144} = 0.166$ for the dice-tossing experiment, and $\frac{40}{156} = .254$ for the voting-income tabulation.

The chi-square statistic is computed to compare these proportions. The computation shows that the null hypothesis is rejected, i.e., there is a significant relation between income and voting in the election.[22]

The second part of the analysis was directed at estimating the extent to which income influenced the voting pattern. Clearly, there were variables other than income affecting the vote on "Proposition A." It is therefore desirable to establish how much differences in income explain interprecinct voting differences. To estimate the explanatory power of income, a simple statistical equation was formulated, such that its parameters could be computed with the available voting data. The equation is as follows:

$$P_n = A + B \cdot Y, \qquad (1)$$

22. For those with a background in principles of statistics, the test was conducted at the 99 percent level of confidence with

$$\chi^2_{5,.01} = 15.09$$

$$\chi^2 \text{ computed} = \sum_{d=0}^{5} \frac{(\text{Od} - \text{Ed})^2}{Ed} = 16.44$$

where Od = observed frequency
Ed = expected frequency under a uniform distribution

where

> $P_n$ = ratio of the vote against the total on "Proposition A" for each income level (interpreted as the probability of voting "no" on the issue);
>
> $A$ = a constant, which expressed the fraction of $P_n$ that does *not* vary with income (other factors in the election decision);
>
> $B$ = the amount a given increase in income will *increase* the probability, $P_n$, of voting against "Proposition A." (Note that if the estimated value of $B$ were negative, then the hypothesis would have to be rejected);
>
> $Y$ = symbol for the income level expressed in thousand dollar units.

The coefficients were computed using the least-squares regression method applied to the data given in Table 10–2.

Several important facts can be gleaned directly from Table 10–2. "Proposition A" went down to defeat by a margin of more than 13,000 votes, so that the Santa Barbara voters as a whole were in close agreement on the final decision. The only group of precincts approving the development were those in the lowest income group—precincts with median incomes of $5,000

Table 10–2
Data for Quantitative Estimation of the Effect of Income on Voting

| $P_n$* | Y (in thousands of dollars) | Total number of voters in each income class |
|---|---|---|
| 0.493 | 5 | 897 |
| 0.539 | 6 | 824 |
| 0.524 | 7 | 1,538 |
| 0.552 | 8 | 2,688 |
| 0.540 | 9 | 6,566 |
| 0.591 | 10 | 3,833 |
| 0.542 | 11 | 9,161 |
| 0.565 | 12 | 9,092 |
| 0.575 | 13 | 5,527 |
| 0.606 | 14 | 5,392 |
| 0.592 | 15 | 3,642 |
| 0.572 | 16 | 949 |
| 0.565 | 17 | 700 |
| 0.617 | 18 | 851 |
| 0.595 | 20 | 786 |

*This is the ratio of "no" votes to total votes for each income class.

or less. Another pattern is that as the precincts become more affluent, the proportion opposing the development increases, but not uniformly at each thousand-dollar increase. What explanation could be given for this from the voting model (Figure 10–5)? Remember that the model, in its simplest form presented above, does not give us much information on which way the middle-income voter will go on the election because we cannot say whether he benefits or loses from a policy change if his preferred combination is *between* those combinations of community income and level of environmental quality presented as alternatives in a voting decision. Middle-income voters, for instance, may be more uncertain than the highest or lowest income people about the relative benefits of the two alternatives.

Table 10–2 shows a significant difference between the voting proportions for the highest and lowest income groups of more than ten percentage points. Even though the voting proportions do not increase uniformly with income, the estimate of the $Pn$ from Equation 2 gives the *average* rate of increase by fitting the equation to the data in Table 10–2.

$$Pn = 0.49 + 0.006Y \tag{2}$$

The equation fits the data fairly well and can be interpreted in the following way: The 0.006 estimate for $B$ implies that if the population had been partitioned by income class (all citizens with the same income were put into the same thousand-dollar class), the probability of voting "no" rises by 0.6 percent as the average income of the voters in a precinct increases by $1,000. The constant 0.49 is the probability of voting against the measure which would depend on factors not related to differences in income, possibly including the community's view of the legal precedents set by the election results.

## Implications of El Capitan to Broader Issues of Environmental Protection

A $1,000 difference in income resulted in a 0.6 percent difference in the probability of voting for the preservation of environmental quality. This seems a paltry difference to be making such a great fuss about. Indeed, it is a small difference in a small, isolated community. So what if the poor of Santa Barbara County had a stronger preference to see the El Capitan development proceed than did the rich? Santa Barbara is a small community; of what relevance is the El Capitan vote to the more important issue of a deteriorating worldwide environment? After all, the citizens by a democratic process chose to protect their environment. If all such questions were so rapidly and easily settled, would we not have a much better environment?

A question of personal preference will put the El Capitan issue in proper perspective: Do you feel a tax system, designed in such a way that the poor bear the heaviest burden, is fair? If not, El Capitan demonstrates a real moral dilemma. Furthermore, this dilemma underlies almost all decisions affecting the environment. In the El Capitan election the voters were choosing between additional income and environmental quality. With the issue of air pollution, for instance, citizens are forced to make other such choices. Perhaps the alternatives are not as immediately clear as with El Capitan; but they are invariably similar. The controversy could involve closing down a mill to protect a body of water or, perhaps, requiring everyone to install improved exhaust-emission devices on his automobile at some personal expense. As people are confronted with such choices, the result is similar to the El Capitan referendum.

The Santa Barbara community decided to protect the environment by prohibiting the development of the El Capitan Ranch. At other times other communities through other sorts of democratic processes have moved to improve environmental quality, and frequently at the expense of foregone income. Invariably, there is some sacrifice of real goods and services required—either by individuals directly, or through the community. What the El Capitan election implies, and other studies seem to verify, is that the major burden of environmental protection policies is borne by the lower income classes. Commonly the decision to engage in an environmental protection policy is made by the middle-class and upper-class majority at the cost of the less affluent members of the community.

How does it happen that the poor bear the major burden of an environmental policy when they usually carry a smaller tax burden than do the rich? The poor bear the burden in ways that cannot be measured only in terms of their money loss. Their burden comes from a loss in what economists call their total welfare.

The El Capitan referendum provides a good example of the concept of burden. It is a small issue, well understood by the community. For a more lucid example consider the El Capitan referendum if it were to be decided by the votes of three people (or three groups of people). The first, A, has the lowest income and will receive the smallest share of the income generated by the building project; the second, B, has the middle income amount; and the third, C, has the largest share of the additional income. Their perceived budget constraints are illustrated in Figure 10–9 as $A$, $B$, and $C$. As before, shown in Figures 10–1 through 10–6, the level of environmental quality is measured along the horizontal axis and the level of income along the vertical axis. The symbol $E_Y$ is the level of environmental quality that would result from an approval of the project; $E_N$ would result from defeating the proposal (it is the quality level that is already in existence); and $E_*$

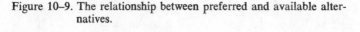

Figure 10–9. The relationship between preferred and available alternatives.

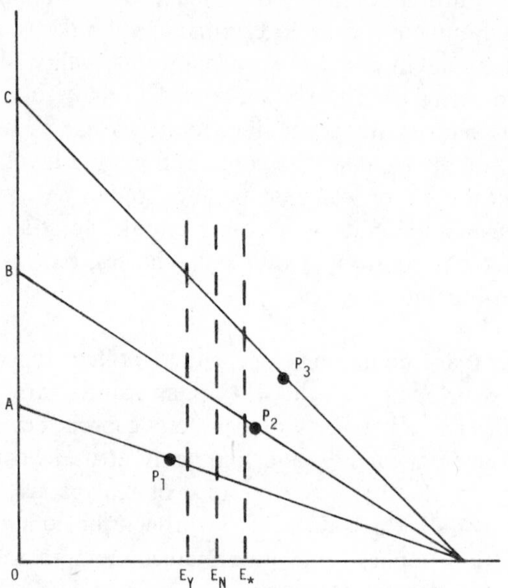


is some arbitrary higher level. If each individual were allowed to choose his most preferred alternative along his own budget constraint, A would choose $P_1$, B would choose $P_2$, and C would choose $P_3$.

Clearly, individual A would vote "yes" and individuals B and C would vote "no." In a democratic process the "no" votes represent 67 percent of the total, and the development is not allowed. What really happened in Santa Barbara was an overwhelming vote for the preservation of the status quo. In this example each member of the community suffers a welfare loss in the sense that neither alternative represents a most preferred position for any of the voters. However, $E_N$ represents a smaller welfare loss for the rich members of the community than does $E_Y$. Since the rich are in the majority in the community, they force the poor citizen to also have $E_N$, which represents a substantial welfare loss to him over $E_Y$. Furthermore, since $E_N$ was won by such a large majority, the community may try, through popular referendum, to raise its environmental quality even more—say to $E_*$.

If the issue of $E_*$ were ever presented to the voters, it would easily pass. It again represents a substantial gain for B and C. They, of course, would vote in favor of $E_*$ over the status quo $E_N$. This example points up the question of moral judgment raised earlier. As the community moves toward the higher environmental standard $E_*$, it increases the happiness of the middle- and higher-income classes while continually diminishing the welfare of the poor. For the good of a relatively affluent majority, the society taxes its poor minority.

Although there is not a direct money transfer, a tax has nonetheless been exacted. It is a tax in terms of individual well-being. What the El Capitan study most definitely shows, and what other studies seem to imply, is that the social measures which trade the growth in the production of real goods and services (i.e., income) for environmental quality are measures that impose a regressive tax: they impose a tax whose burden lies most heavily upon the poor.

A commonly accepted ethical principle, and one that is espoused by liberal politicians, is that regressive taxes are unfair. Yet those who would argue that position most strongly are often the same citizens who are fighting hard for better environmental quality. For the egalitarian mind the only way to reconcile concerns over the state of the environment with concerns about regressive taxes is to combine the programs for environmental protection with other programs to redistribute income in a substantial way. If the rich really do benefit most from an improved environment, let them pay for it by giving up a substantial portion of their material possessions for redistribution to the poorer members of the community as compensation for *their* losses suffered as a consequence of environmental protection.

The results of the El Capitan study, with the light they throw on other known results, should make the environmentalist gloomy even if he is not an egalitarian. In Santa Barbara upper-class tastes predominate in the electoral process. Therefore, in Santa Barbara, it is possible to convince the community to commit its resource to preserve the natural setting. In most urban areas the political power (at least the voting power) rests with the poor. Such areas are major contributors to pollution, but as the El Capitan referendum election demonstrated, it will be very difficult to get the commitment of resources necessary from the urban areas so they can clean up their own pollution.

El Capitan highlights a weakness in the environmental crusade. The drive for a better environment conflicts with society's aim to eliminate poverty. Perhaps the resolution to the apparent conflict in social goals is to combine the two policies. Environmentalists have traditionally taken a narrow view of their campaign. They could enlarge their efforts and combine their environmental protection policies with policies of income redistribution.

## Commentary

Chapter 10 deals with an area of increasing interest to economists: the satisfaction of social desires for publicly produced goods where output decisions are determined by majority voting. While this is a traditional democratic approach to social decision-making, it does not afford the protection to minorities that is permitted in market decision-making. The problem evolves from the constricted nature of typical economic issues which are put to a vote, combined with the all-or-nothing nature of the outcome. That is, the project is either approved (for example, a bond issue for a school is passed and the school built) or rejected (no school is built). The quantity produced (size of the school) is not precisely determined by the election. Because of the indivisibility of the project (school) and the nature of balloting, only a limited range of alternatives can be presented directly to the voter in any given election. Furthermore, it may turn out that no one can purchase precisely the amount of the output (schooling) he would like, and the minority voter does not in any way receive what he desires for the resources he gives up. As citizens we accept the principle of majority control, but as economists we must be concerned with the economic effects of such an approach to decision-making with respect to individuals or specific subsets of the population.

Shapiro and Barkume present us with some rather important results concerning the public's desire to forestall environmental degradation. In doing so they introduce the concept of hypothesis testing, giving an example of how a theory may be tested so that we can then decide whether it is a useful theory for the purposes of shaping public policy. They add to our tool kit in another way as well by introducing a technique for representing societal as well as individual preferences. The chapter that follows will make use of and expand on this representation of social preferences. It deals with one of the most fundamental of decisions: the determination of population size.

In economics we generally consider the problems of providing the best possible level of goods and services. As has already been seen, if effective markets exist, the decision-making process is virtually automatic. If markets are less than perfect, the problems multiply, and, finally, when markets are nonexistent, reaching optimum choices is a most difficult achievement. No markets, in the normal sense, exist for the determination of population size. With the natural determination of population, i.e., without markets or some conscious efforts for control, a disastrous outcome has been predicted in terms of the quality of life that man, either collectively or individually, could and would choose as an alternative if he were in full control of the decision. While economic analysis can offer no assurance of a desirable outcome to the population problem, it does provide the framework for a conceptualization in such a manner that an optimum collective decision would be facilitated. Perhaps a more satisfactory collective outcome in terms of the quality of life can be achieved if economists, in concert with biologists and other scientists, can assist man in perceiving his alternatives.

# 11

# Population Pressure and the Quality of Life

Harold L. Votey, Jr.

## Public Concern

Concern with mounting population pressures is widespread. For example, in January 1969, U Thant, then Secretary-General of the United Nations stated, "We must conclude from the demographic projections that the task of providing opportunities for the world's as yet unborn children and developing their talents and their capabilities to the full appears in a number of countries to be well nigh insuperable, unless action is taken to moderate the population growth rate."[1] Robert S. McNamara, president of the World Bank, in a speech at Notre Dame University in May of that same year, noted that the rate of population growth in most of the underdeveloped world is so great that even the most energetic and resourceful governments can do no more than stand still, maintaining an uneasy status quo in their totally inadequate standards of living. Most are actually slipping backwards.[2] In March 1971 the President's Commission on Population Growth and the American Future, under the chairmanship of John D. Rockefeller, III, submitted its first interim report to the President and Congress.[3] It raised the question,

> Do we wish to continue to invest even more of our resources and those of much of the rest of the world in meeting demands for more services, more classrooms, more hospitals, and more housing as population con-

1. *San Francisco Chronicle,* Friday, January 17, 1969, p. 17.
2. Ibid., Monday, May 5, 1967, p. 24.
3. "Interim Report," Commission on Population Growth and the American Future, May 16, 1971, abridged text in *Family Planning Perspectives* (New York: Planned Parenthood—World Population, 1971).

tinues to grow? Or should we concentrate our energies and resources on improving the quality of existing services and extending them to large number of our people for whom the 'quality of life' still means getting a square meal?

The point is that national population growth and geographical distribution cannot be treated as an either-or affair. The distribution of population is problematic in many ways. But the choice among ways to redirect growth does not eliminate the necessity of [deciding] when the Nation could best accommodate 300 million people or whether it should accommodate 400 million.

While concern over the problem appears to be growing, we are also finding evidence that we have the power, even in underdeveloped nations, to slow the growth of population by voluntary measures. In November of 1967, Frank W. Notestein, president of the Population Council, released a report which stated that in Taiwan and South Korea (where the Council has an advisory role in large-scale family planning programs) the birth rate declined by approximately 3 to 5 births per thousand in Taiwan, and by 3.7 to 5.3 births per thousand in Korea. The report went on to contrast this result with recent history where declines of birth rates had occurred only as a result of industrialization. No nation in the past few centuries, with the exception of Ireland, it said, has dropped its birth rate without first industrializing. Despite the fact that population control appears possible we find in the 1965 National Fertility Study, reported in January of 1970, that in the United States for the period 1960–1965, estimates based on married women's own reports about their childbearing experience showed that 22 percent of all live births were unwanted by at least one parent.[4]

In summary, there appears to be grave concern regarding population growth. Mankind has the ability to control population growth, and yet even where families could be expected to be able to control their own output, they are less than successful. It would seem that population pressures are effectively thwarting the achievement of social goals on a world front.

This chapter will consider the impact of alternative population levels on the standard of living, the notion of an optimum population size, and finally, some possible options with respect to controlling population and the quality of life.

## Historical Experience of Population Growth

To understand the concern about population growth and the apparent difficulty of the problem one should be aware of two sets of forces. One of these

4. A report on the research of Charles Westoff and Larry L. Bumpass, Princeton Office of Population Research, *Parade,* January 18, 1970, p. 10.

forces is the apparent natural pattern of population growth as countries develop. The second is the clamor for economic progress on the part of all the world's less advantaged peoples. The combination of these two forces places demands upon a limited resource base with which our advancing technology may not be adequate to cope. In a UN study on population growth a number of years ago, C. P. Blacker, A. Landry, Frank Notestein, W. F. Thompson and others wrote on the "theory of economic stages."[5] Their ideas may be summarized as follows:

When one investigates the pattern of fertility or mortality rates for a given developed country over its past history, a typical pattern emerges. Beginning early in history and extending over a long period of time a country remains relatively static in terms of population growth, technological change, and economic development. Fertility rates and mortality rates remain approximately equal over time, so that despite occasional plagues, famines, and other seemingly random shocks to the system, a static equilibrium with zero population growth prevails. This is illustrated in Figure 11–1a by the time period labeled "high stationary" (*HS*) in Blacker's terminology. Anthony Barnett's *The Human Species* supports this picture by showing the estimated European population to be relatively constant at a level of 50 million persons over the 1000 years leading up to 1400 A.D., at which time growth began to accelerate so that by 1900 the population was approximately 400 million.[6]

As technological advances and organizational innovations evolve, mortality rates decline. This decline can be explained by advances in medical knowledge and increases in productivity. Medical knowledge leads to better personal hygiene. Higher productivity permits improved levels of subsistence which facilitate better nutrition. The higher incomes resulting from higher productivity also permit greater leisure leading to greater concern for public welfare, which society can now afford with its higher incomes. The effect of all this is to create an early expanding (*EE*) stage in population development. In this stage population grows at an increasing rate, with no change in fertility rates (see Figure 11-1b). In the past this rapid rise in population for developing economies progressed into a third "late expanding" (*LE*) stage in which population, while still increasing, grew at an ever diminishing rate.

There is an "economic theory of population growth," developed in large measure by Harvey Leibenstein, which provides us with a more complete economic explanation of this stage of the pattern.[7] Taking account of a host

5. *The Determination and Consequences of Population Trends,* Population Studies No. 17, Department of Social Affairs, United Nations (New York: 1953), pp. 73–97.

6. Anthony Barnett, *The Human Species* (London: MacGibbon and Kee, 1961).

7. A brief introduction to his theory can be found in Harvey Leibenstein, *Economic Backwardness and Economic Growth* (New York: John Wiley & Sons, 1963), pp. 159–169.

Figure 11–1a. Pattern of fertility and mortality rates over time.

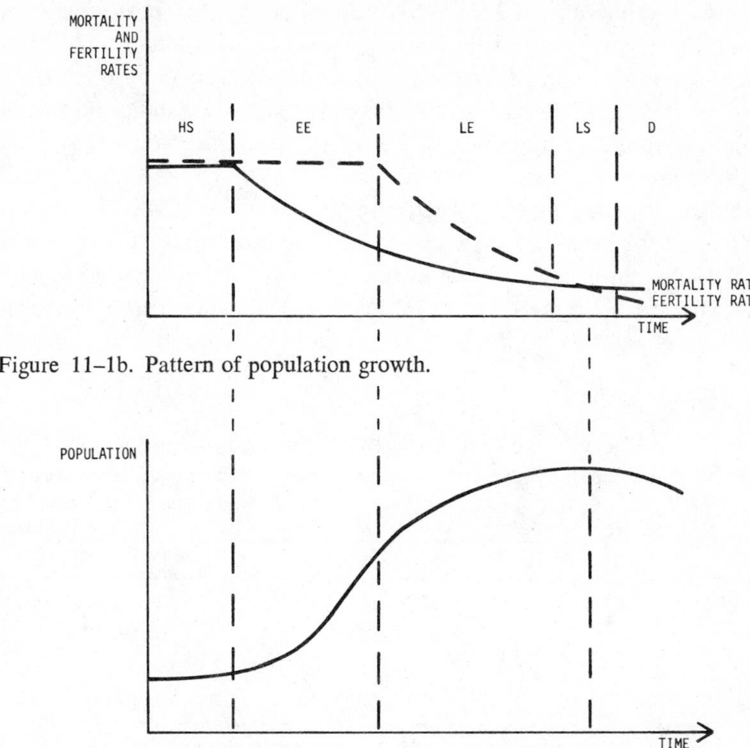


Figure 11–1b. Pattern of population growth.

of causal factors, he suggests that the urge on the part of individual families to procreate becomes diminished partly because families move out of agriculture into industrial activities as development takes place. This follows because the advantages of large families in supplying labor for family agriculture no longer exists. Increasing requirements for education, the lack of jobs for young children, and the tendency for women to seek industrial or at least nonfarm occupations have the effect of raising the cost to families of added children while the benefits of having children diminish. In addition, the development of collective saving schemes, such as private insurance and public social security programs reduces the relative benefits of having numerous children to provide security in old age. This resulting stage of population development is referred to as "low stationary" (*LS*). Population growth is curtailed and we have "zero population growth."

A continuing decline in fertility rates at a time in which it becomes increasingly difficult to lower mortality rates further could lead to a "declining" (*D*) stage of population. The existence of this latter stage is largely speculation, although Ireland is an example of a country that may have reached this stage. Some of the Western European countries appear to be approaching the low stationary (*LS*) stage. Most of the world's population, however, resides in countries in which population is still growing rapidly. We note that for the years 1958–1962 most Western European countries had population growth rates below 1.0 percent; Ireland's rate was −0.3 percent; African and Asian countries, in contrast, ranged from 0.5 to 5.1 percent with the majority above 2.0 percent.[8] The apparent maximum growth rate in some countries appeared to approach or even exceed 4.0 percent per annum.

It has been estimated that the world population in 1967 was 3.4 billion and growing at the rate of 2.0 percent.[9] With such a large existing world population level this rapid growth cannot go on unchecked. Some UN projections for the shorter term are presented in Table 11–1. Mathematical

Table 11-1

Summary of UN World Population 1960, and Projections, 1980, 2000, 2050 (in billions)

| | 1960 | Constant Fertility | | | High Variant | | Medium Variant | | Low Variant | |
|---|---|---|---|---|---|---|---|---|---|---|
| | | 1960 | 2000 | 2050 | 1980 | 2000 | 1980 | 2000 | 1980 | 2000 |
| World | 3.0 | 4.5 | 7.5 | 30.0 | 4.6 | 7.0 | 4.3 | 6.1 | 4.1 | 5.5 |
| Developed countries | 1.0 | 1.2 | 1.6 | | 1.2 | 1.6 | 1.2 | 1.4 | 1.2 | 1.3 |
| Less developed countries | 2.0 | 3.3 | 5.9 | | 5.4 | 3.1 | 3.1 | 4.7 | 3.0 | 4.2 |

Source: World Population Prospects as Assessed in 1963, New York: United Nations, 1968.

projections would indicate standing room only in a couple of centuries, an obvious physical impossibility. Natural processes will prevent such an extreme outcome over the long run. In the short run, however, we need be concerned with pressing problems which can be expressed in terms of simple economic realities.

## Production and Population

A primary economic problem is that of feeding and clothing the growing world population. This problem is compounded by the humanitarian concern that the living standards of poor peoples ought to be raised so that they can enjoy the same level of living as people in advanced nations. Thus, even if we accept the notion that advanced countries are well enough off and

8. These figures were drawn from United Nations, *Demographic Yearbook, 1963* (New York: 1964), pp. 123 ff.

9. Goran Ohlin, *Population Control and Economic Development* (Paris: Development Center of the Organization for Economic Cooperation and Development, 1967), pp. 11 ff.

need no higher standard of living, total output would have to increase in order to satisfy our humanitarian ideals even if population ceased to grow. To better understand the burden of added population it is useful to examine the relationships which prevail between food production, resource use, and population.

### The Nature of Production

Economists characterize the production process in simple functional notation in which the relationship between economic inputs and the resulting product or output is specified as

$$Y = f(K, L, R, T) \tag{1}$$

where $Y$ represents the total output of food and clothing, $K$ is capital, $L$ is labor, $R$ is resources, and $T$ represents the existing state of technology. If, for a given state of technology, all of the inputs were increased by some given percent it might be reasonable to expect output to increase by approximately the same percentage. Empirical studies of production processes the world over tend to substantiate this expectation.[10] Likewise, if none of the inputs ($K$, $L$, or $R$) increased, but there is what we define as an advance in technology, output will rise.

In the event that factors are substitutable in production, we would expect augmentation of any one of the inputs individually to lead to an increase in output as well. By this we mean that production can usually be organized so that, on a given plot of ground ($R$), the addition of farm laborers ($L$) will raise output. This process would be facilitated, of course, if as we increased farm laborers we added to our stock of tools ($K$) or experienced advances in technology. Examples of changes in technology ($T$) might be a new hybrid seed, the development of superior tools, or simply an organizational change such that men, instead of being in each other's way, find ways of effectively helping one another and reducing wasted motion. If production works as depicted here, and if the working proportion of the population remains fairly constant, then an increase in population can be expected to lead to a rise in output. Unfortunately, while this rise in utput is observed to be an empirical fact, such an outcome is not go .

### The Law of Diminishing Returns

While there is strong evidence that proportional increases in all will result in an approximately equal change in output, anothe must be recognized. If we increase one or more inputs but hold a

10. Some of the earlier evidence was accumulated by Paul H. Douglas, "Ar Laws of Production?" *American Economic Review* 38, no. 1 (March 1948).

other input constant we can expect to find diminishing returns to those inputs which are increased. That is, if land in our example is fixed, and the state of technology doesn't change, then each addition to the labor force may be expected to yield an ever smaller addition to output. We can imagine a truck garden of a single acre on which we can add family workers until finally an added worker will add nothing to total output, if all workers' hours are based on some standard working day. At this point we say the marginal product per worker has fallen to zero, i.e., an additional unit of work at the margin will add nothing to output. Production characterized by diminishing returns (and it is hard to conceive of production which is not) might be depicted graphically as in Figure 11–2. Here we show output ($Y$)

Figure 11–2. Output as labor is increased, holding all other inputs constant.

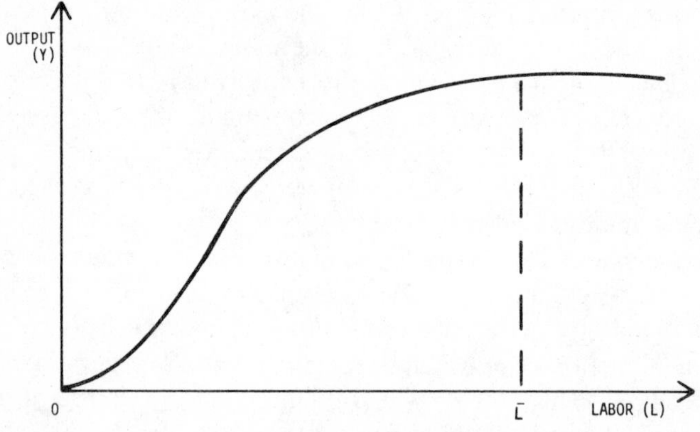


on the vertical axis with labor ($L$) represented on the horizontal axis. As we increase labor up to $\bar{L}$ we see that we reach a point where additions to output are zero. Note also that we have depicted the lower region in terms of the level of the input $L$ as one of *increasing* returns. While this may not be characteristic of all production we might expect that frequently, at very low levels of output, cooperation between inputs of the same sort may lead to increasing benefits in terms of output.

## Predictions of Thomas Malthus

Thomas Malthus was a leading scholar of his time for whom the first professorship in political economy was created in England. As noted an economist as John Maynard Keynes has said of him, "If only Malthus, instead of Ricardo, had been the parent stem from which nineteenth-century economics proceeded, what a much wiser and richer place the world would be today."[11] Although he was one of the outstanding thinkers of his time, Malthus is perhaps best known for suggesting that population can grow geometrically whereas food production increases at arithmetic rates. He did not intend this to be a scientific statement on how the world works but rather an indication of what appeared to be possible based on the early American experience.

Malthus's theorizing was unusual in that his model of economic growth included growth of population as an endogenous variable. That is, population growth was not independent of, but changed in response to, economic development. For our purpose we can define economic development as the sustained rise in the output of all those things which give us satisfaction in consumption, relative to the number of persons who are consuming, i.e., development is the rise in $Y/N$ over time, where $N$ represents the number of people. In terms of functional notation we can write this relationship

$$\frac{\Delta N}{N} = g(Y/N), \tag{2}$$

where $\Delta$ designates a one period change so that $\frac{\Delta N}{N}$ represents a one period change in population (or the labor force) divided by the existing population.[12] Thus $\frac{\Delta N}{N}$ is the instantaneous percentage rate of growth of population. Malthus postulated that the higher a family's income, the greater number of children it will have and, consequently, the faster population will grow.

Malthus's understanding of the growth process ignored technology, but it did take into account the need for capital. He recognized that capital will be invested in production if the profit from its use is high. Profit in this case is simply the difference between output ($Y$) and the wage bill $w \cdot L$. Thus

$$\frac{\Delta K}{K} = k(\pi), \tag{3}$$

and

$$\pi = Y - w \cdot L, \tag{4}$$

i.e., the rate of growth of capital is a function of the level of profits as we have defined them above.

11. J. M. Keynes, *Essays in Biography* (New York: Norton, 1963), pp. 140–144.

12. For simplicity we will assume, at this point, that the labor force is proportional to population.

He also recognized the effect of labor supply on the wage, given the demand for output. We might express this as

$$w = h(L,Y), \tag{5}$$

where the larger the labor force (for a given level of output), the greater the competition for jobs and, hence, the lower the resulting wage.

If we combine the relationships of Equations 1, 3, 4, and 5, for the production function, thus incorporating the effects of profits on the capital stock and hence on output, those with a mathematical bent can see that by substitution we will end up with two relationships: an equation for ever-increasing output, which is a function of the level of population and the capital stock; and an equation for population growth, which depends jointly on the output level and the existing level of population.

The process of growth, as Malthus and other classical economists of his time described it, is illustrated in Figure 11–3. On the horizontal axis capital and labor are growing proportionally. The vertical axis represents the wage bill and total product (after the payment of rents). The curve $OY$ is our now familiar total product curve when land is fixed and technology is given. Line $OS$ represents the subsistence wage bill, below which competition cannot force the wage for any given level of population.

Figure 11–3. The Malthusian growth process.

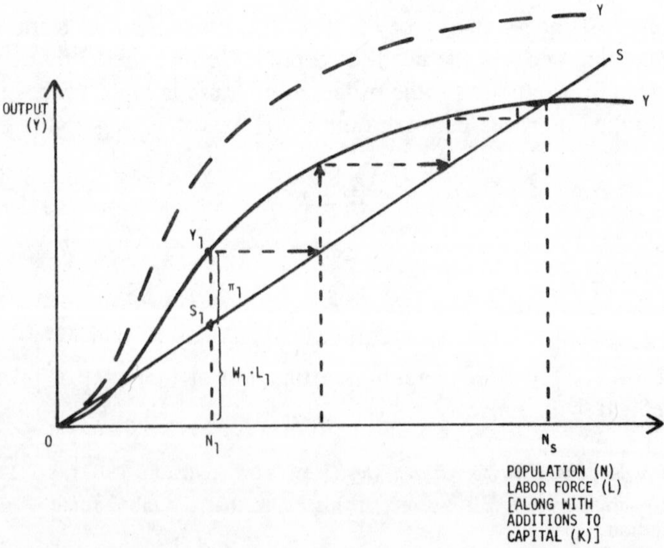

The classical growth process may be illustrated by starting with population level $N_1$. At this level of population, output $(Y_1)$ exceeds the wage bill at the subsistence wage $s \cdot N_1$ $(=w_1L_1)$. Employers will simultaneously do two things. They will invest in added capital and try to hire more workers. As they attempt to hire more workers, given the population level $N_1$, wages will rise toward $Y_1$, tending to absorb all output. The rise in living standards will, however, lead to a rise in population, tending to prevent a sufficient rise in wages to eliminate profits and hence investment. Thus we find ourselves moving to the right in terms of $N$ and to successively higher levels of income $(Y)$. The process must eventually come to a halt, however, because of diminishing returns. At some point $N_s$ we will reach a condition in which profits are wiped out at a subsistence wage. Consequently, population growth will no longer be induced nor will there be any inducement for further capital accumulation. We will be in a low-level stationary state at a subsistence level of income, with zero population growth and zero economic growth.[13] This is indeed a dismal outcome.[14]

## Technology, Discovery, and Economic Development

### The Process of Discovery

For many years the gloomy predictions of Malthus were ignored and even held up to ridicule. The long-term secular trend in wages, capital accumulation, and population was upward. In the past, there was little evidence that population growth would outstrip food supplies. True, many people existed at subsistence levels over the intervening period, but people in the countries where this was true had always existed at near subsistence levels. In other (developing) countries living standards rose steadily. Thus, the problem of the less fortunate countries appeared to be simply one of adopting the methods of the more advanced ones so that all the world's people could be better off.

There are several reasons for the failure of the Malthusian predictions. One has been the steady opening of new lands to cultivation in the western hemisphere, in Australia and New Zealand, in Africa, and even in the older lands in Europe and Asia. As the need for food and other agricultural products rises in the world, lands which are marginal in an economic sense will be brought into production in a process that tends to slow down crowding on the land. This is what David Ricardo, a contemporary of Malthus, referred

13. A more detailed presentation of Malthus's and the classicists' dynamic model of growth can be found in William Baumol, *Economic Dynamics*, 2nd ed. (New York: Macmillan, 1965), ch. 2.

14. It was this outcome which probably prompted Thomas Carlyle to refer to "respectable professors of the dismal science . . ." in *Latter Day Pamphlets*, No. 1, 1850, an appellation that economists have been trying to live down ever since.

to as moving toward the "extensive margin." Adding more of other factors to already cultivated land was a movement toward the "intensive margin." The combination of these two activities would indeed ultimately bring us to Malthus's low-level stationary state if it were not for another phenomenon occurring subsequent to Malthus's prediction.

### Accelerating Technological Change

While new lands and natural resources were being made available to the world, an equally important phenomenon was taking place. The technology of production was advancing at a remarkable rate following the period which initiated what we refer to as the "industrial revolution." This technological change took many forms. The science of animal husbandry led to improved strains of stock for producing food, animal fibers, and a host of by-products. Similar advances in knowledge led to improved strains of crops and better agricultural techniques to utilize land and other factors. Organizational changes based on a better understanding of the nature and contribution of inputs have had a tremendous impact on our ability to produce the necessities of life. Technological change has created economic assets out of substances that previously had no value to man. The potential for economic production has increased as a result.

The recent "green revolution," a technological advance which Lester Brown attributes almost completely to scientific research funded by the Ford and Rockefeller foundations, provides evidence that we have not reached the bounds of scientific capacity to forestall the seemingly inevitable limits of diminishing returns.[15] Biologists caution us that this advance is marred by weaknesses in insect and disease control to which new strains of wheat, corn, and rice are susceptible. Nonetheless, the success of scientists in technological solutions has led Lester Brown, Goran Ohlin, and others to argue that the real issue has less to do with food supply than with the emergence of great social problems associated with crowding.[16] They believe there are natural forces less severe than those postulated by Malthus which will bring population into equilibrium with productive capabilities.[17]

15. Lester Brown, *Seeds of Change* (New York: Frederick A. Praeger, 1970).

16. In part this is based on the observed history of population change as countries develop. The reasons for this pattern and thus the logic behind their position will become more evident after some of the observed functional relationships between economic variables and population change are discussed.

17. There are others who believe that a similar outcome may be the result of continuing present policies of resource management and permitting environmental pollution, both of which will have the effect of reducing population considerably below levels presently prevailing. Prominent among these are Jay W. Forrester and Dennis L. Meadows of MIT. Their studies culminated in the Club of Rome's Project on the Predicament of Mankind which is reported in D. H. Meadows et al., *The Limits to Growth* (New York: Universe Books, 1972).

**The Malthusian Prediction and the Impact of Resource Growth and Technological Change**

The foregoing changes have not in any way altered the logic of the Malthusian prediction but have only pushed back the barrier of diminishing returns. In terms of the Figure 11–3 diagram the effect would be to push $OY$ upward and outward to a position like $OY'$ at a later point in time as the resource factor ($R$) and the state of technology ($T$) are augmented. For those countries who mastered the technology and for those who possess the capability to expand their base of economic resources, steady growth of income and population has taken place in such a manner that living standards have risen at gratifying rates.

The relationship between living standards, income growth, and population growth can be expressed in terms of a simple mathematical identity

$$\frac{\Delta(Y/N)}{Y/N} \equiv \frac{\Delta Y}{Y} - \frac{\Delta N}{N}. \tag{6}$$

This says that the percentage rate of growth of per capita income ($Y/N$) is the difference between the percentage rate of growth of output (or income) and the percentage rate of growth of population. For the countries which have been gaining steadily in living standards, output has simply been growing more rapidly than population. If we incorporate our production relationship into this identity along with the assumptions that (1) production of output grows proportionally to the rate of growth of inputs, (2) the rate of growth of the labor force is the same as the rate of growth of population, and (3) the resource base is fixed, then we have the result that

$$\frac{\Delta(Y/N)}{Y/N} = \alpha\left(\frac{\Delta K}{K} - \frac{\Delta L}{L}\right) + T'. \tag{7}$$

In this result $T'$ is the effect of technological change on economic development and $\alpha$ is a factor which represents the relationship between changes in the capital stock and changes in output.[18]

In the absence of technological change, we see that capital must grow at a greater rate than population for development to take place. In the advanced countries it appears that the capital stock has been growing at a rate close to that for population, so that much of the development which has taken place has been the consequence of technological change.

This expression is obviously an oversimplification of the relationship between the production of goods, people, and technology, but it is useful

18. Derivation of this result can be found in James Meade, *A Neo-Classical Theory of Economic Growth,* (London: Allen & Unwin, 1961).

to highlight key elements of our present problem. There are basically three ways to raise the standard of living of those existing close to subsistence levels. We can increase the capital stock through saving and investment, we can continue to achieve technological advances, or we can reduce the rate of population growth. The difficulty may be that these three alternatives are not independent of one another. While each may be influenced by national policy, changes in the rates of any of the three are nonetheless, a consequence of individual activities. In a democracy, by definition, collective policy must somehow reflect the sum of individual desires. And for that policy to be workable, it must, of course, take account of the economic and the natural environment, as well as the way individuals will respond to policy. Some of the problems associated with the formulation of national policy are examined below.

## Natural Behavioral Relationships

### Capital Accumulation

Capital accumulation is regarded by students of economic development as one of the keys to raising living standards. It would be hard to find a general text on economic development, or a study of development for a particular country, which does not include at least a chapter on capital formation. Manipulation of investment, and hence the saving rate, has been one of the tools of federal growth and income stabilization policy in this country in recent years. It is the object of much of the policy to influence growth in developing countries as well. Since developing countries, which are at very low levels of income, are constrained with respect to domestic saving by the burden of dependency, it is clear that capital accumulation is not independent of the rate of growth of population. Thus, it appears that an effective reduction in population growth, which in itself will influence the rate of economic development in terms of the degree of dilution of income growth, will also provide a secondary impact on income growth through the influence on capital accumulation.

### Technological Change

Technological change has been much maligned of late by some persons who are concerned with environmental problems. Acceptance of the argument that technological change must be condemned as the destroyer of the quality of life is a mistaken and dangerous position. There is no question that some technological advances have had very destructive side effects, and certainly it would be a mistake to assume that technological change will automatically save us from ourselves. It is equally unreasonable, however, to regard technological change as a set of activities with uniform characteristics. Many changes in technology are merely organizational in nature. They simply permit more effective use of existing resources. For example, when crop rotation was developed, it tended to increase total output, while actually conserving the soil. Reorganization of industrial production can either permit the same output at lower cost or greater output at previous levels of inputs.

A change in technology itself need not imply greater use of resources—it must by definition imply a more efficient use of resources. This does not mean to suggest that the implementation of some technologies may not entail undesirable external diseconomies. Wise decision-making implies that such externalities should be taken into account when choosing a technology.

### Population Relationships

Recall that Malthus postulated that the greater the per capita income, the greater the population growth. Panel studies provide supporting evidence for this position.[19] At the same time, historical evidence seems to suggest that as countries develop, birth rates fall, so that population growth is ultimately slowed. This seeming paradox has plagued demographic researchers for many years. There is a growing body of evidence which can explain this paradox on the basis of a combination of the economics of choice and the natural redistribution of population between economic sectors as development takes place.[20]

That evidence supports Malthus's theorizing that, in any given set of families with a given set of tastes, greater family incomes imply a larger average number of children per family. As Leibenstein and Becker have postulated, families appear to respond to an implicit calculus of benefits and costs to determine their size. This does not mean to imply that changes in tastes among a whole society are unimportant. Nor does it mean that religion or other social factors can be disregarded. However, within each religious group, or for a given set of tastes, the economic calculus will still apply. We find solid evidence that family size will decline as families move from an agricultural to an urban environment, and the benefits of having children to serve as family labor are lost.[21] If population policies are to be fully effective, the nature of the multiple influences on family decision-making

19. Gary Becker in "An Economic Analysis of Fertility," *Demographic and Economic Change in Developed Countries* (New York: National Bureau of Economic Research, 1960) cites a number of such studies in which there is a positive statistical relationship between family size and family income.

20. A summary of this literature is presented in Llad Phillips, Harold L. Votey, Jr., and Darold Maxwell, "A Synthesis of the Economic and Demographic Models of Fertility: An Econometric Test," *The Review of Economics and Statistics* 51, no. 3 (August 1969).

21. This is a major finding of Phillips, Votey, and Maxwell, ibid.

must be taken into account. These include not only individual desires, but also the interdependencies between individuals which complicate the determination of social or collective policy.

## The Population Optimum

### The Economics of Choice

Implicit in virtually all economic analysis is the assumption that man, given the nature of the constraints within which he must operate, will make the best possible decisions. Some choices are obviously denied him because they are simply physically impossible. Some choices will be rejected because there are better alternatives which are easily attainable. Economics does not pretend to tell us what choices we should prefer but rather, given that we can effectively assess our resource availability and our productive capabilities, economic analysis can delineate our alternatives. Then, if we can enumerate our preferences, economics can show the way to reach the best possible outcome.

It is useful for analytic purposes to consider the way economists represent individual preferences. One way is to begin with a set of axioms, i.e., statements which are regarded as true and require no proof, and upon which a theory of behavior can be based. In building a theory of consumer behavior, the first assumption made is that people prefer more of a normal good to less of it. Then we assume people are able to choose between goods or bundles of goods. Finally, we assume that some goods or bundles of goods are equal, in the view of the consumer, so that either good or bundle of goods would be equally satisfying. For a consumer who behaves in this manner, it is a simple matter to represent his preferences with respect to a set of alternatives. The fact that the consumer can make a choice, means that he can designate a rank ordering for all the possible combinations of pairs of goods. If he has a fixed budget to allocate between two goods, and prices of the goods were postulated, we could specify the choices he would make for all conceivable prices. A possible rank ordering is illustrated in Table 11–2 for good *a* (apples) and good *b* (bananas). A choice ranked 3 is obviously superior to those ranked 2 and 1. For example, set A is superior to B, since our consumer can have an equal number of bananas with either set, but more apples with set A. Also, our consumer would be equally satisfied with sets B, C, and D, or with E, F, and G.

As an alternative to using a table to enumerate preferences, the various commodity choices might be plotted on a graph such as Figure 11–4a in which the horizontal axis represents quantities of *a* and the vertical axis represents quantities of *b*. If we connect all of the choices which are regarded as equally preferable by a line, we have two lines *BCD* and *GFE*. If apples and bananas were divisible into infinitely small pieces so that we could

Table 11–2
A Rank Ordering of Commodity Choices

| Budget | Amount of Apples | Amount of Bananas | Rank Ordering |
|---|---|---|---|
| A | 6 | 6 | 3 |
| B | 3 | 6 | 2 |
| C | 4 | 4 | 2 |
| D | 6 | 2 | 2 |
| E | 5 | 1 | 1 |
| F | 3 | 3 | 1 |
| G | 2 | 5 | 1 |

Figure 11–4a. A plot of commodity choices.

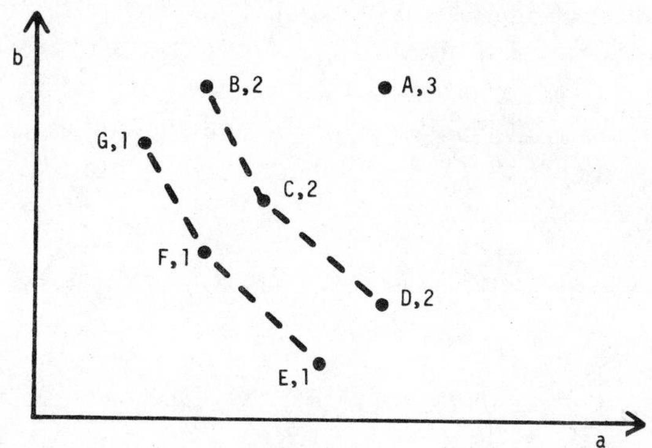


Figure 11–4b. Indifference curves derived from preference orderings.

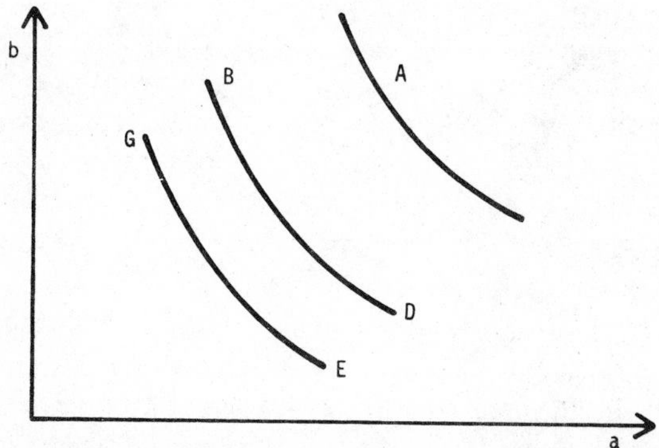


specify alternatives in terms of every conceivable fraction, these two lines might look more like *BD* and *GE* in Figure11–4b. Such curves are referred to by economists as *indifference curves* because a consumer is indifferent as to the choice between (i.e., equally satisfied with) two alternative bundles of commodities on the same line. He would, however, prefer to reach the curve attainable farthest from the origin, since that curve represents combinations containing more goods than curves closer to the origin.

If a more detailed specification of a rational consumer's choices were depicted, the entire space would be filled with curves like *BD*. In this space, movements to the northeast would always represent greater well-being. It might be useful to number these curves with successively higher numbers as we move out from the origin. The numbers then would represent an ordering of *utility* or the relative degree of well-being. Curve 10 need not necessarily represent twice the satisfaction as 5; rather, curve 10 is preferable to 5, i.e., there is no notion of cardinality in the preference ordering.

The curves shown will never intersect if the consumer is rational. So long as we do not entertain the notion of satiation for one of the goods beyond some point, the curves will always have some degree of slope downward and to the right. If, on the other hand, there is an increasing aversion to a commodity as more is available, we might find the curves changing slope as depicted in Figure 11–5. On indifference curve $i_o$, more of *a* beyond the

Figure 11–5. An indifference curve indicating satiation for Good *A*.

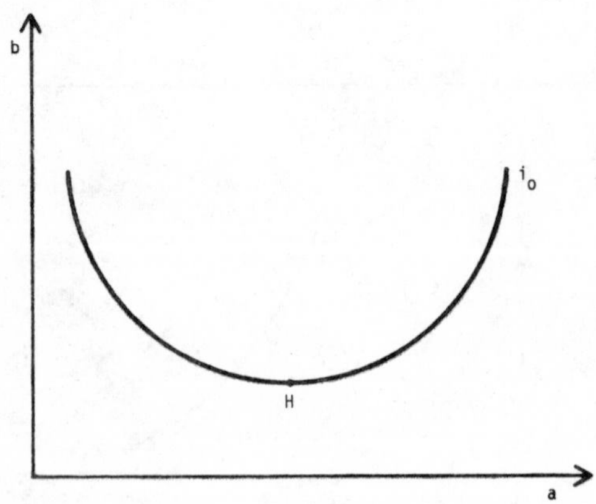


level at *H* results in an increasing aversion to *a*, so that beyond some point our consumer would prefer to move to the northwest with less of *a* and more of *b*.

An alternative way to express the individual's preferences with respect to these two goods would be in terms of a utility function:

$$U = u(a,b) \tag{8}$$

says that a person's well-being or utility is simply a function of the amount of the two goods he possesses. Either more of $a$ or of $b$ would be expected to increase the individual's well-being.[22]

### Social Choice

Turning from a consideration of the way to represent the choices of individuals to social problems, however, we need to think in terms of what society, collectively, prefers between different alternatives. If consumers were all alike and if the preferences of each consumer were independent of the consumption of every other consumer, the representation of social preferences would be quite simple. Preferences could be added up (i.e., simply sum indifference curves), in a manner somewhat similar to the way we add supply and demand to derive aggregate supply and demand curves, to produce a curve representing social preferences. Unfortunately, individuals are not all the same and consumer preferences are not independent. We know that income levels vary between individuals in the same society and even more greatly between societies. We know that tastes are not uniform between people, even within societies. Finally, we know that there are external effects which cannot be ignored. In the case of population we know that individuals have definite feelings about the number of children the rest of the families in society have. As a consequence, if we took social preference with respect to population to be simply the sum of the family size each individual wanted, we would probably be wrong. Taking all this into account the curve representing social preferences will look very much like the curve used to illustrate individual preferences. We will assume, despite the complications associated with attempting to derive it, that it is possible to represent social preference in a manner analogous to the way we represent individual preferences. This curve is called a social welfare function.

### The Arguments in the Welfare Function

One might expect social welfare to be simply a function of all the things society consumes, i.e.,

$$W = w\,(X_1, X_2, \cdots X_n), \tag{9}$$

that is, all the different commodities (the $X$'s, some of which may not be things which can be evaluated easily in monetary terms) that society con-

22. Further discussion of the theory of consumer behavior can be found in P. A. Samuelson, *Economics,* 8th ed. (New York: McGraw-Hill, 1970), pp. 921–25. For a more detailed analysis the student can refer to C. E. Ferguson, *Microeconomic Theory,* 3rd ed. (Homewood, Ill.: Richard D. Irwin, 1972), chs. 1 and 2.

sumes will add to social welfare. If we are concerned with economic development, which has been defined as a sustained rise in real income per capita, we might simply choose as our welfare function

$$W = w(Y/N). \tag{10}$$

While this is an adequate representation of social welfare for the consideration of a number of development problems, it will soon be apparent that it is not an appropriate way to deal with population questions.

### The Possibilities Enumerated

The concept of the production possibility frontier was developed in Chapter 1 of this book. Such a curve is a way of representing the alternatives available to society as a consequence of the choices we make about production levels of alternative commodities. To consider the population problem, a similar concept can be derived that represents the available alternatives between population and living standards, simply by making use of our production function and the development goal expressed in terms of per capita income. We shall do this, continuing to assume that there is a fixed relationship between population and the labor force.

First, referring to the total product curve presented in Figure 11–2, recall that the vertical axis measures total output and the horizontal axis measures labor input. So long as labor is proportional to population, we can (using a different scale) also represent population on the horizontal axis. If we were to divide the output by the number of people for every level of population, we could derive a new curve which represents the per capita income that would be available for every level of population, given levels of resources ($R$), the capital stock ($K$), and the level of technology ($T$). This curve is presented in Figure 11–6. If labor were used instead of population, the curve could be referred to as the average-product-of-labor curve. This curve will serve nicely for the purpose of representing the production (or consumption) possibilities where we are choosing between alternative levels of population and per capita income. If we have diminishing returns, as was assumed to be the case when we drew our original total product curve, this translates into the alternative of more people at lower levels of living or fewer people at a higher standard of real income.[23]

### A Simple Model of the Population Optimum

If we represented social preferences as a function of only per capita income, as in Equation 10, the optimum population would be that level of

23. Note that this is precisely the trade-off with which the President's Commission on Population Growth and the American Future was concerned when it questioned the advisability of having more people vs. fewer people and a higher quality of life.

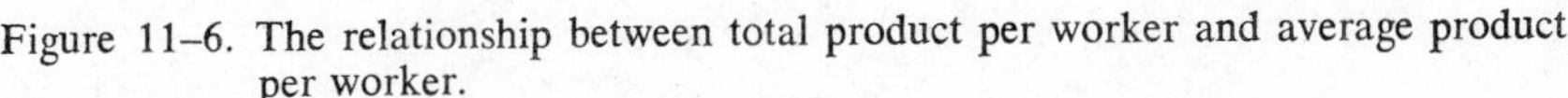

Figure 11–6. The relationship between total product per worker and average product per worker.

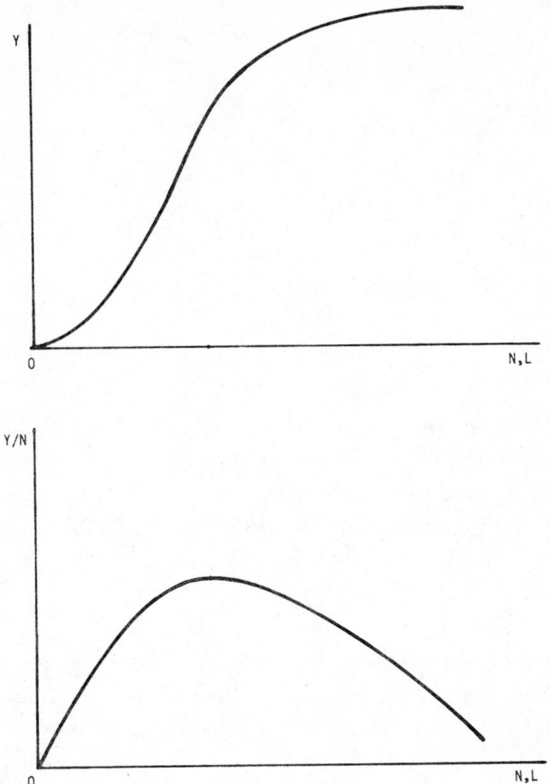


population which maximizes per capita income.[24] In Figure 11–7 this can be represented by population level $N_o$. Suppose, however, that we take account of the notion that most societies place great emphasis on family size. Children represent a kind of consumption good which families choose as an alternative to spending greater amounts of income on other things.[25] Coun-

24. So many writers have in the past discussed the population optimum in terms of this single objective that such a formulation might be regarded as the traditional or classical view. Representative of these writings are W. Arthur Lewis, *The Theory of Economic Growth* (Homewood, Ill.: Richard D. Irwin, 1955), pp. 320–330, James E. Meade, *Trade and Welfare* (London: Oxford University Press, 1955), and Joseph J. Spengler, "Population Optima" in *The 99th Hour* (Chapel Hill, N.C.: University of North Carolina Press, 1967).

25. This argument is consistent with the economic theory of the determination of family size set forth by Leibenstein, *Economic Backwardness*, and Becker, *Analysis of Fertility*. If, in fact, families do regard their family size as an argument in their individual utility or welfare functions, then there is a cogent argument for including population size in the aggregate social welfare function.

Figure 11–7. Optimum population with different welfare functions.

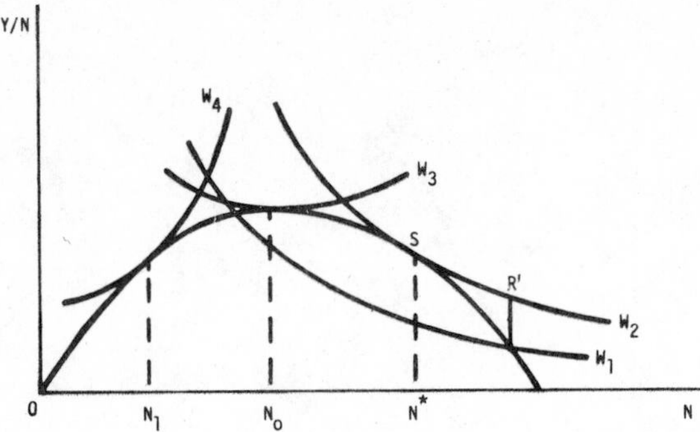


tries associate population size with power, either for defense or aggression. In similar fashion, a large labor force may be associated with national economic power. Should any of these arguments reflect social views in a given country, the welfare function would then include the level of population as an argument. Thus

$$W = w(Y/N, N). \qquad (11)^{26}$$

If society regards added people as a normal good, it is very simple to represent the trade-off between per capita income and population with welfare contours that are shaped similarly to indifference curves. A set of these, labeled $W_1$, $W_2$, is plotted in Figure 11–7. As can be seen, the population level at which we can reach the highest attainable welfare level consistent with our ability to produce output is at $N^*$. Recalling how we defined indifference curves and hence the social welfare function, we see that being on welfare curve $W_2$ is a more desirable state of affairs than being on curve $W_1$. Note, for example, that one can go from point $R$ on $W_1$ to $R'$ on $W_2$, maintaining an equal level of population ($N_1$), but reaching a higher level of per capita income ($Y/N$). Point $S$ is the highest level of welfare we can reach consistent with being on the average product or production possibilities curve $OP$. Thus $N^*$ is the optimum population, given the welfare function (Equation 10), the technical constraint of the production function

26. If our outcome is to be the correct social optimum, we should specifically include elements of the quality of life (on which a monetary value is not usually placed) by attempting to impute monetary value to them, so that Y/N does not simply measure the output of market goods. If there were a market for children there would be no need to include $N$ as a separate argument. An alternative way of handling such externalities as open space vs. congestion and a pollution-free environment is discussed later.

(Equation 2), the existing resource levels (R), the capital stock ($K$), and technology ($T$). Either a greater or a smaller population, for example at $T$ or $R$, would result in a loss of welfare. Note that including population in the welfare function does not preclude the possibility that the optimum may be at the population level that maximizes per capita income. This would be the result if the welfare contours looked like $W_3$ in Figure 11–7. The inclusion of the level of population as an argument in the welfare function does, however, permit the possibility that welfare contours like $W_2$ or $W_4$ could determine the optimum. If the welfare contours look like $W_4$, welfare could be increased by a rise in income per capita accompanied by a lower level of population. In countries where there is social approval of large families for economic reasons, such as those discussed by Leibenstein, Becker and others, or because of what appear to be noneconomic social values like *machismo,* it is likely that the social optimum population is like $N^*$ rather than like $N_o$.[27]

### More Complex Models of the Population Optimum

It is conceivable that members of a society would have a sufficient aversion to other people to prefer a population level like $N_2$, determined by a welfare function of which $W_4$ is the relevant contour. A formulation that effectively explains such an outcome is, however, probably much more complex than our welfare function (Equation 10). The complications are most likely to be of the nature of nonmarket considerations, which are the substance of much of our environmental concern. For example, we might think of including in the welfare function the notion of open space, leisure, pollution levels, and perhaps even life expectancy. The welfare function, after all, includes all the components of what we refer to as the quality of life. Our welfare function might then appear as follows:

$$W = w(Y/N, N, R_s, L_e, P, E, \cdots) \tag{12}$$

where $R_s$ represents resources devoted to open space, $L_e$ represents leisure, $P$ stands for pollution, and $E$ represents life expectancy. Technical constraint, represented by the production function, would have to take account of the effects of these additional arguments in determining the attainable alternatives. For example, land used for open space would have the effect of reducing the resource base for the production of material goods ($Y/N$). More leisure implies less output of material goods per member of the labor force or fewer units of labor input relative to population size. Reducing

27. A more detailed analysis of the nature of the population optimum when a preference for population is included in the welfare function is presented in Harold L. Votey, Jr., "The Optimum Population and Growth: A New Look (A Modification to Include a Preference for Children in the Welfare Function)," *Journal of Economic Theory* 1, no. 3 (October, 1969).

pollution entails costs which may be expressed in terms of opportunity cost, i.e., output of material goods foregone. Greater life expectancy probably requires more resources going into public health research, as well as other forms of public health measures, at the expense of material goods production. Taking account of these additions, our production function might take the form

$$Y = f(K, \phi N, \psi R, \rho, \theta) \tag{13}$$

where $\phi$ represents the proportion of the population's time spent in producing material goods, $\psi$ is the proportion of resources devoted to material goods production, $\rho$ is the proportion of output which is pollution, and $\theta$ is the proportion of output which is public health activity.[28]

The notion of the trade-off between added population and the other things we value in the welfare function should become clear from this analysis. An increase in the per capita levels of almost any of the other elements in the welfare function will reduce the output of material goods given the level of population, since we have a limited resource base ($R$), and given the existing levels of capital ($K$), and technology ($T$). Put another way, to maintain living standards for the advanced nations, raise living standards for the less developed nations, and limit pollution at the same time, we will need to increase our stock of capital and/or raise our level of technology; otherwise we will have to reduce population. It goes without saying that to maintain existing levels of open space, population must cease to grow.

The achievement of the population optimum as defined here, brings society to the point which is "best" in terms of its own choice. As a consequence, the result is not arbitrary. It will be difficult to ascertain correct population targets to effectively achieve the social will. The task should not, however, be regarded as insurmountable. The first step in making social choices is to be able to provide a complete enumeration of the feasible alternatives. We know that scientists are presently able to inventory our resource base. Econometric techniques permit estimates of alternative output possibilities. Experience with space technology shows that we can anticipate technological advances and place estimates on the cost of their achievement. With these capabilities alternative paths for population levels and the life qualities associated with them can be projected. To be sure, such estimates cannot be made without error, but there are accepted sta-

28. An analysis that includes these additional arguments in the welfare function and takes account of the interdependence in production between pollution and material goods is Harold L. Votey, Jr., "The Optimum Population and an Affluent Society (A Formulation Which Considers Shifts in Preferences for Leisure, 'Open Space', and Pollution)" (unpublished paper, 1971).

tistical techniques for making error estimates or for placing probabilistic bounds around them. With these estimates correct goals can be approached so long as governments are able to translate social preferences into policy.[29] Since governments act to control population, economists would argue that sufficient research should be undertaken to assure that the goals they seek are feasible and the choices optimal.

### Affluence and the Population Optimum

We can expect, from the study of the economics of choice, that there are influences on people which will tend to reduce the population optimum. At the same time we can expect additions to the capital stock and to the level of technology to facilitate the maintenance of a larger optimum population. For example, we tend to regard open space and a pollution-free environment as luxury goods.[30] (Recall that a luxury good is defined to be one that a person will consume proportionately more of as his income rises.) If such environmental concerns are luxuries, we can expect that as countries develop and individual incomes rise there will be a tendency for people to prefer more environmental benefits to added population. In other words, the effect of rising income will be a declining population optimum. A host of other factors mentioned by Leibenstein also tends to reduce the desire for added births as development takes place. Given the existence of such forces one might ask why there is any justification for policy measures to control population. A few of the problems involved in allowing natural forces or uncontrolled individual behavior to determine population merit our attention.

## Alternatives for Population Control

There are three notions of population size which are useful for the purposes of this analysis. (1) The realized population size, (2) the privately desired level of population, and (3) the socially desired level of population. Knowing the differences between the magnitudes of these alternative measures will provide an indication of the sort of actions required for population control.

The realized level of population is the simplest of the measures and the one most easily obtained. It is the sum which would be derived from any

29. Efforts are moving in this direction. Two good examples are L. T. Taylor, ed., *The Optimum Population for Britain* (London: Academic Press, 1970) and S. Fred Singer, *Is There An Optimum Level of Population* (New York: McGraw-Hill, 1971). Both are outgrowths of symposia on the problem. Each is at the stage of conceptualizing the problem rather than attempting specific calculations with respect to feasible alternatives.

30. This is a conclusion reached in Chapter 10.

population census, and a useful measure upon which to base estimates of per capita income levels. Projections of the realized population based on assumptions about mortality and fertility rates permit us to make estimates of future needs for food, housing, recreational space, etc. Projections actually made by demographers have resulted in the conviction that, unless there are radical changes in fertility rates, the quality of life must decline for all of us. Levels of, and changes in, fertility rates depend upon our next concept of population.

The privately desired level of population, our second measure, is the sum total of the membership all families would desire for themselves at a particular point in time. The fact that there are differences between the privately desired and the realized population level are not difficult to explain. Because of accidents, disease, and war, some family members meet an untimely end. In addition, while family fertility levels are subject to family control, we know that through ignorance, carelessness, and miscalculation unwanted children are conceived. As noted on page 279, the 1965 National Fertility Study estimated that for the years 1960–1965 approximately 22 percent of all children born in the United States were unwanted by at least one parent. If this is the case in the country where birth control technology is perhaps the most advanced, and educational attainment and the dissemination of information reach the highest levels, it would be reasonable to presume that the proportion of unwanted births is even higher in many countries of the world.

Our third measure, the socially desired level of population, is the most complex and difficult to determine. This is the level defined earlier as optimum. Just as we might expect the privately desired level of population to be less than the realized level, the socially desired level of population in all likelihood will be smaller than the privately desired level. Such will be the case if families have more children than would be consistent with achieving the social optimum. This might happen even among those who accept a particular population level as socially optimal. One can always find examples of active advocates of zero population growth who have five children of their own. In less developed countries there are families who desire greater levels of development, yet have numbers of children inconsistent with achieving economic growth with the limited resources available to the country. If such cases are the rule rather than the exception, we might expect the privately desired level of population to be in excess of the socially desired level.

### Who Has the Right to Determine Population Size?

The complex philosophical issues associated with population control are, to a large degree, the crux of the problem. Distinctions need to be made between individual rights, family rights, and social rights. Can women refuse to bear children or husbands insist upon wives bearing children? Can society overrule private decisions to have children? Appropriate social policy depends upon the point at which we are willing to concede that social rights supersede individual or family rights.

Economists as such cannot provide simple solutions for ethical questions. They can, however, enumerate the effects of accepting one position over another. Note that the three measures of population size coincide with three recognized ethical positions. First is the ethical position that conception and birth are acts of God with which humans should not interfere, i.e., that neither private nor social rights exist with respect to the determination of population size. If we all believed this, then the realized population would be that which is privately desired and there would be no divergence between social and private goals. Few people accept such a position, however, and even religious groups who have advocated such a position in the past have recently tended to modify their beliefs.

A second ethical position which has adherents in many countries holds that individual rights are supreme. Such a position permits the possibility of population control but leaves the choice to the individual family.[31] If all people adhered to this viewpoint we might find a divergence between the realized population level and the privately desired level. But there would not be a divergence between private and socially desired levels where this ethical position prevails.

Finally, we might adopt the ethical position that permitting unrestrained family decision-making with regard to births may encroach upon the rights of others when resources are scarce. In this view, society, collectively, should make the ultimate decision as to the appropriate level of population. This is the position adopted by those who would use more than persuasion to regulate family and, hence, total population size. They argue that the determination of the number of people on earth is too important to be left to unrestrained human behavior. To justify their position they point out that many other aspects of resource allocation are regulated by collective decision. Health, education, public safety, even to some extent incomes are regulated by the people through their governments. Since population size affects all of these things it may need to be controlled as well.

Malthus's solution to the population problem was delayed marriage and the abstinence from sexual activity. While this may have worked effectively for the Irish, it does not appear that such a solution will be volun-

31. If we pursue the notion of individual rights to its logical conclusion we would not even accept the family as the decision unit, but would require that both husband and wife, as individuals, must decide on the appropriate family size.

tarily adopted elsewhere. Consequently, it seems appropriate to consider other measures designed to compel the population to utilize the biological techniques of control available to it.

### Some Means of Control

The appropriate measures of control will depend upon the ethical position adopted, and the extent to which the three measures of population differ. Obviously, under the first ethical judgment, no controls would be appropriate. If we believe that laissez-faire should prevail, i.e., that each family has the exclusive right to determine its own family size independent of social constraints, some degree of control may still be appropriate. This will be true if, as we find in the United States, private desires for children are for fewer children than are actually born. If the divergence between desired and realized population is a matter of misinformation or ignorance regarding contraceptive techniques, it might be appropriate to initiate private voluntary birth control clinics where birth control devices are demonstrated and perhaps even distributed. Such measures would help families to have the number of children they wish.

If the problem is considered to be a social one, i.e., that there are external diseconomies which would result in an excessive number of births, then a different sort of measure is indicated.

### Economic Techniques for Population Control

Where externalities exist, the usual economic solution is to impose a system of taxes and subsidies to entice producers to generate the socially desired level of output. For example, if it is felt that not enough oil is being produced, we institute a depletion allowance to increase the profitability of drilling for oil, with the consequence that more oil is produced relative to the production of other goods. If it is later decided there was an overproduction of oil, we could reduce the level of output by eliminating the depletion allowance (subsidy). Alternatively, we could impose production quotas. The subsidy measure has the advantage that it is impersonal and thus reduces the possibility of political favoritism which is a weakness of a quota system under which the rights to produce are allocated by bureaucrats.

When it is considered desirable to provide economic incentives for birth control, we can consider the implications of various forms of taxation. An obvious subsidy to childbirth is the family exemption in the federal income tax. The elimination of such a subsidy would raise the cost of children relative to other things and fewer births might be expected. It has been argued that such a measure would place greater burdens on the poor. This need not be so, however, if a truly progressive tax structure is devised. A greater problem is that childbirths may be fairly inelastic with respect to price. A change in the family exemption may have little effect on the number of births. If this turned out to be the case other measures would be required.

Another problem area may be that many births are simply a matter of misinformation. This problem is easily dealt with by the subsidization of birth control education. Along with this subsidy we might also subsidize contraceptive devices to reduce the cost of birth control itself. The latter measure has the same weakness as the elimination of tax subsidies for child-bearing if childbirths are inelastic with respect to price.

Some countries have experimented with positive incentives to use birth control measures. India pays women a subsidy to use an intrauterine device. Men have been paid 20 rupees to submit to a vasectomy.[32] Both of these measures can be effective if properly administered.[33]

As suggested earlier, it may be that financial incentives or disincentives are not adequate to bring about socially desired reductions in fertility rates. Should it turn out that social preferences or tastes are only moderately controlled by the usual forms of economic control, some sort of quota system might be required. The question then becomes, how do we administer a quota system without the usual problems of political administration of quotas.

An interesting solution has been proposed which has particular appeal to economists. Actually, it amounts to the creation of a market for children in which total output is rigidly controlled. A society begins by determining the appropriate number of births in a given period. Then it coins tokens in that amount to be divided equally among families formed in this period.[34] Each token entitles a family to have one child. Families who desire fewer children than the number of tokens they possess could sell their tokens and thus earn a subsidy for having fewer children. Families who desire a larger number of children can pay the price of purchasing extra tokens on the market. In this way there is no absolute restriction on

32. The choice between techniques may be a subject for economic study as well as for study by physicians and physiologists. For a detailed analysis of the economic appropriateness of alternative birth control techniques, see Stephen Enke, "The Economic Aspects of Slowing Population Growth," *Economic Journal* 76 (March, 1966).

33. The vasectomy incentive program, as administered, had a number of weaknesses. Frequently, old men who had no further desire for children would submit to the operation for money. Furthermore, men could have the operation more than once without medical technicians being aware of the unneeded procedure so the bonus could be collected more than once. Obviously, improvements could be made in administrative rules.

34. Where divorces are numerous or under any system in which families are formed and reformed frequently, the tokens could simply be allocated among women reaching child-bearing age.

family size. Families with fewer children are not penalized because other families have greater numbers of children. Freedom of choice is preserved consistent with the overall social constraint. It has been argued that this is a solution which penalizes the poor in favor of the rich. Under our present tax structure this would tend to be true, but if we adopted measures to eliminate inequalities in economic opportunities, this criticism could be obviated.

An alternative proposal is a quota system that avoids any possibility of favoring high income over low income families. The solution is to allow families to have only a single daughter but as many sons as desired. This puts a biological upper limit on the number of births but would permit a substantial once-and-for-all increase in population size, since birth rates in most countries fall far short of biological limits already. Population could not continue to rise beyond this limit because the number of women of child-bearing age would be fixed.

There are a number of problems with such a solution. First of all, the technology that can control the sex of children conceived is yet to be perfected. Furthermore, this proposal is more restrictive than the token system in that it regulates the composition of families, thus reducing freedom of choice. Even when the technology for controlling sex is perfected, it is likely to be more costly to regulate the sex of a conception than to simply regulate the total number of births by economic measures. Finally, it does not prevent all families from having large numbers of children, unless a quota is put on male births as well, thus reverting to an overall quota with less flexibility than the token system.

There has been no attempt here to be all-inclusive in terms of enumerating the alternative socioeconomic schemes for controlling population growth.[35] Rather, the intent is to point out the nature of economic solutions. Those solutions are best that provide the greatest net social benefits. This is a difficult area of decision-making because neither costs nor benefits are easily evaluated in monetary terms. Once more the role of the economist should be to point out alternatives by means of an evaluation of the social consequences (both costs and benefits) of each, so that a society is in a position to make a choice.

## Conclusion

In summary, a number of points should be emphasized. We noted that population pressures exacerbate the problem of economic development.

35. An interesting list of alternative socioeconomic measures for population control is presented in P. R. and A. H. Ehrlich, *Population, Resources, Environment* (San Francisco: W. H. Freeman, 1972), pp. 335–341.

Furthermore, they create a burden on resources in other ways which affect the quality of life for all. Any notion of an optimum population size must take into account our resource base, productive capabilities, and technology, as well as social preferences. Social preferences involve ethical choices which society must agree upon if a population optimum is to be defined. Once this is done, the nature of control measures depends upon where the divergence between desired and realized population lies, and upon our ethical judgments. Population control is feasible and could be easily administered within a framework of maximum individual choice, if there were agreement on the appropriate level of population.

### Suggested Reading

Cipolla, Carlo M. *The Economic History of World Population.* 3rd ed. Baltimore: Penguin Books, 1965.

Coale, Ansley J. "Population and Economic Development." In *The Population Dilemma.* 2nd ed. Edited by Philip M. Hauser. Englewood Cliffs, N.J.: Prentice-Hall, 1963.

Keyfitz, Nathan. "The Numbers and Distribution of Mankind." In *Environment: Resources, Pollution, and Society.* Edited by William W. Murdock. Stamford, Conn.: Sinauer Associates, 1971.

Malthus, Thomas Robert. *An Essay of the Principle of Population.* Harmondsworth, England: Penguin Books, 1970.

Robinson, Warren C. and David E. Horlacher. *Population Growth and Economic Welfare.* New York: The Population Council, 1971.

# Commentary

Chapter 11 has presented us with an economist's view of the nature of the population problem. Professor Votey suggests a way in which we might conceptualize the notion of a socially optimum population, and presents some of the alternatives for policy which might facilitate population control. In doing so he utilizes many of the tools presented earlier and adds more. We see, for example, how the production function, introduced in Chapter 1, can be combined with an investment function, a profit function, and equations representing the supply and demand for labor to create a growth model. In such a model the paths of production, investment, population growth, and wages are determined; it can also help to explain the historical concern over population increase.

The presentation of preferences for alternatives in consumption, introduced in Chapter 10, is expanded upon. From this evolves the concept of indifference curves, a useful tool in evaluating how individuals choose between goods and services. Finally, the concept of a social welfare function is developed, representing aggregate preferences with respect to society's alternatives. The use of production functions is extended by the introduction of the total and average product curves, which are alternative ways to present production possibilities. These new concepts are put together to illustrate optimization when there are resource and production constraints. Thus we see standard tools of the economist used in connection with a problem given little attention until fairly recently.

In the final chapter, Llad Phillips deals with "the war on crime," an old war, but one being fought with new vigor. In dealing with this problem Professor Phillips makes use of the notion of simultaneous systems in which the effects of interacting forces are registered. He will show how optimization techniques once again can assist in the formulation of social policy for improved resource allocation in an area where markets are nonexistent.

# 12

# The War on Crime: Prevention or Control

Llad Phillips

Crime is one of the major concerns in the United States. In the election year of 1972 it ranked third behind the Vietnam War and the cost of living in a July Gallup poll on vital issues; in 1968 it ranked second behind Vietnam.[1] Fear of crime and violence causes many city dwellers to live in home fortresses, makes nervous air travelers wish they had the time to take the Greyhound, and inspires more than a few students to ride old bikes worth little more than the chains and locks used to shackle them. Despite the country's concern about crime, there appears to be a growing resignation to the inevitability that crime will get worse. A recent quote by the Chief of the California Bureau of Criminal Statistics reflects this attitude: "In this annual report, we again note the dismal increase of crime in California. The rise in crime seems to have joined those other traditional certainties—death and taxes—in American life."[2] On the other hand, some observers argue that reports of increasing crime are exaggerated, largely as a consequence of reports by the FBI and the news media.

Despite the pledges of politicians to do something about crime, there seems to be no consensus on why crime is increasing or on effective action to arrest it. Certainly, at this time, there are but few among us who conceive of crime as an economic problem. That is to say, the crime problem is seldom thought of in terms of spending money to control crime or eliminate its causes as opposed to suffering the losses that crime imposes. This may in part result from the emphasis by social scientists on understanding

1. *Santa Barbara News Press,* July 1972; July 1968. Gallup polls on issues.

2. State of California Department of Justice, Bureau of Criminal Statistics, *Crime and Delinquency in California,* 1966.

the social, psychological, and cultural basis of crime. As a consequence, scholars are still arguing about the degree to which crime is controllable, and on how to construct a predictive model which will identify the factors that cause crime and its costs to vary from one community to another.

In basic terms, the crime problem from an economic point of view is a matter of prescribing the proper amount of resources that society should allocate to crime prevention and control. We shall attempt to define the magnitude of the crime problem, identify those causes of crime which can be alleviated through social programs, and determine whether or not crime is subject to control by the instruments of apprehension, prosecution, and correction. Our concern will not be with why one individual engages in deviant behavior and another does not. Instead, we shall examine why some groups in our society are more criminal than others, and why crime varies from the South to the West and from San Diego to Sacramento, with a view toward answering the question: what policies are in the best interests of society?

First, to view the dimensions of the crime problem, it must be set in perspective. The information about the major index felony crimes (robbery, burglary, larceny, auto theft, rape, aggravated assault and homicide) is most complete. The task then is to view crime as an economic problem and identify the policy variables and causal factors which determine the choice between crime control and crime alleviation. With the general framework of analysis established, some specific evidence is examined on whether crime is controllable. For balance, we next focus on why crime is a phenomenon disproportionately associated with the young black male city dweller. Finally, we consider the prospects for the future.

## U.S. Crime in Perspective

Like the men in the Hindu fable of "The Blind Men and the Elephant," one's impression of crime depends upon whether one has hold of "the trunk or the tail." To provide perspective, crime statistics need to be approached from several directions: (1) the estimated costs of crime and crime control to see how crime in general compares to other social problems and which crimes cost us the most; (2) the trends in crime and police effectiveness, reported for the crimes on which the FBI index is based, to see why both citizens and public officials have become increasingly concerned with crime in the last decade; (3) how crime and its rate of increase vary by age and race; (4) the reliability of crime statistics and the reasons that led former Attorney General Ramsey Clark to suggest in 1968 that "there is no wave of crime in this country."[3] Some of the phenomena

3. Fred P. Graham, "A contemporary history of American crime," *Violence in America: Historical and Comparative Perspectives,* vol. II, edited by Hugh Davis Graham and Ted Robert Gurr (Washington, D.C., U.S. Printing Office, July 1969).

identified here will then be rationalized by models developed for that purpose (see pp. 324–336).

## Social Costs of Crime and Crime Control

Viewing crime from a cost perspective we get an indication of how much society loses because of criminal activity and how much it spends for crime control. In addition, such a view calls attention to the fact that the nature of the loss varies from crime to crime. Some crimes involve the destruction of property or the loss of life; some involve the unwanted and illegal transfer of resources; and some involve the provision of desired but illegal services.

The monetary losses that citizens suffer because of criminal activity are substantial. The President's Commission on Law Enforcement and Administration of Justice estimated the losses in 1965 from homicide alone at $750 million.[4] Assault and rape cost another $65 million. The other FBI index crimes of robbery, burglary, larceny, and auto theft resulted in losses of $600 million. Fraud and driving under the influence of alcohol were even more costly. Table 12–1 lists the estimated losses from these crimes.

Losses of life (resulting, for example, from murder) or losses of property (due, for example, to vandalism) result in a net loss of resources to society. Losses resulting from crimes such as robbery, auto theft, or embezzlement are principally of the nature of a transfer of resources or ownership, a sort of illegal income redistribution or antiwelfare program. Crimes involving narcotics, loan sharking, gambling, and prostitution provide a service where the victim is willing, but resources are drained from socially sanctioned activities and add to the economic and political power of the criminal sector. Altogether, the estimated total loss of approximately $15 billion to criminal activity compares to the $21 billion of national income generated by legitimate activity in agriculture, forestry, and fisheries.

Controlling and preventing crime cost additional money. For example, expenditures for police cost $2.8 billion in 1965; prosecution and public defense took an additional $125 million; operation of the courts cost $261 million; and funds for correctional institutions amounted to another $1 billion. Altogether public efforts at crime control absorbed $4.2 billion of resources. In addition to this, private prevention services and equipment (including bicycle chains and locks) plus insurance and other costs amounted to another $1.9 billion. Public and private costs of controlling and preventing crime are listed in Table 12–2. Altogether, the losses to

4. President's Commission on Law Enforcement and Administration of Justice, *Task Force Report: Crime and Its Impact—An Assessment* (Washington, D.C., U.S. Government Printing Office, 1967).

Table 12–1
Economic Impact of Crimes, 1965

| | $ Millions | |
|---|---|---|
| Crimes against the person | | 815 |
| Homicide* | 750 | |
| Assault, rape* | 65 | |
| Crimes against property | | 3,932 |
| Robbery, burglary, larceny, auto theft* | 600 | |
| Unreported commercial theft | 1,400 | |
| Embezzlement | 200 | |
| Fraud | 1,350 | |
| Forgery | 82 | |
| Arson and vandalism | 300 | |
| Other crimes | | 2,036 |
| Driving under the influence | 1,816 | |
| Tax fraud | 100 | |
| Abortion | 120 | |
| Illegal goods and services | | 8,075 |
| Narcotics | 350 | |
| Loan sharking | 350 | |
| Prostitution | 225 | |
| Alcohol | 150 | |
| Gambling | 7,000 | |
| | Total | 14,858 |

*FBI index crimes

Source: The President's Commission on Law Enforcement, *Task Force Report*, Ch. 3.

crime and the costs of controlling and preventing crime amounted to nearly $21 billion in 1965.

### Trends in Crime and Police Effectiveness

The decade of the sixties, with its assassinations of public figures and riots in the cities and on the campuses, engendered a great deal of soul searching in American society. Are we a violent society? Are we becoming more violent? And, to expand a little on H. Rap Brown, are crime and violence as American as apple pie? The assassination of Senator Robert F. Kennedy in 1968 precipitated the formation in June 1968 of the National Commission on the Causes and Prevention of Violence to investigate questions such as these. An examination of the trends in crimes classified as FBI index crimes, shows that per capita offense rates for these crimes (so classified on the basis of their supposed reliability) have been increasing dramatically for the last two decades. Of even greater alarm and potential significance, the data reveal that the ability of the police to clear (to their satisfaction) crimes by means of arrest has been dramatically falling.

Table 12–2
Public and Private Expenditures
for Crime Control and Prevention

| | | | $ Millions |
|---|---|---|---|
| **Public expenditures on criminal justice** | | | |
| Police | | | 2,792 |
| Local | 2,201 | | |
| State | 348 | | |
| Federal | 243 | | |
| Prosecution | | | 105 |
| Public defenders | | | 20 |
| Courts | | | 261 |
| Local | 173 | | |
| State | 51 | | |
| Federal | 37 | | |
| Corrections | | | 1,034 |
| Local | 343 | | |
| State | 632 | | |
| Federal | 59 | | |
| | | Total | 4,212 |
| **Private expenditures** | | | |
| Prevention services | | | 1,350 |
| Prevention equipment | | | 200 |
| Insurance | | | 300 |
| Court costs | | | 60 |
| | | Total | 1,910 |
| | | Grand Total | 6,122 |

Source: Ibid., footnote 2.

The offense rates per 100,000 people are plotted for the years 1952 to 1970 in Figure 12–1.[5] These data show both the relative frequency and the increase in crime, with larceny being the most prevalent and homicide the least. Note that during this period all of the offense rates have at least doubled from their lows. Robbery has increased nearly fivefold. This crime is particularly indicative, since it is a crime against persons as well as property and usually involves strangers, in contrast to aggravated assault, which occurs principally among family, friends, or acquaintances. As such, robbery is regarded as a bellwether of proclivity toward violence.

The ability of the police to clear crimes through arrest is reflected by the clearance ratios plotted for the years 1952–1970 in Figure 12–2.[6] These ratios are the fraction of offenses cleared (in the view of the police) by arrest of suspect. They are a measure of the average likelihood or

5. Data obtained from U.S. Department of Justice, Federal Bureau of Investigation, *Uniform Crime Reports,* Washington, D.C.

6. Ibid.

Figure 12–1. Offense rates per 100,000 people for seven major felonies.

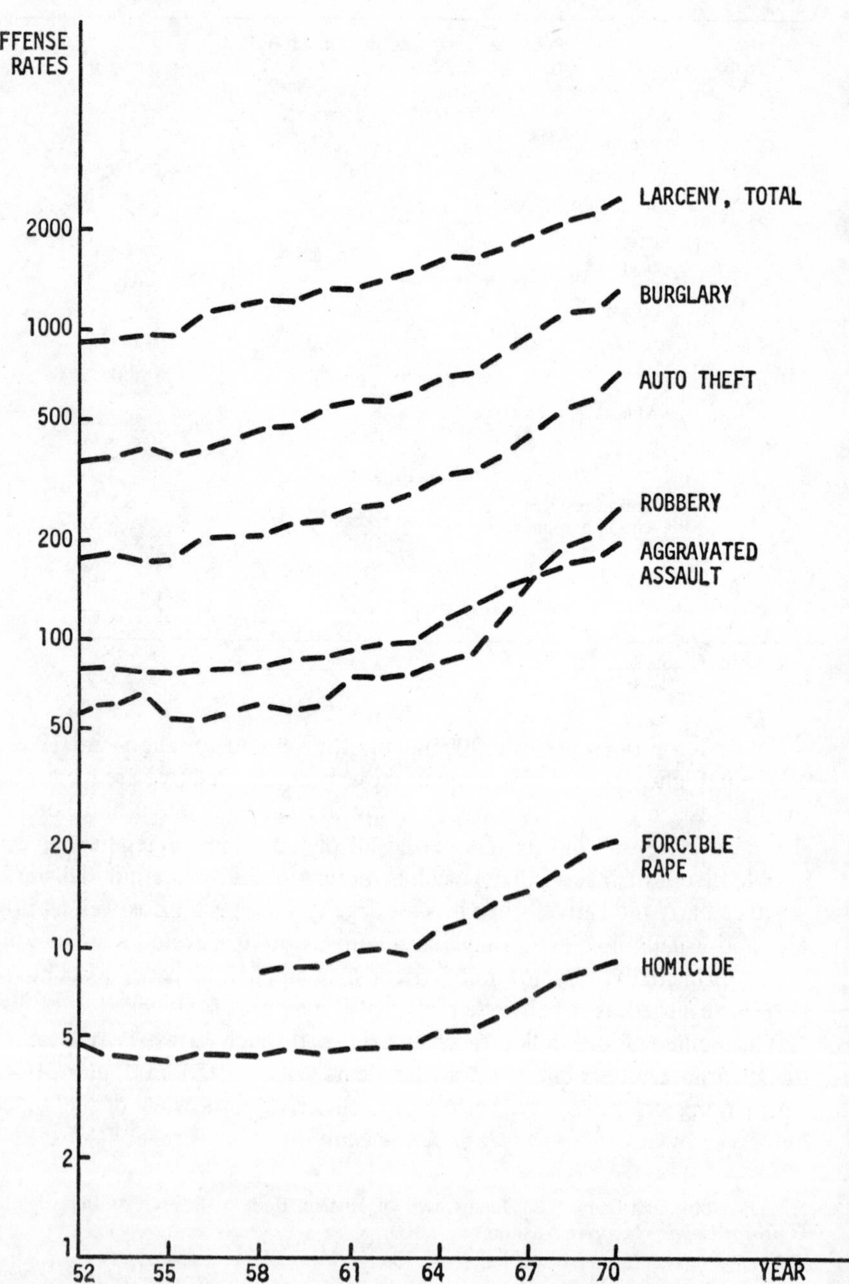

Figure 12–2. Clearance ratios for seven major felonies.

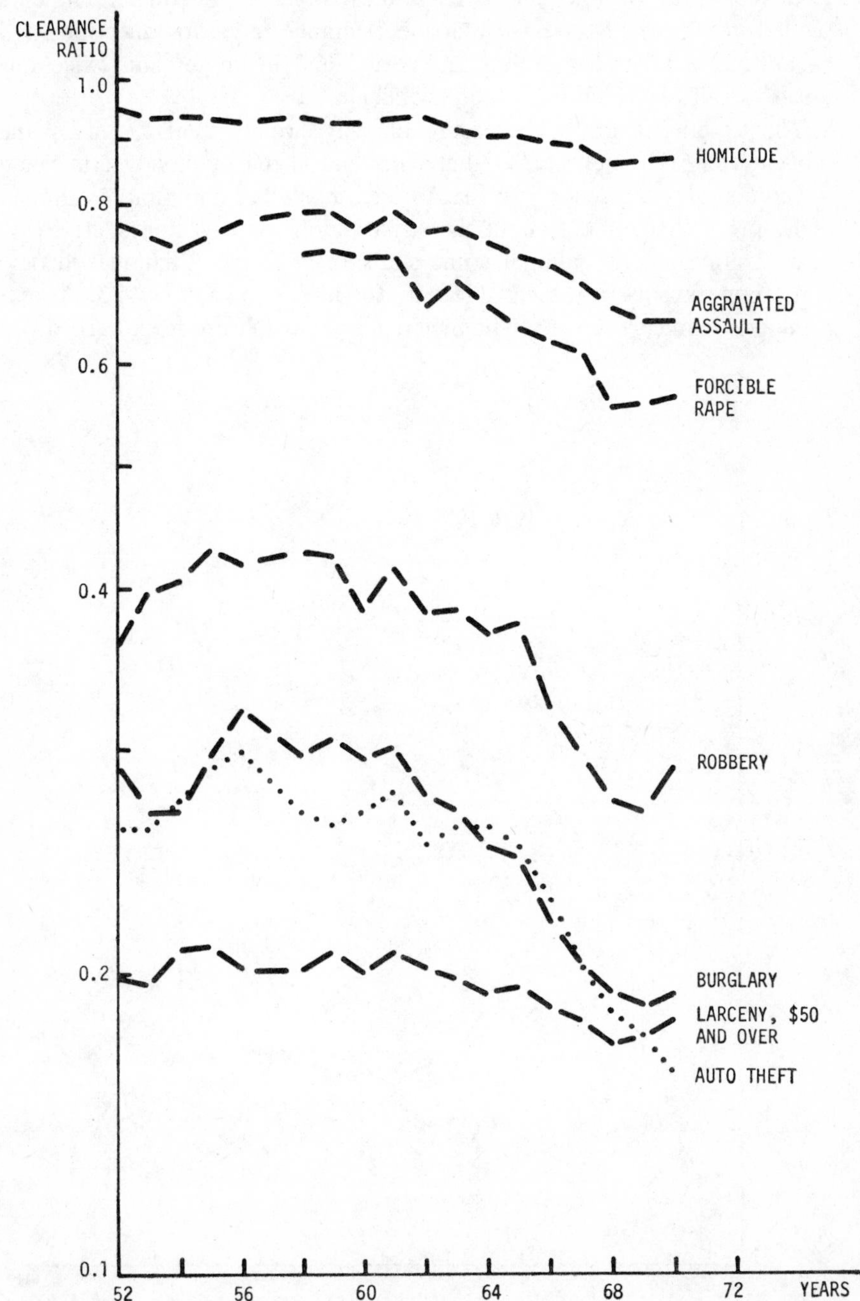

probability of the criminal being apprehended. Viewed in this light, police effectiveness may be particularly significant. If criminal activity is deterrable and varies inversely with the likelihood of punishment, then offense rates should rise if police effectiveness falls (other things equal). The data plotted in Figure 12–2 reveal that the clearance ratios for all crimes fell by at least 8.5 percent during this period and by more than twice this much for all of the crimes except homicide.

The experience in the last score of years would seem to justify the biblical view (Ezekiel vii:23) that "the land is full of bloody crime and the city is full of violence." But is America really becoming more criminal and more violent? What about the strikes, riots, and lynchings of yesteryear? Unfortunately, national crime statistics (like many national income and labor statistics) are available only for the period since 1933. An exception is homicide. Data for homicide are obtainable from the records on

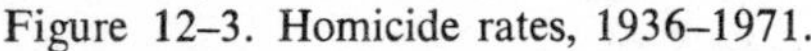
Figure 12–3. Homicide rates, 1936–1971.

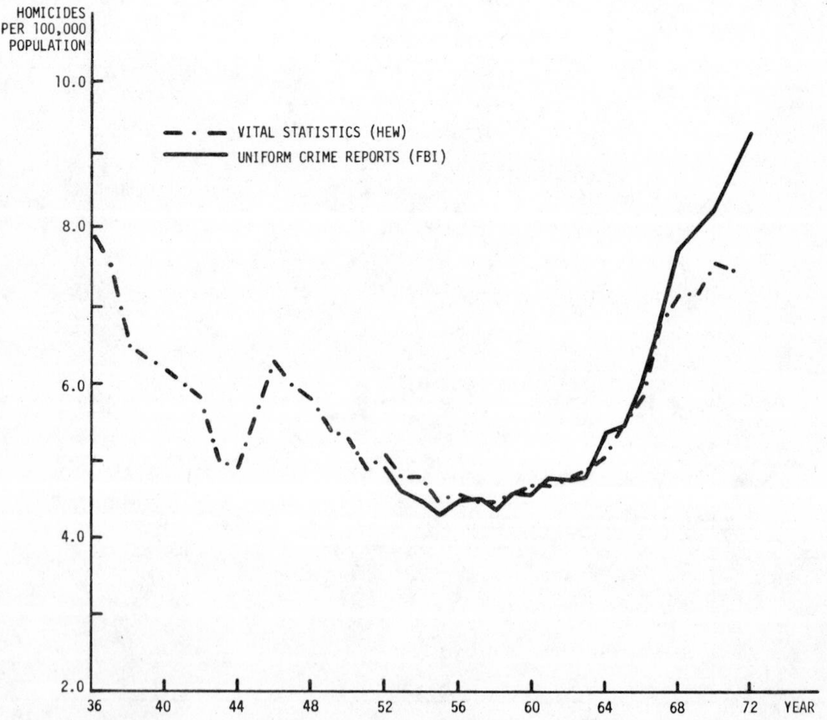

vital statistics, and the rate per 100,000 people is plotted in Figure 12–3 for the period 1936–1971.[7] It is noteworthy that the 1970 homicide rate is not a new phenomenon. It was this high in the 1930s. The homicide rate has risen before and fallen. Perhaps a steady increase in "bloody crime and violence" is not inevitable after all.

### Patterns in Crime: Age, Sex, Race, and City Size

Arrest data show that crime is predominantly an urban, youthful, male phenomenon with nonwhites more than proportionately involved. Youth play a particularly important role in the four economic felonies: robbery, burglary, larceny, and auto theft. Arrest rates for these crimes are one or two orders of magnitude higher for groups between age 14 and age 24 than for males a generation older. It is interesting to note that youths under 18 account for over 54 percent of total arrests for larceny committed by each race. The youthful nature of crime is illustrated in Figures 12–4 and 12–5, where arrest rates per 1000 persons are plotted by age for four of the seven index crimes.[8] Also observe in Figure 12–6 that the trends in crime rates plotted by age show that youths have a higher rate of increase than older age groups for homicide and aggravated assault. This tends to be true for the other index crimes but to a lesser degree.[9]

The high rate of increase in aggregate arrest rates could be explained, in part, by the post-World War II baby boom and the consequent shift in the age distribution of the population in the direction of a more youthful population. The median age of the population declined from 30.3 years in 1952 to 27.7 in 1967. If arrest rates by age are held constant at the 1952 levels, the shift toward a younger population accounts for 15 percent of the rise in the aggregate arrest rate for larceny over the years 1952–1967. This leaves a considerable rise in arrest rates over this period to be explained by other factors.

The observation that economic crimes may be regarded essentially as a male phenomenon is attested to by the fact that more than 94 percent of those arrested for the crimes of burglary, robbery, and auto theft in the 18–19-year-old age group were males. For larceny the percentage was 75 percent.

7. U.S. Department of Health, Education, and Welfare, Public Health Service, Office of Vital Statistics, *Vital Statistics Rates in the United States,* Government Printing Office, Washington, D.C., various issues.

8. Data obtained from FBI *Uniform Crime Reports* and analyzed in Harold L. Votey, Jr. and Llad Phillips, *Economic Crimes: Their Generation, Deterrence and Control* (Springfield, Va.: U.S. Clearinghouse for Federal Scientific and Technical Information, 1969). Votey and Phillips contains a plot similar to Figure 12–5 for aggravated assault, auto theft and rape.

9. Plots similar to Figure 12–6 may be found in Votey and Phillips, *Economic Crimes,* for burglary, robbery, larceny and auto theft.

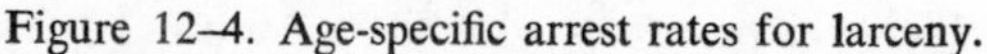


Figure 12–4. Age-specific arrest rates for larceny.

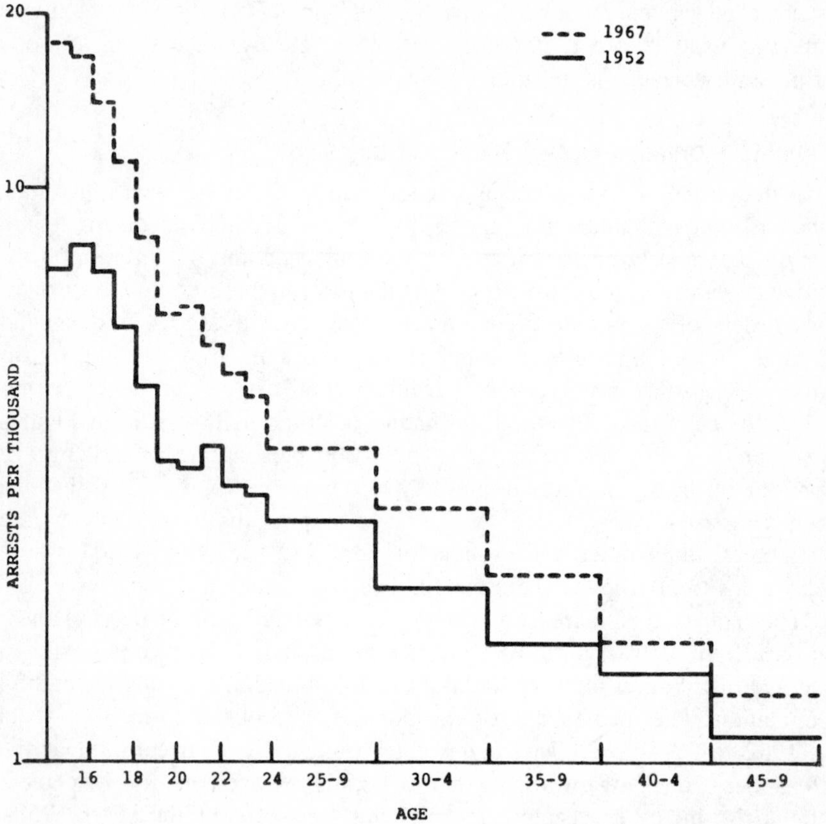

The high incidence of crime by nonwhites is illustrated in Figure 12–7 using larceny as an example.[10]

Comparing arrest rates for young people only, in 1967 for youths under 18 the urban arrest rate per 10,000 population for larceny is 268.0 for nonwhites, and 93.1 for whites. For the remaining FBI index crimes the differences are of a comparable or greater magnitude. The impact of the racial difference gains more significance when one observes that the proportion of nonwhites to total population has been rising secularly, so that for males under 18 the proportion in 1967 was greater than one-seventh.

10. Plots similar to Figure 12–7 may be found in Votey and Phillips, *Economic Crimes,* for burglary, robbery and homicide.

Figure 12–5. Age-specific arrest rates in 1967.

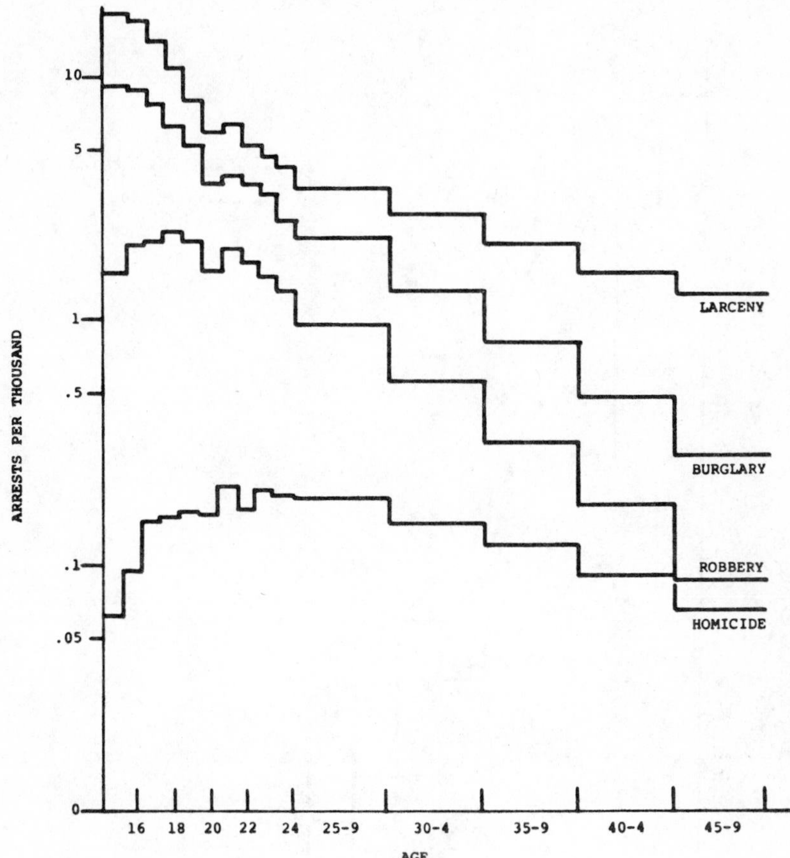


The variation of crime with color suggests why, in the words of T. H. White, the issue of "law and order" contains a "racial edge that disturbs conservatives and liberals alike."[11]

It is well to keep in mind that crime tends to be an urban phenomenon. The cores of American cities are the most crime prone and violence ridden, and they are increasingly becoming predominantly black. There are also suburban black communities which are communities in the true sense and are safe.

11. See Theodore H. White, *The Making of the President, 1968* (New York: Pocket Books, 1968), p. 241.

Figure 12–6. Percentage rates of growth of arrest rates per capita.

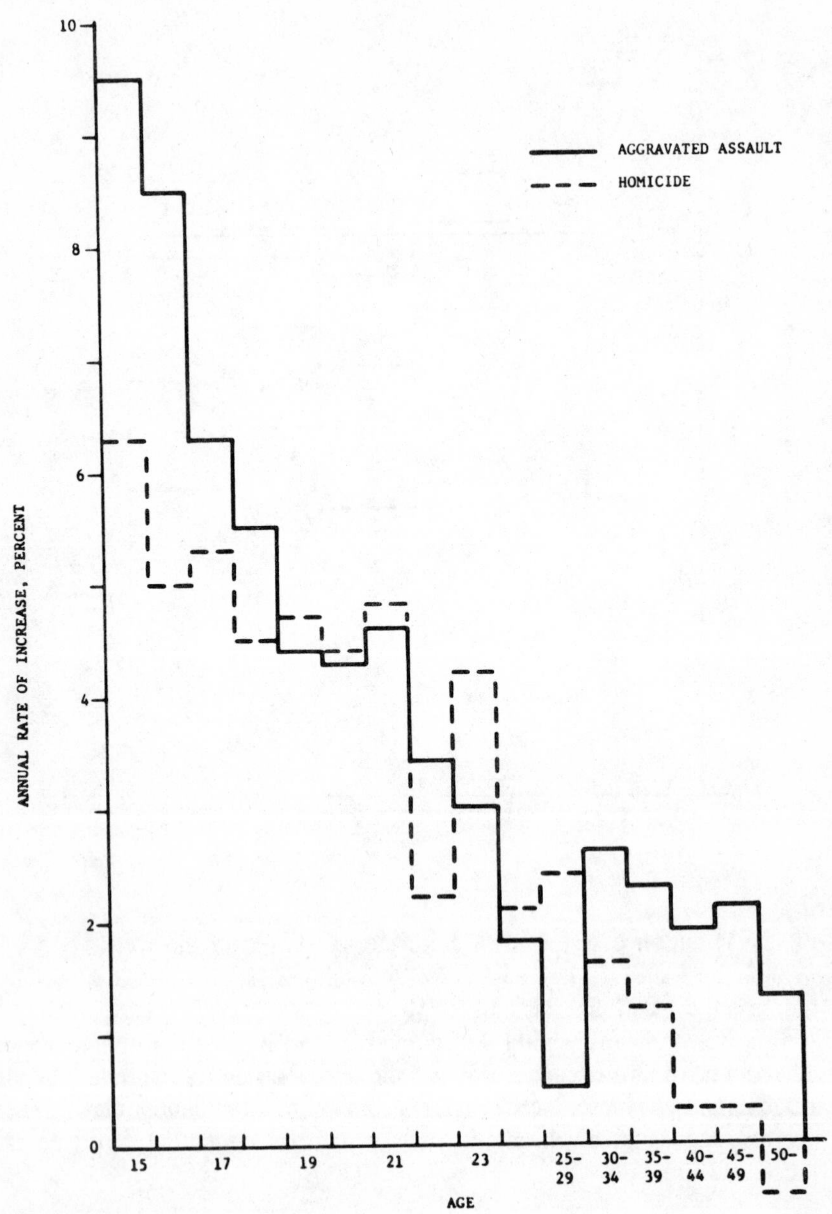

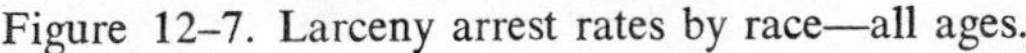

Figure 12–7. Larceny arrest rates by race—all ages.

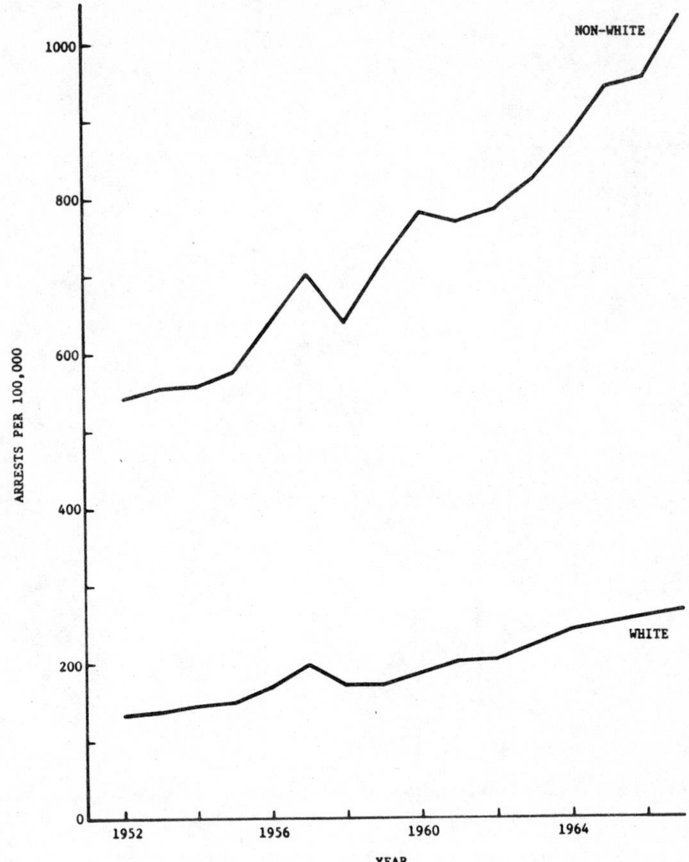


The variation of crime with city size is illustrated in Figure 12–8.[12] Since the nation is continuing to urbanize, the aggregate crime rate tends to naturally increase as a result.

## Validity of U.S. Crime Statistics

Donald R. Cressey has discussed six principal criticisms of general crime statistics.[13]

12. The data are obtained from FBI *Uniform Crime Reports.*

13. Donald R. Cressey, "Measuring crime rates," in *Criminal Behavior and Social Systems,* edited by Anthony L. Guenther (Chicago: Rand McNally, 1970).

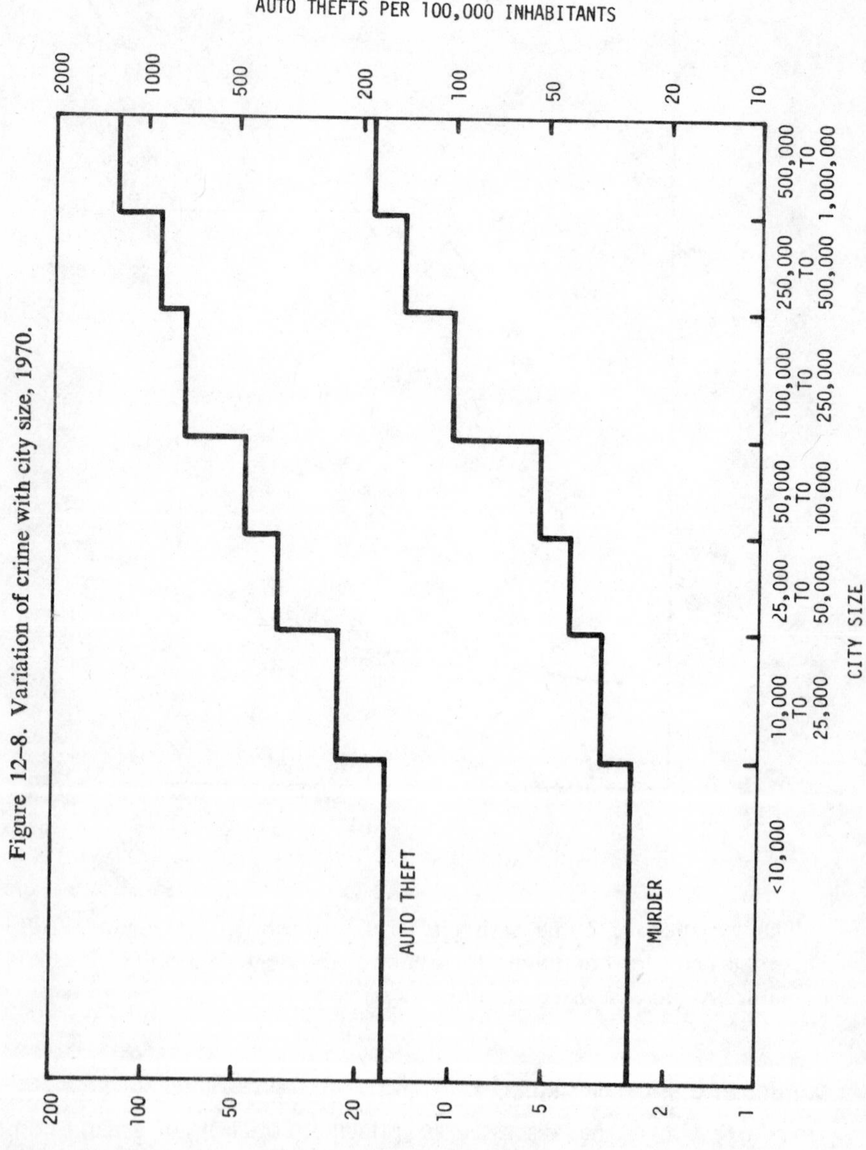


Figure 12–8. Variation of crime with city size, 1970.

(1) The true crime rate remains unknown; only reported or discovered crime becomes known.

(2) The ratio of reported crime to true crime does not stay constant.

(3) It is hazardous to compare crime rates between jurisdictions, or even over time for the same jurisdiction, because reporting practices are subject to wide variation.

(4) Crime statistics are compiled for administrative (not research) purposes, and the statistical reliability is unknown.

(5) Statistics for many crimes, such as white-collar crimes, are not compiled.

(6) Statistics on juvenile delinquency suffer all the foregoing faults and, in addition, are not precisely defined.

Regarding points (5) and (6), it is certainly true, as revealed by the cost statistics on pages 311–12, that the index offenses present an incomplete picture of crime in America. Nonetheless, they are a window on the criminal world.

Concerning points (3) and (4), while it may be hazardous to examine individual reporting units, the national statistics are averages based on many reporting units. Hence, by the law of mass averages, variation due to random errors in individual reporting units decreases with the number of units.

It may appear difficult to deal with points (1) and (2), since "true" crime is unknown. However, there are some benchmarks on the FBI index crime data provided by outside sources. Reporting is not generally a problem for homicide. In the preponderance of cases there is a corpse. Furthermore, the circumstances leading to the crime involve family, friends, or acquaintances in approximately three-fourths of the cases. Consequently, the clearance ratio is highest for this crime. It is the exceptional homicide which goes undetected. The homicide rate compiled independently from the U.S. Vital Statistics compares favorably to the rate reported by the FBI (see Figure 12–3).

There is another benchmark for the index crimes. The President's Commission on Law Enforcement and the Administration of Justice commissioned a victimization survey conducted by the National Opinion Research Center (NORC). The NORC rate of 206.5 per 100,000 population for auto theft for 1965–66 does not differ appreciably from the 1965 rate reported by the FBI of 226.0. Perhaps citizens take the theft of a car seriously enough to report it.

Benchmarks exist for homicide and auto theft—both index crimes; one violent and the other property. Referring back to Figures 12–1 and

12–2, it is significant to note that the patterns for offense rates and clearance ratios for the other index crimes are comparable to those for these benchmark crimes. The qualitative conclusions of rising crime rates and falling police effectiveness drawn from these figures seem valid. It would seem reasonable to look for systematic causes relevant for all index crimes.

### Programs to Minimize the Social Cost of Crime

Society can fight crime by operating directly against it, using the resources of criminal justice; or it can support programs designed to alleviate the conditions which generate crime. Former U.S. Attorney General Ramsey Clark hit the nail on the head when he said, "Law enforcement can only deal with the symptoms of crime. It's like bailing out the basement without turning off the water." The irony of it all is that no matter how many social programs society mounts, it may never be able to get the faucet completely off. We shall always need some bailers. Furthermore, the cost of trying to turn the faucet off may, at some point, rapidly become more expensive than bailing the water. The best solution for society is to find the proper balance between programs to control crime and programs to prevent crime.

### Detention and Rehabilitation versus Deterrence

The essential controversy about the nature of criminal justice is whether apprehension, prosecution, and punishment are only effective in controlling the individual unfortunate enough to be caught, or whether through the expectations of sanctions, these consequences deter criminal behavior in the general populace. The notion of deterrence can be traced at least as far back as Aristotle, who reasoned that "the generality of men are naturally apt to be swayed by fear rather than by reverence, and to refrain from evil rather because of the punishment that it brings, than because of its own foulness." Jeremy Bentham, writing in the latter part of the 18th century, suggested that "deterrence would vary with the 'certainty' (likelihood), 'proximity' (swiftness), and 'magnitude' (severity) of punishment.[14] The question of course is whether (and which) deviant behaviors are deterrable.

At the minimum the resources of criminal justice can be used to reduce crime by putting the criminal out of circulation. In this case effectiveness depends on the length of detention or the prospects for rehabilitation. This view of the role of criminal justice is central to the notion of pre-

14. Jeremy Bentham, *The Principles and Morals of Legislation* (New York: Hafner, 1948).

ventive detention and to programs which emphasize rehabilitation. In this case the way to reduce crime is to lock up criminals and try to persuade them to go straight.

The difficulty with this custodial view of criminal justice is that it lacks leverage. Individual behavior is presumed to be independent of the experience of others. The emphasis of the custodial view is on the individual criminal rather than on group behavior. Consequently, the policy alternatives are to rehabilitate the criminal, or to keep him out of mischief if that fails.

On the other hand, if deviant behavior is (on the average) deterrable because of the expectation of punishment, then leverage or control over the entire population is gained from the example of the apprehension, prosecution, and punishment of the few. The best interests of society shift from concern with the individual offender to the effect that society's sanctions will have on group behavior. The interests of society and of the individual offender may no longer be the same, but in conflict. Less severe sentences, probation, and rehabilitation may diminish the deterrent effect of punishment. Bentham's criterion of "the greatest happiness" for the community may be a thorn to the champion of the individual.

## The Systems Approach to Crime Control

The interaction of crime generation and crime control is illustrated schematically in Figure 12–9. Let us assume, for example, that socioeconomic

Figure 12–9. A schematic illustration of crime generation and crime control.

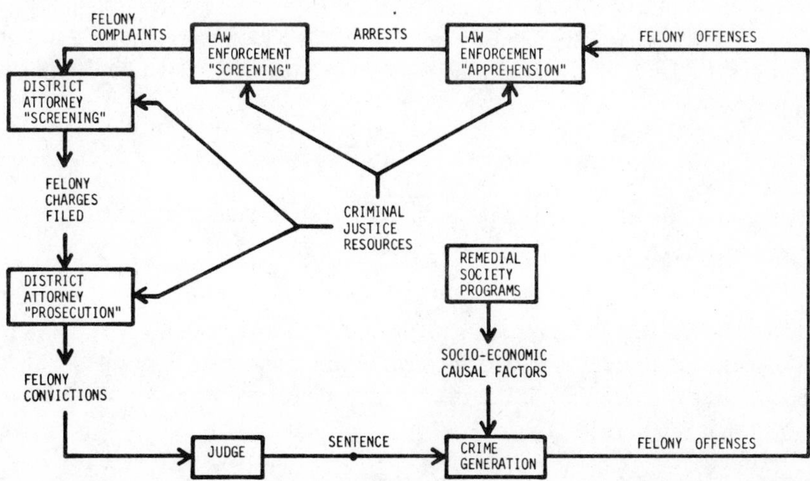

causal factors $SE$ generate crime—felony offenses $OF$. These causal factors can be alleviated by remedial society programs $SP$, which cost money, $C_1(SP)$. The offense rate (in per capita terms) is a burden or load on society and on the criminal justice system. Criminal justice resources $L$ are devoted to law enforcement and to prosecution. Law enforcement engages in apprehending suspects through arrests and weighs the quality of the case against suspects, resulting in felony complaints, lesser charges, or release. The district attorney screens the complaints, identifies cases which justify the filing of charges in superior court, and strives for a felony conviction. The ratio of felony convictions to felony offenses, i.e., the conviction ratio $CR$, is a measure of the "certainty" of punishment considered a deterrent factor by Bentham. In this simplified schema, we shall abstract from consideration of the swiftness of justice and consider only the "severity" of the sentence $SV$ imposed on the convicted offender. "Severity" $SV$ is also considered to be a deterrent factor (based on Bentham) and occasions the costs of corrections and incarceration, $C_2(SV)$.

Increasing criminal justice resources $L$ can increase the conviction ratio $CR$, given the offense rate $OF$, but at the going price per resource $w$, costs $wL$. If the loss rate per offense is $r$, the total social cost of crime to society (\$) is the sum of 1) losses to crime $rOF$, 2) the cost of criminal justice resources $wL$, 3) the cost of corrections $C_2(SV)$, and 4) the costs of programs to alleviate causal factors $C_1(SP)$, i.e.,

$$\$ = rOF + wL + C_1(SP) + C_2\,(SV). \tag{1}$$

If crime is controllable, it will decrease with "certainty" (the conviction ratio $CR$) and "severity" (the sentence $SV$). The more deterrable a crime, the greater the effect increases in certainty and severity will have on diminishing the offense rate. Of course, increases in the socioeconomic causal factors will increase the offense rate. The influence of these causal and control factors on crime generation is summarized in the functional relationship $g$,

$$OF = g(CR, SV, SE). \tag{2}$$

The causal factors $SE$ can be reduced by increasing the remedial social programs $SP$ represented by the relationship $h$,

$$SE = h(SP). \tag{3}$$

The conviction ratio $CR$ will increase if criminal justice resources $L$ increase and will decrease if the offense rate increases, as represented by the functional relationship $f$,

$$CR = f(OF,L). \tag{4}$$

In this simple scheme, society has three means or instruments to reduce crime: criminal justice resources devoted to law enforcement and prosecution $L$; remedial social programs to alleviate causal factors $SP$; and sentences or corrections $SV$. The task is to consider and compare the costs of using these alternative instruments and to choose the mix that will minimize the total social cost.

Suppose we hold fixed the severity of the sentence (and consequently, the corrections resources needed) as well as the resources devoted to social programs to alleviate the causes of crime. If we increase the resources allocated to law enforcement and prosecution $L$, we can increase the conviction ratio $CR$, and thereby decrease the offense rate $OF$. This is indicated in Figure 12–10 by the downward sloping solid line depicting the combina-

Figure 12–10. Minimizing the social costs of crime—police and prosecution.

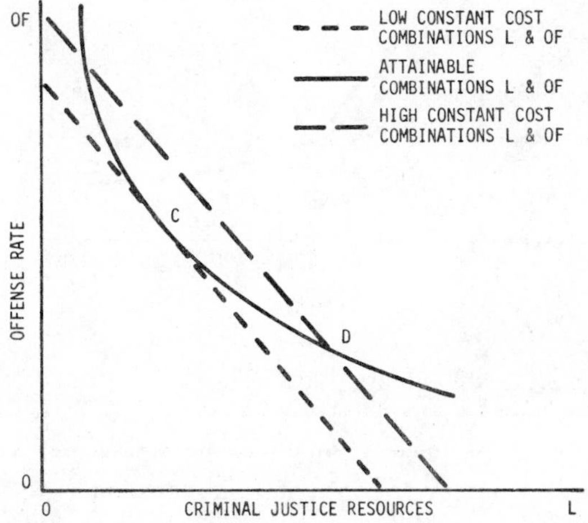


tions of crime $OF$ attainable by applying criminal justice resources $L$, given severity $SV$ and causal factors $SE$. The continued application of resources to criminal justice has a diminishing impact on reducing the offense rate as implied by the curvature. For a presumed constant cost per unit resource $w$ and a dollar loss rate per offense $r$, the combination of offense rates and crime fighting resources with a constant total social cost $TC$ (net of the costs of corrections and social programs held fixed by assumption) is

$$TC = wL + rOF \tag{5}$$

and is illustrated by the shorter dashed line in Figure 12–10. The minimum attainable social cost of crime is indicated by point *C*. A lower offense rate could be obtained by allocating more resources to criminal justice, as indicated by point *D*, but only at a higher cost (longer dashed line). Thus, the optimal crime rate and effort towards law enforcement and prosecution are determined.

A similar analysis can be undertaken to trace the effects of varying the

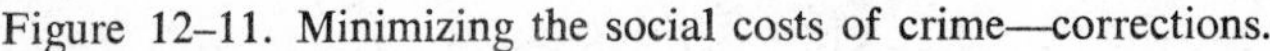
Figure 12–11. Minimizing the social costs of crime—corrections.

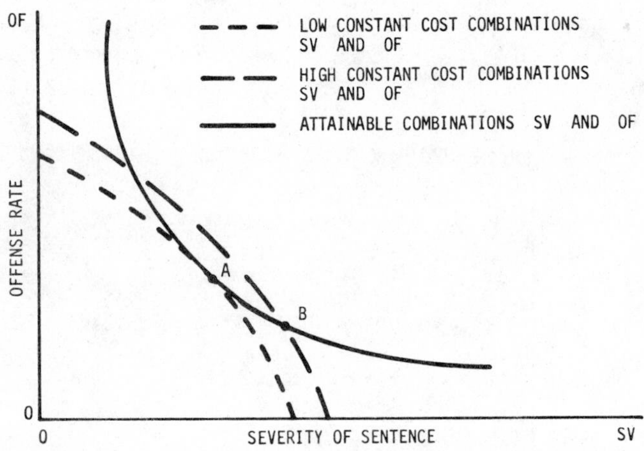


severity of penalties on offense rates. This is illustrated in Figure 12–11 where the solid line once again indicates the offense rates attainable as the severity of the penalty is varied, this time holding social programs *SP* and criminal justice resources *L* constant. The constant cost combinations of crime and corrections are illustrated assuming the average cost of corrections increases with the severity of the penalty. The minimum attainable social cost of crime is indicated at point *A*, and determines the optimal crime rate and length of sentence. Clearly, a lower offense rate could be achieved by lengthening the sentence, as indicated by point *B*, but only at a higher cost. The increased cost of corrections would overbalance the decrease in losses to crime.

Of course, the three instruments to control crime (criminal justice resources, severity of sentence, and social programs) should be varied simultaneously to determine the offense rate which will minimize the sum of the losses to crime and the costs of prevention and control. This involves simply an extension in several dimensions of the partial two-dimensional graphical analysis above.

## Scientific Questions for Investigation

If public policies are to be based on crime control or crime prevention, there must be available a better operational knowledge of which criminal behaviors are controllable through deterrence and which are preventable by changing socioeconomic conditions. The controversy over the death penalty is a current example of the lack of knowledge about deterrence.

The death penalty is a specific case of attempting to use an extremely severe sentence to deter crime. Opponents of the death penalty have argued that it is cruel, unfairly or unequally applied to various socioeconomic groups, immoral, and ineffective.[15] The evidence on ineffectiveness is based on studies which show little difference in homicide rates between contiguous states or regions, regardless of whether their statutes allow the death penalty or not.[16] In general, these studies do not control for variations in causal factors (other than using contiguous jurisdictions), and they do not control for the variation in the likelihood of application of the death penalty. Nonetheless, the evidence suggests there is no strong relationship between the death penalty and the murder rate. Given the volume of books, editorials, and rhetoric on the subject (which indicate public concern), one might expect more scientific studies as a basis for public policy on this issue.

Evidence on the deterrent effect of imprisonment is scant.[17] Many criminologists have evidently accepted the argument that (a) the death penalty is not a deterrent and (b) since it is a severe penalty, lesser penalties must be ineffective also. Since criminologists have been preoccupied with studying the causes of crime, they have neglected investigating the means to control it. As a consequence, society has insufficient information on which to base the design of the criminal justice system. (See pp. 331–334 for evidence developed by this author supporting the deterrent effect of the certainty and severity of punishment on the frequency of gun use in assault.)

Notwithstanding the preoccupation of criminologists with the study of the causes of crime, it is still difficult to explain why San Diego has a lower crime rate than Sacramento. The reason for this difficulty is evident. Referring to Figure 12–9, we recall that crime generation is affected by both control or deterrent factors and causal forces. To sort out the causal factors which lead to different crime rates in San Diego and Sacramento, one must standardize for differences in control factors, i.e., one must study both control and causal factors simultaneously. Since the study of control has been

15. Hugo Adam Bedau, *The Death Penalty in America* (New York: Doubleday, 1964).

16. See Edwin H. Sutherland and Donald R. Cressey, *Principles of Criminology,* 7th ed. (Philadelphia: J. B. Lippincott, 1966), p. 346ff.

17. For a discussion of this point see Jack P. Gibbs, "Crime, punishment, and deterrence," *Southwestern Social Science Quarterly,* 48, no. 4 (March 1968), p. 515; and Sutherland and Cressey, *Principles,* ch. 14.

neglected, the information obtained from studies of causes is sadly deficient. The possibilities for studies of crime using sophisticated research strategies and advanced statistical techniques are only presently being realized and were urgently needed by society yesterday. In the words of Fedor Dostoevski, "with ready-made opinions one cannot judge crime. Its philosophy is a little more complicated than people think."

## A Policy Toward Crimes Without Victims

The cost to society of crimes without victims may be largely avoidable. The major cost may arise from considering such activities as crimes in the first place. The revenues from gambling, prostitution, etc. could be denied to organized crime and the criminal sector simply by legalizing and, if necessary, regulating such activities.

Recall from Table 12–1 that nearly half of the economic impact of crime in 1965 was attributable to the provision of illegal goods and services to willing victims. The costs are based on the revenue going to the criminal sector. If these activities were legalized, much of this revenue could be denied the criminal sector. Organized crime would tend to wither on the vine. It would no longer receive the resources to maintain its program of social and political corruption. Rather than trying to combat organized crime with a crimebusting, G-man approach (which has shown no signs of notable success in the last fifty years), it could be cut off at the source. The leaders of organized crime, of course, tend to be conservative fellows, who oppose legalizing such sinful practices as gambling and prostitution. Furthermore, they may have bought enough corrupt political influence to see that such views prevail. Changing the laws against the crimes without victims may have to be accomplished by means of public initiatives.

If the crimes without victims were no longer crimes, would society suffer any losses? What would be the loss rate per offense $r$? One can argue that the loss would be small. Gambling and prostitution cannot offend your moral sensibilities, if you are ignorant of their occurrence. Of course such activities can also have a nuisance value, or worse, if they are not sufficiently private. Society may wish to prohibit some individual and group activities in public which it permits in private.

The logic of social policy toward crimes without victims can be illustrated in Figure 12–12 (similar to Figure 12–11). If the social loss rate per offense $r$ of a crime without a victim is very small, then the line of constant cost combinations of criminal justice resources $L$ and offense rates $OF$ will be quite steep. This is illustrated by the dashed line. The minimum attainable social cost of crime, as represented by point $C$, indicates that few resources should be devoted to law enforcement. Of course, if the social loss rate per offense were zero, no resource should be allocated to criminal justice for that offense.

Figure 12–12. Minimizing the social costs of crime—low loss rate offenses.

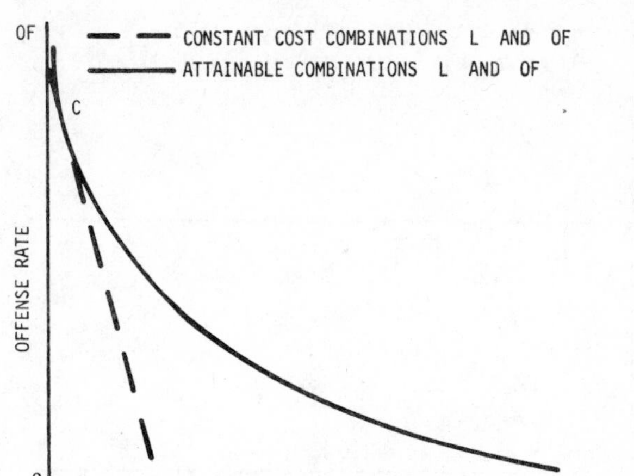


## Policy Toward Undeterrable Crimes

Some crimes may not be deterrable. This category might include difficult-to-detect crimes, such as minor cheating on income tax and some instances of white-collar crime. Activities which might be considered illnesses rather than crimes, such as drunkenness and narcotic addiction, may also fall into this category. In these cases, arrest and incarceration for a short period of time may have little effect on the offense rate. The relationship between the offense rate and criminal justice resources for crimes which are difficult to deter is illustrated by the nearly horizontal solid line in Figure 12–13. Here the offense rate is determined principally by factors other than control, such as opportunities and/or social malaise. The minimum attainable social cost to society involves no use of criminal justice resources, as indicated by point *C*. Society must rely on other social programs such as education and health care for these crimes.

## Deterring Gun Use in Assault

In recent years the homicide rate has been increasing dramatically. (See Figure 12–1.) There are two major factors affecting homicide: social proclivity towards violence (as measured by the assault rate) and the use of firearms. The latter increases both the feasibility of attack and the fatality rate. Gun use has been increasing. Between 1961 and 1969 the fraction of homicides involving guns increased from .525 to .645, and the rate of homicides (per capita) involving guns more than doubled.[18]

18. See various issues of FBI *Uniform Crime Reports*.

Figure 12–13. Minimizing the social costs of crime—undeterrable crimes.

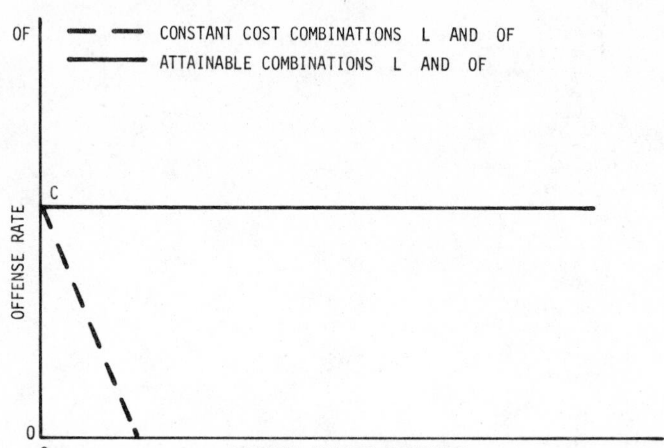


Studies of the circumstances that lead to homicide indicate that most cases involve family or acquaintances who became involved in a fight. In 1969 known and suspected felonious murders (defined as killings resulting from robberies, sex motives, gangland slayings, and other felonious activities) comprised only 27 percent of total murder offenses.[19] Furthermore, the circumstances leading to crime are similar whether the weapon used was a gun or a knife.[20] Thus, it is reasonable to assume that a major source of homicide is aggravated assault, and the fraction of these offenses in which guns were involved has increased from 12.7 percent in 1960 to 23.8 percent in 1969.[21] The fatality rate of firearms attacks is approximately five times the fatality rate of attacks with a knife, the most frequently used weapon.[22]

The importance of gun use as a contributing factor in homicide can be illustrated by relating (1) the *ratio* of homicides committed with a gun to assaults and (2) the *fraction* of assaults committed with firearms. States with a high rate of homicides relative to assaults tend to have a large fraction of assaults committed with a gun. This is illustrated in Figure 12–14.

Given the importance of gun use in determining the seriousness of violence, it is important to ask whether gun use is controllable. While the

19. Ibid., 1969, p. 8.

20. See George D. Newton and Franklin E. Zimring, *Firearms and Violence in American Life,* National Commission on the Causes and Prevention of Violence, Staff Report (Washington, D.C.: U.S. Government Printing Office, 1969), p. 43.

21. See various issues of FBI *Uniform Crime Reports.*

22. See Newton and Zimring, *Firearms,* p. 41 and FBI *Uniform Crime Reports,* 1969, p. 10.

Figure 12–14. Gun use in assault and violence.

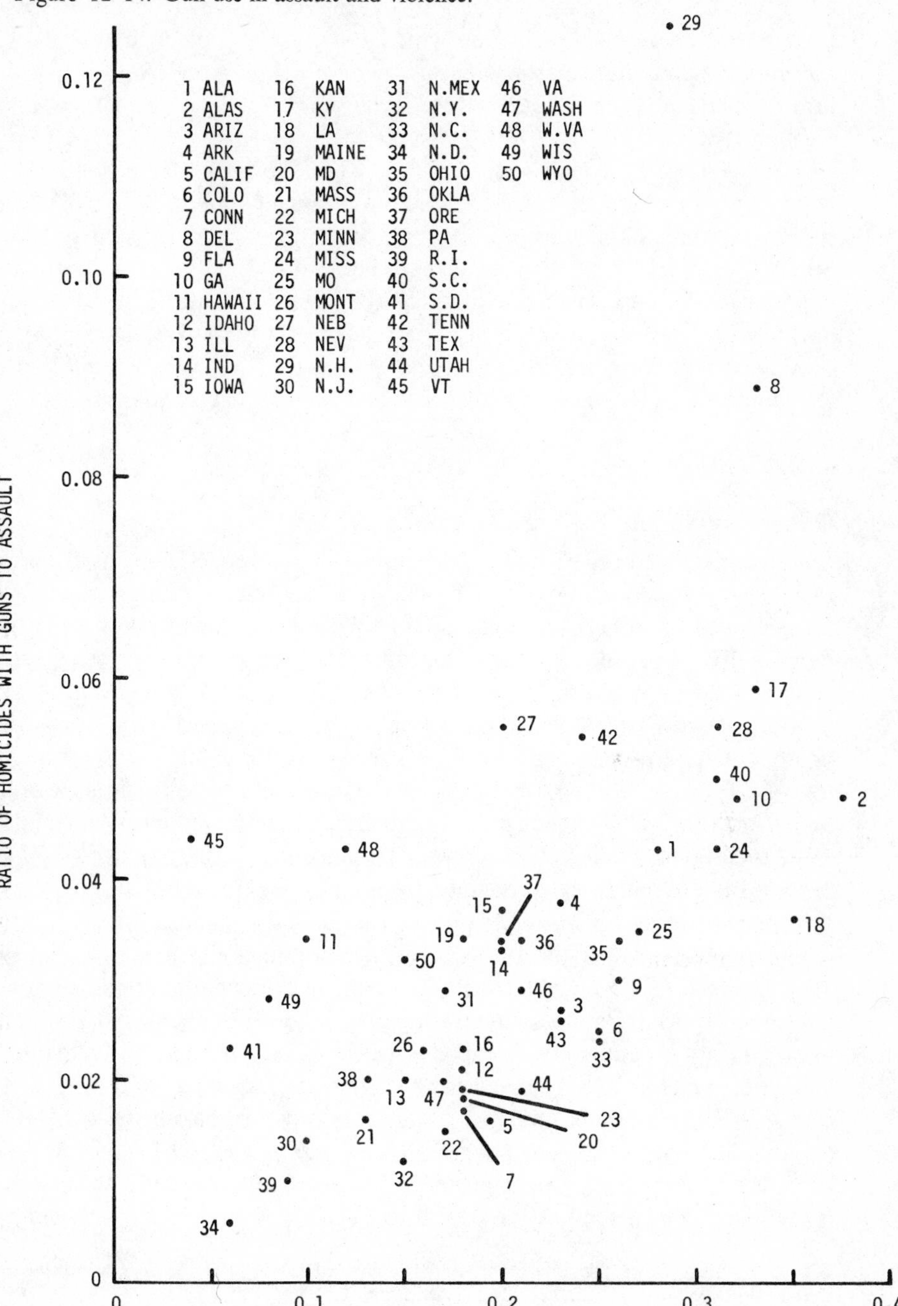

causes of fights are manifold, and their eruption somewhat spontaneous, the severity or seriousness of the fight may be more subject to control. If the punitive consequences of lethal assault (which is more likely if a firearm is used) are certain and severe, attacks with a firearm may be less frequent.

The odds of not using a gun in assault (i.e., the ratio of the fraction of assaults not involving a gun to the fraction of assaults involving a gun) can be related to the likelihood of imprisonment and the length of sentence for criminal homicide. These two deterrent factors of certainty and severity accounted for 37 percent of the variance from state to state in the odds an assailant will not use a gun.[23] The results are statistically significant and provide strong support for the view that gun use in assault is deterrable. In the words of the French dramatist Racine, "Crime, like virtue, has its degrees."

## Crime, Youth, and the Labor Market

The arrest data reviewed under Patterns in Crime (pp. 316–321) showed that crime is predominantly an urban, youthful, male phenomenon with nonwhites more than proportionately involved. An examination of the evidence will support the hypothesis that increasing crime rates for youth can be explained by deteriorating economic opportunities for this group.

It is interesting to observe that while crime rates were skyrocketing for youths, unemployment rates for 18–19-year-old white males rose from a low of 7.0 percent in 1952 to a peak of 16.5 percent in 1958, and were still 9 percent in 1967. For nonwhite males the situation was even worse. In 1952 their level of unemployment was 10 percent; it rose to a high of 27.2 percent in 1959, and recovered to the level of 20.1 percent in the prosperity year of 1967.[24] (See Figure 12–15.) During the same period, the aggregate unemployment rate started at 2.8 percent, rose to a peak of 6.8 percent in 1958, and fell to 3.1 percent by 1967. Thus, by comparison, youths in general, and nonwhites in particular, were clearly in a disadvantaged position in our society. Examination of labor force participation rates reinforces this view. For white youths 18–19 years old, this rate declined from 72.9 percent in 1952 to a low of 65.4 percent in 1966, then rose somewhat to 66.1 percent in 1967. For nonwhites the 1952 figure was 79.1 percent and dropped steadily to 62.7 percent in 1967. (See Figure 12–16.) In relating labor market opportunities for youths to their arrest rates, it is particularly

23. See Llad Phillips, "Crime Control: The Case of Deterrence," *The Economics of Crime and Punishment* (forthcoming), American Enterprise Institute.

24. Labor force data are from U.S. Department of Labor, *Manpower Report of the President* (Washington, D.C., Government Printing Office, 1970).

Figure 12–15. Male unemployment rates by race—selected age groups.

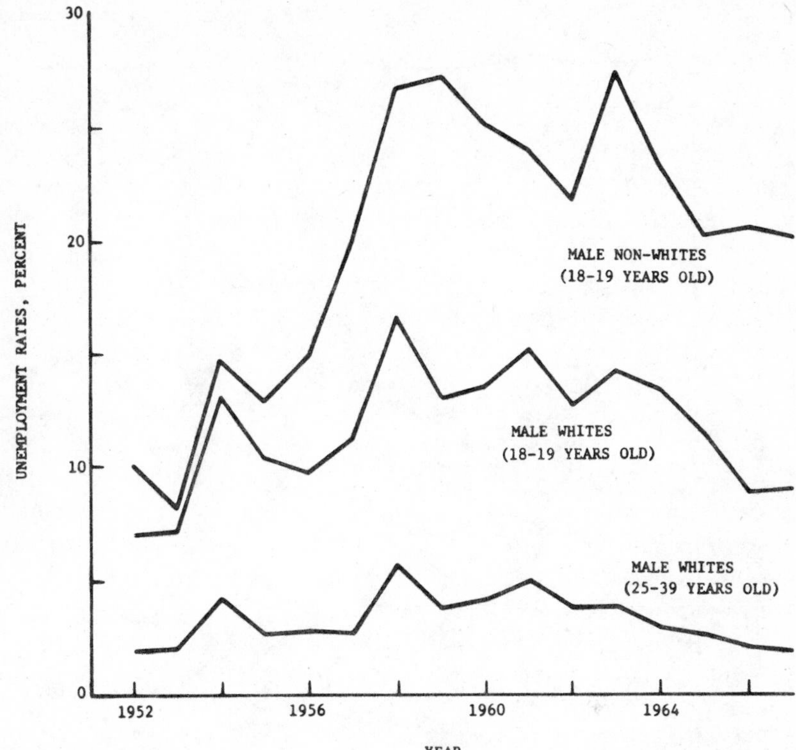


important to consider labor force participation as well as unemployment rates. Since youths have low participation rates, unemployment rates will have less weight because of the considerable fraction of youths outside the labor force. In addition, while unemployment rates reflect cyclical and short-run conditions in the labor market, participation rates capture secular changes including the influence of past unemployment rates.

To test the hypothesis that increasing crime rates for youth can be explained by deteriorating economic opportunities, we can relate crime rates to labor force status. The 18–19-year-old population can be classified by whether they are in the labor force or not. We hypothesize that those *in* the labor force will have a lower crime rate (on the average) than those *outside* the labor force, which tends to be a status associated with more crime. Since labor market opportunities for youths have been worsening, and the fraction participating in the labor force has been shrinking, the crime rate for 18–19-year-olds should increase.

Figure 12–16. Male labor force participation rates by race—selected age groups.

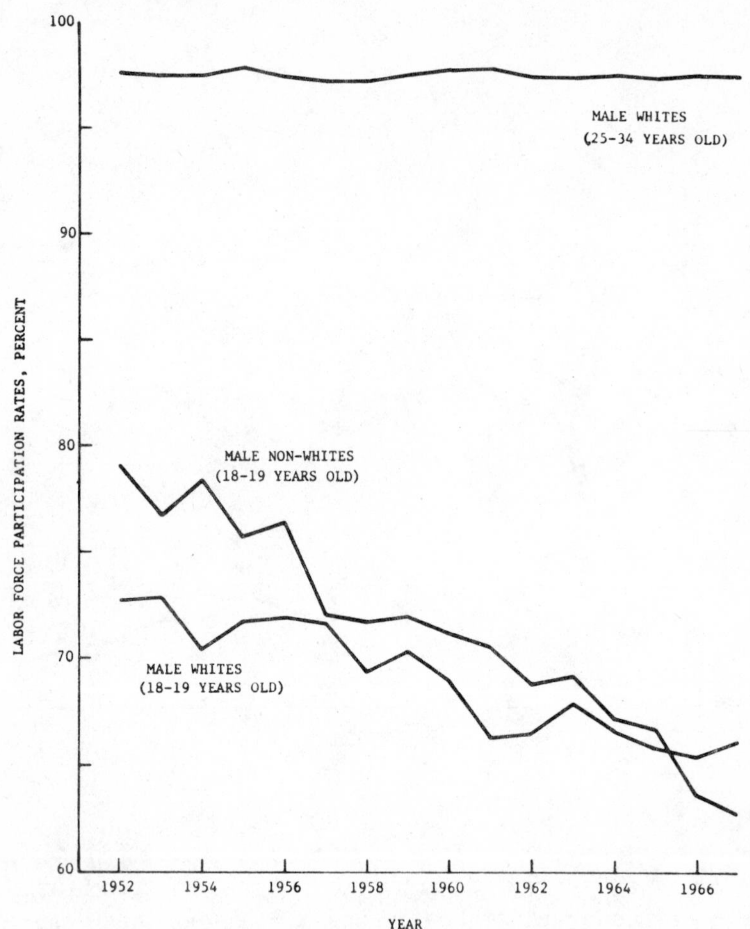


Age-specific arrest rates (ASAR) were related to labor force status for four crimes: larceny, burglary, auto theft and robbery. The changing labor-market opportunities for youth were sufficient to explain the increasing crime rates.[25] The results of the analysis are illustrated in Figure 12–17, which displays plots of the actual crime rates as well as the crime rates estimated and forecast on the basis of labor force status. The evidence indicates that a successful attack on rising crime rates must consider the employment problems facing young people.

25. Llad Phillips, Harold L. Votey, Jr., and Darold Maxwell, "Crime, youth, and the labor market," *Journal of Political Economy*, 80, no. 3 (May/June 1972).

Figure 12–17. Actual, estimated, and forecast arrest rates for 18–19-year-olds, 1968–1970.

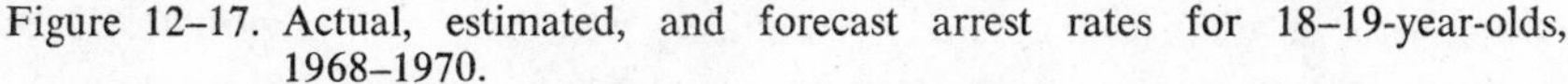

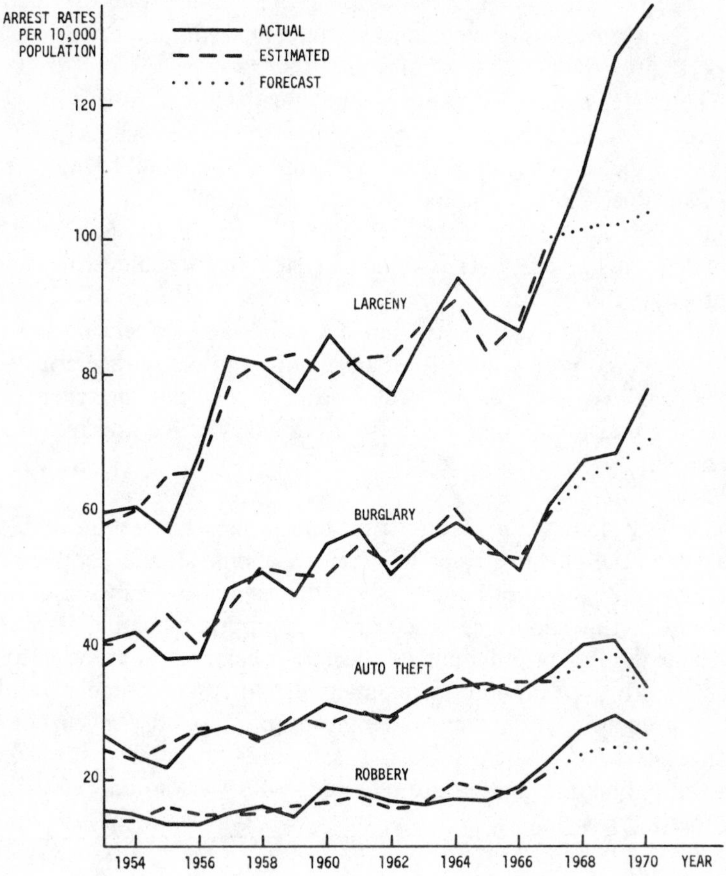

## Conclusions

The average citizen is likely to be concerned with the crimes that affect him directly, such as burglary at his residence or theft of his car. He is also disturbed by the sensational crimes of violence, about which he hears and reads a great deal. From a review of the data in this chapter, it would appear that per capita rates for these felony crimes have been increasing significantly. Our analysis of the crime problem suggests several reasons for this increase:

> Crime is predominantly an urban phenomenon. Since the nation is continuing to urbanize and population density is continuing to rise, we should anticipate a long-run tendency for crime to increase.

Crime is disproportionately associated with youths and nonwhites. A deterioration in their economic opportunities is sufficient to explain the increases in their crime rates since the 1950s. To alleviate the conditions which generate crime, society must be concerned with improving economic opportunities for the disadvantaged.

There is evidence that crime can be effectively controlled. In the case of homicide, an increase in the likelihood of imprisonment and/or the length of the sentence appear to deter gun use in assault. Unfortunately, the data since 1950 reveal a decrease in the effectiveness of law enforcement ability to clear crimes (including homicide) through arrest. This decline in police effectiveness could be stemmed by allocating more resources to criminal justice.

Society should examine its changing values and reflect on the wisdom of continuing to use criminal justice resources to discourage crimes without victims. We should ponder the wisdom of diverting the revenues from gambling and prostitution away from organized crime and into the public treasury.

The steady increase in "bloody crime and violence" is not inevitable. Our society can take effective steps to protect the right of the people to "life, liberty, and the pursuit of happiness." A domestic program to insure justice and control crime should be based on an appropriate combination of policies. Expenditures on programs to alleviate the causes of crime need to be balanced with expenditures to maintain the forces of crime control. We need to promote rehabilitation where promising, support punishment where effective. To execute these policies wisely, more scientific knowledge and improved public information are required. With wisdom and effort it need not come to pass that

> "Lost is our old simplicity of times,
> The world abounds with laws,
> and teems with crimes."
>
> Anon.

# Summary

## Goals of Our Analysis

Two fundamental goals have been sought in this volume. The first has been to acquaint those unfamiliar with the nature of the substance of economics with at least a partial understanding of what economics is all about. This has been done by example, using not the most ordinary applications of economics to social problems, but rather by selecting a diverse set of topics which might illustrate the versatility of economic tools in yielding greater understanding of complex problems. By now it should be evident that these examples are only samples of a much broader array of problems which are amenable to the use of economic analysis for devising policy prescriptions.

The second goal has been to provide a set of analytical tools which the reader may utilize for his own decision-making. He is encouraged to apply these tools to similar problems encountered in making personal resource decisions or in determining how to vote on public issues.

## Pressing Social Problems in Review

The pressing social problems we have dealt with can be divided into two broad classifications: decision-making via the market mechanism and nonmarket decision-making. In many cases, however, such a breakdown is not clear-cut and, in fact, it may be more helpful to think of problems along a continuum, running from cases in which there is pure competition and in which markets function perfectly, through cases of market failure, and finally to situations in which markets are nonexistent and society must search for other mechanisms as instruments of social policy.

### Perfect Competition

Perfect competition is characterized by many buyers and many sellers, all free to choose whether or not they wish to buy or sell a product. In addition, no participants in the market can, by their own actions alone, influence prices or the quantities of goods produced. It is hard to find examples of a perfect market, and even if found, it would not provide an example of a pressing social problem. This is because buyers and sellers would both be well served with no unmet demand or excess production.

Economists are somewhat like physicians—interested only in patients with problems. Consequently, this volume does not include a chapter dealing with a market that is functioning perfectly. What we find more interesting is the next kind of situation along our continuum: that in which markets are naturally competitive but in which governments intervene in ways generally contrary to the interests of consumers and society as a whole.

### Competitive Markets with Intervention

When markets are competitive but subject to various forms of intervention, the effects of the intervention must be considered in relation to what might have existed in its absence. The justification generally provided for intervention, of course, is that it corrects an inequitable situation. Economists would argue, however, that market interference is not, in general, an effective way to improve equity. What is more likely to be true is that when one group is benefited via market intervention, other groups in society are harmed and resource allocation is interfered with such that inappropriate quantities of some goods are produced. If we truly believe that one group should be aided by society in general, a tax and direct subsidy would probably be a more equitable way to do so. In this manner, third parties are less likely to be penalized and resource allocation will be efficient.

Chapter 1 illustrates this effectively in the case of agricultural output. Various schemes to improve the well-being of farmers neither help poor farmers nor control overproduction. Instead, they generally lead to double taxation of consumers: taxes to pay subsidies to farmers and storage operations, and higher than appropriate prices for food. The effect of government intervention is illustrated again in Chapter 2 in the case of interference in international markets for oil. Instead of providing greater protection to U.S. citizens, oil quotas raise fuel costs to consumers and lead to the consumption of high-cost domestic reserves. Water use provides a third example. As Chapter 5 shows, without efficient price allocation too much water will be consumed, water resources will be depleted, and inappropriate decisions will be made in regard to investment in water producing facilities. Even the market for international exchange, as Chapter 7 points out, may be prevented from best serving public interests by market intervention. Evidence is mounting that the claimed undesirable effects of a freely fluctuating market in international currencies may be more myth than reality.

This does not mean to suggest that market intervention is always bad or that generally those who interfere are anything but well-meaning. It does suggest, however, that extreme care should be taken to consider all other alternatives before intervening to correct alleged market imperfections. Market intervention can be as detrimental to production and consumption efficiency as the market failure which motivated the intervention. Perceived income distribution problems arising out of market situations may be handled in ways preferable to market intervention.

**Free Private Markets Where Competition is Limited**

An alternative situation in which the outcome may be equally unfortunate for consumers and society is that in which the free enterprise system has facilitated the establishment of monopoly or at least the concentration of economic power in the hands of a few producers. Chapter 3 indicates the extent to which this is characteristic of production in the United States. What is the result of market concentration? We find that insufficient amounts of goods are produced in those industries where power is concentrated and goods are overpriced. Those with market power are in a position to "exploit" consumers and society. This would seem to provide an obvious justification for government intervention. However, as Robert McGuckin points out, such a conclusion is an oversimplification. Without favoring such exploitation in any way, the economist may recommend leaving well enough alone in some cases. This is simply because regulation may be more costly to society than the losses from concentration of power. Even more disturbing is the likelihood that regulation may be easily subverted by those regulated so that it is not only costly but almost totally ineffectual. As McGuckin makes clear, time, invention, and competition will tend to erode monopoly power. Thus, we must learn to select policies which, while they may not lead to a "best" solution, at least leave us better off than we would be in their absence.

**Joint Products: Market Goods and Nonmarket Outputs**

Moving along our scale from perfect markets to no markets, cases occur where some outputs are produced for market jointly with goods which are unwanted and for which markets do not exist. Examples are the desired outputs of iron and steel which are produced along with effluents in the form of air and water pollution.

Chapter 2 introduces us to this type of problem for the case of energy production; and this externality problem is taken up in greater detail by Robert Deacon in Chapter 6. One class of solutions for achieving an appropriate balance between undesirable nonmarket outputs and market goods is to attempt to create markets or quasi markets for the nonmarket outputs. Other alternatives making use of the assignment of property rights or the assessment of appropriate penalties will be more appropriate in some cases. Only recently has society seriously taken up consideration of such problems, and our experience in dealing with these matters is limited. Nevertheless, economic theory is clearly in a position to point the way to a variety of policy alternatives.

Another case which might fall under this general heading relates to the labor market. While there is a market for labor services, there is no market for evaluating the aesthetics of work. Often the market is competitive, but more often it is dominated by opposing power groups. Despite the power of unions to achieve high wages, however, workers do not perceive themselves as well-off even where living standards are, at least on a world scale, very high. Here is an instance where market intervention would probably be powerless to achieve a satisfactory result. As Chapter 9 points out, workers are becoming increasingly disillusioned with their role in industrial society. Neither higher pay nor greater leisure seem to provide satisfactory compensation for the unaesthetic qualities of some classes of work. It is as if there is no conceivable rate of exchange between the undesired nonmarket drudgery that is an output of some classes of work and real goods produced in response to market demands. William Kennedy would argue, however, that aesthetic values of work constitute a third good which is ignored in the market process. Such a situation is a challenge to decision-makers who cannot neglect the nonmarket concerns of the most important factor of production: the worker. Economists, psychologists, sociologists and scholars from other disciplines have thus far done little beyond recognizing the problem in this area. The challenge of designing policy to successfully deal with it is yet to be fully met.

### Publicly Produced Goods in the Absence of Markets

As a final category on our continuum, we find a wide variety of situations in which decision-making is typically conducted in an almost complete absence of markets. In the case of a pure public good such as a flood control dam, protection is common property and individual consumption does not diminish protection to others. As a consequence, individual consumption cannot be excluded and, therefore, it is difficult to charge for the good. There is no incentive for private production and supply is achieved by public action rather than through markets. Examples of pure public goods are rare and most publicly produced goods could be produced privately. Our examples of pressing problems fall into this category. At one end of the scale we find some of the peak load pricing problems discussed in Chapter 4. M. Bruce Johnson presents some examples in which markets, as normally constituted, do not make short-run adjustments of price to relieve congestion but where such adjustments could easily be achieved. In other cases that he examines, such as congestion on highways, it might be very difficult to put into operation a peak load pricing scheme that is practical. Once again, our overriding concern should be whether the cost of instituting a more effective pricing mechanism would be justified by the benefits in terms of improved allocation.

Much of higher education might seem to fall in the nonmarket publicly produced good category, but it is clear from Chapter 8 that college education is produced in a "market" in which there is much intervention, and in which information is not effectively transmitted to purchasers. It has been suggested that freedom of choice of purchasers of education be increased by allocating existing subsidies in such a way that purchasers can spend them at the institution of their choice. This proposal is referred to as a voucher system. The market will still be imperfect, however, in the sense that those who benefit may not pay their appropriate share of the costs. Thus, the problem is not simply one of economic efficiency, but one of equity as well. Society already uses a nonmarket device (subsidy) to attempt to correct inequity, but Donald Winkler believes that the evidence indicates not enough is being done. This is a debate that is not likely to be resolved in the immediate future.

As Chapter 10 points out, there are kinds of environmental degradation which also are not likely to be resolved through a market situation. The determination of social choice over an issue not obviously economic seems a natural one for a democratic voting process. Shapiro and Barkume show that there are economic overtones to such decision processes which can only be evaluated by economic analysis—and such analysis may help to prevent social inequities in the future resolution of environmental problems.

Another nonmarket decision-making problem is that of achieving a desirable level of population through social control. One possible way of achieving a socially desired level of control is through the establishment of a quasi market for babies. Chapter 11, in presenting this and other alternatives for policy implementation, illustrates that a rigorous conceptualization of the problem of optimum population involves the economics of choice and the notion of constrained optimization. Econometric evaluation combined with planning techniques, where no markets exist, can lead us to the same outcome as would result from an efficient market.

Chapter 12 presents another case in which economic resources are involved and in which no market is available to guide us to efficient output levels. Crime generation and control are both economic activities. Here is probably the best example of the need for econometric evaluation and the planning techniques of the economist for the implementation of efficient public policy. Law enforcement protection and the process of crime control through deterrent actions of police are matters best handled by public officials. Yet the processes involved require the effective allocation of society's resources to minimize the total social cost of crime. It is no wonder that authorities in the area of criminal justice are turning more frequently to economic techniques for evaluation of alternatives for social control.

## The Economist's Tool Kit in Review

As we have traced a path through the chapters in this volume repeated reference has been made to the economist's tool kit (see next page). This term is perhaps a trifle narrow to convey a picture of the devices used by the economist to evaluate society's real problems, since their implementations involve an intellectual rather than physical process. Nonetheless, the economist has a set of instruments at his disposal which are, for the most part, unique to the discipline of economics and which are powerful devices for diagnosing and prescribing for social problems. In the appendix, those elements of the set which have been utilized in this volume are briefly inventoried. This is done in the form of a table (interspersed with comments) which attempts to distinguish between concepts and diagrammatic and algebraic techniques for depicting and analyzing these concepts in particular cases.

# The Economist's Tool Kit

| Chapter | Economic Concepts | Expository and Analytical Tools |
|---|---|---|
| 1 | Market | Supply, demand curves |
| | Excess demand | |
| | Price | |
| | Production—inputs, outputs | Production function |
| | Production alternatives | Transformation curve |
| | Elasticities—price, income | |
| | Technological change | |
| | Market interference | |

Because the demand curve is derived from consumer desires and the supply curve is based on the available production technology and resource availability, the equilibrium price is, in a perfect market, an accurate representation of social value.

| Chapter | Economic Concepts | Expository and Analytical Tools |
|---|---|---|
| 2 | Market interference—(cont.) | |
| | Externalities | |
| | Investment | |
| | Marginal costs | Marginal cost curve |
| | Marginal benefits | Marginal benefit curve |
| | Optimum (level of pollution) | |

In addition to analytical and expository tools, there is another class of tool: those which are used to effect policy. In this class would fall tariffs and quotas (including acreage allotments mentioned in Chapter 1 as one form of attempted control of agricultural output).

| Chapter | Economic Concepts | Expository and Analytical Tools |
|---|---|---|
| 3 | Competition | |
| | Monopoly | |
| | Marginal revenue | Marginal revenue curve |
| | Average revenue | Demand curve |
| | Marginal cost | Marginal cost—supply curve |
| | Dead-weight loss | |

A rule that a good decision-maker should never forget is to equate marginal revenue to marginal cost if he wishes to maximize his net return. Under perfect competition this is equivalent to setting price equal to marginal cost.

| Chapter | Economic Concepts | Expository and Analytical Tools |
|---|---|---|
| 4 | Capacity per unit of time | Long-run vs. short-run marginal cost (supply) curves |
| | Peak load demand | |
| | Congestion | |
| | Externalities | |

Implicit in Johnson's analysis is the idea that time is an economic asset which has value and thus should appropriately be taken into account in determining price, and hence, value to producer and consumer.

| Chapter | Economic Concepts | Expository and Analytical Tools |
|---|---|---|
| 5 | Requirements fallacy | |
| | Public vs. private goods | |
| | Average cost pricing | |
| | Promotional pricing | |
| | Flat rate pricing | |
| | Investment | Benefit-cost analysis |
| | Discounting | |
| | Present value | |

Investment decisions depend on the correct evaluation of both present and anticipated future market situations. Correct pricing is essential to correct investment decisions.

| Chapter | Economic Concepts | Expository and Analytical Tools |
|---|---|---|
| 6 | Environmental goods | Transformation curve |
| | Opportunity cost | |
| | Externalities (again) | |
| | Shadow prices | |
| | Property rights | |
| | Public goods | |
| | Rights in common | |
| | Internalization (of externalities) | |

The determination of output becomes much more complex when we receive some "goods" which are produced whether we want them or not and when rights to resources cannot be easily assigned to individuals. Even here, however, a market framework for conceptualization helps to clarify the issues and to evaluate policy alternatives.

| Chapter | Economic Concepts | Expository and Analytical Tools |
|---|---|---|
| 7 | Money supply | |
| | Money creation | |
| | Monetary reserves | |
| | Quantity theory of money | |
| | Purchasing power parity | |
| | Exchange rates | |
| | Fixed (pegged) | |
| | Flexible (freely fluctuating) | |
| | Gold standard | |

Since money is a medium of exchange and a standard of value, and since virtually every country has its own unique currency system, it should not be surprising that in each country there will be a market for the currencies of the others. These markets adhere to the same economic "laws" that govern markets for commodities, and again price represents social value.

| Chapter | Economic Concepts | Expository and Analytical Tools |
|---|---|---|
| 8 | Human capital | Cost benefit analysis (again) |
| | Private vs. social costs | |
| | Private vs. social benefits | |
| | Future income stream | |
| | Direct costs | |

| Chapter | Economic Concepts | Expository and Analytical Tools |
|---|---|---|
| | Opportunity costs (again) | |
| | Capital market | |
| | Income redistribution | |
| | Transfer payments | |
| | Adapting the notion of capital investment to activities in which human beings indulge for the purposes of increasing future earnings provides a powerful tool for resolving crucial social questions pertaining to educational policy. | |
| 9 | Ethics vs. efficiency | |
| | Consumption ethic | |
| | Production (work) ethics | |
| | Wage | |
| | A wage is a price—and it is determined via a bargaining process. It is willingly accepted by a worker in exchange for services. Therefore, it must be a measure of value. The question remains, are there other values which cannot be measured by price alone. We must ask ourselves, where is a market price sufficient for decision-making purposes and where is it not? | |
| 10 | Opportunity cost | Transformation curve between |
| | Trade-offs | market and nonmarket goods |
| | Null hypothesis | Hypothesis testing techniques |
| | Burden concept | |
| | A democratic voting process is an alternative device for determining output and price. While it lacks some of the fine tuning powers of a competitive market, it works where markets are infeasible. | |
| 11 | Demographic concepts | |
| | Mortality, fertility rates | |
| | Production functions (again) | Total product curve |
| | Diminishing returns | |
| | Growth rates | Growth models |
| | Technological change (again) | |
| | Per capita income | |
| | Utility function | Indifference curves |
| | Welfare function | Social indifference curves |
| | Production possibilities | Average product curve |
| | Social value can refer to people as well as things and if we wish to control the output of people we cannot avoid that fact. Economists didn't create the fact, but only make use of it in attempting to find ways to evaluate and determine socially desirable population policy. | |
| 12 | Social cost (of crime) | |
| | Criminal justice concepts | |
| | Clearances of crimes by arrest | |
| | Offenses per capita | |

| Chapter | Economic Concepts | Expository and Analytical Tools |
|---|---|---|
| (12) | Clearance ratio | |
| | Deterrence | |
| | Age distribution of crime | |
| | Crime generation function | Use of schematic diagrams |
| | Crime control (production) function | |
| | Simultaneous systems | Cost minimization techniques |

Economists always are concerned with optima: e.g., society achieving maximum social value by setting price equal to marginal costs, the optimum population, or in this case, minimum total social cost of crime so that we have the maximum resources left to spend on other desirable things.

The list of concepts and tools provided above is broader than that generally provided in a typical introductory course in microeconomics because the topics are wider ranging than those usually presented in a traditional course. This is simply a sign of the times. Economists are reaching out—seeking to provide solutions to an ever-widening range of problems. As mentioned earlier the list presented here is simply an introduction to typical problems yielding to economic analysis. We are all concerned with matters which affect the quality of life and, hence, with social optimization. It is clear that decision-makers can benefit by an understanding of the methods and tools of economics. Since all of us are decision-makers in one way or another, this means we all will be benefited if we are able to utilize at least the rudiments of economic analysis. When the reader has mastered the use of this kit, he will have come a long way in mastering key aspects of microeconomic analysis.